THIRD EDITION

THE SOCIOLOGY OF CHILDHOOD

Sociology for a New Century Series

SOCIOLOGY FOR A NEW CENTURY

THIRD EDITION

THE SOCIOLOGY OF CHILDHOOD

◆

WILLIAM A. CORSARO

Indiana University, Bloomington

Los Angeles | London | New Delhi
Singapore | Washington DC

For information:

Pine Forge Press
An Imprint of
  SAGE Publications, Inc.
2455 Teller Road
Thousand Oaks, California 91320
E-mail: order@sagepub.com

SAGE Publications India Pvt. Ltd.
B 1/I 1 Mohan Cooperative
  Industrial Area
Mathura Road, New Delhi 110 044
India

SAGE Publications Ltd.
1 Oliver's Yard
55 City Road
London EC1Y 1SP
United Kingdom

SAGE Publications Asia-Pacific Pte. Ltd.
33 Pekin Street #02-01
Far East Square
Singapore 048763

Printed in the United States of America

Library of Congress Cataloging-in-Publication Data

Corsaro, William A.
The sociology of childhood / William A. Corsaro. — 3rd ed.
    p. cm.
(Sociology for a new century series)
Includes bibliographical references and index.
ISBN 978-1-4129-7943-6 (pbk.)
    1. Children. I. Title.

HQ767.9.C675 2011
305.23—dc22   2010035772

This book is printed on acid-free paper.

12   13   14   10   9   8   7   6   5   4   3   2

Acquisitions Editor:	David Repetto
Editorial Assistant:	Maggie Stanley
Production Editor:	Karen Wiley
Copy Editor:	Barbara Corrigan
Proofreader:	Rae-Ann Goodwin
Typesetter:	C&M Digitals (P) Ltd.
Cover Designer:	Candice Harman
Marketing Manager:	Erica DeLuca
Permissions Editor:	Karen Ehrmann

Contents

Preface

This third edition of *The Sociology of Childhood*, like the first two editions (published in 1997 and 2005), is about children and childhood from a sociological perspective. It brings together my ideas and experiences gained from research and teaching in this area during the past 30 years. Sociology has now established a tradition for studying children and childhood; although still understudied, these are no longer relegated to the margins of the field. There are now, in addition to *The Sociology of Childhood*, other basic texts in sociology on children or childhood, and a growing number of courses on the sociology of childhood are now offered at colleges and universities. In short, much has changed during the past 13 years.

New and important theoretical and empirical work has been done by a number of scholars who advocate the conceptual autonomy of children and childhood (Alanen, 2000, 2009; Alanen & Mayall, 2001; Boocock & Scott, 2005; Corsaro, 2003; M. Honig, 2009; James, Jenks, & Prout, 1998; N. Lee, 2001; Mayall, 2002; Prout, 2005; Qvortrup, 2009; Shanahan, 2007; Thorne, 1987). Their work focuses on children as the basic units and categories of study. Children and childhood become the center of analysis; they are no longer linked to other categories, such as families or schools, on which they are supposedly dependent (Qvortrup, 1994a, 2009). In addition, we have seen substantial growth in membership in the research section of Sociology of Children and Youth in the American Sociological Association and in the thematic group Sociology of Childhood in the International Sociological Association.

In this new edition, I have updated the explosion of new research on children, focusing especially on studies of peer relations, friendship, children's peer culture, and the social problems of children. I have also updated statistical indicators on the quality of children's lives in both developed and developing societies. In addition, I have greatly expanded the coverage of children's symbolic and material culture—especially related to media and new technologies—in Chapters 6 and 9. Even though much is new in this edition, I must point out that it is not possible to cover what is now such a vast quantity of theory and research highly relevant to a new sociology of childhood. For example, there is a great deal of reflection regarding various theoretical approaches in the new sociology of childhood and children's media and culture that is addressed in much detail in other books and handbooks (Drotner & Livingstone, 2008; Prout, 2005; Qvortrup, Corsaro, & Honig, 2009). Therefore, my coverage of the topic is by no means all encompassing. I focus much more on children's relationships with peers than with adults, and my coverage of children's peer cultures generally ends in preadolescence, at the age of 12. Furthermore, I offer an interpretive perspective to the sociology of childhood, which I contrast with more traditional socialization or outcome approaches to children and child development. In the process, I slight much of the good work in the socialization tradition, but this does not mean I feel there is no place for socialization studies in the sociology of childhood (see Handel, Cahill, & Elkin, 2007, for a more traditional approach to childhood socialization).

Another challenge in writing about children concerns doing justice to both micro (social psychological) and macro (structural) approaches to the sociology of childhood. My main theoretical orientation of interpretive reproduction is clearly social psychological; however, at times I felt I needed to write two books, just as many of us who teach courses on childhood feel we need two courses or at least two semesters to cover both micro and macro issues. Nevertheless, I do give much attention to historical, demographic, and socioeconomic aspects of childhood.

Part One of the book reviews traditional approaches to socialization and child development and contrasts them with my perspective of interpretive reproduction and my focus on children's peer cultures. I present an orb web model of children's developing memberships in their cultures, and I integrate this model, along with the concept of interpretive reproduction, with structural approaches to childhood. Here I also include an updated chapter on studying children and childhood.

Part Two places the new sociology of childhood in historical and cultural perspective. I present what I feel is a much-needed detailed review and evaluation of classic work on the history of childhood, and I introduce the new history of childhood and present some representative examples of it.

I then consider children and childhood cross-culturally by examining children, families, and social change in industrialized and developing societies, updating the discussion to capture recent trends.

Part Three discusses the importance of children's peer cultures for a new sociology of childhood. I have made major revisions. In the first chapter in this section (Chapter 6), I present a much extended discussion of children's introduction to symbolic and material aspects of peer culture in their families and from the media and focus on how new technology has had major effects on the peer cultures of children and youth. In the next two chapters, I consider the basic themes of control and communal sharing in children's initial peer cultures. In Chapter 9, I explore these same themes and consider the importance of autonomy, self, and identity in preadolescent peer cultures. In this chapter I also describe and discuss important changes in what has been called the new media of, for example, video games, cell phones and texting, and social networking on Internet sites by preadolescents and adolescents. In addition to the major revisions of Chapters 6 and 9, the other chapters in Parts Two and Three have been updated in my introduction to, review of, and discussion of some of the best work recently published in the various areas covered.

Part Four brings us back to more macro issues. Here I consider children as social problems and also the social problems of children. I first examine growing levels of anxiety about children's potential victimization in rapidly changing industrialized societies in which adults feel they have less control over their children's lives. I then explore the reverse of this phenomenon, the tendency in modern societies to blame some children, most especially poor children and youth, for their own vulnerability. Chapters 10 and 11 provide a detailed discussion of the nature and extent of social problems of children (including disturbing global trends in poverty, family instability, and violence). In these chapters I present updated social indicators related to the quality of the lives of children and youth and note where some progress has been made, and I indicate where much more needs to be done in regard to both research and social policy. Updating these chapters is a challenge as we are still in the midst of a global recession that began late in 2007. The ultimate effects of this recession on the quality of children's lives are still unknown, as are possible improvements in what appears to be a slow economic recovery. In the last chapter I present some proposals (both major and more modest) to begin to address the social problems of children. In this last part of the book, my appreciation and celebration of children's lives and childhoods develop into clear political advocacy. I am aware that many readers may disagree with some of the specifics of my positions. Others (I hope a minority) will see them as misguided. In either case, I challenge all of you to join the debate.

I am indebted to a number of people for both the first edition and now this new edition of the book. Several scholars were influential in my developing a theoretical interest in children, and others have inspired me to expand and refine my theoretical approach. The first group includes Aaron Cicourel, whose work on socialization started me on the quest. The late Leonard (Slats) Cottrell was very important in providing me with support in my graduate student days. Slats convinced me that I should do the research I believed in and wanted to do even if it was out of the mainstream. He encouraged me to swim against the tide, and I have not drowned yet. A central intellectual role model for me has been Shirley Brice Heath, whose ethnographic work with children and families shines through with rigor, compassion, and integrity. Most recently I have been inspired and challenged by the theoretical views and writings on children and childhood of Lena Alanen, April Brayfield, Pia Christensen, Cindy Dell Clark, Candy Goodwin, Michael-Sebastian Honig, Allison James, Chris Jenks, Anne Trine Kjørholt, Randi Dyblie Nilsen, Barry Mayall, Steve Mintz, Alan Prout, Jens Qvortrup, Barbara Rogoff, Barrie Thorne, James Wertsch, and James Youniss.

I was pretty much a loner in my early work, but during the past 20 years a number of collaborators have helped me clarify, refine, and sharpen my thinking. Many of these collaborators have also assisted me in the field, and all are good friends. They include Art Alderson, Hilary Aydt, the late Sigurd Berentzen, Ana Carvalho, Jenny Cook-Gumperz, Donna Eder, Franca Emiliani, Ann-Carita Evaldsson, Laura Fingerson, Suzanne Gaskins, Kathryn Hadley, Dave Heise, Berit Johannesen, Doug Maynard, Peggy Miller, Fernanda Müller, Elizabeth Nelson, Tom Rizzo, Kathryn Brown Rosier, Jürgen Streeck, Heather Sugioka, the late Graham Tomlinson, Silvia Zetti, and most especially Luisa Molinari. I also want to thank my colleagues in the Department of Sociology at Indiana University, Bloomington, who have always strongly supported and encouraged my work with young children. Finally, I wish to thank the reviewers of the manuscript who provided a number of helpful and insightful comments.

I wish to thank several people who have worked with me through Pine Forge Press, most especially Steve Rutter, who was the editor for the first edition, and Jerry Westby, who worked with me as the editor of the second edition. The two people who have put up with me the most throughout all three editions of this book are my wife, Vickie Renfrow, and my daughter, Veronica. Finally, I wish to thank all the teachers and children who have allowed me to enter and be a part of their worlds in my research during the past 35 years. Their friendships have enriched my life and given me strong optimism concerning the present and future of childhood.

William A. Corsaro

To Veronica,
il mio Tesoro

PART ONE

The Sociological Study of Childhood

It was a bright, sunny day, and I was sitting with a group of boys who were digging in the outside play area of an Italian preschool. This was my second time doing research at the school. I had spent 9 months with the children and their teachers in the previous year, and now I was back for a 2-month follow-up. The boys were talking about military matters—the navy, warships, and the boss or *il capo* on such ships—as they dug holes and buried rocks in the dirt.

At some distance I saw three children marching around the yard carrying a large, red milk carton. The teachers used the carton to carry play materials to the yard, and I had seen the children playing with it before. What I did not know was that the carton was now a forbidden object. As I was to find out later, earlier in the year, before my arrival, a child had placed the carton on her head and chased after several other children. She eventually fell and suffered a minor injury. After this incident, the children were prohibited from playing with the carton.

(Continued)

(Continued)

But they were playing with it today. In fact, they were now marching in my direction, and I could begin to make out their chant. It sounded like *Arriva la barca! Arriva la barca!* (Here comes the boat! Here comes the boat!) I was not sure about the last word, though; it could have been *barca* or *banca* (bank). They were right up close to me now; Antonio was leading the way, and Luisa and Mario were helping him carry the carton. There was a bucket inside the carton, and it was filled with rocks.

"*La barca?*" I asked Antonio.

"*No, la banca coi soldi!*" (The bank with money!), he said as he cupped his hand in a familiar Italian gesture.

I was intrigued. These kids had created a whole new dimension in banking, a bank that makes house calls! "Give me some money," I said to Antonio.

The children now put the carton down, and Mario took out the small bucket with rocks and said, "I'll give the money to him." "How much do you want?" he asked. "There are thousands. . . ."

"Forty thousand," I quickly responded. (This sounds like a lot, but 40,000 lire was only about 25 dollars.)

Mario began counting out the rocks, doing exactly as they do in Italian banks by announcing the final sum as he counted out each 10,000 lira note: "Forty thousand, forty thousand, here's forty thousand."

But he counted only three rocks. "No, no, three—thirty thousand. I said forty!"

"Four," said Luisa. "Four!"

Mario then reached in the bucket to get more rocks and counted, "Thirty, forty, here," and handed me three more rocks and then a fourth.

"Sixty now," I said laughing. "Seventy. I said forty!"

"How many?" Mario asked.

Luisa was now getting impatient with Mario and seemed to think she could be a better bank teller. "Four, he said four!" she exclaimed as she reached to take the bucket from Mario.

The three children now began to struggle over the bucket, and Antonio scooped the rocks from my hand and dropped them back into the bucket. "Let's go," he commanded. And the children marched off again, chanting, *"Arriva la banca! Arriva la banca!"* I waved and called out, *"Ciao la banca!"*

Oklahoma City, Oklahoma—April 1995

At 9:02 a.m. on April 19, 1995, a major explosion destroyed the Alfred P. Murrah Federal Building in Oklahoma City. In the blast, 168 lives were lost, including the lives of 19 children and a nurse who was killed during the rescue attempt. More than 600 people were injured. The explosion was caused by a car bomb containing an estimated 4,800 pounds of explosives. The children ranged in age from 6 months to 5 years old and attended the America's Kids Day Care Center in the building. Two teachers and the administrator of the day care center were also killed.

Two suspects, Timothy McVeigh and his accomplice Terry Nichols, were arrested, and their trials began in June 1996. McVeigh was convicted of the bombing and received the death penalty. He was executed on June 11, 2001. Terry Nichols was convicted and is now serving a sentence of life imprisonment. The reason for the bombing was linked to McVeigh's deep anger at the federal government's raid on a religious group in Waco, Texas, that left some 80 members dead. It appears that all of the victims in Oklahoma City, including the children, died because they happened to be in a U.S. government office building that was targeted for destruction.

I purposely selected these two incidents because of their stark contrast. (I should point out that events like the first [children's joyful and creative reproduction and embellishment of the adult world within their peer cultures] and the second [the vicious and cowardly taking of children's lives by adults] can occur anywhere in the world.) My reason for presenting them is to illustrate two central concepts of a new sociology of children.

First, children are active, creative social agents who produce their own unique children's cultures while simultaneously contributing to the production of adult societies. Take the Italian preschoolers. They were not supposed to play with the milk carton. But they did not like the adult rule, so they played with it anyway. They created a unique "traveling bank"— an idea taken from the adult world but extended and given new meaning. (After this incident, one of the teachers told me that she saw the children playing with the carton but overlooked the rule violation because, like me, she was so impressed by the children's ingenuity.)

Second, childhood—that socially constructed period in which children live their lives—is a structural form. When we refer to "childhood as a structural form," we mean it is a category or a part of society, like social class and age groups. In this sense children are members or incumbents of their childhoods. For the children themselves, childhood is a temporary period. For society, on the other hand, childhood is a permanent structural form or category that never disappears even though its members change continuously and its nature and conception vary historically. It is somewhat difficult to recognize childhood as a structural form because we tend to think of childhood solely as a period when children are prepared for entry into society. But children are already a part of society from their births, as childhood is part and parcel of society.

As a structural form, childhood is interrelated with other structural categories such as social class, gender, and age groups (Qvortrup, 1994a). Thus, the structural arrangements of these categories and changes in these arrangements will affect the nature of childhood. In modern societies, for example, changes in social structural arrangements of categories such as gender, occupation or work, family, and social class have resulted in many mothers' working outside the home and their young children's spending much of their time in institutional settings such as day care centers and early childhood education programs, which did not exist in the past. The young Oklahoma City victims and the kids in the Italian preschool inhabited such settings; their experiences remind us that children both affect and are affected by society.

The first part of this book further develops these two basic tenets of a new sociology of childhood: Children are active agents who construct their own cultures and contribute to the production of the adult world, and childhood is a structural form or part of society. Chapter 1 contrasts the first tenet—that children are active social agents—with traditional views of socialization in sociology and psychology. Here, the notion of interpretive reproduction—the idea that children actively contribute to societal preservation (or reproduction) as well as societal change—is offered as an extension of the heretofore almost exclusive focus on the individual child's development and adaptation to society. Chapter 2 integrates the notion of interpretive reproduction with the general assumptions of the second tenet, which holds that childhood is a structural form or part of society. The importance of children's contributions to their own childhoods (and to childhood as a more abstract structural form) through their negotiations with adults, and through their creative production of a series of peer cultures with other children, is examined. Chapter 3 reviews and evaluates a variety of research methods for studying children's peer cultures and documenting the quality of children's lives in contemporary society.

1

Social Theories of Childhood

This chapter examines the reasons for the resurgent interest in children in society and, especially, in sociology. I review traditional theories of socialization and child development and examine basic assumptions in these theories that have now been called into question. Finally, I present an alternative theoretical approach to childhood, one that reconceptualizes the place of children in the social structure and stresses the unique contributions that children make to their own development and socialization.

Sociology's Rediscovery of Childhood

As recently as 23 years ago there was a near absence of studies on children in mainstream sociology (Ambert, 1986; for recent reflection on childhood studies also see Prout, 2005; Qvortrup, Corsaro, & Honig, 2009). Today the situation is very different. A large and growing number of monographs, edited volumes, and journal articles addresses theoretical issues and reports empirical findings related to the sociological study of children and childhood. Childhood socialization has been given expanded coverage in basic introductory texts in sociology, new journals and sections of national and international associations devoted to the sociology of childhood have been established, and courses on the sociology of childhood now frequently are offered.

These developments are long overdue and very encouraging. But why have children been so long ignored in sociology? Jens Qvortrup (1993a) aptly noted that children have not so much been ignored as they have been marginalized. Children are marginalized in sociology because of their subordinate position in societies and in theoretical conceptualizations of childhood and socialization. As I will discuss more fully in this chapter, adults most often view children in a forward-looking way, that is, with an eye to what they will become—future adults with a place in the social order and contributions to make to it. Rarely are they viewed in a way that appreciates what they are—children with ongoing lives, needs, and desires. In fact, the current lives, needs, and desires of children are often seen as causes for alarm by adults, as social problems that are threatening, that need to be resolved. As a result, children are pushed to the margins of the social structure by more powerful adults (including social theorists), who focus instead on the potential and the threat of children to present and future societies.

Another question prompted by the resurgence of interest in childhood is why ideas are now being put forth that reconsider, challenge, refine, and even transform traditional lay and theoretical approaches to children and childhood. One reason is that consideration of other subordinate groups by sociologists (for example, minorities and women) has drawn attention to the lives of children. Unlike other subordinate groups, children have no representatives among sociologists; however, the work of feminists and minority scholars has, at least indirectly, drawn attention to the neglect of children. Barrie Thorne noted that in some ideological constructions, *"women are closely and unreflectively tied* with children; womanhood has been equated with motherhood in a mixing of identities that simply does not occur for men and fatherhood" (1987, p. 96). Indeed, feminists who find themselves labeled (most especially by political conservatives) as selfishly negligent of children have responded that children should be the responsibility of women and men. In their call for recognition of more diverse and equitable roles for women and men, feminists have been slow to note the marginalization of children in sociology. However, feminist analyses of gender ideologies have provided a lens for what Thorne (1987) has called the "re-visioning of children," resulting in a number of important recent studies of children, gender, and identity (Alanen, 1994; Eder, 1995; Mayall, 2002; Thorne, 1993).

New ways of conceptualizing children in sociology also stem from the rise of constructivist and interpretive theoretical perspectives in sociology (Connell, 1987; Corsaro, 1992; James, Jenks, & Prout, 1998; Prout, 2005).

From these perspectives, assumptions about the genesis of everything from friendship to scientific knowledge are carefully examined as social constructions rather than simply accepted as biological givens or obvious social facts. What this means is that childhood and all social objects (including things such as class, gender, race, and ethnicity) are seen as being interpreted, debated, and defined in processes of social action. In short, they are viewed as social products or constructions. When applied to the sociology of childhood, constructivist and interpretive perspectives argue that children and adults alike are active participants in the social construction of childhood and in the interpretive reproduction of their shared culture. In contrast, traditional theories view children as "consumers" of the culture established by adults.

Traditional Theories: Socialization

Much of sociology's thinking about children and childhood derives from theoretical work on socialization, the processes by which children adapt to and internalize society. Most have focused on early socialization in the family, which views the child as internalizing society. In other words, the child is seen as something apart from society that must be shaped and guided by external forces to become a fully functioning member.

Two models of the socialization process have been proposed. The first is a deterministic model, in which the child plays a basically passive role. In this view the child is simultaneously a novice with potential to contribute to the maintenance of society and an untamed threat who must be controlled through careful training. In the second, a constructivist model, the child is seen as an active agent and eager learner. In this view, the child actively constructs his or her social world and his or her place in it. Let's look first at the deterministic model.

The Deterministic Model:
Society Appropriates the Child

Early theorists of socialization had a problem. In their day, the philosophy of individualism held sway; it was popular to focus on how individuals relate to society. Yet society was also recognized as a powerful determinant of individual behavior. How were these theorists to resolve the contradiction (Wentworth, 1980, pp. 38–39)? The solution to this problem was a theoretical view describing appropriation of the child by society.

Appropriation means the child is taken over by society; he is trained to become, eventually, a competent and contributing member. This model of socialization is seen as deterministic because the child plays a primarily passive role. Within the deterministic model, two subsidiary approaches arose that differed primarily in their views of society. The functionalist models, on the one hand, saw order and balance in society and stressed the importance of training and preparing children to fit into and contribute to that order. The reproductive models, on the other hand, focused on conflicts and inequalities in society and argued that some children have differential access to certain types of training and other societal resources.

Functionalist Models. Functionalist models, which were popular in the 1950s and 1960s, focused on describing rather superficial aspects of socialization: what the child needed to internalize and which parental childrearing or training strategies were used to ensure such internalization. Functionalists had little concern for why and how children become integrated into society. Alex Inkeles, for example, maintained that the study of socialization must be inherently "forward looking," specifying what the child must become to meet requisites for the continued functioning of society (1968, pp. 76–77).

The major spokesperson of the functionalist perspective, Talcott Parsons, set the tone for Inkeles's forward-looking view of socialization. In Parsons's view, the child is a threat to society; he must be appropriated and shaped to fit in. Parsons envisioned a society as an "intricate network of interdependent and interpenetrating" roles and consensual values (Parsons & Bales, 1955, p. 36). The entry of the child into this system is problematic because, although she has the potential to be useful to the continued functioning of the system, she is also a threat until socialized. In fact, Parsons likened the child to a "pebble 'thrown' by the fact of birth into the social 'pond'" (Parsons & Bales, 1955, pp. 36–37). The initial point of entry—the family—feels the first effects of this "pebble," and as the child grows older the effects are seen as a succession of widening waves that radiate to other parts of the system. In a cyclical process of dealing with problems and through formal training to accept and follow social norms, the child eventually internalizes the social system (Parsons & Bales, 1955, p. 202).

Reproductive Models. As sociological theory developed, the functionalist view of socialization lost favor. Some social theorists argued that the internalization of the functional requisites of society could be seen as a mechanism of social control leading to the social reproduction or maintenance of class inequalities (Bernstein, 1981; Bourdieu & Passeron, 1977). These reproductive models, as they are known, focus on the advantages enjoyed by those with greater access to cultural resources. For example, parents from higher social-class groups can ensure that their children receive quality education in prestigious academic institutions. Reproductive theorists also point to differential treatment of individuals in social institutions (especially the educational system), which reflects and supports the prevailing class system.

Weaknesses of the Deterministic Model. Reproductive theorists provide a needed acknowledgment of the effect of social conflict and inequality on the socialization of children. However, both functionalist and reproductive theories can be criticized for their overconcentration on the outcomes of socialization, their underestimation of the active and innovative capacities of all members of society, and their neglect of the historical and contingent nature of social action and reproduction. In short, these abstract models simplify highly complex processes and, in the process, overlook the importance of children and childhood in society.

A key question is, Where do children and childhood fit into these abstract theories of social structure? Not surprisingly, some of these social theorists downplayed the importance of children's activities, which they considered to be inconsequential or nonfunctional. Other determinists looked to theories of child development and learning that fit their views for explanations about the mechanisms of socialization. Parsons, for example, linked his views on socialization to Freud's theory of psychosexual development. In his model, socialization takes place as the child learns to act in accordance with social norms and values rather than according to innate sexual and aggressive drives. Inkeles opted for another type of determinism, behaviorism, and pointed to the importance of explicit training in the skills needed for living in society, supported by a system of rewards and punishments (1968, pp. 97–103).

Both functionalist and reproductive models overlook the point that children do not just internalize the society they are born into. As we saw in the example of the Italian preschoolers' traveling bank at the beginning of this part, children act on and can bring about changes in society. Reproductive theorists are, however, more inventive than functionalists in their views of socialization. Bourdieu (1977), for example, offers the complex and intriguing notion of the habitus to capture how members of

[handwritten margin note: LIFESTYLE, THE VALUES, THE DISPOSITIONS + EXPECTATION OF PARTICULAR SOCIAL GROUPS ACQUIRED THROUGH EVERYDAY LIVING]

society (or social actors), through their continual and routine involvement in their social worlds, acquire a set of predispositions to act and to see things in a certain way. This set of predispositions, this habitus, is inculcated in early socialization and plays itself out reproductively through the tendency of the child and all social actors to maintain their sense of self and place in the world (Bourdieu, 1993).

Bourdieu is on a track that usefully leads us away from determinism and provides a more active role for the child. However, this conceptualization of socialization limits children's involvement to cultural participation and reproduction while ignoring children's contributions to cultural refinement and change. For a model that truly incorporates an active child, we must consider the rise of constructivism.

The Constructivist Model: The Child Appropriates Society

Much of the early sociological study of childhood socialization was influenced by the dominant theories in developmental psychology at the time. The theories that sociologists most often turned to, most especially varieties of behaviorism, relegate the child to a passive role. In these theories development is basically unilateral, with the child being shaped and molded by adult reinforcements and punishments. Many developmental psychologists, however, have come to see the child as active rather than passive, involved in appropriating information from his or her environment to use in organizing and constructing his or her own interpretations of the world.

Piaget's Theory of Intellectual Development. Perhaps the best representative of the constructivist approach is the Swiss psychologist Jean Piaget. He studied the evolution of knowledge in children, which was a way of integrating two of his enduring interests: biology and epistemology (the study of knowledge) (Ginsburg & Opper, 1988). Piaget's many empirical studies of children and their development had a major impact on the image of the child in developmental psychology. Piaget believed that children, from the first days of infancy, interpret, organize, and use information from the environment and come to construct conceptions (known as mental structures) of their physical and social worlds.

Piaget is perhaps best known for his view that intellectual development is not simply an accumulation of facts or skills but rather a progression through a series of qualitatively distinct stages of intellectual ability. Piaget's notion of stages is important for the sociology of children because it reminds us that children perceive and organize their worlds in ways qualitatively different from the ways of adults. Consider, for example, the following incident, which occurred in my very first ethnographic study of young children. A 3-year-old boy, Krister, drew a squiggly line on a chalkboard. I asked him what it was, and he responded, "A snake." "A snake!" I replied and then asked, "Have you ever seen a snake?" "Sure," said Krister, pointing to his squiggly line, "right there!" I then realized that my perspective of the squiggly line as a representation of a snake was different than Krister's perspective of his creation, which was that the line was exactly what he said it was—a snake!

As a result of many similar experiences, I have gotten much better at adopting children's perspectives in my fieldwork. I have also come to appreciate, in line with Piaget's theory, that any sociological theory of children and childhood that attempts to explain children's understanding and use of information from the adult world as well as children's participation in and organization of their own peer worlds, must consider the child's level of cognitive development.

Although Piaget's conception of stages of development is the best-known element of his theory, the most important element of his theory is his conception of equilibrium. Equilibrium is the central force that propels the child through the stages of cognitive development. Unfortunately, not only is this concept often overlooked; it is also frequently misunderstood. Many sociological and psychological theorists (such as Parsons) use the idea of equilibrium to explain societal, behavioral, or attitudinal change as a return to a state of balance (in other words, an occurrence that creates disequilibrium will be followed by attempts on the part of a society or an individual to regain balance). Piaget, however, is concerned with the process of equilibration, or the actual activities the child undertakes to deal with problems in the external world. Piaget conceives of equilibrium as the "compensation resulting from the activities of the subject in response to external intrusions" (Piaget, 1968, p. 101). Intrusions are compensated for only by activities, and the maximum equilibrium involves not a state of rest but rather a maximum of activity on the part of the child.

Piaget believes that the tendency to compensate for disequilibriums is innate. This biological or nativist assumption does not mean, however, that Piaget is a biological determinist. Biological determinists hold that things such as innate tendencies, processes, or knowledge are the causes or determiners of children's development. For Piaget, the innate tendency to compensate for disequilibriums is just one part of his complex model of intellectual development. Although Piaget believed children have an innate tendency to compensate for environmental intrusions, the nature of the compensations is dependent on the activities of children in their social-ecological worlds.

We can get a more concrete understanding of Piaget's concept of equilibrium as well as his developmental stages by considering the following case study of a Piagetian experiment of children's understanding of the conservation of mass.

Children's Understanding of Conservation of Mass

In a classic experiment, Piaget would present a child between the ages of 4 and 9 with two identical balls of clay. The child would be asked if each ball contains the same amount of clay. If the child did not think so, he or she would be asked to take away or add some clay to make the balls identical. Then, Piaget would change one of the balls into a sausage shape as the child watched. The child would then be asked if the ball and sausage now contain the same amount of clay. This experiment can be seen as illustrating the process of equilibration, with the child attempting to compensate through a series of strategies. We can capture the nature of the series each child will go through by examining how children of different ages deal with the problem:

1. The very young child, age 4 or 5, concentrates on one characteristic or dimension of the objects, usually length, and is apt to say with a great deal of conviction, "This one has more 'cause it is longer!" The child is unaware of the notion of conservation of mass and refers only to one dimension. Again, the child shows a great deal of certainty, and there is limited mental activity or thinking. In fact, the child may even claim that the problem is too easy, silly, or possibly a trick.

2. The slightly older child, age 6 or 7, tends to reverse his or her original claim because he or she notices a second dimension (width or thinness). At this point a new strategy becomes probable because the uncertainty of the child leads to more activity in dealing with the intrusion. In thinking about the intrusion, the child oscillates back and forth in his or her thinking and may become vaguely aware of the interdependence of the sausage's elongation and its thinness. Here a child might start out with confidence: "This one has more 'cause it's longer. No, no wait, this one 'cause it's fatter. Oh, I don't know!"

3. The 7- to 9-year-old child acts on the insight of interdependence. He or she places a mental emphasis on the transformation rather than the static configuration with dimensions. He or she will make them both the same and

will now claim that they are equal. Here the child will often be very careful, rolling the ball into a second sausage and holding the two next to each other to see if they match. If not, he or she will go back to work, shortening one or lengthening the other until convinced that they are the same. Here there is a maximum of activity in the equilibration process as the child approaches the mental insight of conservation of mass.

4. For the 9- to 11-year-old, the strategy begins with the discovery of the compensations of the transformation (that is, as clay lengthens it becomes thinner; as it broadens it becomes shorter). Here the child may scoff at the question, saying, "They are obviously the same!" or, "See, it makes no difference. I can make this ball a sausage or the sausage a ball," doing so as he or she talks. At this point, conservation is accepted, and the child understands reversibility. Certainty now returns, and related problems in the future will seem simple (adapted from Piaget, 1968, p. 112; Ginsburg & Opper, 1988, pp. 150–151).

Vygotsky's Sociocultural View of Human Development. Another important constructivist theorist is the Russian psychologist Lev Vygotsky. Like Piaget, Vygotsky stressed children's active role in human development. Vygotsky, however, believed that children's social development is always the result of their collective actions and that these actions take place and are located in society. Therefore, for Vygotsky, changes in society, especially changes in societal demands on the individual, require changes in strategies for dealing with those demands. For Vygotsky, strategies for dealing with changes in societal demands are always collective; that is, they always involve interaction with others. These collective strategies are seen as practical actions that lead to both social and psychological development. In this sense, the child's interactions and practical activities with others lead to her acquisition of new skills and knowledge, which are seen as the transformation of previous skills and knowledge.

A key principle in Vygotsky's view is the individual's internalization or appropriation of culture. Especially important to this process is language, which both encodes culture and is a tool for participating in culture. Vygotsky argues that language and other sign systems (for example, writing, film, and so on), like tool systems (for example, material objects such as machines), are created by societies over the course of history and change with cultural development. Thus, argued Vygotsky, children, through their acquisition and use of language, come to reproduce a culture that contains the knowledge of generations.

Vygotsky offered a quite different constructivist approach to human development than that of Piaget. Although both theorists viewed development as resulting from the child's activities, Vygotsky made no nativistic assumption similar to Piaget's notion of equilibrium to account for the motivating factor that generates the child's activities. Vygotsky saw practical activities developing from the child's attempts to deal with everyday problems. Furthermore, in dealing with these problems, the child always develops strategies collectively—that is, in interaction with others. Thus, for Piaget human development is primarily individualistic, whereas for Vygotsky it is primarily collective.

Other differences exist between the two theorists. Piaget concentrated more on the nature and characteristics of cognitive processes and structures, whereas Vygotsky emphasized their developmental contexts and history. As a result, rather than identifying abstract stages of cognitive development, Vygotsky sought to specify the cultural events and practical activities that lead to the appropriation, internalization, and reproduction of culture and society.

How, specifically, do these processes of internalization, appropriation, and reproduction occur? Two of Vygotsky's concepts are crucial. First is the notion of internalization. According to Vygotsky, "every function in the child's development appears twice: first on the social level, and later on the individual level; first, between people (interpsychological) and then inside the child (intrapsychological)" (1978, p. 57). By this, Vygotsky meant that all our psychological and social skills (cognitive, communicative, and emotional) are always acquired from our interactions with others. We develop and use such skills at the interpersonal level first before internalizing them at the individual level.

Consider Vygotsky's conceptions of self-directed and inner speech. With *self-directed speech*, Vygotsky is referring to the tendency of young children to speak out loud to themselves, especially in problematic situations. Piaget saw such speech as egocentric or emotional and serving no social function. Vygotsky, on the other hand, saw self-directed speech as a form of interpersonal communication, except that in this case the child is addressing himself as another. In a sense, the child is directing and advising himself on how to deal with a problem. In experimental work, Vygotsky found that such speech increased when children were given tasks such as building a car with construction toys or were told to draw a picture. Vygotsky believed that over time, self-directed speech was transformed or internalized from the interpersonal to the intrapersonal, becoming inner speech or a form of thought. We can grasp his ideas when we think about how we first learn to read. Most of our early reading as young children is done out loud as we read to ourselves and others. Over time we begin to mumble and then to mouth the words as we read, and eventually we read entirely at a mental level. In short, the intrapsychological function or skill of reading has its origins in social or collective activity—reading out loud for others and oneself. For Vygotsky, internalization occurs gradually over an extended period of time.

In a second important concept, Vygotsky builds on his view of language as a cultural tool. According to Vygotsky, human activity is inherently mediational in that it is carried out through language and other cultural tools. A significant proportion of children's everyday activities take place in what Vygotsky calls the "zone of proximal development": "the distance between the actual developmental level as determined by independent problem solving and the level of potential development as determined through problem solving under adult guidance or in collaboration with more capable peers" (Vygotsky, 1978, p. 86). Let's go back to our example of learning to read. A child's actual level of reading ability would be measured by his or her ability to read, summarize, and talk about a story such as *Cinderella* or *Snow White*. A child's potential level of development would be estimated by his or her ability to read, summarize, and discuss the story with help from teachers, parents, and more-developed peers. The first indicates the child's full mastery of a particular ability or skill, whereas the latter indicates his or her potential level of mastery. The distance between the two levels is the zone of proximal development, as depicted in Exhibit 1.1.

As we can see in this exhibit, the child in interactions with others is always a step ahead in development of where she is alone. In this sense, interactions in the zone of proximal development

> are the crucible of development and culture, in that they allow children to participate in activities that would be impossible for them alone, using cultural tools that themselves must be adapted to the specific activity at hand, and thus both passed along to and transformed by new generations. (Rogoff, Mosier, & Göncü, 1989, p. 211)

Thus, the model of development is one in which children gradually appropriate the adult world through the communal processes of sharing and creating culture (Bruner, 1986).

Weaknesses of the Constructivist Model. Although the general acceptance of constructivism moved theory and research in developmental psychology in the right direction, its main focus still remains squarely on individual development. We can see this in repeated references to the *child's* activity, the *child's* development, the *child's* becoming an adult. In Piaget's theory, the focus is on the individual child's mastery of the world on her own terms. Constructivism offers an active but somewhat lonely view of children. Even when others (parents, peers, and teachers) are taken into account, the focus

Exhibit 1.1   Vygotsky's Zone of Proximal Development

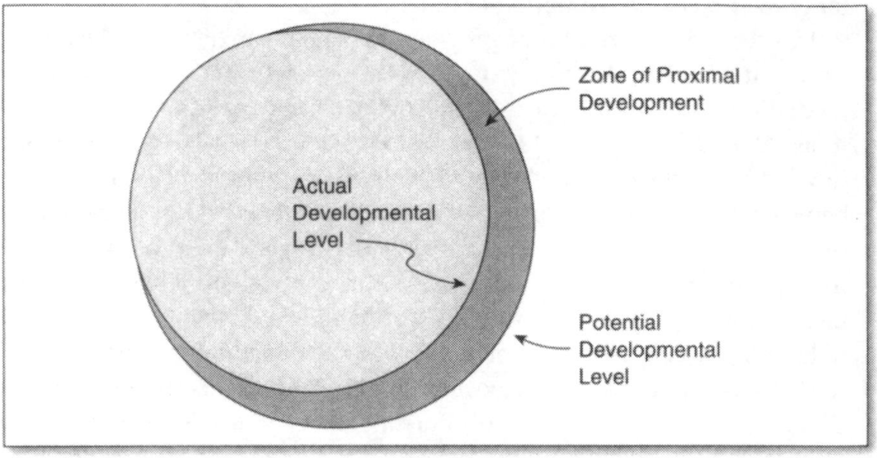

remains on the effects of various interpersonal experiences on individual development. There is little, if any, consideration of how interpersonal relations reflect cultural systems, or how children, through their participation in communicative events, become part of these interpersonal relations and cultural patterns and reproduce them collectively.

Another limitation of constructivist developmental psychology is the overwhelming concern with the endpoint of development, or the child's movement from immaturity to adult competence. Take, for example, research on friendship. The focus of nearly all of the research is on identifying stages in the child's abstract conceptions of friendship. These conceptions are elicited through clinical interviews, and a child's underdeveloped conceptions are compared to those of the competent adult (Damon, 1977; Selman, 1980). Yet few psychologists study what it is like to be or to have a friend in children's social worlds or how developing conceptions of friendships are embedded in children's interactions in peer culture.

This emphasis on the endpoint of development is also apparent in many developmental psychologists' interest in Vygotsky's notion of internalization. As we saw previously, Vygotsky stressed both children's collective interactions with others at the interpersonal level and their internalization of these interactions at the intrapersonal level in his theory of children's appropriation of culture. Yet much research by constructivists places so much emphasis on the second phase of internalization that many view the appropriation of culture as the movement from the external to the internal. This misconception pushes children's collective actions with others to the background and implies that an individual actor's participation in society occurs only after such individual internalization.

Extensions of Piaget and Vygotsky. Recent theoretical discussions and research by both Piagetians and sociocultural theorists influenced by Vygotsky have extended constructivist theory to focus more on children's agency in childhood and the importance of peer interaction. For example, Tesson and Youniss (1995) argued that there has been too much emphasis on the details of stages in developmental psychology. They maintain that Piaget did not place great importance on the stages and that his later work investigated the interrelationship between the logic and social qualities of children's thought. Expanding on Piaget's work on moral development, Tesson and Youniss argued that Piagetian operations enable children to make sense of the world as a set of possibilities for action. Thus, Piaget attributed agency to children and further argued that children's relationships with peers were more conducive to the development of cognitive operations than the authoritative relationships with adults. Along these lines, Piaget made a distinction between practical and theoretical modes of behavior.

> The practical occurs on the plane of direct action, the theoretical on the plane of consciousness. Piaget proposed a developmental relation between the two. First the child works out the conception of rules in the course of actual play with peers, then later the child grasps in consciousness a symbolic representation of this once practical concept. (Youniss & Damon, 1994, p. 417)

As we will see later, the interpretive approach to childhood socialization gives special emphasis to children's practical activities in their production of and participation in their own peer cultures.

Recent work by sociocultural theorists develops the theoretical work of Vygotsky in a similar vein, also stressing children's collective activities with peers and others. Rogoff, for example, building on Vygotsky, argues that "human development is a process of *people's changing participation in sociocultural activities of their communities*" (2003, p. 32). To capture the nature of children's involvements in sociocultural activities, Rogoff (1996) suggested that they be studied on three planes of analysis: the community, the interpersonal, and the individual. However, Rogoff noted that these processes must be analyzed not separately but together in collective activities. In line with this view of human development, Rogoff introduced the notion of "participatory appropriation" by which she meant that "any event in the present is an extension of previous events and is directed toward goals that have not yet been accomplished" (Rogoff, 1995, p. 155). Thus, previous experiences of collectively produced and shared activities are not merely stored in individual memory and called on in the present; rather, the individual's previous participation contributes to and primes the event at hand by having prepared it.

Here again, in this extension of the constructivist approach, we see new emphasis on collective actions in social context as essential for the development of children and all humans. To capture more fully the importance of collective action and children's construction of their own peer cultures, we now turn to a discussion of the notion of interpretive reproduction.

Interpretive Reproduction: IMPORTANT SECTION
Children Collectively Participate in Society

Sociological theories of childhood must break free from the individualistic doctrine that regards children's social development solely as the child's private internalization of adult skills and knowledge. From a sociological perspective, socialization is not only a matter of adaptation and internalization but also a process of appropriation, reinvention, and reproduction. Central to this view of socialization is the appreciation of the importance of collective, communal activity—how children negotiate, share, and create culture with adults and each other (Corsaro, 1992; James, Jenks, & Prout, 1998).

However, to say that a sociological perspective of socialization stresses the importance of collective and communal processes is not enough in constructing a new sociology of childhood. The problem is the term *socialization* itself. It has an individualistic and forward-looking connotation that is inescapable. One hears the term, and the idea of training and preparing the individual child for the future keeps coming to mind (Thorne, 1993, pp. 3–6; also see James, Jenks, & Prout, 1998, pp. 22–26). Instead, I offer the notion of interpretive reproduction. The term *interpretive* captures the innovative and creative aspects of children's participation in society. In fact, as we shall see throughout this book, children create and participate in their own unique peer cultures by creatively taking or appropriating information from the adult world to address their own peer concerns. The term *reproduction* captures the idea that children are not simply internalizing society and culture but are actively contributing to cultural production and change. The term also implies that children are, by their very participation in society, constrained by the existing social structure and by societal reproduction. That is, children and their childhoods are affected by the societies and cultures of which they are members. These societies and cultures have, in turn, been shaped and affected by processes of historical change.

As we can see from the above discussion, there is a central focus on children's peer cultures in interpretive reproduction. I define peer culture as a stable set of activities or routines, artifacts, values, and concerns that children produce and share in interaction with peers (Corsaro, 2003, 2009b; Corsaro & Eder, 1990).

Let's pursue this notion of interpretive reproduction and children's peer cultures further by looking at two of their key elements: the importance of language and cultural routines and the reproductive nature of children's evolving membership in their culture.

Language and Cultural Routines. Interpretive reproduction places special emphasis on language and on children's participation in cultural routines. Language is central to children's participation in their culture both as a "symbolic system that encodes local, social, and cultural structure" and as a "tool for establishing (that is, maintaining, creating) social and psychological realities" (Ochs, 1988, p. 210). These interrelated features of language and language use are "deeply embedded and instrumental in the accomplishment of the concrete routines of social life" (Schieffelin, 1990, p. 19).

Children's participation in cultural routines is a key element of interpretive reproduction. The habitual, taken-for-granted character of routines provides children and all social actors with the security and shared understanding of belonging to a social group. On the other hand, this very predictability empowers routines, providing a framework within which a wide range of sociocultural knowledge can be produced, displayed, and interpreted. In this way, cultural routines serve as anchors that enable social actors to deal with ambiguities, the unexpected, and the problematic while remaining comfortably within the friendly confines of everyday life (Corsaro, 1992).

Participation in cultural routines begins very early, almost from the minute children are born (see Stern, 1985, 2004). Early in infancy, at least in Western societies, when children's language and communicative

SOMETHING THAT CONSISTS OF 2 ELEMENTS OR PARTS.

abilities are emerging, social interaction proceeds in line with an "as-if" assumption. That is, infants are treated as socially competent (as if they were fully capable of social exchanges). Over time, because of this as-if attitude, infants quickly move from limited to full participation in cultural routines.

Consider, for example, the well-known parent-infant game of peeka-boo. In their study of six mother-infant dyads, Bruner and Sherwood (1976) identified four basic phases in peekaboo: (a) initial contact or shared attention (usually established by the mother through vocalization and/or gaze); (b) disappearance (usually the mother hiding her or her child's face with her hands or a cloth, accompanied by vocalizations such as "Where's baby?"); (c) reappearance (removal of hands or cloth, usually by the mother); and (d) the reestablishment of contact (usually with vocalizations such as "Boo," "There's the baby," and so on by the mother, gaining a response such as a smile or laugh from the child). Bruner and Sherwood noted that what the child appears to be learning "is not only the basic rules of the game, but the range of variation that is possible with the rule set" (1976, p. 283). Thus, by participating in the routine, children are learning a set of predictable rules that provide security, and they also are learning that a range of embellishments of the rules is possible and even desirable. In this way, children gain insight into the generative or productive nature of cultural participation in a play routine from which they derive great pleasure. Furthermore, we know from later work (Ratner & Bruner, 1977) that there is a movement from the as-if function of these games in the first months of life, when children's participation is often limited to a responsive role, to a point when the same children at 1 year old are initiating and directing the games and even creating and participating in other types of disappearance-reappearance games alone and with others.

To say that adults always strive for shared understanding with children and that the adoption of an as-if attitude in parent-child games is crucial in attaining joint activity does not mean that shared understanding is always achieved and maintained in adult-child interaction. What is important is not that shared understanding is always achieved but rather that attempts by both the adult and the child to reach such understanding are always made. Often, especially in adult-child interaction, children are exposed to social knowledge and communicative demands they do not fully grasp. Interaction normally continues in an orderly fashion, and any persisting ambiguities must be pursued over the course of the children's experiences with adults and peers.

DO CHIPS HAVE BLOOD ON THEM?

To illustrate the power and importance of cultural routines, let's consider a real-life example: an everyday interactive routine between a 2-and-a-half-year-old boy, Buddy, and his mother, which I video recorded in their home as part of my dissertation research a number of years ago. Buddy and his mother talked every weekday at this time as she prepared lunch. During this conversation, Buddy was still curious about blood from his cut finger the day before:

Mother: What?

Buddy: Chips [potato chips] have blood on them? Do they have blood on 'em?

Mother: No, I don't believe so.

Buddy: Kids and people do.

Mother: Um-hum.

Buddy: And monsters.

Mother: Yeah.

Buddy: Like Grover has blood on him.

Mother: Well, Grover's a pretend monster. He's really a puppet, you know?

Buddy: Yeah.

Mother: So he wouldn't have any blood on him.

Buddy: But Harry does.

Mother: Well, they're just like your puppets. Your Big Bird and your Cookie Monster.

Buddy: Yeah.

Mother: They're made out of cloth and furry things.

Buddy: Yeah, like—

Mother: Somebody made them—

(Continued)

(Continued)

Buddy: Harry has blood.

Mother: I don't think so. Pretend blood maybe.

Buddy: Yeah, maybe—maybe Grover and Cookie Monster and Harry have pretend blood. Maybe they do—maybe they have real blood.

Buddy: Mommy, someday I wanna go to Sesame Street and we can see if those monsters have blood.

Mother: You do?

Buddy: Yeah.

Mother: I don't know. We'll have to see about that. But you know what? Sesame Street is really a make-believe land.

Buddy: Oh, I didn't notice that.

Mother: You can pretend a lot of things about Sesame Street.

A number of issues are raised in this short episode that are relevant to interpretive reproduction:

1. Why is this a routine?

   Everyday talk of this type and at this time of day is recurrent and predictable in this family. In fact, this recurrence and typicality provides an opportunity to pursue issues that are problematic and confusing in the everyday activity of having lunch. Through their very participation in this everyday routine, the mother and child reaffirm their relation to one another and address problems and confusions about the world.

2. How is Buddy using the routine?

   First, Buddy uses the opportunity to address his curiosity about blood and who does and does not have it. At a surface level, his confusion about blood concerns a distinction between animate and inanimate objects. But soon the discussion moves beyond that distinction, to a discussion about real and pretend animate objects. Second, the routine allows Buddy an opportunity to display his knowledge and to discuss his interests with a receptive and supportive adult caretaker. In this sense, the repetitive enactment of such routines reaffirms these bonds and Buddy's status as an active member of the family.

3. How does Buddy's mother use the routine?

    First, on one level the routine provides her with information about a confusing concept that Buddy is trying to deal with (the distinction between animate and inanimate objects). On another level, however, Buddy's mother gains insight into the tie-in (for Buddy) between this distinction and a more general and complex distinction between real and pretend in modern culture. Consider the complexity: animate versus inanimate; pretend animate objects (dolls, puppets, and so on) versus inanimate objects (potato chips, apples, a flower pot); and the dramatic characters from a familiar television show. Second, the mother sees that the issue has a larger cultural significance when Buddy proposes to go to Sesame Street. She sees that her knowledge of the Sesame Street culture is different from her child's: She knows it is a fabricated television culture; he does not. She must now decide how far to push in addressing these distinctions given our culture's beliefs and values (and her interpretation of and commitment to such beliefs and values) regarding the existence of certain pretend figures (such as Santa Claus, the tooth fairy, and Big Bird). Third, the mother uses the routine to reaffirm the close relationship and bonding she has with her son. She takes the opportunity to display openness to his curiosity and concerns. In fact, this routine of talking at lunchtime may have been created by Buddy's mother for this very reason.

4. The emergent nature of routines

    This example demonstrates how the very predictability of routines provides a framework for producing, displaying, and interpreting cultural knowledge, values, and beliefs. We see how quickly the participants move from a basic question about blood to a discussion of a wide range of cultural facts, values, and relationships. Although the general framework of the routine itself (talking at lunchtime) is recurrent and predictable, what emerges in this talk (extensions and embellishments of the routine) is not. What we see here is that children, as they become part of their cultures, have wide interpretive latitude in making sense of their places in the world. Thus, almost any everyday routine interaction is ripe for children to refine and extend their developing cultural skills and knowledge.

5. Remaining ambiguities

    As in most cases involving young children, confusions are addressed but not resolved in routines. In some cases, the confusion may increase. However, the structure of routines allows participants to move ahead (in this case to go on with lunch) while the confusions are left behind to be pursued at other points in time.

From Individual Progression to Collective Reproductions

As we discussed earlier, many theories of child development focus on the individual child. These theories take a linear view of the developmental process. In the linear view, it is assumed that the child must pass through a preparatory period in childhood before he or she can develop into a socially competent adult. In this view, the period of childhood consists of a set of developmental stages in which cognitive skills, emotions, and knowledge are acquired in preparation for adult life (see Exhibit 1.2).

Interpretive reproduction views children's evolving membership in their cultures as reproductive rather than linear. According to this reproductive view, children do not simply imitate or internalize the world around them. They strive to interpret or make sense of their culture and

Exhibit 1.2   The Linear View of Development

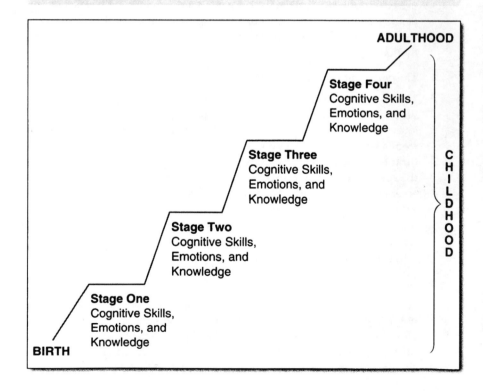

to participate in it. In attempting to make sense of the adult world, children come to collectively produce their own peer worlds and cultures.

The Orb Web Model

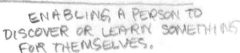

ENABLING A PERSON TO DISCOVER OR LEARN SOMETHING FOR THEMSELVES.

The notion of interpretive reproduction can be presented graphically in a way that captures its productive-reproductive characteristics. The key is to use a model that captures interpretive reproduction as a spiral in which children produce and participate in a series of embedded peer cultures. I've found the "spider web" to be an effective heuristic device or metaphor for conceptualizing interpretive reproduction (Corsaro, 1993). Of the different varieties of webs that spiders produce, the orb web, produced by common garden spiders, is the most useful for my conceptual needs. A number of features of the orb web make it a useful metaphor for conceptualizing the process of interpretive reproduction. Let's look at Exhibit 1.3. The radii or spokes of the model represent a range of locales or fields that make up various social institutions (family,

Exhibit 1.3   The Orb Web Model

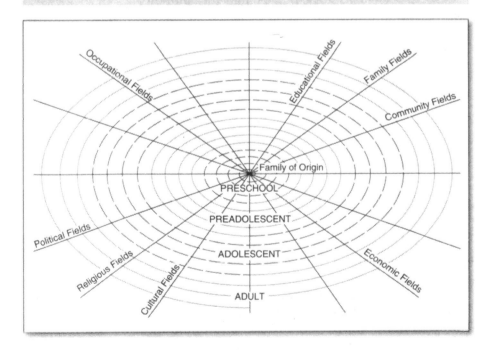

economic, cultural, educational, political, occupational, community, and religious). The fields illustrate the diverse locations in which institutional interaction or behavior occurs (Bourdieu, 1991). For example, family interaction takes place in a wide range of actual locales such as in the home; in the family car; at neighborhood parks; at family reunions, weddings, and funerals; and so forth, whereas educational activities take place in classrooms, libraries, gymnasiums, music practice rooms, and many other locations. It is important to note that these institutional fields (the radii of the web) exist as stable but changing structures on which children will weave their webs. Cultural information flows to all parts of the web along these radii.

At the hub or the center of the web is the family of origin, which serves as a nexus of all cultural institutions for children. Children enter the culture through their families at birth. Thus, families are very important to the notion of interpretive reproduction. Children in modern societies, however, begin to participate in other institutional locales with other children and adults who are not family members at an early age. It is in these institutional fields, as well as in the family, that children begin to produce and participate in a series of peer cultures.

The differently shaded spirals represent four distinct peer cultures, which are created by each generation of children in a given society: preschool, preadolescent, adolescent, and adult. Although aspects of peer culture may be passed on to younger children by older children, peer cultures are not preexisting structures that children encounter or confront. It is in this sense that these cultures differ from the institutional fields (radii) on which they are woven. Although affected by the many experiences that occur through interactions with the adult world and encounters in institutional fields (or crossings of the various radii), children's peer cultures are innovative and creative collective productions. In this sense, the webbing or spirals of peer cultures are collectively spun on the framework of the cultural knowledge and institutions they come in part to constitute.

These collective, productive, and innovative features of children's peer cultures are captured in the basic features of spiraling and embeddedness in the orb web model. Peer cultures are not stages that individual children pass through. Children produce and participate in their peer cultures, and these productions are embedded in the web of experiences children weave with others throughout their lives. Therefore, children's experiences in peer cultures are not left behind with maturity or individual development; rather, they remain part of their life histories as active members of a given culture. Thus, individual development is embedded in the collective production of a series of peer cultures that in turn contribute to reproduction and change in the wider adult society or culture.

Finally, it is the general structure of the model that is most crucial. As is the case for garden spiders, whose webs vary in terms of number of radii and spirals, when we use the web as a model for interpretive reproduction, the number of radii (institutional fields or locales) and the nature and number of spirals (the makeup or age diversity of peer groups and cohorts, the nature of the encounters and crossings of institutional locales, and so on) varies across cultures, across subcultural groups within a particular culture, and over historical time.

Children's Two Cultures

MAKE SOMETHING ABSTRACT MORE REAL OR CONCRETE.

Although the orb web model is useful for visualizing the nature of interpretive reproduction, like any metaphor it tends to reify a highly complex process; in other words, it regards as concrete something that is, in fact, an abstract concept. However, the model does capture the idea that children are always participating in and are part of two cultures— children's and adults'—and these cultures are intricately interwoven. To capture the complexity of children's evolving membership in these two cultures, we need to examine their collective activities with each other and adults. We also need to consider children part of a social group that has a place in the larger social structure. Here our focus will be on childhood as a structural form that has a permanent place in society. In this book we will continually shift back and forth between these micro and macro levels, examining both children and childhood.

SUMMARY

Until recently, sociology has paid relatively little attention to children and childhood. The neglect or marginalization of children in sociology is clearly related to traditional views of socialization, which relegate children to a primarily passive role. Most of these theories were based on behavioristic views of child development that have been severely challenged by the rise of constructivism in contemporary developmental psychology. Best represented in Piaget's cognitive developmental theory and

Vygotsky's sociocultural approach, constructivism stresses the child's active role in her development and her eventual participation in the adult world. Although constructivist theories of individual human development provide sociology with a lens for refocusing our images of children as active agents, these theories until recently have focused primarily on developmental outcomes and failed to seriously consider the complexity of social structure and children's collective activities. Interpretive reproduction and its emphasis on the importance of children's peer culture provide a basis for a new sociology of childhood. Interpretive reproduction replaces linear models of children's individual social development with the collective, productive-reproductive view that is illustrated in the orb web model. In the model, children spontaneously participate as active members of both childhood and adult cultures.

In Chapter 2 we will extend the notion of interpretive reproduction by examining its relationship to structural and relational approaches to children and childhood.

2

The Structure of Childhood and Children's Interpretive Reproductions

In Chapter 1 we discussed how interpretive reproduction argues that children affect and are affected by society. As a group, children are in a subordinate position in society in relationship to other groups. Therefore, even though children are active agents, the nature of their activities, power, and rights must be considered in relation to their role as a generational group in society and their place in the generational order (Alanen, 2000, 2009; M. Honig, 2009; Mayall, 2002). To capture these generational relationships, we must examine childhood from a structural perspective.

Assumptions of the Structural Perspective

In a series of theoretical papers stemming from his work on the international project "Childhood as a Social Phenomenon," the Danish sociologist Jens Qvortrup (1991, 1993a, 1993b, 1994a, 1994b, 2009) has outlined a structural perspective to the study of childhood. The approach is based on three central assumptions: (a) Childhood constitutes a particular structural form, (b) childhood is exposed to the same societal forces as adulthood, and (c) children are themselves coconstructors of childhood and society. Let's examine each of these assumptions.

Childhood as a Structural Form

We earlier discussed the notion of childhood as a social form, noting that childhood is both a period in which children live their lives and a category or part of society, like social class. We also discussed the idea that although childhood is a temporary period for children, it is a permanent structural category in society. Qvortrup further develops the notion of viewing childhood as a structural form by contrasting it with perspectives that focus on childhood only as a period of life. He places these perspectives in three general categories. The first is the typical psychological view, which is individual and personality oriented. In this view, childhood is forward looking or anticipatory and is determined by an adult perspective. The second is the psychoanalytic view, which is also individual and personality oriented, but here the interest in individual adulthood requires the retrospective examination of the individual's childhood experiences. A third view is the life course perspective. This perspective is a mix of individual and nonindividual approaches in that it follows single individuals from childhood to adulthood or vice versa while at the same time stressing the impact of historical and societal events. All of these views are similar to the traditional theories of socialization we discussed in Chapter 1 in that (a) they focus on the anticipatory outcomes of childhood (that is, children's becoming adults) and (b) they consider childhood and adulthood as necessarily belonging to different historical periods.

Qvortrup (2009) argued that, by conceptualizing childhood as a structural form, we can move beyond these individualistic, adult-oriented, and time-bound perspectives to pose and answer a wide range of sociological questions. Consider just a few possibilities: How is childhood like, different from, and related to other age groups at any given time and place? (For example, consider the interrelationships of childhood, adulthood, and old age in the 1950s compared to the 1980s in the United States.) How has the conception and nature of childhood changed over different historical periods in particular societies (for example, childhood in the 1890s compared to the 1990s in the United States)? How do conceptions and the nature of childhood vary across cultures at particular points in time (for example, childhood in the early years of the 21st century in Western industrial societies compared to non-Western developing societies)? We will examine these and related questions in detail in Chapters 4, 5, 9, and 10.

Let's now move to a consideration of the general effects of societal forces on childhood.

Effects of Societal Forces on Childhood

A key feature of Qvortrup's structural approach is that it sees childhood as integrated in society (Qvortrup, 1991, p. 14). Children in their particular childhoods are, like adults, active participants in organized activities (for example, they engage in economic production and consumption). They both affect and are affected by major societal events and developments. Consider, for example, recent changes in Western societies such as higher divorce rates, greater female participation in the labor force, and lower fertility levels (especially among the middle and upper classes). Sociologists have increasingly documented the effects of these factors on the family and to some extent on individual children. But how are the lives of children—that is, contemporary children's childhoods—affected by such changes? Furthermore, how might children, through their collective activities, contribute to society's accommodation to such changes?

We will examine children, families, and social change in Chapter 5, but first let's address one of the issues posed earlier, the interrelations of different age groups in a given society and how these may change over time. In particular, how has increased longevity due to modern technology affected the interrelationships of the generations and the lives of children in American society? Let's consider the following case study of the new American grandparent.

THE NEW AMERICAN GRANDPARENT

In their book *The New American Grandparent*, sociologists Andrew Cherlin and Frank Furstenberg (1986) charted the modernization of "grand-parenthood." They noted that a number of trends such as changes in mortality, fertility, communication, transportation, retirement, social security, and standards of living have transformed grandparenthood since World War II. As a result, "more people are living long enough to become grandparents and to enjoy a lengthy period of life as grandparents" (p. 33). Furthermore, noted Cherlin and Furstenberg, grandparents "can keep in touch more easily with their grandchildren; they have more time to devote to them; they have more money to spend on them; and they are less likely still to be raising their own children" (p. 35).

(Continued)

(Continued)

Cherlin and Furstenberg (1986) interviewed grandparents to pursue the effects of this modernization of grandparenthood and to examine grandparenting styles, careers, and the effects of divorce on grandparenting. They also studied the influence of grandparents on grandchildren. For this topic, the authors supplemented their interviews of grandparents with survey items from a larger study of adolescent grandchildren and their parents. Here the findings were somewhat surprising. Even though grandparenthood has seemed to change for the better, there was little evidence from the grandchildren's responses that greater involvement by grandparents had any major impact on their lives. In qualification of these findings, Cherlin and Furstenberg recognized the limits of their survey data, noting that surveys can "not reveal the subtle forms of influence that occur when grandparents and grandchildren interact over long periods of time" (p. 182). Nevertheless, they argued that the results are persuasive and lead them to see grandparents in America as "volunteer firefighters" who are "required to be on the scene when needed but otherwise keep their assistance in reserve" (p. 184).

Like most traditional sociological research that involves children, Cherlin and Furstenberg's (1986) study focuses on the effects of a social phenomenon (in this case grandparenting) on individual children. Although the authors' acknowledgment of subtle forms of influence hints at the complexity of the worlds of children and their grandparents, the authors failed to push their study to fully consider children's perspectives. For example, they did not consider the possible counterpart of the conception of grandparenthood, which we can term *grandchildhood*. Just as adults are grandparents, children are grandchildren, and as the nature of grandparenting changes, so does the nature of being a grandchild. The very difficulty of the word *grandchildhood* is due to the tendency of social scientists to think of children as individually affected (as dependent variables) rather than as agents of complex collective actions.

Surely the intergenerational lives of grandchildren have changed in ways that parallel those of their grandparents. We can consider a whole new set of vantage points: styles of being a grandchild, grandchild careers, and variations in these styles and careers by gender, class, race, and ethnicity (see Mayall, 2009). An important factor to keep in mind in this regard is the influence of parents on their children's lives as grandchildren (or, for that matter, the lives of their parents as grandparents). At least for younger children, for instance, parents control access to grandparents, and they both actively and reactively support children in their interpretation and appreciation of their interactions with grandparents. Finally, children's interactions with grandparents occur often in multigenerational settings (for example, in the presence of grandparents, parents, aunts, uncles, and cousins). These occasions provide an ideal setting for priming activities in which children are prepared for transitions into a variety of social relations in their lives (Corsaro & Molinari, 2000). One such family obligation—to serve as the adult child caretaker of elderly parents—may indeed be a long and demanding one for the present generation of children.

Children's Activities and Contributions to Society

Like all theories that focus primarily on how the structural features of society affect individual societal members, a structural approach to the sociology of childhood runs the risk of undervaluing how the collective actions of individuals (including children) can affect society. Qvortrup is well aware of this tendency, and he argued that "children are themselves coconstructors of childhood and society" (1993a, p. 14). While acknowledging the historical trend of an increasing sentimentalism and overprotectiveness of children, as noted by Zelizer (1985) and others, he challenged their accompanying contention that children have moved from being useful to useless. On the contrary, Qvortrup maintained that children have always been useful and that it is the nature of their contributions to society that have changed (1991, pp. 25–26). A wonderful example of Qvortrup's point in this regard is research conducted by the anthropologist Enid Schildkrout (1975/2002) in her study of a certain African culture.

AGE AND GENDER IN HAUSA SOCIETY

In her study of Hausa culture in the Nigerian city of Kano in the 1970s, Enid Schildkrout (1975/2002) found that children were essential in maintaining an institution known as *purdah*. Purdah relates to Hausa beliefs about male/female interaction and places specific limits on both men's and women's spatial mobility. The vast majority of married Hausa women in Kano were in purdah, which meant that they generally did not leave their compounds except to visit relatives or close female friends;

(Continued)

(Continued)

to attend ceremonies for births, marriages, and funerals; to go for medical treatment; or to visit the sick. Men also did not have free access in and out of each other's houses. A man could not, for example, enter the household of his younger married sister. Adhering to the rules of purdah meant there was very little daily interaction between men and women, even between spouses, because most men worked away from their homes.

Although purdah strongly affects the spatial mobility of adults,

> Hausa children enjoy a freedom that no other group in the society commands—the right to wander in and out of people's houses. Children are not expected to observe formal greetings behavior, and they casually walk into the houses of neighbors, relatives, friends, and even strangers, to look for playmates, to make purchases, to offer things for sale, or to carry messages. (Schildkrout, 1975/2002, p. 357)

Children's freedom in this regard is essential for the institution of purdah because, if this were not the case, women (except for the very wealthy, who could replace children with paid labor) could not remain in purdah and still carry out their domestic responsibilities. Furthermore, children's freedom allowed women to be involved in independent economic activities. With their own children or those of relatives or neighbors to serve as street traders and messengers, "women sell cooked food outside their houses, and may invest in other commodities such as detergent, kola nuts, sugar, salt, fruit— just about anything that can be transported on a tray and sold in small quantities" (p. 352). Money from these economic ventures serves as insurance for divorce, which is frequent; it also can supplement the income of husbands. As a result of the experiences in this cash economy of adults very early in life, many girls and boys develop their own "children's economy." They use allowance money provided for their work for their mothers and for running errands for other adults to set up their own small businesses.

> By ten, many girls cook for sale on their own. With initial help from their mothers, or other adult female relatives, who may give them a cooking pot, charcoal, or a small stove, they purchase small amounts of ingredients and prepare various snack foods. These are then sold in very small quantities to other children. (p. 360)

It is clear that Hausa women's and men's sex roles could not be defined as they were without the children performing roles that were distinct from but complementary to those of adults.

By the time this study was first published in 1975, Schildkrout found that the development of Western educational beliefs and increasing primary school enrollment was viewed by adult members of the Hausa culture as threatening the institution of purdah and the complex socioeconomic relations and complementary roles of adults and children in these relations. Although very few people objected to what were seen as the long-term benefits of Western education, the resistance that did exist was "very often based upon those very realistic appraisals of its immediate socio-economic consequences" (Schildkrout, 1975/2002, p. 365).

Although this case study is generally in line with functionalist views of society, which we criticized in Chapter 1, there is an important difference in this particular case from traditional functionalist views of children and socialization. In the Hausa culture, children do not simply internalize the norms of their society like those in line with purdah and then behave in accordance with them in later life. On the contrary, children are active contributors to society in that they cooperate with adults in the enforcement of norms and values. In the process of carrying out activities related to purdah, children do, of course, come to understand its significance, and in this way they contribute to societal maintenance.

Overall, this case study vividly illustrates the ways in which children serve as active contributors to society and how children and adults are complementary participants in the social system. Qvortrup points to other activities of children from industrialized societies—in school, the workplace, the home, and organized sports, play and leisure settings—through which children make similar contributions.

Children's Schoolwork. In line with historians and sociologists of education, Qvortrup notes children's movement from primarily agricultural labor in preindustrial society, to a wide range of types of work during the transition to industrial capitalism (on farms, in factories, in mills, on city streets), and finally to formal schooling in modern industrial societies. He argues, however, that this last movement should not be seen as a break from the past, because schooling is a continuation of children's work (albeit of a different type); it is an investment in the future economic health of any modern society. Furthermore, schooling has some immediate payoff in that children, along with their teachers, are coproducers of knowledge. This point is especially true in modern societies where children and youth spend long periods of time (stretching well into young adulthood) in educational institutions.

The notion of schooling as work is not widely recognized by adults, including social scientists. Qvortrup links this "collective amnesia" regarding the usefulness of schoolwork to the bureaucratic nature of schools—to their focus on functioning as accrediting devices that shape immature and unskilled children into productive adults. Such views are clearly related to the traditional theories of socialization and child development; the focus is on preparing children for their future as adults rather than appreciating their present contributions.

Children's Work Outside the Home. Given the amount of time children in Western societies spend on schoolwork, opportunities for work outside the home would seem to be limited. In fact, youth employment has declined in much of western Europe and in Japan. The trend in the United States has been different, with youth employment rising steadily into the 1970s and then declining in the 1980s because of economic downturns. After the decline there was again a rise but not to the level of the 1970s (Blanchflower & Freeman, 2000; Harrisson, Reubens, & Sparr, 1983; U.S. Department of Labor, 2000). In developing countries the pattern is somewhat different because children have always worked either for their families or for others to supplement family income. Although educational expansion has somewhat curtailed the number of hours children and youth can work, demanding work with long hours normally supplements school work for even young children in these countries (see Katz, 2004; Nieuwenhuys, 2009).

In theory, children's work outside the home should have benefits. It can, for example, add variety to childhood experiences and prepare children for future work roles. For both developing and industrialized societies, however, there is much debate about what children gain from work outside the home today, and they can be exploited (Greenberger & Steinberg, 1986; Nieuwenhuys, 2009). We will discuss why work outside the home is seldom beneficial for children in contemporary society in later chapters.

Children's Work in the Home. As increasing numbers of women have entered the workforce, the study of domestic labor or housework has become an important research topic in American sociology. Most studies document the heavy work demands and stress on dual-income and single-parent families, most especially for women. In fact, study after study documents that women perform most of the housework in what Arlie Hochschild (1989) termed the "second shift." Beth Shelton (1992), for example, found that in 1987 employed women spent an estimated 33 hours a week on housework compared to employed men's 22 hours a week.

In many of the early studies of domestic labor carried out in the 1970s and early 1980s, children were seen primarily as sources of additional work for mothers. More recently, however, researchers have begun to take children's contributions into account. Most of these studies do not use children as respondents but rather use parental (usually mother's) reports of children's work in the home. Nonetheless, most of the studies reported a similar pattern, with younger children (8- to 13-year-olds) contributing 2 to 4 hours a week to domestic chores and older children (14- to 18-year-olds) 6 to 9 hours a week. In accounting for differences by age, the studies also consistently documented gender differences, with girls contributing more domestic labor than boys. Moreover, chores were highly gender typed, with girls doing cooking, cleaning, and other indoor tasks and boys more often engaging in outdoor tasks such as yard work. In one study of parental reports of the household labor of 5- to 18-year-old children, Sampson Blair found that "daughters perform significantly more total labor than sons (5.62 versus 4.63 hours) per week" and that daughters spent "the majority of their time in those tasks traditionally defined as 'female-dominated'" (1992, pp. 187–188).

An interesting aspect of these studies is how the relationship between children and domestic labor is conceptualized. Although psychologists often consider the effects of such labor on children's cognitive, emotional, and social development (see Goodnow, 1988), sociologists focus primarily on adult members of the family and on implications for the reproduction of current gender inequalities. In neither case do we learn much about children's perspectives on household chores or how domestic labor relates to other features of children's daily lives. We will pursue these topics in Chapter 5.

Children's Play and Leisure Activities. In his book *Childhood's Future* (1990), the journalist Richard Louv recounts an episode when he was playing catch with his son in a city park. The park was filling with children's soccer teams, and as Louv and his son Jason threw the ball back and forth, they were approached by the mother of one of Jason's classmates. Louv reports the following conversation:

"Whatcha doing? Waiting for a team?" she said with a friendly smile.

"Nope. Just playing catch," I answered, tossing the ball to Jason.

"Killing time, eh?" she said. (p. 109)

This exchange captures the recent trend in Western societies toward the institutionalization of increasingly more children's leisure-time activities; the woman assumed the father and son would not be in a park with a ball and a mitt unless they were waiting for an organized event to take place. Qvortrup reported that in all of the 16 industrialized countries participating in the international project "Childhood as a Social Phenomenon," more than 50% of children are involved in organized sports and leisure activities, with many involved in several such activities (Qvortrup, 1991, p. 29).

Commentators such as Louv and Qvortrup challenge the assumption that such activities are voluntary on the part of the children, pointing to the highly structured, closely supervised, and rigidly scheduled nature of what Qvortrup termed "planned spontaneity" (Qvortrup, 1991, pp. 29–30; see also Chudacoff, 2007; Louv, 1990, pp. 109–116). Children interviewed by Louv echoed this theme. One fifth grader commented,

> I don't really have much time to play at all because I have piano lessons. My mom makes me practice for about an hour every day, and then I have my homework, and that's about an hour's worth, and then I got soccer practice, and that's from 5:30 to 7:00, and then there's no time left to play. On weekends we usually have soccer games, and I have the chores, and then I'm free to play—which is only about two hours, three hours something like that. (Louv, 1990, p. 110)

This child's distinction between planned activities, such as soccer and piano practice, and play is intriguing. Kids seem to have less and less time to be kids. In fact, many commercial establishments (pizza restaurant chains, indoor playgrounds, or amusement areas) try to convince parents that they can provide "kid play" for their children. But why aren't kids allowed to find their own fun, to set out on their own play quests in the neighborhood, in nearby parks and playgrounds, or even in their own backyard? This shift toward the institutionalization of childhood and less opportunity for children to have time for free play—especially outdoors— has led to what Louv (2008) called nature-deficit disorder. Louv has many wonderful suggestions in his international back-to-nature campaign to combat children's separation from nature. However, he is fighting an uphill battle as there are many structural and cultural reasons for the institutionalization of childhood in modern society.

The major reason for an increase in organized activities for children may well be an accompanying increase in parental concerns regarding children's safety. Given modern conditions, parental preoccupation with children's well-being, even while playing in their own neighborhoods, is understandable. Such fears have been heightened in recent years by the media's reporting and depiction of children as victims of kidnappings and physical and sexual abuse.

Much debate exists about the accuracy of descriptive accounts and statistical reports of child victimization and other threats to children (J. Best, 1990; Glassner, 2010). Violent crimes in general have declined after peaking in the 1980s. Yet there is little doubt that concerns about the physical safety of poor children in the United States and throughout the world are justified. However, the general anxiety about children's safety runs much deeper, beyond big-city streets to affluent suburbs and small towns. This uneasiness about our children is probably related to the state of modern societies more generally: We have less time for our children and for family interaction and activities, we do not know our communities and neighborhoods well, and we rely more on the media for information and advice (Stephens, 1993).

A second reason for the increased institutionalization of children's activities is that structured leisure activities and lessons provide parents with needed child care. In a national child care survey in the United States conducted by the Urban Institute, Sandra Hofferth and her colleagues found that "many parents use lessons as a way to care for school-age children after school, as well as to expand their academic, physical, social, and cultural skills" (Hofferth, Brayfield, Deich, & Holcomb, 1991, p. 67). The percentage of families relying on lessons for after-school care is highest for households with working mothers, where 22.4% rely on such care for their 10- to 12-year-old children. This is the most frequent type of arrangement, except for "father care"—or care by fathers—which was the type of care in 33% of households with working mothers. Hofferth and colleagues pointed out the "two for one" advantage of after-school lessons: The child gets to pursue an area of interest, and at the same time the parent benefits from child care. The data also suggest that lessons may become a necessary replacement for child center care as children move from preschool into elementary school. For example, 42.8% of families with employed mothers rely on center care (child care at an institutionalized setting) for 3- to 4-year-olds, 16% for 6- to 9-year-olds, and only 3.2% for 10- to 12-year-olds; the corresponding figures for families relying on after-school lessons is 0.6% for 3- to 4-year-olds, 13.6% for 6- to 9-year-olds, and 22.4% for 10- to 12-year-olds (Hofferth et al., 1991, p. 50). Older children may be more interested in pursuits such as piano and tennis lessons; however, it is also true that after-school care for school-age children is not available in many communities.

A third reason for an increase in organized activities for children may be demographic changes in American families. As social demographer Don Hernandez (1993a, 1993b) recently documented, children have experienced a dramatic shift from large to small families during the past 100 years. For example, noted Hernandez,

> the typical child born in 1890 lived, as an adolescent, in a family in which there were about 6.6 siblings, but the typical child born in 1994 is expected to live in a family that is only one-third as large—with 1.9 children. (1993b, p. 418)

Although there was a brief lull in this dramatic shift during the baby boom period from about 1945 to about 1957, it was more than offset by the baby bust period in later years. As Hernandez noted, this shift has drastically reduced the number of siblings who are available for companionship. Without siblings to integrate them into informal neighborhood activities and children's cultures (or to serve as caretakers and protectors), children find they have to rely more on parents. And for the two reasons we just discussed, parents often turn to organized (and often age-segregated) activities.

Childhood, Children's Activities, and Interpretive Reproduction in Peer Culture

Qvortrup's approach to childhood as a social phenomenon and his emphasis on children as active coconstructors of their social worlds reflect an important shift away from individualistic views of socialization in which the individual child internalizes adult skills and knowledge. His view leads us to a better understanding of children's place, stake, and importance in both cultural production and cultural maintenance. Children do not just actively contribute to the adult culture and their own childhoods in a direct way, however. Children creatively appropriate information from the adult world to produce their own, unique peer cultures. As we saw in Chapter 1, the process of interpretive reproduction enables children to become a part of adult culture—to contribute to its reproduction and extension—through their negotiations with adults and their creative production of a series of peer cultures with other children. Let's turn now to a more detailed discussion of this notion of interpretive reproduction within children's peer cultures.

In Chapter 1 we discussed examples of young children's participation in cultural routines in the family. For example, we considered the importance of parent-infant games such as peekaboo for providing infants with opportunities to participate in everyday family life and to develop a sense of security in belonging to a social group. Also, in the case study of the 2-and-a-half-year-old child (Buddy) and his mother, we saw that the everyday routine of conversation at lunch helped establish a strong emotional bond between mother and son, and it also provided Buddy with numerous opportunities to explore and to learn about his social world. Through their participation in such cultural routines in the family with parents and siblings, young children initiate their evolving membership in their culture. We can see this evolving membership as a process in which children refine and expand their place in the culture over time and with experience (Lave & Wenger, 1991). This process continues as children, from very young ages, begin to participate in cultural routines and other collective activities outside the family. By interacting with playmates in playgroups and preschools, children produce the first in a series of peer cultures in which childhood knowledge and practices are gradually transformed into the knowledge and skills necessary to participate in the adult world.

We will consider children's peer cultures in detail in Chapters 6 through 9. Here I want to stress that children's production of peer cultures is neither a matter of simple imitation nor direct appropriation of the adult world. Children creatively appropriate or take information from the adult world to produce their own unique peer cultures. Such appropriation is creative in that it extends or elaborates peer culture; children transform information from the adult world to meet the concerns of their peer world. In this way they simultaneously contribute to the reproduction of the adult culture. Thus, children's peer cultures have an autonomy that makes them worthy of documentation and study in their own right.

Three Kinds of Collective Action

In Chapter 1, I referred to the process of creative appropriation as *interpretive reproduction*. This is made up of three types of collective action: (a) children's creative appropriation of information and knowledge from the adult world; (b) children's production and participation in a series of peer cultures; and (c) children's contribution to the reproduction and extension of the adult culture. These activities follow a certain progression: Appropriation enables cultural production, which contributes to reproduction and change. The activities are, however, not historically partitioned. That is, children do not proceed through a specific period in which they appropriate all the needed information to produce a peer culture and only then make contributions to reproduction and change in adult culture. Instead, these collective actions occur both within the moment and over time. To better understand this idea, it is helpful to consider how children acquire and use language. Children do not first learn all the rules of grammar, phonology, and semantics; practice these rules; and only then begin to use them to communicate with others. Instead, children use their developing language skills to communicate at specific moments in time, and they refine and further develop the skills through repeated use in interaction over time. It is the same for the creation of and participation in peer culture. Children appropriate information from the adult world to create and participate in a peer culture at specific moments in time. These same collective actions, through their repetition in peer culture over time, contribute to children's better understanding of the aspects of the adult culture they have appropriated. Furthermore, these repetitions over time can even bring about changes in certain aspects of the adult culture. Let's consider the following case study.

↗ IMPORTANT

PRESCHOOL CHILDREN'S SECONDARY ADJUSTMENTS TO TEACHER'S RULES

In my 20 years of ethnographic research in nursery schools in the United States and Italy, I found that children attempt to evade adult rules through collaboratively produced *secondary adjustments*, which enable children to gain a certain amount of control over their lives in these settings. According to Goffman, secondary adjustments are "any habitual arrangement by which a member of an organization employs unauthorized means, or obtains unauthorized ends, or both, thus getting around the organization's assumptions as to what he should do and get and hence what he should be" (1961, p. 189).

In my studies I found that children produced a wide variety of secondary adjustments in response to school rules. For example, the children employed several concealment strategies to evade the rule that prohibited bringing toys or other personal objects from home to school. This rule was necessary: Personal objects were attractive to other children simply because they were different from the everyday materials in the preschools, and as a result the teachers were constantly settling disputes about these items. Therefore, such objects could not be brought to school; if they were, they had to be stored in the child's locker until the end of the day. In both the American and Italian schools, the children attempted to evade this rule by bringing small personal objects that they could conceal in their pockets. Particular favorites were small toy animals, model cars, candies, and chewing gum. While playing, a child often would show his or her "stashed loot" to a playmate and carefully share the forbidden object without catching the teachers' attention. The teachers, of course, often knew what was going on but simply ignored minor transgressions. The teachers overlooked these violations because the nature of the secondary adjustment often eliminates the organizational need to enforce the rule. Children shared and played with smuggled personal objects surreptitiously to avoid detection by the teachers. If the children always played with personal objects in this fashion, there would be no conflict and hence no need for the rule. That is not the case, however; the careful sharing took place only because the adult rule was in effect. Thus, in an indirect way, the secondary adjustment endorsed the organizational need for the rule. We see, then, that children's secondary adjustments (which are innovative and highly valued features of the peer culture, as we shall see in Chapter 7) often contributed to the maintenance of the adult rules.

The story does not end here, however. The children's secondary adjustments to school rules often led to the teachers' selective enforcement of the rules and, in some cases, to changes in the rules and in the organizational structure of the nursery school. I often found that teachers relaxed the enforcement of school rules because they recognized the creativity of certain features of peer culture. For example, in an American school, teachers first relaxed a rule prohibiting children from moving objects from one play area to another; they allowed the children to use string and blocks from a worktable to create a "fishing" game by dangling the string from an upstairs playhouse to their peers below, who then attached the blocks. The teachers then actually endorsed the secondary adjustment by joining in the play (see Corsaro, 1985, p. 257). In these instances the teachers themselves appeared to be engaged in a secondary adjustment to their own rules and exposed children to a basic feature of all rules—that is, knowledge of the content of a rule is never sufficient for its application; rules must be applied and interpreted in social context (Wootton, 1986).

SUMMARY

In recent years we have seen the beginnings of a new sociology of child-hood, one that breaks free from the individualistic doctrine that regards socialization as the child's private internalization of adult skills and knowledge. In this new approach the focus is on childhood as a social construction resulting from the collective actions of children with adults and each other. Childhood is recognized as a structural form and children as social agents who contribute to the reproduction of childhood and soci-ety through their negotiations with adults and through their creative pro-duction of a series of peer cultures with other children. This new view of childhood as a social phenomenon replaces the traditional notion of socialization with the concept of interpretive reproduction. Interpretive reproduction reflects children's evolving membership in their culture, which begins in the family and spirals outward as children create a series of embedded peer cultures based on the institutional structure of the adult culture. Overall, the notion of interpretive reproduction challenges sociology to take children seriously and to appreciate children's contribu-tions to social reproduction and change.

3

Studying Children and Childhood

The resurgence of interest in children in sociology has led to numerous studies of children and childhood using a variety of methods (for discussion and reviews, see A. Best, 2007; Christensen & James, 2008b; A. Clark, Kjørholt, & Moss, 2005; Greene & Hogan, 2005; Lange & Mierendorff, 2009; V. Lewis, Kellett, Fraser, Ding, & Robinson, 2003). One general trend in this research during the past 20 years has been a movement from *research on* to *research with* or *research for* children. This trend "repositions children as the subjects, rather than the objects of research" (Christensen & James, 2008c, p. 1; also see Nilsen, 2005). Thus, the research process reflects a direct concern with capturing children's voices, perspectives, interests, and rights as citizens. In doing so, researchers have not devised new methods for studying children that differ from traditional methods used to study adults. Rather, they have maintained that methods for studying any group should include a rigorous application of techniques applied to that group with special attention to the group's specific needs and particularities (Christensen & James, 2008b; Corsaro & Fingerson, 2003). Therefore, instead of studying adults as representatives of children (for example, relying on parents', teachers', or clinicians' perceptions and reports about children), researchers view children as social actors in their own right and adapt and refine methods to better fit their lives.

Childhood is a Permanent Structural form [handwritten annotation]

In line with the notion of interpretive reproduction, which stresses that children affect and are affected by society, this chapter reviews, at a micro level, methods for capturing children's everyday lives as participants in their cultures, and the nature of their childhoods in time and space at a more macro level. Although the renewed interest in children grew primarily from fine-grained ethnographic studies, over time research on children has become more diverse and has come to reflect sociology's general aim of studying social phenomena at multiple levels of analysis.

Macrolevel Methods ☆ IMPORTANT [handwritten annotation]

Macrolevel methods of research enable us to explore the variability and nature of childhood and children's experiences and quality of life as macrophenomena (Qvortrup, 2000). These methods are primarily comparative and are essential for identifying factors that contribute to the diversities of childhood and children's daily lives. They include demographic, large-scale surveys and social historical studies that can involve comparisons across communities, across generations, across nation-states, and over historical time.

Demographic Studies

Demographic studies using census data have documented changes in family structure and children's lives. The work of Hernandez (1993a; also see Hernandez & Charney, 1998) captures the face of childhood in terms of race, ethnicity, and class and also how patterns of immigration affect childhood in the United States and other developed countries. Hernandez's work is especially important in the United States because he uses the child (rather than the family) as his unit of analysis to describe profound changes in families and childhood during the past 150 years. We consider Hernandez's work in Chapter 5 when we discuss social change, families, and children.

Other demographic research studies equity of distribution of resources across age and generational groups in society. The United States and most modern industrialized societies have seen a trend in social policies that invest more resources in the elderly than the young. For example, in 1995 the U.S. federal government dispensed nearly 10 times as much in benefits to adults aged 65 and older than to children 18 and younger (Peterson, 1999, p. 110). This trend has led to a decrease in poverty and an increase in the quality of life (especially due to better medical care) for the elderly, whereas the reverse has been the case for children.

Demographers have found that as investment in the elderly has risen and the cost of having children has increased, fertility rates in developed countries have dropped. In some cases, especially in Italy, Germany, and Japan, the decrease in fertility has been dramatic, and the viability of pension schemes, social security, and medical care for the elderly will be severely threatened in the near future due to a lack of workers to contribute to such programs (Qvortrup, 1994b; Sgritta, 1994, 1997). The drop in fertility in the United States has not been as severe compared to the drop in other countries, but the fertility rate in the United States is slightly below replacement level, and a large number of people from the baby boom generation will reach retirement age by 2014. Therefore, major social programs such as social security and Medicare will be hard to maintain at current levels.

We will discuss, in Chapters 11 and 12, the equity across generations and the need to invest more in children. Here, in this chapter, I want to stress that important work by demographers demonstrates the interdependence of the generations and how demographic changes demand greater investments in children.

Large-Scale Surveys

Several authors have worked with large-scale survey data sets involving the direct participation of children (for example, the 1997 Child Development Supplement of the Panel Study of Income Dynamics, a 30-year longitudinal survey of men, women, and the families in which they reside [see Hofferth & Sandberg, 2001a] and the Children of the National Longitudinal Surveys of Youth, a biennial survey of the children of female Children of the National Longitudinal Surveys of Youth respondents [see Wu & Li, 2005]) or reports by parents and other caretakers about the quality of life of children in the United States and Europe (for example, the 1990 National Child Care Survey of the Panel Study of Income Dynamics and the Profile of Child Care Settings in 1989–1990 [see Hofferth, 1995; also see R. Jones & Brayfield, 1997]). Survey data sets on adolescents are central to the study of adolescent experiences and the transition to adulthood in the United States (for example, the National

Longitudinal Study of Adolescent Health [see Resnick et al., 1997] and the National Longitudinal Survey of Youth 1997 [see Paternoster, Bushway, Brame, & Apel, 2003]). The collection and analysis of large-scale survey data sets and census data, both in the United States and in other countries, help to gauge the effects of globalization on children's lives, welfare, and social trajectories to adulthood.

Surveys of children must, however, be interpreted with caution, given the special demands faced by researchers using such methods with children. We must also remember that parental and other caretaker reports about children's behaviors, beliefs, and values may differ considerably from reports by children themselves. In detailed reviews of methodological and empirical literature, J. Scott (2008) outlined the benefits of using children in quantitative survey research and evaluated a number of research studies that used such methods. She found that children, even young children, are good questionnaire respondents if they are asked about events that are meaningful in their lives. Children can be willing and able to answer questions about their experiences if the response alternatives are appropriate and ordered well. Additionally, children are motivated to give truthful and careful answers if the interviewers and children have good relationships and if the children feel secure in the confidentiality of the responses.

Specific issues that need to be addressed, however, include language use, literacy, and cognitive development. Pretests of the survey instrument are particularly important when doing research on children to ensure that the children's understanding of questions is the same as the researcher's. One way to develop good instruments is through the use of focus group interviewing to elicit children's ideas and language and to uncover what is most salient to them. J. Scott (2008) argued that until recently, children have been neglected from survey research and that their parents or teachers have responded for them instead. This technique not only eliminates the children's own voices but also may give researchers false data because adults do not always provide the same responses their children would.

Children aged 11 and up are particularly able to respond to standardized questionnaire instruments (J. Scott, 2008). Scott listed several successful surveys used to interview children in Britain. Included in the methods of data collection are a self-administered questionnaire using a personal tape recorder (ages 11–15), face-to-face interviews (ages 12–19), diaries (ages 9–15), and self-completion written interviews (school-aged children 7–12). She also described a Computer Assisted Personal Interviewing Program for even younger respondents. The computer program incorporates both visual and audio stimuli that decrease the need to rely on only verbal or written questions and answers. (See Corsaro & Fingerson, 2003, for further discussion of the use of survey methods with children.)

Historical Methods

were categorized w/ families

Historians all but ignored children in their research until the 1960s, when Philippe Ariès's *Centuries of Childhood* (1962) led to a debate about the historical development of the conception of childhood. We will consider that debate, and what is called the "new history of childhood" that eventually emerged from it, in Chapter 4. It is fair to say, however, that early work following that of Ariès was concerned primarily with adult conceptions of childhood and not the lives of children. Only later did historians consider children and adolescents important actors in past societies.

These studies in the new history of childhood have relied on a variety of sources for documenting and interpreting the nature of children's lives in the past (see Fass, 2003, for a broad collection of historical studies of children and reviews of previous work; also see Mintz, 2004). Sources include public records, such as wills and coroners' reports, as well as oral testimonies, school log books, child-rearing manuals, memoirs, family correspondence, legal transcripts, autobiographies, paintings, photographs, and diaries, to name a few (Hendrick, 2008). As we will see in Chapter 4, many historians are now using such materials in creative ways to sketch and interpret the nature of children's lives in the past. They are finding that children contributed much to history and that the neglect, until recently, of children in many historical accounts is a result of the inequality of power between children and adults. In fact, such inequality is a key issue in much recent historical research on children. As Hendrick argued,

> Our purpose, as historians, is not simply to describe—however "objectively"— past cultures, it is to unmask the hidden and apparently "natural" structures of inequalities that existed (and continue to exist) between adults and children, to show how these affected the latter as historical subjects, to examine their influence on the evolution of age relations and to illustrate their significance for the varying concepts of childhood. (2008, p. 49)

Microlevel Methods

Microlevel methods such as formal and informal face-to-face interviews and ethnographic research are especially appropriate for documenting and appreciating children's peer relationships and cultures and for demonstrating how they make sense of and contribute to processes of social reproduction and change. These methods, if used carefully and appropriately, give voice to children's concerns and provide detailed descriptions and interpretations as children live their childhoods. These methods have great potential because they do not focus so much on how children become adults (which is the goal of most traditional research on socialization) but rather on what children can teach and tell us about their shared life experiences and their struggles to gain some control over more powerful adults and adult rules.

Individual and Group Interviews

Eder and Fingerson (2002) contended that using individual and group interviews with children is one of the strongest methods of exploring children's own interpretations of their lives. Using interviews, researchers can also study topics in children's lives that are highly salient yet are rarely discussed in everyday interactions—such as divorce, family relationships, violence, or other sensitive issues. However, researchers must be aware that as with any other research method, the power imbalance between the researcher and respondent is heightened because of the age and status difference. Ways of reducing this power difference include group interviewing, peer interviewing, creating a natural context, using multiple methods, and engaging in reciprocity (Eder & Fingerson, 2002; Hagerman, 2010; Schäfer & Yarwood, 2008). Using a child-centered interview approach, Hagerman found that the children interviewed enjoyed the experience, maintained serious attitudes toward their inclusion in social research, and wished to be participants in future research (2010, p. 61).

For example, Mayall (2008) used the "research conversation" to learn about children's health and health care. She engaged small groups of 5- to 9-year-old children in conversations during their everyday school activities. The children felt secure in this familiar setting and engaged in discussions similar to their own "natural" conversations that Mayall heard in the school's classrooms and corridors. The children selected topics for discussion and controlled the pace and direction of the conversation. In this way, Mayall was able to understand the issues that were important to the children rather than having the children respond to questions directed by her.

In Davies's (1989) research on children's understandings of gender, Davies held "study groups" of fifth and sixth graders. The groups met once per week for 90 minutes for more than 12 months. Activities included having discussions, sharing photos of family, taking pictures with disposable cameras, making collages, reading traditional and feminist stories, and writing stories and autobiographies. Through this wide variety of activity, the children explored discourses of gender from multiple angles.

Adler and Adler (1998) studied their own children and the children of their friends (the ethics of which I discuss later in this chapter) in both their home and in the children's school. Having developed close ties and good rapport with the children in what they describe as their natural role of concerned and "cool" parents, the Adlers were able to engage preadolescents in informal and formal interviews about their concerns regarding friendships, clique structures and dynamics, peer relationships, and cross-sex activities.

Ethnography and Sociolinguistic Analysis ☆ READ CAREFULLY

Ethnography is an effective method for studying young children because many features of their interactions and cultures are produced and shared in the present and cannot easily be obtained by way of reflective interviews or surveys. Three central features of ethnography with young children are that it be sustained and engaged, microscopic and holistic, and flexible and self-corrective (Gaskins, Miller, & Corsaro, 1992). Ethnography usually involves prolonged fieldwork in which the researcher gains access to a group and carries out intensive observation for a period of months or years. The value of prolonged observation is that the ethnographer discovers what daily life is like for members of the group—their physical and institutional settings, their daily routines, their beliefs and values, and the linguistic and other semiotic systems that mediate all these contexts and activities.

Sustained and Engaged Research. In my work on peer culture, I have conducted six intensive studies, in preschool settings in the United States and

Italy, of peer interaction and culture over the course of an academic year. In several of these projects I returned for shorter periods to observe some members of the children's groups who spent successive years in the preschool, and in others I continued ethnographic observation as children made the transition from preschool to elementary school and then through elementary school (Corsaro, 1985, 1993, 2003; Corsaro & Molinari, 2000, 2005, 2008). The sustained nature of these and other ethnographic studies of young children (Evaldsson, 1993; Goodwin, 1990; Thorne, 1993; Waskler, 1991) documents crucial changes and transitions in children's lives, which are essential for understanding socialization as a process of production and reproduction.

To carry out prolonged and intensive observations of young children, one must first be accepted into the group and acquire participant status. Gaining acceptance into children's worlds is especially challenging given that adults are physically larger than children, are more powerful, and are often seen as having control over children's behavior. Several authors have discussed techniques for overcoming these obstacles, being accepted into children's worlds as adult friends, and participating in children's worlds to varying degrees (Corsaro, 1985, 2003; Corsaro & Molinari, 2008; G. Fine & Sandstrom, 1988; Holmes, 1998; Mandell, 1988). The work of Holmes is especially interesting because it considers how researchers' sex and ethnicity can affect their ability to be accepted by children and to carry out participant observation in their worlds.

In my ethnographic research in preschools in the United States and Italy, my goal has always been to discover the children's perspectives, to see what it is like to be a child in the school. To do this I have to overcome the children's tendency to see me as a typical adult (see Corsaro, 2003). A significant problem is physical size; I am much bigger than the children. In my early work I found that a reactive method of field entry into children's worlds works best. In simple terms, I enter free play areas, sit down, and wait for the kids to react to me. (I should point out that this is pretty much the opposite of what most adults do in such settings. Teachers, parents, and other adults normally do not sit down in play areas, and when they enter it is usually to ask questions, give advice, or settle disputes. In short, they are more active in their dealings with children.) I find that the reactive method does work, but in American schools it normally takes some time. After a while the children begin to ask me questions, draw me into their activities, and gradually define me as an atypical adult. Size is still a factor, however, and the children come to see me as a big kid, often referring to me as "Big Bill."

When I have used the reactive method in Italian preschools, things have gone somewhat differently. To the Italian children, as soon as I spoke in my fractured Italian I was peculiar, funny, and fascinating. I was not just an atypical adult but also an incompetent one—not just a big kid but sort of a big, dumb kid (Corsaro, 1996, 2003). From these experiences I began to see what it was like for children when those around them assume they are incompetent, incomplete, and in need of training. For example, long after my Italian improved, I was still teased about my mistakes and failure to understand something someone had said. The youngest kids in the schools especially enjoyed this teasing, often saying, "Bill, *lui capisce niente!*" (Bill, he doesn't understand anything!). Of course, the children knew this was not true, but they enjoyed turning the tables on an adult. The issue runs deeper than this, however. The children often extended my incompetence in language to other areas of social and cultural knowledge. Once on a field trip to a zoo that had scale models of dinosaurs, I pointed out to a small group of kids (in very good Italian, I might add) that the dinosaur we were looking at had lived in the same place where I now lived in the United States (I was certain I was right about this because the map accompanying the exhibit clearly indicated as much). The kids laughed uproariously, and one, Ramano, said, "Bill, he's crazy! He says the dinosaur lived in the United States." Then, pointing to the dinosaur, he added, "But you can see it lived right here!"

It was a new experience for me to be on the receiving end of the power differential between kids and adults. Adults, of course, are quick to dismiss children's insights, knowledge, and contributions to the culture all the time. We usually do not do this in a mean way (although the ill treatment of children in modern society seems to be increasing); it is more that we take children's perspectives for granted and our own views as the truth. Gaining acceptance and being accepted into children's worlds requires that ethnographers overcome these tendencies and puts them in a position to document children's peer cultures.

Microscopic and Holistic Ethnography. To ensure that ethnographic interpretations are culturally valid, they must be grounded in an accumulation of the specifics of everyday life. But simply describing what is seen and heard is not enough, as ethnographers must engage in a process of "thick description" (Geertz, 1973). This mode of interpretation goes beyond the microscopic examination of actions to their contextualization in a more holistic sense, to capture actions and events as they are understood by the actors themselves.

For example, through observation and audiovisual records I documented that preschoolers often resist the access of peers into established play routines. At the level of thin description (and from an adult perspective), this behavior is seen as a refusal to share. Given features of preschool settings, however, I interpreted this behavior as the "protection of interactive space" and argued that it was not that children did not want to share. Instead, they wanted to keep sharing the fragile play activities they were already sharing. They knew from experience that their activities were often easily disrupted by the entry of others who were not aware of the nature of play. In fact, through careful observation I found that children who used more indirect access strategies, like watching from a distance and discovering the nature of play and then going in and contributing to the play verbally or nonverbally, were readily accepted—because they showed they could play. On the other hand, more direct strategies, like simply asking to play or demanding that others must share their play, were frequently met with resistance. We discuss children's tendency to protect their interactive space in detail in Chapter 7.

Flexibility and Self-Correction. An important feature of ethnography is that it provides continual feedback in which initial questions may change during the course of inquiry. This flexibility in inquiry is accompanied by self-correction when the ethnographer searches for additional support for emerging hypotheses, including negative cases, which can lead to refinements and expansions of initial interpretations. It is this feature of ethnography that fits with my earlier discussion of research *with* rather than *on* children. Over the course of research, children, like adult ethnographic informants, come to reflect on the nature of the ethnography and its place in their lives. For example, in my work with Italian preschoolers (Corsaro & Molinari, 2008), the children often wanted to display their art and literacy skills by drawing and printing in my notebook. What the children were doing, in fact, given my interest in children's literacy and in their preparation for and transition to first grade, was inscribing field notes directly into my notebook (Corsaro & Nelson, 2003). Over time, however, it went further than this as the children became coresearchers, even suggesting things I needed to record about them in my notes. Consider the following example from my field notes.

A LETTER FOR LUCIANO'S LITTLE SISTER

I am sitting at a worktable with Luciano, Stefania, and several other children. Luciano is printing a letter to his sister. Stefania tells me to write what Luciano is doing in my notebook. So I do so in Italian and show it to her.

Luciano scrive una lettera per la sua sorellina. (Luciano is writing a letter for his little sister.)

Luciano then suggests that Stefania also write a letter to his sister, which she does with Luciano's help. It reads,

CARA LUISA,

TANTI BACIONI DA STEFANIA LUCIANO E DA BILL. (Many big kisses from Stefania Luciano and from Bill.)

This example nicely captures how literacy activities (like printing one's name or a short letter), first presented in teacher-directed tasks, are appropriated and used by the children in the peer culture. Furthermore, the children document these priming activities directly into my notebook. We see here an excellent example of research *with* rather than *on* children. Finally, this documentation by children of data directly relevant to my research interests demonstrates the value of longitudinal ethnography. It was the result of my acceptance, participation, and evolving membership in the school and peer cultures (see Corsaro & Molinari, 2008).

Sociolinguistic Analysis. Many ethnographies of young children include audiovisual recording of play activities and routines such as fantasy play, dramatic role play, debates and disputes, and games with rules. Audiovisual recording is useful in documenting children's culture because much of children's play is nonverbal, fast moving, and highly complex. As a result, it is very difficult to capture the density and complexity of play in field notes. Researchers rely on fine-grained sociolinguistic, discourse, and conversational analysis to document the meaning of children's play and activities in their peer culture as well as variation in styles of play activities across gender and across ethnic and cultural groups (Blum-Kulka & Snow, 2004; Butler, 2008; Corsaro, 1985; Cromdal, 2001, 2004; Evaldsson, 2002, 2003; Goodwin, 1990, 1998, 2006; Hoyle, 1998; Hutchby, 2005). We will examine examples of sociolinguistic analyses of children's play activities and routines in Chapters 7, 8, and 9.

Nontraditional Methods in Studying Children

Although one can gather rich data on children and childhood from traditional methods, there is a need in childhood research to develop and practice new and "child-centered" methods to encourage children to present their own images and representations of their lives (Williams & Bendelow, 1998).

Several researchers, including Williams and Bendelow, use drawings to elicit stories and understandings of children's everyday lives. For example, Holmes (1995) asked kindergartners to draw self-portraits while telling her about what they were drawing, so as to understand how they construct race and ethnicity. She argued that through drawing, children can express themselves about subjects and ideas they have difficulty conveying verbally to adults, such as complex notions of race. Christensen and James (2008a) used drawings to explore similarities and differences in 10-year-olds' daily experiences and organization of their time. Each child was given a piece of paper inscribed with a large circle titled "My Week." Then, the children were asked to divide the circles to represent their weekly activities and how much time they spent in each activity. The children had complete freedom to fill in the circles however they felt best represented their experiences. During the activity, which was completed in small groups, the researchers were both present and had a tape recorder running. Christensen and James thus collected a wide variety of data that were meaningful to each child, both on the paper drawings and in their dialogue about the process of doing the activity.

In my own research I have often incorporated children's drawings and visual culture to capture their developing literacy as well as their friendships and peer relations (Corsaro & Molinari, 2005; Corsaro & Nelson, 2003). In a recent 6-year longitudinal study my colleague Luisa Molinari and I followed a group of Italian children as they finished preschool and made the transition to elementary school and then to middle school (Corsaro & Molinari, 2005). After a year of intensive ethnography when the children finished preschool and entered elementary school I observed the children over shorter periods during the spring of each year in elementary school. During the periods when I was away from the field I sent letters and cards to each of the children of four classes in elementary school. The children answered my letters by sending me individual artistic productions along with messages and letters. The artwork was very impressive and reinforced the messages about what was going on in their classrooms and lives. One picture and message I received from a girl in first grade (Class D) wonderfully captured our correspondence and the importance of the children's artwork in the longitudinal ethnography (see Exhibit 3.1).

Exhibit 3.1 A Picture and Message From a Child in *Prima D*

We can see the girl, Stefania, has divided the picture into two frames. On the left she drew a picture of me throwing letters for the children in *Prima D* (first grade Class D) into the sky as I say, "Hi kids from Prima D and long live Prima D." She also drew a picture of my daughter, Veronica, in the background, as I often talked about my daughter and all the children had met her. In the right panel the teacher of Prima D catches the letters as they fall from the sky and says, "Our letters are arriving." Next to the teacher is Stefania, and she holds up one of the letters and says, "Hi Bill. Long live Bill." Stefania, using artwork and messages captured in talk bubbles similar to those in comic books, communicates her and the other children's strong personal relationship to me as both a researcher and a friend. She also invents a method of transporting the letters that seems a lot faster than the slow American and Italian postal services!

Children can also be used as research assistants and informants, helping the adult investigators with interviews and with understanding children's local culture and analyzing the data. Thus, the children become coproducers of the data and findings. Alderson (2000) argued that in research, children are an underestimated and underused resource. For example, in her empirical work, Alderson explored children's everyday projects done in school as sources of data, such as a project in which 9- to 11-year-olds ran small-group brainstorming sessions to design a pond for their school playground. In her ethnography of Black males' experiences in elementary school, Ferguson (2000) used Horace, age 12, as a research assistant. Horace both helped Ferguson understand aspects of the boys' cultures, music, and worlds that were otherwise inaccessible to her and helped her design the topics for her interviews with other boys. As an insider, Horace knew about aspects of his culture that were most salient to him and his peers. Similarly, in his study of street children in Brazil, Hecht (1998) used children as interviewers. He found they asked questions he would not have thought about and received responses that he, as an adult and an outsider, would not have been able to elicit. The child-interviewers had a deep understanding of street life and could connect with other street children on a level inaccessible to Hecht.

Some researchers have used children as assistants and informants by providing them with cameras and asking them and their parents and teachers to take pictures of what they feel are important aspects of the children's lives. For example, Cindy Dell Clark (1999) used what she termed the "autodriven interview" in which photographs (taken by children or parents) served as the basis for child-directed interviews about their chronic illnesses (asthma and diabetes). The method encouraged children's "free recall, sense of personal control, and ability to reflect upon photographed events" (C. Clark, 1999, p. 39). A similar method was employed by Johanna Einarsdottir (2005) in an Icelandic preschool. One group of children used digital cameras to take pictures while they showed the researcher important places and things in their preschool, and another group was given disposable cameras, which they used unsupervised for a period of time. The method captured the ways children think about the early childhood educational setting and experiences from their own perspectives.

Finally, some researchers use their own children as research participants, thereby blending the parent and researcher roles (which can lead to role conflict). Greenwood (1998) set up tape recorders in her home for

1 year to record her three children and their guests. She contended that some of the benefits of such recording were that there were no adults in the room and the recorder was out of sight of the children. Thus, she felt she was able to gather more "natural" interaction data than possible with other methods.

Adler and Adler (1998) called this practice "PAR," or "parents as researchers," and used this method as the basis of their research on preadolescent culture and identity. They argued that there are three primary benefits to such research. First, parents can gain access to children's worlds through their own children, who thereby act as informants. Second, the role of parents is an existing social role with which children are already very familiar. In other research settings, such as ethnography in a classroom, researchers must spend time explaining their unique role as not a teacher but clearly not a child. Third, parents have easy access to a variety of children's settings in their recreational and social lives such as the home, playground, and school.

Ethical Issues in Researching Children's Lives

In addition to the ethical issues of power and representation already discussed, doing research with children has institutional review board (IRB) implications (Stanley & Sieber, 1992). IRBs set the standards for research with human participants. With the tightening of IRB standards for research with human participants, research with children has undergone even higher scrutiny. Review board rules vary from institution to institution, and even federal requirements are changing rapidly, but one consistent and important feature is the requirement of active parental consent. Such consent forms usually contain guarantees of privacy (through the use of cover names and restrictions on the display of audiovisual data) and give parents the right to inspect field notes and audiovisual data on request and to demand that certain data not be included in analysis. Previously, consent could be obtained by a letter's being sent home to the parents; if parents did not want their children to participate, they could send a negative reply. Currently, active consent is required whereby each child must have a signed consent form to participate in research. For example, when research is being conducted in a classroom, each child's parent or guardian must sign an informed consent form, which, in addition to the guarantees just discussed, details the research plan and provides contact information for the researcher and the research institution's IRB. Often, if the child is 10 years old or younger, her own signature is not required, although I believe the child's own consent is a necessary step regardless of age. If any of the children do not have signed consent forms, they must be excluded from all data collection, whether it be from field notes or audio or video recordings. Although this safeguards children's and parents' rights, requiring active consent makes ethnography in particular a much more difficult research endeavor. It also means that ethnographers or interviewers may have to sacrifice important data collection opportunities (for example, alter or restrict field notes or stop videotaping if a child without consent enters an interactive event). Most ethnographers have little trouble dealing with these challenges, however, given the large amount of rich data that they normally collect in intensive fieldwork.

One strategy some researchers have employed to work around this requirement is to use their own children, often together with children of friends and neighbors, as research participants. However, the parent-as-researcher strategy (as previously discussed) is one of the most widely critiqued methods of studying children. Parents can frequently face ethical and role conflicts in deciding which events are public and therefore available to be recorded as data versus which events are private and confined to the parental role. Additionally, traditional ethnographers attempt to see the world through the children's eyes and become a member of children's cultures as much as possible. Parents, on the other hand, cannot ethically cross the boundary between child and adult to become "one of the kids," because they are in an inherently supervisory position.

As in any research, unanticipated ethical issues will arise even after the researcher has fulfilled IRB requirements. Such unforeseen problems can often be the case in sociological studies of young children, especially given the subtle implications of the power differential between adults and children and the fact that children are an understudied group (Christensen & Prout, 2002; Morrow, 2008). For this reason, those who carry out ethnographies, interviews, or surveys with children should carefully document the research process as it unfolds and pay special attention to unanticipated ethical problems. When they occur, researchers should discuss decisions in dealing with them with IRBs, parents and other gatekeepers, and children themselves. Also, researchers should discuss such issues in as much detail as possible (while preserving privacy) in research reports so that other researchers can learn from their experience.

SUMMARY

In this chapter we discussed research methods for studying children and childhood. We noted the general trend toward research with as opposed to research on children. To fully explore childhood and children's worlds and activities, researchers use both macrolevel methods (for example, large-scale surveys, demographic studies, and historical analyses) and microlevel methods (for example, interviews, ethnographies, and sociolinguistic analyses). All of these methods are also used in research on adults and demand innovative strategies for adapting the various methodological strategies and techniques to the nature and needs of children's physical, social, cognitive, and emotional worlds. We also discussed some new and nontraditional methods such as using children's drawings and audiovisual recordings and including children as active informants or coresearchers. Finally, we noted the special nature of ethical issues in work with children and the nature of IRBs regarding the standards for children as participants in research. We showed that researchers must not only meet these standards, gain informed consent from parents, and in many cases gain informed consent from the children themselves but also be prepared for possible unforeseen problems and circumstances once research is under way. Those who do research with children can contribute to the demanding ethical requirements of such research by keeping careful records of the research process to discuss with children, parents, IRBs, and other researchers.

PART TWO

Children, Childhood, and Families in Historical and Cultural Context

M any years ago in my first ethnographic study in a preschool, a 4-year-old girl asked me, "Bill, do you remember the good old days?" This was during the early years of my research with young children, and I was still getting used to the surprising things children say and ask. Nowadays kids still ask surprising things, but I'm less surprised by this fact and know that I do not always have to have a good answer. Back then I thought I did, and I was taken aback. A 4-year-old is asking me about the good old days. Whose good old days? I was a lot older than she. But not that old. Where did she hear this line? From her parents? A television commercial? Does her grandpa or grandma talk about the good old days? Does she really expect an answer? All this was going through my head, and she was there, smiling, looking up at me.

So I sort of mumbled, "Well, let's see, the good old days. Do you mean—well, like when I was a kid?"

"Ah, the good old days," she said. Then she turned and walked away. It was as if any response I gave would have been sufficient. I did not have to take the question so seriously.

When it comes to the study of children and childhood, few psychologists and not many more sociologists have taken questions about the good old days very seriously either. Neither psychologists nor sociologists have routinely placed their work in sociohistorical context. The situation is a little better when it comes to cross-cultural studies of children and childhood, but not much. There are exceptions, but for most psychologists and sociologists, the focus has been on the individual development of children in Western societies from the mid-20th century or so.

A new sociology of childhood has to correct this tendency. We need to place the theoretical notion of interpretive reproduction in historical and cultural context. This section of the book will do just that. Chapter 4 explores Philippe Ariès's groundbreaking work on the history of childhood. Ariès's subtle and innovative analysis and his bold interpretations of a range of historical materials generated intense interest in the history of conceptions of childhood, as well as a good bit of criticism. We will look at both the related work and the criticisms. We will also consider several examples from the new history of childhood, which captures the perspectives of children and youth from medieval times to the early 20th century. Although this review is selective and does not capture many important, recent historical studies of childhood and children, it does place the notion of interpretive reproduction in historical context.

The topic of Chapter 5 is children in families from a global perspective. Here we'll look at how children and childhood are affected by recent social changes in families, and we'll also ponder the growing diversity of families in both industrialized and developing societies. Although much of the work on families fails to consider seriously the activities and contributions of children, we'll focus on research that has directly investigated young children's experiences in families in both Western and non-Western or developing societies. We'll also examine how social changes in Western and developing societies affect childhood. We'll focus on general experiences of children as a social group to discover how their childhoods have been affected by key social and economic changes in families.

4

Historical Views of Childhood and Children

In medieval society the idea of childhood did not exist; this is not to suggest that children were neglected, forsaken or despised. The idea of childhood is not to be confused with affection for children: it corresponds to an awareness of the particular nature of childhood, that particular nature which distinguishes the child from the adult, even the young adult. In medieval society this awareness was lacking.

Philippe Ariès, *Centuries of Childhood* (1962, p. 128)

This quote, the central claim in Philippe Ariès's historical account of family life and the conception of childhood, sparked the attention of historians, who, like sociologists, had long neglected children. Ariès's approach to the history of childhood was complex and powerful. Using a contingent sense of time, he traced changes in ideas about the organization of family, children, and age relationships from the Middle Ages to the end of the 18th century. Although Ariès never claimed these stages were inevitable, his book soon spawned evolutionary theories of the family and conceptions of childhood (deMause, 1974; Shorter, 1977; Stone, 1977) and, in turn, fired heated debate about the historical evidence for such assertions.

Although a number of elements of Ariès's position are now considered untenable, his overall work is of major importance for the history of childhood. Most important, he argued that childhood was a social construction and that historians should take children and their lives seriously. As a result, a growing number of historians have come to adopt children's perspectives and voices in their studies of children and childhood.

In this chapter we will consider Ariès's theory, the related evolutionary views of others, and the methodological debates about the adequacy of their evidence and interpretations as presented in the work of Linda Pollock. We will then look at several examples from the new history of childhood that capture the perspectives of children and youth from medieval times to the early 20th century. Most current discussions of the sociology of childhood give only brief mention of children of the past. We will look beyond these accounts to examine a more extensive review of work on the history of childhood and to place the notion of interpretive reproduction in historical context.

Philippe Ariès's *Centuries of Childhood*

For Ariès the "idea of childhood" corresponded to an awareness of the particular nature of childhood, that particular nature that distinguishes the child from the adult. According to Ariès, this awareness was lacking in medieval society. That is why, as soon as a child could live without the constant attention of his or her mother or nanny, he or she belonged to adult society. Ariès's support for this contention is drawn primarily from his interpretations of medieval art. Children were almost totally absent from medieval paintings, and where they were depicted they looked much like miniature adults. Ariès presented only references to paintings, and his book has no actual pictures. Exhibit 4.1 is a picture I took of a mosaic constructed in an archway in Taoromina, Sicily, in the 12th century. Here we can see that Jesus is not quite a miniature adult but has the proportions of a very small young man.

Ariès did notice a gradual change in the depiction of children beginning in the 13th century. He pointed to the introduction, in paintings, of the *putto*, the naked child. These *putti*, or "semi-pagan angels," were not seen as real children; rather, they were used as an ornamental motif in the work of great masters such as Titian. The ubiquity of putti during this period, however, argued Ariès, "corresponded to something far deeper than the taste for classical nudity," something that can be ascribed only to a broad surge of interest in childhood (1962, p. 44).

Ariès believed that this first recognition and interest in childhood eventually led to the coddling period, which fully emerged in the 16th century,

Exhibit 4.1   Mosaic in Taoromina, Sicily

when childhood was seen as a time of innocence and sweetness. Children were idolized and valued as a source of amusement or escape for adults, especially women. Consider, for example, this quote from a letter that Madame de Sévigné wrote to her son in 1672:

gendernom?

> I am reading the story of Christopher Columbus's discovery of the Indies, which is entertaining me greatly; but your daughter entertains me even more. I do so love her . . . she strokes your portrait and caresses it in such an amusing way that I have to kiss her straight away. (Ariès, 1962, p. 130)

The moralistic period (from the 16th through the 18th centuries) was in large part a negative reaction to the coddling period, most especially from scholars and moralists of the time. The French essayist Montaigne wrote, "I cannot abide that passion for caressing new-born children, which have neither mental activities nor recognizable bodily shape by which to make themselves lovable," noting further that he could not accept the idea of loving children "for our amusement like monkeys or taking pleasure in their games and infantile nonsense" (Ariès, 1962, p. 130). This attitude was taken up and extended by other moralists, who emphasized that childhood is a period of immaturity and that children must be trained and disciplined.

Ariès argued that such early writings on morals and education laid the groundwork for the development of child psychology, which has had tremendous influence on conceptions of childhood and child rearing in contemporary times. Thus, Ariès saw a progression from no conception of childhood, to coddling, and then to the moralistic period in which childhood was seen as a time for discipline and preparation for adulthood. It is a mistake, however, to assume that Ariès felt that this evolution was inevitable or that it was a positive occurrence, as some interpreters of his work have done.

For Ariès the modern world is "obsessed by the physical, moral, and sexual problems of childhood," which have developed from moralist propaganda that "taught parents that they were spiritual guardians, that they were responsible before God for the souls, and indeed the bodies too, of their children" (1962, pp. 411–412). Ariès bemoaned the removal of the child from adult society, arguing that the

> solicitude of family, church, moralists, and administrators deprived the child of the freedom he had hitherto enjoyed among adults. It inflicted on him the birch, the prison cell—in a word, the punishments usually reserved for convicts from the lowest strata of society. (p. 413)

Clearly, then, Ariès did not believe that things had gotten better for children. In fact, Ariès saw the progressive separation of children and adults as part of more general cultural changes that have resulted in separations by social class and race in modern society. He argued that the old society "concentrated the maximum number of ways of life into the minimum of space" and in doing so accepted the mixing of widely different social class groups (1962, p. 415). Modern society, on the other hand, provides "each way of life with a confined space in which it [is] understood that the dominant features should be respected, and that each person [has] to resemble a conventional model, an ideal type" (p. 415).

Although some researchers have found problems with ambiguity and sweeping generalizations in his work, Ariès generated a great deal of interest in the history of childhood, perhaps even more so because of his bold interpretations and conclusions. His recognition of the contradiction in denying children their freedom in the name of their own protection and moral education is directly related to the present-day conception of children as social problems that we discuss in Chapter 9.

The Debate Regarding Grand-Stage Theories of the Family and Childhood

Ariès offered a constructivist argument about institutional changes and their effects on conceptions of children. He saw these changes as phases of the unique history of Europe, which involved shifting configurations in the family and educational institutions. For example, he pointed to the general movement from extended families that were very much a part of the surrounding community to nuclear families that were more isolated from the rest of society and to the emergence of age-graded schools as having important effects on both conceptions of childhood and the lives of children. Other theorists pushed these ideas much further, proposing grand-stage theories of the family (deMause, 1974; Shorter, 1977; Stone, 1977; see Hendrick, 2008, 2009, for a review). These theories hold that there are specific, universal, and in some cases, predestined stages in the evolution of the family, children, and childhood.

For example, Lloyd deMause (1974) offered a "psychogenic theory of history" in which historical changes in the conceptions and treatment of children result from individual parents' working out their own anxieties and psychological problems in their interaction with their children. deMause saw a pattern shifting from the vicious mistreatment of children in medieval times to more humane care and nurturing of children in the present. He maintained that "the further back in history one goes, the lower the level of child care, and the more likely children are to be killed, abandoned, beaten, terrorized, and sexually abused" (deMause, 1974, p. 1).

A number of historians have criticized the work of both deMause and other grand-stage theorists and have offered impressive historical evidence in support of their critiques (Garnsey, 1991; Hanawalt, 1993; Pollock, 1983; Shahar, 1990). Perhaps the best known of these critiques is that of Linda Pollock.

In her book *Forgotten Children* (1983), Pollock carefully (at times laboriously) challenged the conceptions of the history of childhood in the work of Ariès and most especially grand-stage theorists such as deMause. She was especially critical of the indirect evidence (for example, paintings, philosophical and religious tracts, advice literature, and letters) on which much of the earlier work on the history of childhood is based. Pollock believed a history of childhood could be pursued with more direct primary sources such as diaries, autobiographies, and newspaper reports of court cases regarding child abuse. She noted, first, that when direct sources are used, a much less negative picture of childhood emerges. Second, many who have used diaries to supplement less direct sources have done so selectively and anecdotally, which Pollock felt led to a distortion of how children were viewed and treated in the past. Pollock pointed, for example, to the many references in Puritan Samuel Sewall's diary—written between 1673 and 1729 but published in 1878—of "whipping" his son Joseph as typical of the practice of selective analysis. Although many accounts stress Sewall's report of the whipping as evidence of the strict discipline of the time, few note that this is the only statement, in a long and detailed diary, in which Sewall mentions physically punishing his son. It is also important to consider social and cultural context in interpreting such cases. As Pollock pointed out, "parent-child interaction is a continuing process, not a series of isolated events" (1983, p. 66). In the Sewall case, it turns out that the father resorted to physical punishment after admonishing his son several times for inappropriate behavior during prayer and other quiet times within the household. The actual whipping came about when the boy "threw a lump of brass at his sister, bruising and cutting her forehead" (p. 66).

Aware of the need to examine sources thoroughly and systematically, Pollock undertook an intensive analysis of 500 British and American diaries, autobiographies, and related sources. She found little support for Ariès's thesis that there was an abiding indifference to children or deMause's contention of widespread mistreatment and abuse of children until the enlightenment of the 18th and 19th centuries. Rather, Pollock discovered that "nearly all children were wanted, such developmental stages as weaning and teething aroused interest and concern, and parents revealed anxiety and distress at the illness or death of their children" (1983, p. 268). Acknowledging some reports of physical punishment in her materials, Pollock nevertheless concluded that diaries and newspaper reports of abuse suggest that cruelty to children was not widespread and that a "large section of the population—probably most parents—were not 'battering' their children" (p. 268). Finally, Pollock found that the parent-child relationship was not formal and one-sided. Children were close to their parents and were influenced by them, but parents were influenced by their children as well. From these and related findings, Pollock ended her book with the following challenge to historians: "Instead of trying to explain the supposed changes in the parent-child relationship, historians would do well to ponder just why parental care is a variable so curiously resistant to change" (p. 271). Unfortunately, Pollock never developed this idea. As one review argued, the book "bulldozes the standard literature, but leaves the task of reconstruction to others" (Gillis, 1985, p. 143; also see Hendrick, 2009, for other critical reactions to Pollock's work).

Pollock did provide some support for the idea of continuity of parental care when she argued that qualitative aspects of care such as protection, love, and socialization are essential for human survival. In the actual analysis of her materials, she began to see, but did not fully develop, the notion that the care and socialization of children as prerequisites for cultural survival must always be culturally constructed through the collective actions of adults and children. There are some weaknesses in Pollock's evidence, though: The diaries and autobiographies are limited primarily to the literate upper classes, the authors may have selectively omitted information that would put themselves in a bad light, and it is possible that some materials may have been edited by others. Other researchers have criticized Pollock for overstating her case. For example, in responding to Pollock's claim that "parents have always tried to do what is best for their children within the context of culture" (1983, p. 64), Horn has countered, "To youngsters harshly disciplined . . . it was doubtless small consolation to know that this was taking place within the context of their culture" (1994, p. 46, quoted in Hendrick, 2008).

Even so, Pollock's work has been very well received for its careful and painstaking scholarship. Her intensive analysis of diaries allowed her to go beyond the focus on adult sentiments that characterized the earlier work of others, and it set the stage for subsequent historical studies of childhood, which attempt to reconstruct the everyday activities and cultural practices of children themselves.

The New History of Childhood

The new history of childhood, like the new sociology of childhood that we discussed in Chapters 1 and 2, focuses directly on the collective actions of children with adults and with each other. In doing so, it begins to address a long-ignored defect in the historical record. Even in the accounts of authors such as Ariès, deMause, and Pollock that we discussed previously, the focus remains on adult conceptions of childhood, their sentiments toward children, and their methods of child rearing. What is left out is a consideration of "children and adolescents as influential actors in past societies" (West & Petrick, 1992, p. 1). This is what the new history of childhood is all about (see Fass, 2003; Levi & Schmitt, 1997; West & Petrick, 1992).

A pioneering historical study of American childhood that bridges the early work on conceptions of adults to a more direct focus on children's lives is Steve Mintz's *Huck's Raft* (2004). Mintz saw the image of Huck's raft from Mark Twain's classic *The Adventures of Huckleberry Finn* as encapsulating "the modern conception of childhood as a period of peril and freedom; an odyssey of psychological self-discovery and growth; and a world apart, with its own values, culture and psychology" (p. 5). Mintz pushed the image further, noting that "much as the raft is carried by raging currents that Huck can only partly control, so, too, childhood is inevitably shaped and constrained by society, time, and circumstances" (p. 5).

Mintz's nuanced analysis of a wide array of literary and secondary sources makes numerous contributions not just to historians of childhood but also to policy makers, parents, and children and youth themselves. First, Mintz set out to debunk five myths that "have clouded public thinking about the history of American childhood" (2004, p. 2). The first of these myths is the fantasy that once upon a time childhood was a time of carefree adventure. Mintz showed instead that for most young people in the past growing up was anything but easy as they faced disease, family disruption, and early entry into the workforce. A second myth is that home and the family serve as "a bastion of stability in an ever-changing world" (p. 2). Like Stephanie Coontz (1992, 1997) before him, Mintz showed that through much of American history family stability was the exception rather than the norm. A third myth is that childhood is more or less the same for all children regardless of race, ethnicity, gender, or class. Mintz showed instead that child-rearing practices, schooling, and the age at which a young person leaves home are all profoundly affected by particular social and cultural circumstances. Myth 4 is the general belief that the United States is an especially child-friendly society, but Mintz showed that Americans are deeply ambivalent about children. Although adults may envy the youth and vitality of the young, they also resent children's intrusions on their time and resources and often fear their passions and drives. Further in line with Ariès, Mintz found that many reforms designed to protect or assist the young were also instituted to insulate adults from children, leading to increasing age segregation in American society. The final myth includes the contrary beliefs of progress and the decline of childhood. Although Mintz showed that things have not always gotten better for children as the first part of this myth holds, he also challenged the notion that childhood is disappearing and that children and youth are growing up too quickly and losing their innocence and imaginations.

Mintz's historical narrative goes about debunking these myths and exploring myriad other aspects of the lives of American children and youth. Again like Ariès, his story is one of periods or overlapping phases, but not inevitable stages. The first, the premodern childhood, which roughly coincides with colonial times, was a period that stressed the training of children for adulthood. Mintz noted that in this period it was the parent's duty "to hurry a child toward adult status" (2004, p. 3) and into the world of work in the home and the outside world. In the middle of the 18th century a new set of attitudes defined the modern period of American childhood. Children were now seen as innocent, malleable, fragile, and in need of special care and protection. Children now stayed longer in the home, and the discovery, or what Mintz called the invention, of adolescence occurred around the turn of the 20th century. This sheltered period was uneven, however, again mainly in terms of social class but also race and gender. It was not until the 1950s that the norms of modern childhood defined the experiences of most American children and youth. But by this time a new period was already developing what Mintz called postmodern childhood. Now the dominant norms about family, gender roles, and age were called into question, and major changes occurred at a rapid pace. Mintz noted that in today's postmodern period,

> children are more likely than the Baby Boomers to experience their parents' divorce, to have a working mother, to spend significant amounts of time unsupervised by adults, to grow up without siblings, and to have sexual relations during their mid-teens. (p. 4)

Like the children of the premodern period, postmodern children are also growing up fast, but not to enter the adult world of work (Gillis, 2009). Rather, postmodern children are independent consumers and participate in what Mintz called a separate, semiautonomous youth culture. Much of what Mintz described and discussed about these three periods of American childhood we will also examine directly in later chapters of this book when we consider social change, families, and children (Chapter 5) and children, social problems, and the future of childhood (Chapters 10, 11, and 12).

Although Mintz's important history of American childhood brings children and youth to the center of his narrative, other work focuses even more directly on what it was like to be a child in different historical periods. The following is a consideration of some of the work of these new historians of childhood.

Barbara Hanawalt's *Growing Up in Medieval London*

Relying on evidence from court records, coroners' rolls, literary sources, and advice books, Barbara Hanawalt captured the lives of London children and youth in the 14th and 15th centuries. Hanawalt grounded her discussion of the rights, treatment, and everyday activities of children in careful exploration of the evidence. She also dramatized these facts in what some see as a daring narrative style, however. At the end of each chapter in her book *Growing Up in Medieval London* (1993), Hanawalt penned composite stories about real children that summarize the main points of the chapter.

The following are some of Hanawalt's main themes.

Treatment of Children and Their Quality of Life. Hanawalt acknowledged that life in 14th- and 15th-century London was difficult for children and adolescents. The mortality rate among infants and young children was high, and disease and accidents presented many dangers. However, she noted that "play, rather than serious work, was still very much part of children's lives" (1993, p. 66). She also disputed the notions that it was common practice to neglect or abuse young children, that there was a general callousness about the death of children, and that there was no conception of children beyond the infancy period. First, she noted that no court records show widespread abandonment or infanticide and that the ecclesiastical court records for London reveal allegations of fewer than one infanticide case per year (p. 44). Second, she acknowledged that it is safe to assume that children spent a good part of their 1st year of life swaddled and in cradles, but she pointed out that given the cold and damp environment, swaddling prevented chills and kept the children from crawling about the filth of London or moving outside onto dangerous streets. Third, she produced numerous examples to illustrate that young children clearly were seen as being different from adults and required different treatment. In one court case, for example, a mother complained that a man had wrongfully made her 7-year-old daughter a servant with a 7-year contract. The mayor's court agreed and returned the child to her mother "out of charity for the youth of the infant" (p. 66). Hanawalt pointed to a second case wherein neighbors came to the rescue of a child being beaten by adults. This boy was carrying water near a shop when he was accosted by a cook and a clerk. Neighbors intervened, but the cook and the clerk said they could beat the boy if they liked. A fight ensued in which the neighbors defended the boy (whom they did not know) and beat up the other two. Later the vanquished bullies sued but lost the case. Neighbors and the court felt that the cook and the clerk deserved the beating they received for mistreating the youth (p. 67).

Finally, Hanawalt presented a great deal of data about the laws and procedures regarding the care of orphans. The laws and courts monitored the fortunes of orphans, oversaw their estates, and guarded against any abuse or mistreatment by foster parents. In fact, Hanawalt argued that "London's laws granted medieval orphans more protection than our own courts give today's children" (1993, p. 89).

The Play of Young Children and Youth. Hanawalt maintained that London adults knew that children must and would play. Children "played ball and tag, ran races, played hoops, and imitated adult ceremonies such as royal entries, Masses, and marriages" (1993, p. 78). Sadly, much of Hanawalt's support for claims about children's play comes from court or coroners' records of injuries and deaths. She reported that one young boy fell to his death when he climbed out a window to retrieve a ball that had landed in a gutter while he was playing with it. In another case, a 7-year-old boy was playing with two other boys on pieces of timber when a piece fell on him and broke his right leg. Using one of her composite stories, Hanawalt presented a moving account of a third case. In this composite, she dramatized the story of 8-year-old Richard Le Mazon. Richard was on his way back to school from his midday meal when he met up with friends to play a favorite and daring game—hanging by one's hands from a beam that protruded from the side of London Bridge. Richard was feeling brave on his turn in the game,

> but when he swung himself out on the beam, he felt his hands slipping. As Richard plummeted toward the river, he prayed to St. Nicholas to save him, promising that he would always obey his parents. His satchel pulled him down, and Father Thames claimed another victim. (p. 82)

Children's Participation in Public Celebrations and Folklore. In addition to games the children organized among themselves, the urban environment of many cities, including London, prompted a number of parades and pageants that involved children and certainly entertained them. Some celebrations were reserved for children. The most notable was that of the boy bishops, which coincided with St. Nicholas Day. St. Nicholas was a favorite of young students because of a legend about two young boys on their way to study in Athens. One of the boys' fathers had instructed them to stop and visit Bishop Nicholas in the city of Myra. When the boys arrived in Myra, they decided to spend the night at an inn and visit the bishop the next day. The innkeeper, seeing the boys' wealth, killed them and cut them into little pieces to sell as pickled pork. Bishop Nicholas had a vision of the murder and rushed to the inn. He reprimanded the innkeeper and sought his forgiveness from heaven. Nicholas's wish was granted, and the pieces of the boys emerged from the brine tub and reassembled. The bishop sent the boys off to Athens amid great rejoicing (Hanawalt, 1993, p. 79).

In the boy bishop celebration, Hanawalt related, it was the bishops rather than the boys who got disassembled. The best scholar from each school was elected to impersonate the bishop, and the rest of the boys formed his clergy. The boys took over the church for the services and sermon, ousting the real bishop. As Hanawalt noted, "It was one of those medieval, world-turned-topsy-turvy events. The boys, whose life seemed all discipline, were given a taste of the power to discipline" (1993, p. 79). The boys traveled in style with ceremonial capes, rings, and crosses, and their clergy stopped at parish homes for offerings, gracious meals, and gifts. It is no wonder that Richard Le Mazon, before he drowned, looked forward to the event and aspired to be the boy bishop.

The Importance of Hanawalt's Study. Hanawalt's historical work on children in medieval London is important for a new sociology of childhood for several reasons. First, it challenges prior work, which claimed that children were treated harshly in the medieval period and that they were forced to enter adult society at an early age with little opportunity to have or enjoy their childhoods. Second, Hanawalt's detailed descriptions of children's play, games, and involvement in public rituals and celebrations show that children created and participated in their own peer cultures as far back as the 14th century. Especially interesting in this regard was the children's fascination with St. Nicholas and their clear enjoyment of the boy bishops celebration. In activities such as the boy bishops ritual, children gained control over adult authority and celebrated their autonomy in a highly public fashion. As we will see in Chapters 5 through 8, children's challenging of adult authority is also a key feature of the peer cultures of children in contemporary societies. Overall, these aspects of Hanawalt's study demonstrate the value of taking children seriously as active agents in their cultures.

Slave Children in the Pre–Civil War South

Recently, several reports have attempted to reconstruct the lives of slave children in the United States, including an article by Lester Alston (1992) titled "Children as Chattel" and another by David Wiggins (1985) titled "The Play of Slave Children in the Plantation Communities of the Old South, 1820–60." These authors rely on narratives, testimonies, autobiographies, and diaries. The bulk of the data comes from the 1936–1938 Federal Writer's Project, which compiled the slave narrative collection. As Wiggins pointed out, though, there are some inherent problems with narratives from the Federal Writer's Project. Because nearly two thirds of the former slaves who were interviewed were 80 years old or older, there is the obvious concern of failing memory. A second problem relates to "the question of whether longevity was the result of unusually good rather than typical treatment as slaves" (Wiggins, 1985, p. 174). Also, in recalling childhood memories (probably the best of times for most slaves), there may be a tendency to paint a more favorable picture (especially when compared to the former slaves' memories of their adult lives). Possible biases, procedures, and methods of the predominantly White Southern interviewers may also have come into play. Wiggins argued, however, that the narratives do represent the voices of slaves themselves rather than the speculations of commentators.

What follows is a look at the nature of childhood in slavery based on these historical records.

The Nature of Childhood in Slavery. As Alston noted,

> Children were born into slave communities that were as distinct from the African communities of their forebears as they were from the social communities of their white owners. Their experiences of childhood were shaped by an African American slave subculture that, by the time of the Civil War, was four to six generations old and was peopled by parents and elders who themselves had been born on these shores into slave families and slave communities. (1992, p. 208)

A sense of community was central to both adult slaves and their children. Wiggins noted that members of slave quarters viewed themselves "as a familial group" with a "common need to stay together no matter what the circumstances" (1985, p. 174).

Slave mothers worked in the fields until shortly before their babies were born. They were then given a "lying-in period" of just a few days to a few weeks to spend with their newborns before returning to their regular sun-up-to-sun-down work schedule. After that time, care of the infants was given over to older slave women, with mothers returning from the fields for just a short period each day to nurse their children. When the children reached toddler age (around 2), they were placed in the care of siblings and other children in the slave community. This type of communal child rearing was continued by the practice of having 8- to 12-year-old slave children tend to younger children (Alston, 1992, p. 211).

Wiggins reported similar patterns of communal child rearing and linked it to the work requirements for slave children. Slave children were not expected to work full-time in the fields until about the age of 13. Alston argued that this delay was for economic and not humanitarian reasons. He pointed out that

> the [economic] reality was that many slave holders believed that a slowed maturity during childhood guaranteed maximum productivity later, that work during childhood weakened the foundation for physical health in adulthood, and that a slow breaking-in reduced the trauma of going to the fields and facing the whip. (Alston, 1992, p. 360; also see Genovese, 1974, pp. 504–505)

During this transition period, slave children were expected to perform chores such as hauling water, fetching wood, tending gardens, cleaning the yards, and feeding livestock. The care of younger children was seen as part of these work obligations. An especially interesting aspect of this pattern of communal child care primarily by older siblings and other children in the slave community is its striking similarity to child care practices in many regions of contemporary Africa (see Harkness & Super, 1992).

Children's Activities and Play in Slave Communities. There was more to the everyday lives of slave children than chores and caretaking. They also had some freedom to explore their physical world and to play. Older children especially had a good deal of autonomy. Boys and, less often, girls also made good use of their explorations by hunting and fishing with peers during the day and with their fathers at night to supplement the quarters' food supply. Not only were hunting and fishing enjoyable, but they also generated feelings of self-worth in the children because of their contributions to the family table. Perhaps more important, such activities also provided limited, shared interaction and support between fathers and their children.

Slave children engaged in both traditional and improvised games. They were especially attracted to dramatic role-play, a type of play commented on by Hanawalt (1993) in her study of children in medieval London. Both Wiggins and Alston believed the evidence strongly suggests that slave children attempted to relieve particular anxieties and fears through the medium of dramatic role-play. These children especially liked to emulate social events such as church services, funerals, and auctions (Alston, 1992, p. 225). One former slave from Texas described the game of auction, where one child would become the auctioneer and conduct a simulated slave sale. The fact that slave children knew early on that they themselves could be sold and separated from their families certainly displays the power of such play for dealing with fears and anxieties. In another game, Hiding the Switch, several children would look for a switch hidden by another child. The one who found the switch would run after the others, attempting to hit them. The relationship of this type of play to certain brutal treatment of adults in many slave quarters should be obvious.

The slave children played a number of organized games such as jump rope and various chasing games. However, Wiggins reported the apparent absence of any games that required the elimination of players: "Even the various dodge ball and tagging games played by the children contained designed stratagems within their rule structure that prevented the removal of any participants" (1985, p. 181). Wiggins linked this finding to real fears among these children that members of their families (and eventually themselves) could be "indiscriminately sold or hired out anytime" (p. 181).

Although slave children also frequently participated in games and played together with the White children of the plantation, "a caste system frequently operated within the 'play world' of the slave and white children just as it did in the everyday affairs of the plantation community" (Wiggins, 1985, p. 184). Interview data from the Federal Writer's Project indicates that the White children often took the role of master of the plantation or overseer of slave workers in their play with slave children. Still, slave children were not passive in their play with White playmates. They often took great pride in standing up to the plantation children and especially in outwitting them in verbal play and physical contests. In fact, Wiggins reported that most slave children felt both morally and physically superior to White children. "'We was stronger and knowed how to play, and the white children didn't,' recalled Felix Heywood of Texas" (Wiggins, 1985, p. 185).

Slave Children and the New Sociology of Childhood. The work of Alston and Wiggins contributes importantly to our understanding of the lives of families and children in slavery. It captures the major roles that children played in building and maintaining strong communal bonds in slave communities under extremely challenging circumstances. Especially important were older children's contributions to the care and socialization of younger children, which is very similar to child care practices in contemporary African societies. These historical studies also provide insights into how children's play and games can provide secure arenas in which children can deal with anxieties and fears that can be extremely difficult to confront directly. As we will see in Chapters 5 through 8, many routines in the peer cultures of children in contemporary societies serve these same functions. Overall, we see, as we did with the work of Hanawalt, that the documentation of children's activities and lives in the past contributes a great deal to our understanding of history and of children in present-day societies.

American Pioneer and Immigrant Children at the Turn of the 20th Century

Two recent historical studies bring to life, from the perspectives of children and youth, the exciting, challenging, and rapidly changing worlds of the American frontier at the end of the 19th century and of American cities in the early 20th century. Elliott West (1992) described the lives of children who migrated to and settled with their families on the Great Plains (Nebraska, Kansas, the Dakotas, and Oklahoma) in the period from about 1880 to the turn of the 20th century. He relied primarily on diaries to tell the children's stories, but he also made good use of interviews, autobiographies, and written "reminiscences" of a wide range of experiences. David Nasaw's (1985) study covers the period from approximately the late 1890s until about 1920 and focuses on children's lives in cities across the United States, with a concentration on the large urban areas of the Northeast. The children Nasaw described were for the most part preadolescents; lower working class; of various ethnicities such as Irish, Italian, and so forth; and recent immigrants to the United States. His primary materials include detailed reports of children's work activities by child reformers, oral histories, and autobiographies, but he also used secondary sources such as biographies and novels to supplement and extend his interpretations. These two studies document the important roles children played in their families' economic survival, and they identify the importance of children's autonomy and pioneering spirit as they became the first generation to grow up in a new world.

Children's Contributions to Family and Societal Production. The Euro-American conquest of the frontier in the second half of the 19th century was accomplished primarily by hardworking families. Children contributed significantly to the central tasks of production (the breaking, plowing, and planting of the land and the caring for and harvesting of crops) and subsistence (providing food and clothing and caring for daily needs) in bringing about the transformation of the vast plains region. In fact, West argued that children "generally labored at a wider variety of tasks than either mothers or fathers"; in that sense, they were "the most accomplished and versatile workers of the farming frontier" (1992, p. 30).

Although men usually carried out the physically taxing work of breaking the thickly rooted sod, children were intricately involved in the remaining phases of production. As West noted, the revolution in agricultural technology during this period allowed children to take over some jobs that were previously carried out only by men. Boys and girls as young as 8 years old plowed fields in the spring. West quoted Percy Ebbut, who, as a young child, had observed full-grown men having much difficulty using old-style plows in his native England, whereas he "plowed acre after acre from the time I was twelve years old" with a new steel-tipped plow in the fields of his family farm in Kansas (1992, p. 28).

no "play"

Once fields were plowed and crops planted, children were responsible for their care and protection. They worked "as living scarecrows, patrolling the fields for hours a day, dispersing the grazing cattle and horses, and shooing away the whirling birds that threatened to devour the family's future" (West, 1992, p. 29). Finally, children played a major role at harvest time, with their contributions increasing and becoming more diverse with the advent of new methods. For example, when the horse-drawn thresher arrived, "a small girl might lead the animals around the circle, while one brother cut the bands of sheaves about to be threshed and another kept the machine cleared of straw to keep it from clogging" (p. 29).

The children's contributions to the families' subsistence were probably even more important than their work in farm production. Girls and boys helped in preparing and caring for gardens. However, it was mainly girls who helped with household chores (cooking, cleaning, and so on) and mainly boys who tended to farm chores (tending cattle, haying, and so on). Both boys and girls supplemented the family food supply by gathering wild plants, fruit, and berries and by hunting and fishing. Adults, according to West, had little time for hunting. Children, on the other hand, "some as young as seven or eight," stalked and killed "antelopes, raccoons, ducks, geese, deer, prairie chickens, bison, wild hogs, and, above all, rabbits" (1992, p. 30). As was the case for the slave children discussed earlier, the children of the frontier felt a sense of autonomy, as well as pride, for their contributions to the family—all while they were having fun!

Like the children on the plains frontier, working-class urban children contributed in important ways to the economic health of their families. At the turn of the 20th century, most working- and lower-class children of American cities moved from full-time work to schooling because of child labor laws. These children continued to work both in and outside the home for the majority of their nonschool hours, however. Like farm children, these girls and boys worked in a wide variety of jobs. Some of these jobs were the urban equivalents of those performed by the children of the plains. In addition to foraging for food (in this case, discarded and decaying fruits and vegetables and stale bread and bakery goods), urban children also scavenged backyards, alleyways, train yards, construction sites, and most especially city dumps for anything of value: rags, old furniture and dishes, bottles, tires, pieces of wood, metal, and coal. At first glance, scavenging and junking in inner cities would seem much less enjoyable than collecting berries, hunting, and fishing on the frontier. As Nasaw observed, however, children felt a sense of autonomy scavenging in the streets and dumps. He cited the photographer Lewis Hine, who observed that dumps (especially those that contained only nondecaying refuse) were natural meeting places for children. "Since no adults frequented the dumps except the hoboes, who were seldom any trouble," noted Hine, the children could do as they pleased: run and chase, dig for buried treasure, build forts, "start a warming fire or throw rocks at old bottles without raising the ire of property owners or the cops" (quoted in Nasaw, 1985, p. 93).

Although girls engaged in scavenging and in other types of work, their primary work responsibilities kept them near or in the home. Because homes lacked modern conveniences, girls' work responsibilities were many, varied, and extremely challenging. Household chores required hours of preparation and multiple steps:

> The laundry had to be done by hand from beginning to end: sorted, soaked, rubbed against the washboard, rinsed, boiled, rinsed again, wrung out, starched, hung to dry, ironed with irons heated on the stove, folded, and put away. Cooking involved not only preparing the food and cooking it but hauling coal for the fire, dumping the ashes afterwards, and keeping the cast-iron stove cleaned, blacked, and rust-free. Housecleaning was complicated by the soot, grime, and ashes released by coal-burning stoves and kerosene and gas lamps. Shopping had to be done daily and in several different shops; there were no refrigerators to store food purchased earlier in the week and no supermarkets for one-stop marketing. (Nasaw, 1985, p. 105)

The household work did not end here, however, as many families had boarders to look after and took in "homework" (usually involving sewing or sorting of various goods) from jobbers and contractors. This work was done by mothers but always with help from daughters. In addition to helping with all these demanding chores, girls as young as 7 years old assumed their major responsibilities as "little mothers" (Nasaw, 1985, pp. 101–114). These girls took full responsibility for younger siblings, often while tending to other chores such as shopping. "In many working-class families," argued Nasaw, "the babies and small children were effectively raised by their older sisters" (p. 107).

Unlike the frontier, where technology expanded the role of children in family production and income, in American cities at the turn of the 20th century technological change, industrialization, and growing urbanization continually created and eliminated part-time jobs outside the family for children (Nasaw, 1985, pp. 39–47). Early in the period, retail businesses and working-class children were perfectly suited for each other. Children needed and wanted part-time work, and shopkeepers and department store owners needed children to run errands, carry messages, and deliver goods. For example, in large department stores "cash" boys and girls carried the item sold and the customer's money to an inspector, who took the money and sent the children back with a wrapped package and change. By the turn of the century, however, these jobs were all eliminated as the "pneumatic tube [a device in which receipts and money could be transferred by air pressure from sales clerks to cashiers], followed swiftly by cash registers at each sales counter, made the children superfluous" (p. 43).

As quickly as jobs were eliminated, however, children were able to find others. Many jobs were created by the rapid rate of urbanization. With the expansion of streetcar lines and the growing concentration of white-collar workers in central cities, retailers gained an ever-increasing number of customers. Many children were willing to work for retailers in a range of capacities. Others, however, struck out on their own to practice capitalism without the constraints of bosses, supervisors, or even regular hours. Nasaw referred to these children as the "littlest hustlers" who sold candy, gum, fruit, flowers, and just about anything their adult customers would buy. Many of the adults on the streets of the big cities—businessmen on their way to and from work and well-to-do patrons of large department stores—were very different from the adults of the working-class, immigrant neighborhoods of the children.

Perhaps the most famous of all the little hustlers were the "newsies" whose rise and fall is captured in the following case study.

THE NEWSIES

David Nasaw (1985) noted that the rise of a new generation of newspaper hustlers was a product of the boom in afternoon circulation that had been building through the 1880s and 1890s but that took off during the Spanish-American War. The morning newspapers that had been the mainstay of the industry had, by the turn of the 20th century, been eclipsed by the late editions. By 1900, "evening papers, bought on the way home from work, outnumbered morning papers . . . about three to one" (pp. 62–63). Because of such growing demand and the fact that the customers came to the paper rather than vice versa, 20th-century newsies were able to transform what was once full-time work into part-time jobs that conveniently fit their after-school work hours.

Newsies bought papers from circulation managers of various publishers and worked as independent contractors. Thus, they had a great deal of autonomy "to set their own schedules, establish their own pace, and work when and where they chose" (Nasaw, 1985, p. 67). In fact, argued Nasaw, they "experienced more autonomy at work than in school or at home" (p. 67). Still, newsies had to sell all the newspapers they contracted for to make a profit; adult distributors had no pity on children who could not get the job done. The boys (and some girls) had to come up with a "stake" to buy their initial supply of papers and often borrowed money from parents, siblings, or friends. The profits from the first batch of papers were then used to keep going and, in most cases, to begin profitable careers as newsies. Physical, cognitive, and social skills had to be developed and sharpened for a child to become a successful newsie. Newsies also developed strategies to pitch their wares successfully. One such strategy was the well-known "Extra! Extra! Read all about it!" chant, which was designed to capture the attention of potential customers. In most cases, real news was simply exaggerated a bit for extra impact, but newsies were not above true fabrication (p. 78).

Newsies often used the "last paper ploy," pretending to be hungry, cold, and exhausted as they conned sympathetic adults to buy their last paper. Once that customer moved out of sight, another paper was pulled out, and the routine was repeated. Newsies also had a wide range of strategies to cajole tips from customers, often by claiming to lack needed change.

Newsies were so good at their trade that they were in great demand and were often courted by the major newspaper publishers. In fact, the newsies became so powerful and organized that they formed a union and went on strike against the major New York publishers Joseph Pulitzer and William Randolph Hearst in 1899 in protest against a rise in the prices of papers. The publishers did not take the strike seriously at first, but as the newsies held the line and garnered public support, the publishers decided to offer a settlement. As Nasaw noted, by "unionizing and striking to protect their rights and their profits, the children were behaving precisely as they believed American workers should when treated unjustly" (1985, p. 181). Thus, the children were playing an active and major role in their own socialization in preparation for the adult world they were about to enter.

Autonomy, Activity, and Social Reproduction. In Chapter 1 we discussed the notion of interpretive reproduction and the idea of children's evolving membership in their cultures. As illustrated in the orb web model, children enter the culture through the family, but they come to collectively produce and participate in a series of peer cultures. In this view children do not simply develop as individuals; they collectively produce peer cultures and contribute to the reproduction of the wider society or culture. The cyclical processes in the weaving of the web are always situated in cultural time and space. Major cultural or societal changes create reverberations in the web that are experienced differently across generations. Especially important is the idea that children often contribute to two cultures (children's and adults') simultaneously. Children of the plains and cities in turn-of-the-20th-century America, like the Hausa children studied by Schildkrout (1975/2002), whom we discussed in Chapter 2, were active, here-and-now contributors to their families' subsistence.

The experiences and perspectives of parents and children on the plains frontier and in American cities at the turn of the century aptly demonstrate how the process of interpretive reproduction unfolds. In both cases families had relocated to new worlds. Adults continued to weave their webs, but their foundation consisted of new cultural fields that brought with them new demands and challenges. The demands of this new place and time were, however, always perceived and acted on through a lens that focused on past experiences in other places and times. Adult migrants to the frontier and immigrants to the big cities of a new country had high hopes for a new beginning and better lives for themselves and their children. They could not and did not, however, leave their pasts behind—they always retained memories of "family, friends, the millions of details that made up the familiar world of their origins" (West, 1992, p. 32). These adults tended to look back on their pasts in dealing with challenges of their new world, including the raising of their children.

The children of the plains and the cities, on the other hand, were highly engaged in weaving their webs from a present-day perspective. They were native to the frontier and the city "with no memory, no longing, no historic commitment to another land, another way of life" (Nasaw, 1985, p. 195). As West noted, "They were not 'far from home,' they were home" (1992, p. 33). As a result they actively engaged their worlds with energy, excitement, and true pioneer spirit. When not caught up in the moment, children of the frontier and city did not look back but looked forward, spurred on by goals and dreams that were developing in their childhoods.

As we noted earlier in discussing the orb web model, one of its most instructive features is that it reminds us that we do not leave experiences in childhood behind with maturity and development. "We live our lives," argued Nasaw, "moving forward to catch the possibilities we set before us as children" (1985, p. 198). In this sense, the lessons the children learned on the city streets and the frontier plains "were not interred with their childhoods, but were cast forward to frame their perceptions of the society they would join as adults" (p. 198).

SUMMARY

The major goal of this chapter has been to place the new sociology of children into historical context. In doing so, we examined Ariès's highly original and groundbreaking work on the changing conceptions of childhood and children's changing place in society from the Middle Ages to the 18th century. Ariès saw a general movement from a lack of awareness of an idea of childhood, to a coddling period wherein children were idolized and valued as a source of amusement for adults, to a moralistic period in which childhood was seen as a period of training and discipline in preparation for adult life. Ariès saw these changes not as inevitable but rather as related to shifts in institutional arrangements in European societies such as the move from extended to more nuclear families and the emergence of age-graded schools. Overall, Ariès bemoaned the general separations by class and race that have occurred in modern societies.

Unfortunately, many others working in the area of the history of childhood and the family concentrated primarily on Ariès's ideas of changes in conceptions of childhood, causing them to propose grand-stage theories of the family. These theories maintain that there are universal (and, in some cases, predestined) stages in the evolution of the family, children, and childhood. This work has been criticized by Linda Pollock and other historians for its sweeping claims, its reliance on indirect evidence (such as paintings, religious tracts, and letters), and its unsystematic historical analysis. In her own work, relying on more direct sources (such as diaries, newspaper reports, and court records), Pollock found a great deal of support for the idea of continuity in conceptions of children, parental care, and parental-child relations over time. Although Pollock did not offer a satisfactory theoretical explanation for such continuity, her work, along with that of Ariès, influenced many other historians to focus more directly on children's collective actions and contributions to past societies and to seek out sound historical evidence that bore on these concerns. We discussed how Steven Mintz's history of American childhood (in premodern, modern, and postmodern periods) and his debunking of several myths about childhood serve as a bridge between those historians who focused more on changing adult conceptions of children and those who studied history directly from children's perspectives.

We referred to this work as the new history of childhood and examined several examples, including Hanawalt's study of children in medieval London, the research of Alston and Wiggins on slave children in the pre–Civil War South, West's study of pioneer children on the American Great Plains in the 1880s, and Nasaw's depiction of children in American cities at the turn of the 20th century. The historical narratives in all these studies bring children to life and show that they were influential actors in past societies. The importance of these studies goes beyond their documentation of children's contributions to the historical record, however. They are also vitally important for seeing children as actively contributing to societal production and change while simultaneously creating their own child cultures. In this sense, they help us better understand the notion of interpretive reproduction introduced in Chapter 1, which stressed the importance and complexity of children's collective actions in both the adult world and their own peer cultures.

5

Social Change, Families, and Children

Examining Changes in Families From the Children's Perspective

In Chapter 4 we placed the new sociology of childhood in its historical context. In this chapter our focus will be on children in families. We'll look at how children and childhood are affected by recent social changes in families, and we'll examine the growing diversity of families in both industrialized and developing societies. Increased divorce rates, the rise of single-mother and blended families, the increase in births outside of marriage, and the growing gap between the rich and poor have all had profound effects on children. Some people lament what they see as the breakdown of the traditional family and family values; others argue that families are going through an important period of adjustment and redefinition and that there has always been a diversity of family structures.

Although children are often used to frame the discourse, the voices of children are seldom heard amid the polemic posturing on both sides of the debate about changes in family structure. Furthermore, the effects of changes in families on children's everyday lives are seldom considered. We often hear the refrain from conservatives that we must cut government spending (most especially for welfare programs) to ensure the future of our children. However, there seems to be much less concern for children's lives today—for their childhoods—and especially the childhoods of working-class and poor children. This focus on children's futures serves as an excellent example of what the Finnish sociologist Leena Alanen (1990) has referred to as "children negatively defined." By this she meant that children are defined primarily by what they are going to be and not by what they presently are. We will join this debate about children's lives and futures in the last three chapters of this book.

Some sociologists and social historians who take a more liberal position argue for the redefinition of families. They focus primarily on adults' adjustments to changing family roles, especially those adjustments made by women (see Coontz, 1992, 1997). Ruth Sidel (1992) has demonstrated that women and children often come last; by this she meant that they are most negatively affected by postindustrial change. Still, one yearns to hear more of the voices of young children in theoretical and empirical work by those who call for family redefinition. Sociologist Judith Stacey (1991) impressively traced the attempts of two working-class families to cope with domestic upheaval by carving out wide-ranging, supportive kin networks. Stacey's research focuses primarily on two women whose children were grown and had started families of their own. These grown children often were still dependent on their parents, in-laws, and each other as they struggled with unemployment, drug addiction, family conflict and abuse, and failed aspirations. We learn much about the adult kin in these two families, but the young grandchildren are rarely identified by gender or name; nor are they given the opportunity to present their perspectives of their families' lives.

Stacey is not alone in overlooking children's perspectives. All those who comment on the difficulties that families face in contemporary societies must step back a bit from their struggles to preserve or redefine postindustrial families to appreciate more fully how these struggles affect the childhoods of children of the present.

Our goal must be to bring children back into our conceptualizations of social change and families. In this chapter, we will consider some of the research on young children's experiences in families in both Western and non-Western or developing societies. We will focus on work carried out primarily in the United States and some western European societies and in several developing societies, most especially Africa. We'll also examine how social changes in Western and developing societies are affecting childhood. Here the focus is less on specific children and the texture of their everyday lives and more on general experiences of children as a social group to discover how their childhoods have been affected by key social and economic changes in families since the turn of the 20th century.

Children's Everyday Lives in Families

Most studies on children in families concentrate primarily on socialization and on developmental outcomes. For example, the field of psychology has a long history of research on the effects of attachment and emotional bonding, socialization practices and parenting styles, family disruption, and the role of the media on individual development. Sociologists who study families have also investigated these topics, but they usually view them as intervening variables that are affected by social, structural, and cultural conditions and by the processes of social change. Although they are important, we will not review studies such as these; instead we will examine studies that investigate children's actual experiences and participation in family life. We look first at such studies in Western, industrialized societies.

Studies of Families in Western Societies

A few months after my daughter learned to walk, she liked to practice her new mobility by climbing up and onto what seemed to my wife and me to be very dangerous places. We often took to removing her from atop chairs and other furniture, placing her back on solid ground, and admonishing her about the dangers of such behavior. After several repetitions of such episodes, I heard her call out to me one day, and when I turned to look she was standing at the very top of the back of a large cushioned chair. I gasped and jumped up to get her down, but I still had to chuckle at the large smile on her gleeful face. She was clearing communicating, "Hey Daddy, look what I did this time!"

In her book *The Beginnings of Social Understanding*, psychologist Judy Dunn linked episodes such as this one to children's development of humor, referring to the incidents as "amusement of forbidden acts." In her observational studies of young children's behavior in the family, Dunn found that such amusement of forbidden acts increased dramatically from about 1.5 incidents in 2 hours at the age of 4 months to an average of 6.1 in 2 hours at the age of 14 months (Dunn, 1988, p. 154). Perhaps more important, the children were 4 times more likely to express amusement at their own transgressions than they were to express it at those of other people. We can see that a key feature of children's peer cultures, one we discussed in Chapter 2—to challenge the authority of adults—begins at a very early age.

Dunn is one of very few psychologists or sociologists who actually study young children in the family in Western societies. As Dunn noted, children have been rarely studied in the world in which they develop or in a context in which we can capture the subtleties of social understanding. There are at least two reasons for the lack of research on children's everyday life in the family. The first is methodological, and the second has more to do with ethics and practicality. In the social sciences, research methods are normally of two different types: positivist or interpretive. Positivist approaches stress the importance of investigating causal relationships between social and psychological variables and in formulating and testing hypotheses under controlled conditions. Interpretive approaches stress the importance of meaning or interpretive understanding of social processes (that is, what the processes "mean" from the perspective of the social participants involved) and favor the direct study of these processes in natural settings. The positivist thrust of most social science has led researchers to carry out their studies of children in experimental settings with precise controls that give them the ability to test specific hypotheses or to rely on surveys of parents about child-rearing attitudes and behaviors. However, even researchers who take an interpretive approach have rarely studied children in the family in Western society. The lack of study of family interaction and process even by interpretive researchers is related to how the privacy of family life is valued in most Western societies. Researchers face a good deal of resistance and must confront challenging ethical issues when attempting to set up camp in the family. Still, we are beginning to see more observational and ethnographic studies of the family, and we are learning more about children's participation in family life. In this respect, Dunn's work on young children's involvement in family life and with parents and siblings is groundbreaking (Dunn, 1988; Dunn & Kendrick, 1982). It represents one of the few attempts in developmental psychology to examine closely the importance of interpersonal relationships in the context of family life for young children's social and emotional development.

Dunn used a combination of observational and interview methods to capture key processes in children's socioemotional development between the ages of 1 and 3. She found strong evidence for the rapid growth of assertive and resistant behavior by children in their 2nd year in dealings with parents and siblings. These behaviors, in turn, led to conflicts and the display of emotions. Dunn related these findings to children's discovery of misbehavior (including emotional displays) as a means of gaining control over their parents. Dunn further developed the theoretical significance of these findings by arguing that the "urgency of self-assertion in the face of powerful others increases along with the child's understanding" (1988, p. 176). Indeed, according to Dunn, children's self-interest drives much of their behavior in these early years. She argued, however, that it is not that young children simply want their way; it is rather that they want to be effective members of their families. In this view, "children are motivated to understand the social rules and relationships of their cultural world *because they need to get things done in their family relationships*" (1988, p. 189).

In addition to Dunn's research, many important studies of adult–young child interaction in families have focused on language development. Many of the early studies in this area were restricted to tape recordings of children's spontaneous language use over the first 3 years of life. The aim was to document children's development of the form and function of language. Later studies moved to a broader focus on children's development of communicative competence through their involvement in everyday cultural routines in families with both parents and siblings (Dunn & Kendrick, 1982; Heath, 1983; Miller, Wiley, Fung, & Liang, 1997; Ochs, 1988; Pontecorvo, Fasulo, & Sterponi, 2001; Schieffelin, 1990; Schieffelin & Ochs, 1986; Zukow, 1989).

In Chapter 1 we discussed the importance of language and children's involvement in everyday cultural routines for interpretive reproduction. Recent work by psychologist Peggy Miller and her colleagues brings these theoretical notions to life through the careful observation and analysis of language practices in families. Miller examined *narrative practices*, the term she used to describe stories that provide family members with "widely available means by which [they] create, interpret, and publicly project culturally constituted images of self in face-to-face interaction" (Miller, Potts, Fung, Hoogstra, & Mintz, 1990, p. 294). Miller and her colleagues argued that children develop "a means of expressing and understanding who they are through their routine participation in culturally organized narrative practices in which personal experiences are recounted" (1990, p. 295). The emphasis on collective practices is important. Unlike conventional approaches, which focus on how various experiences in families affect children's individual development, this interpretive approach stresses children's active involvement in the joint creation of family experiences through their very participation in families. We learn not only about potential outcomes but also about how children participate in and contribute to the creation of their own childhoods in families. Let's look at an example from Miller's research on working-class families in the eastern United States.

AMY STICKS UP FOR HER MOM

In the following story, told in the presence of 23-month-old Amy and her 5-year-old cousin Kris, Amy's mother, Marlene, relates to the researcher an event involving her boyfriend, Johnny, whom Amy habitually calls "Daddy." The story focuses on Amy's clever, assertive retort to Johnny's efforts to prod her into teasing her mother (italicized words indicate stress).

Mother: Johnny told her the other night, he says to her, "Isn't your mother a creep?"

Amy: Mar! Mar!

Mother: And he kept tellin' her all these things and she says, "*Na huh.*" She says, "*You* are, Daddy. *You're* the creep."

Researcher: [Laughs]

Mother: That's what she told him. He like to come off that chair.

Amy: [Now sitting close to her mother on the sofa] Mar!

Mother: Yeah.

Amy: Yeah.

Mother: Yeah, he says, "Tell your mother she's a creep." And finally she's just sittin' there takin' it and takin' it and he said, "Tell her, tell your mother she's a creep." That's when she said, "*Nuh* uh, Daddy." She said, "*You're* the creep."

Source: Adapted from Miller, Potts, Fung, Hoogstra, and Mintz (1990, p. 296).

A number of elements in this case study are important for understanding how such narratives can be seen as excellent examples of interpretive reproduction in families. Telling stories about young children relays information about the importance and organization of their experiences. Thus, by

> consistently telling stories about some experiences rather than others, caregivers convey which ones are reportable. By creating a particular rendition of the experience, they show what the component events are, how the events are related, and what is important about them. (Miller et al., 1990, p. 297)

For example, Miller found in her work with these working-class families that parents valued their children's being able to stick up for themselves, especially in response to frequent adult teasing (Miller, 1982, 1986). In fact, such teasing was viewed as good preparation for interaction with peers and other adults. In this case, Amy not only resisted Johnny's playful teasing but also demonstrated "quick-witted assertiveness" (especially for a 2-year-old), which was the main "point" of the story (Miller et al., 1990, p. 297).

Such narratives also are multifunctional. The mother is able to convey to the researcher the developing communicative competence of her daughter, the nature of Amy's close relationship with the mother's boyfriend (Amy calls him Daddy and feels comfortable teasing him, and Johnny accepts being put in his place), and the mother's valuing of assertiveness in her child. Amy is present throughout the story and seems attentive to the fact that she is being singled out in a positive way, "as someone whose experiences are tellable" (Miller et al., 1990, p. 297).

In this and other studies, Miller pursued the implications of such narrative practices by examining cases wherein children intervened in narratives produced by their parents. She found that by the age of 2 and a half, children were 4 times more likely to intervene and make comments regarding stories about themselves than regarding other stories. She also found that children appropriate stories they have heard and reproduce them in other settings (Miller et al., 1990, pp. 298–305; also see Miller & Moore, 1989; Miller & Sperry, 1987).

In a detailed ethnography of 12 families, sociologist Annette Lareau (2003) investigated the importance of social class in child rearing and children's life chances. Lareau and her research assistants spent nearly a month in each of the families. The sample was diverse in regard to race and class in that there were two White and two Black middle-class, working-class, and poor families in the study. Lareau first made contact with the families in a larger interview study related to the lives of their third-grade children in an urban and a suburban school. Once accepted in the families, Lareau and her assistants shadowed and observed family members as they went about daily activities in and outside the home (shopping; visiting doctors; going on family outings; consulting with teachers; taking children to soccer, piano, or dance lessons; visiting relatives; and so on). They also spent at least one overnight visit with most of the families. Lareau's aim was to capture the cultures of the families—how they organized their daily lives, talked to and disciplined their children, and dealt with institutions such as schools, churches, and medical facilities.

Lareau found that White and Black middle-class parents engaged in practices of what she called *concerted cultivation.* By this she meant that "parents actively fostered and assessed their children's talents, opinions, and skills. They scheduled their children for activities. They reasoned with them. They hovered over them and outside the home they did not hesitate to intervene on the children's behalf" (Lareau, 2003, p. 238). In short, the middle-class parents made every effort to stimulate their "children's development and to cultivate their cognitive and social skills" (p. 238).

Things were quite different for working-class and poor parents. These parents practiced what Lareau termed a logic of child rearing as the *accomplishment of natural growth.* By this she meant the working-class and poor parents (both White and Black) "viewed children's development as unfolding spontaneously, as long as they were provided with comfort, food, shelter, and other basic support" (Lareau, 2003, p. 238). The lives of the working-class and poor children were less structured and controlled. They were expected to spend time in and around the home and to play informally with peers, siblings, and cousins. Working- and lower-class parents were generally more authoritative with their children, relying on directives and threats to keep them in line. They did not tolerate disrespect, whining, or bad manners, as many of the middle-class parents did. Finally, in institutional encounters, working-class and poor parents seldom intervened and turned over responsibility to professionals. When they did try to intervene on their children's behalf, they often felt intimidated and misunderstood.

Lareau's study is important because she argued that the middle-class practices of concerted cultivation result in an emerging sense of entitlement on the part of middle-class children and a better chance for maintaining or improving their social-class positions. Working-class and poor children, on the other hand, develop an emerging sense of constraint and resignation to the limitations of their life circumstances. Thus, their chances for upward mobility are less likely. In short, the practices of the two social-class groups contribute to social reproduction and social inequality.

The in-depth ethnographic observations of the study also reveal fascinating aspects of family life that go beyond these general patterns regarding social class, however. For example, middle-class children and parents are so involved in school and extracurricular activities that they feel constantly harried and tired. There are fewer opportunities for relaxing family time and for the kids just to be kids (a trend we discussed earlier in

Chapter 2). Working-class and poor families, on the other hand, although often lacking needed resources to make their lives easier or to provide special lessons or training for their children, spent more time together in unstructured family interactions and visiting with relatives. In addition, working-class and poor children had more autonomy and were more independent.

Finally, it must be remembered that Lareau's study is based on a small sample, and other studies of working-class and poor families have found that parents have high educational aspirations for their children (T. Chin & Phillips, 2004; Rosier, 2000; Rosier & Corsaro, 1993). In these studies, researchers argue that working-class and poor parents attempt to act and are sometimes successful in acting on these aspirations, although compared to middle-class parents, they lack financial resources, flexible jobs, and knowledge to better cultivate their children for success.

Overall, in this important observational work of Dunn, Miller, Lareau, and others, families are conceptualized as local cultures in which young children actively participate, contribute to their own socialization, and affect the participation of adults (see Gubrium & Holstein, 1990; see also DeVault, 2000; Thorne, 2001, for other studies of children in the family). Such capturing of important productive-reproductive processes in families is made possible by the use of interpretive ethnographic methods. Earlier we noted that interpretive research methods stress the importance of understanding social processes from the participants' perspectives. These methods involve the careful entry into natural settings such as families and peer groups, observing over long periods of time, and capturing the meaning of social processes from the perspectives of those studied. Such methods are becoming more common in research on families and children in Western societies. However, they have long been employed by anthropologists to understand family life and socialization processes in non-Western cultures. It is to a consideration of such research that we now turn.

Studies of Families in Non-Western Societies

A number of recent, important, cross-cultural studies of early socialization in the family share a definite affinity with the work of Dunn, Miller, and Lareau. A central feature of this work is the focus on children's development of communicative competence through their involvement in everyday cultural routines within families (Briggs, 1998; Ochs, 1988; Schieffelin, 1990; Watson-Gegeo & Gegeo, 1986).

Elinor Ochs's (1988) study of culture and language development in a Samoan village captures many of the strengths of this cross-cultural research. Ochs maintained that participants in verbal interactions draw on linguistic and sociocultural knowledge to create and define what is taking place in any given interactive event. For example, Ochs noted that findings from studies of middle-class families in the United States illustrate that American adults do not hesitate "to guess" at what children are trying to communicate in situations of ambiguity. In such instances, adults offer up reformulations of unclear speech for children to confirm or disconfirm. Although clarification frequently occurs in adult-child interaction in Samoa (and in some rare cases involves guessing and reformulation), Samoan adults show a clear preference for a "minimal-grasp" strategy in which they

> initiate clarification of children's utterances through quizzical expressions, statements of nonunderstanding, WH questions [for example, who/what/ where/when/why questions like "Where's Daddy," "What are you doing?"], and other directives, to elicit from the child a reformulation of all or part of the unclear utterance or gesture. (Ochs, 1988, p. 136)

Although this difference in strategies of clarification may seem minor or even trivial, it is reflective of major differences between Samoan and American societies and demonstrates how children's conversations with caregivers are socially and culturally organized. The White, middle-class, American style of clarification reflects that society's belief that a speaker's intentions are critical to the interpretation of his or her utterances or actions. This is evident in the American legal system, where the notion of intent is important in the characterization of crimes and accompanying sanctions. Ochs argued that this orientation "leads members to take seriously and pursue establishing an individual's motivations and psychological states" (1988, p. 141). Samoans generally display a strong dispreference for guessing at what is going on in another person's mind, and in the Samoan legal arena actions are "assessed almost exclusively in terms of social and economic losses and disturbances" (1988, p. 141). However, personal intentions are important in communicative situations when the speaker is of high social status. At political meetings, for example, high chiefs and high-status orators are entitled to voice personal opinions. In these situations, those of lower status often guess about personal intentions when ambiguities arise. Such guessing rarely is directed toward lower ranking individuals, such as those involved in caretaker-child interactions. In fact, given the low status of children, such guessing is seen not only as inappropriate but also as not worth the time. Because Samoans believe that children learn by listening to and watching (over and over) indications that their actions or responses need clarification, adults elicit redoings and resayings through simple clarification requests.

Although work on sibling relations in Western societies has appeared only recently, there is a long history of the study of sibling interaction in other societies (Harkness & Super, 1992; Nsamenang, 1992a; Weisner & Gallimore, 1977; Zukow, 1989). In a fascinating study of socialization practices of the Kalui people of Papua New Guinea, Bambi Schieffelin (1990) found clear differences in the way mothers encouraged interaction between same-sex and opposite-sex siblings. Same-sex siblings are encouraged to cooperate, and mothers urge younger children to seek the help and company of older siblings just as they urge older children to comply with the wishes of their younger siblings. Cooperation is not fostered between opposite-sex siblings, however, and younger brothers are actually encouraged to tease, provoke, and even hit their older sisters.

Schieffelin argued that these differences in parental socialization practices not only affect the nature of sibling relations but also prepare children for sibling relations, gender identities, and male-female relations in adult life. Whereas men in Kalui society establish cooperative and egalitarian roles with other men (especially brothers), they are socialized to develop an orientation of entitlement regarding the attention and support of women. Schieffelin referred to this process as men's coming to "feel owed." Women, on the other hand, are given less attention as children and "learn quickly that 'feeling owed' as a general orientation is neither valued nor appropriate for them" (1990, p. 248). As a result, "women are the givers of the society, to the appeals and demands of others, particularly men and children; less often women" (p. 249).

In Africa the long tradition of having multiple caregivers for young children is captured in the proverb, "It takes a village to raise a child." This idea runs counter to Western theories of child development, which support the notion of attachment and hold that the child must establish a strong bond with a primary caretaker (normally the mother) for healthy emotional development. In their study of the Efe (Pygmies) of Northeastern Zaire, Edward Tronick, Gilda Morelli, and Steve Winn (1987) documented a distinctive pattern of multiple caretaker child care. Efe infants spend a large percentage of time away from their mothers, who return to work in the fields only a few days after giving birth. At the work site, child care responsibilities are generally shared by several individuals. The infants are nursed by several women, including the mother. In fact, argued Tronick and colleagues, "almost all females attempt to comfort a distressed or fussy infant" (1987, p. 99). Such comforting "includes allowing the infant to suckle and often occurs in the mother's presence. But if unsuccessful the infant is returned to the mother" (p. 99).

Given certain ecological factors, such as the low temperature of the forests in which they dwell, the small size of the infants, cultural values, and their unique cultural history, some researchers see many highly beneficial physical, emotional, and social outcomes of multiple caregiving by the Efe (Tronick et al., 1987, p. 104). These researchers propose that multiple caretaking among the Efe "may function to teach infants about culturally appropriate styles of interactions as well as to expose infants to the culture's valuation of cooperation, mutual support, and gregariousness" (Tronick et al., 1987, p. 103).

Similar patterns of multiple caregiving, most especially of young children by older siblings and peers, can be seen in other parts of Africa. Bame Nsamenang described traditional child care in Cameroon in west-central Africa as a "social enterprise in which parents, kin, sometimes neighbors and friends, and older children were active participants" (1992a, p. 422). He noted, however, that fathers are never assigned routine caretaking duties, and once the children are weaned mothers turn over most of the care to older siblings or peers. The typical pattern is for fathers to be involved in animal husbandry, clearing and fencing farmland, and building dwellings, whereas mothers are responsible for child rearing, food production and processing, and homekeeping. This pattern bears striking similarity to the ones described by Alston and Wiggins in their works on child care by slave children in the pre–Civil War South of the United States, which we discussed in Chapter 4.

The younger, 5- to 6-year-old Cameroonian children take on progressively demanding chores such as running errands, fetching water and firewood, and tending animals under the direction of older children. Nsamenang pointed out the strong communal ethos of these groups and noted that peer cultures involving both work and play emerge from this. He argued further that this pattern of peer socialization and training "seemed relevant and appropriate for the requirements of a subsistent, agrarian economy. The close texture of traditional life and the courtesies and human warmth it engendered and fostered, supported individuals and families" (1992a, p. 426).

Similar patterns of multiage peer caregiving have been documented in the East African countries of Kenya, Tanzania, and Uganda. In these societies, infants as young as 1 to 3 months are often turned over to child nurses, usually young girls between 6 and 10 years of age. These child nurses serve as primary caregivers; the mothers normally return to full-time agricultural work (Harkness & Super, 1992). Although these caretaking practices may seem neglectful by Western standards, the actual pattern of caregiving by child nurses and mothers is quite indulgent. In fact, a comparative study of the caretaking behavior of American mothers and the Kipsigis of Kenya showed "that the African babies received three times the *amount* of attention of the U.S. babies, whereas [the] mothers' *rate* of attention in both samples were similar" (Harkness & Super, 1992, p. 453, italics added). Furthermore, East African caretakers believe that infants should be responded to quickly when they are fussy. As Harkness and Super noted, "it would be unthinkable in the East African context for a baby to cry itself to sleep; this U.S. custom is considered abusive by East Africans" (1992, p. 453). Finally, as was the case with indigenous caretaking practices in Cameroon, the responsibilities given to older siblings and peers in caring for younger children are seen as an *"apprenticeship system in which women and men are well trained in parental roles by the time they actually have children of their own"* (1992, p. 454). Here we see a parallel to the "little mothers" of turn-of-the-20th-century American cities, who were described in Chapter 4. Unfortunately, the comforting sense of traditional community and collective responsibility that occurred as a result of these indigenous child care practices has been disrupted by major economic and social changes in Africa and much of the Third World (Bradshaw & Wallace, 1996).

The Effects of Recent Socioeconomic Changes on Children and Childhood in Western Societies

In Chapter 1 we saw that children enter into their societies or cultures through the family and that families play a central role in children's early lives. As we saw in Chapter 4, the structure of the family and family processes were both alike and different on the frontier and in large cities in turn-of-the-20th-century America. Both frontier and big-city families were large, and children were expected to begin to contribute to their families' economic well-being from an early age. Children in frontier families were directly involved in the subsistence economy of the farms, whereas city children contributed their labor both at home and in employment as newsies, delivery boys and girls, and scavengers. American families have changed dramatically since then, and these changes have brought about major transformations in the everyday lives of young children. The most dramatic changes have been the decline of two-parent farm families and change in family size, coupled with an increase in mothers' labor force participation and in the number of mother-only families. Although this book focuses primarily on childhood up to and including preadolescence, in considering these trends in family structure we will focus on adolescence as well. Let's discuss each of these changes in turn.

The Rapid Decline of Two-Parent Farm Families

As we discussed earlier, the shift from an agricultural to an industrialized economy in Western societies brought about major changes in families. In the United States, these economic changes led to a dramatic family reorganization in a relatively short period of time. In 1830 nearly 70% of children lived in two-parent farm families, but by 1930 this percentage had dropped to less than 30%. During the same 100-year period, the percentage of children living in nonfarm families with breadwinner fathers and homemaker mothers increased from 15% to 55%, and in 1930 this was the most prevalent type of family organization (see Exhibit 5.1). Children no longer worked side by side with their parents and siblings, contributing to the family livelihood. Now fathers spent their workdays away from the home while mothers remained home to care for their children and perform domestic work (Hernandez, 1994, p. 4).

This change did not mean, however, that children and youth no longer worked. It was the nature of children's work that changed. For example, there was an almost complete reversal of teenage employment in what Ellen Greenberger and Laurence Steinberg (1986) term the "old" workplace (crafts, factory, and farm) and the "new" workplace (service and sales) in the United States between 1940 and 1980. Today, in industrialized societies, fewer after-school and summer jobs are available that provide the kinds of experiences that enhance childhood and adolescence or prepare children and youth for the transition to adulthood. In fact, two jobs in particular (store clerks and food service workers) constituted "the core of the new adolescent workplace" for in-school workers in the 1980s (Greenberger & Steinberg, 1986, p. 63). It is a safe assumption that this trend has continued to grow.

On an intuitive level, most adults believe that for today's youth, work—even though clearly different from that of the past—is still valuable and clearly preferable to many other activities such as watching TV or hanging out at the mall. Greenberger and Steinberg presented a set of observational, interview, and survey findings that clearly challenge this view. They found, for example, that

> working is more likely to interfere with than enhance schooling; promotes pseudomaturity rather than maturity; is associated in certain circumstances with higher, not lower, rates of delinquency and drug and alcohol use; and fosters cynical rather than respectful attitudes toward work. (1986, p. 235)

They link these negative effects to the fact that the new youth workplace is educationally irrelevant, economically unnecessary, and largely age segregated.

Of course, many American children and youth have to work to supplement meager family incomes. These youth have fewer opportunities in sales and service positions as compared to middle-class youth, however, because many service and retail businesses have relocated from downtown areas to suburban shopping malls in American cities. In fact, low-income minority youth face high rates of unemployment, and many of those who

Exhibit 5.1   Children Aged 0 to 17 in Farm Families, Father-as-Breadwinner Families, and Dual-Earner Families: 1790–1998

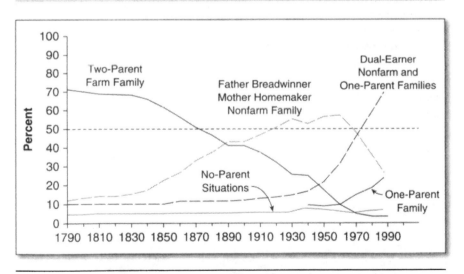

Sources: Hernandez, 1993a, p. 103. Copyright © by Russell Sage Foundation. Reprinted with permission. (Original data from Census PUMS for 1940–1980, CPS for 1980 and 1989, and Appendix 4.1.)

Notes: Estimates for 10-year intervals to 1980, and for 1989.

do find work tend to work 35 or more hours per week while continuing their schooling (Lewin-Epstein, 1981). Limited employment opportunities for poor youth in the United States has led some criminologists to argue that a significant percentage of criminal activity, especially that related to the drug trade, can be seen as a form of employment (see Hagan, 1994).

The Decline in Family Size

Children also have been affected by a dramatic shift in family size during the past 100 years. Although there was a brief lull in this shift during the baby boom period of 1945 to 1957 (see Exhibit 5.2), it was more than offset by the baby bust period in later years. (A recent estimate for 2000 reports further decline in family size, with the average number of siblings dropping to 1.74; Hernandez, personal communication, 2004. This trend toward lower fertility and smaller families is even stronger in most European countries; see Peterson, 1999; Sgritta, 1997.)

This shift in family size has drastically reduced the number of siblings who are available for companionship. Without siblings to integrate them into informal neighborhood activities and children's cultures, children find they have to rely more on parents. Because parental work demands have also increased, especially with many more mothers working, there

Exhibit 5.2 Median Number of Siblings in a Typical American Family, 1865–1994

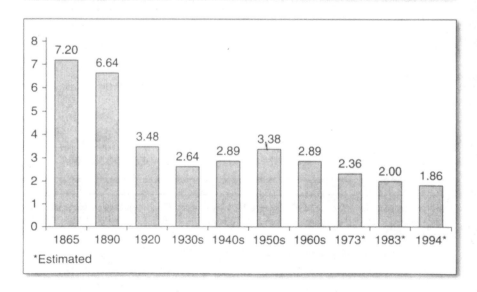

*Estimated

has been a resulting increase in the general institutionalization of children. Many children now enter child care and early education institutions shortly after birth, with the majority of American children now spending several years in such institutions before entering elementary school. Also, as we discussed in Chapter 2, parents in contemporary American society often enroll their children in lessons and organized activities. These often serve a dual function, providing child care and also serving as a substitute for the interactions with siblings and parents that occurred more routinely in the large families of the past.

The Rise in Mothers' Labor Force Participation

Another major change in families began in the 1940s and, as of this writing, is still increasing: the dramatic rise in mothers' labor force participation. As we see in Exhibit 5.3, mothers' labor force participation increased at a steady rate of about 10% each year, from 10% in 1940 to nearly 60% in 1990 and to slightly more than 70% in 2000. It seems to have reached a peak at this point and remained at slightly more than 70% in 2008 (Bureau of Labor Statistics, 2009; Fields, 2003; Hernandez, 1994). In addition to creating a need for child care institutions and for children's leisure activities, the increase in mothers' labor force participation also affected the nature of children's lives when they were at home with parents, especially regarding children's contributions to work in the home. As we discussed in Chapter 2, the increase in mothers' labor force participation often meant that mothers now had two jobs—one in and another outside the home. However, work in the home changed for children and youth as well, and it is important to examine these changes from the perspectives of children.

Take, for example, studies of the relationship between family structure and children's household work. The findings from these studies are mixed (see Y. Lee, Schneider, and Waite, 2003, for a review). In several studies, it was found that children help to pick up the slack when both parents or the single parent is working (Blair, 1992; Hofferth & Sandberg, 2001a, 2001b; Solberg, 1990). However, these and other studies suggest that in families in which mothers work outside the home, gender differences in children's contributions are magnified: Daughters contribute more and perform more gender-typed tasks (Hilton & Haldeman, 1991; Hofferth & Sandberg, 2001b; Larson, Richards, Sims, & Dworkin, 2001). In fact, one study (Benin & Edwards, 1990) found that sons actually contributed less in dual-earner families than they did in traditional families and that the gap between sons' and daughters' contributions was greater (10.2 hours of work per week for daughters compared to only 2.7 hours per week for sons).

Exhibit 5.3   Proportion of Children With Mothers in the Labor Force

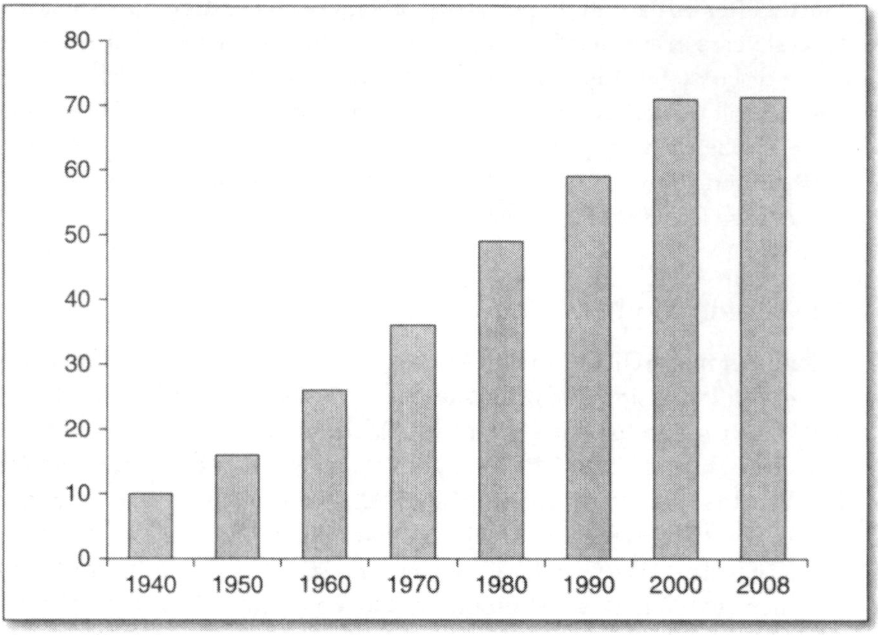

Source: Bureau of Labor Statistics (2009), Fields (2003), Hernandez (1994).

The authors of reports such as these almost always interpret such find-ings from the parents' perspective. For example, they suggest that sons get by with doing less because of the "stereotyped assumption that their daugh-ters can perform housework tasks well, whereas their sons cannot" (Benin & Edwards, 1990, p. 370). Others maintain that hard-pressed, stressed-out mothers have less time to argue with and nag their sons into action, so they pass on the work to daughters or do it themselves. But what of the children's perspectives? In one study, after first noting that the median number of hours of housework per week was only about 6 for older girls, the authors noted, "On top of schoolwork, homework, and extracurricular activities, chores can add a significant additional demand on children" (White & Brinkerhoff, 1981, p. 792). However, neither this study nor any of the other studies I could locate ever controlled for or even considered the effects of children's work outside the home. This was true even in those studies in which it appears that such information was present in the database used.

We know from our earlier discussion of youth employment that, for adolescents, the amount of paid work undertaken outside the home is often extensive. Some studies of youth employment report that boys work longer hours than girls—21.1 mean hours per week for high school senior boys compared to 17.8 for girls (Lewin-Epstein, 1981, p. 74). This difference surely may contribute to gender differences in hours worked in the home; boys are home less often and therefore have less time available for working in the home. Wendy Manning, however, found that the number of hours worked outside the home did not differ by gender (1990, p. 189). Both of these studies are now somewhat out of date, and gender differences in work inside and outside the home may not vary as much today.

Although the evidence suggests that adolescent females may be working even harder than male adolescents overall, the key issue is that adolescent work in school, at home, and on the job is not appreciated as it should be in sociological research (Y. Lee et al., 2003). In their study of teenage workers, Greenberger and Steinberg lamented the amount of time youth invested in outside work, noting that "the student with a half-time job is a very busy person, who commits, at the minimum, fifty hours to school and work; and if after-school activities are substantial, sixty hours or more" (1986, p. 22). This estimate does not include housework. If we factor in chores at home, along with assigned homework, eating, and sleeping, we find that about 18 of the 168 hours in a week are available for leisure and related activities. If housework is the "second shift" for mothers (Hochschild, 1989), then it must be the third shift for adolescents (especially daughters).

Not surprisingly, one of the few studies of parental attitudes toward children's work found that "helping around the house was the domain of greatest disagreement," and children who worked outside the home "were significantly more likely to disagree about helping than nonworkers were" (Manning, 1990, p. 194). Here again, however, the findings were based on parental reports, and the children's behaviors and attitudes were filtered through the perspectives of parents.

Studies of children's perceptions of housework are rare. In her ethnography of adolescent girls growing up in South London, Helena Wulff found that girls begrudgingly accepted the necessity of helping with chores. However, the girls often offered up complaints such as the following: "Parents can be mean when it comes to housework, especially mums. You have to hoover [vacuum] the whole house and polish the furniture" (Wulff, 1988, p. 150). In an innovative study of children's housework, Anne Solberg (1990) first collected questionnaire data from 800 schoolchildren (ages 10 through 12) from across Norway and then followed up with intensive interviews of 10 families living in Oslo. The results from the survey were quite similar to the American studies just discussed concerning number of hours worked, gender differences, and so on. However, the interview study revealed some fascinating insights regarding the children's perspectives. The children were more likely to accept and even enjoy housework in homes where duties were divided up in an egalitarian way, with all family members taking turns fixing evening meals, rotating the laundry duties, and so on (see Elder & Conger, 2000, for similar findings regarding children from rural families in the United States regarding their contributions to housework and farm tasks). Also, children felt that being responsible for certain chores after school gave them more independence. They especially liked having the control and run of the house for a few hours and would often intermesh play and socializing with peers and chores. According to Solberg, the children's negotiated use of domestic space in these instances gave them a sense of autonomy, whereas the parents—although not aware of all that may have occurred while they were away—expressed pleasure at their children's ability to look after themselves and get some work done at the same time (pp. 134–135).

In a recent study of 30 middle-class families in Los Angeles, Klein, Graesch, and Izquierdo (2009) relied on direct observation scans and interviews regarding children's work or chores compared to those of parents. The children in the study ranged in age from 5 to 17, but most were between the ages of 8 and 10. The authors found that on the subset of observations in which parents and children were engaged in household chores, children accounted for an average of 13% of all household work compared to 60% for mothers and 27% for fathers. There was, however, wide variation across families, with children doing no household work in some families and up to 28% of all household work in others. These findings are on the whole similar to studies that rely on questioning of mothers about children's household work. The study differs in gaining the children's perspectives through interviews. The children (especially those 12 and younger) had broad perspectives about how they perceived work or chores. In addition to specific kinds of household work such as cleaning, taking care of pets, or taking out the trash, many of the children pointed to things that contributed to the overall well-being of the household. For example, one girl, Aurora (8 years old) said she didn't have any specific chores but that "it's our job to try to not make a mess, and if we do make a mess, we say sorry and mom forgives us and then we might help her clean up the mess" (Klein et al., 2009, p. 104). Other children, in line with Qvortrup's points about schooling as children's work discussed in Chapter 2, stated that their primary responsibility was to attend school and complete their homework assignments. These children seemed keenly aware that doing well in school and managing school homework by themselves "saved their parents the daily trials of overseeing this activity" (Klein et al., 2009, p. 104).

The Rise in Mother-Only Families

Another change in family organization in Western societies is the marked increase in single-parent families, the overwhelming majority of which are mother-only families. The proportion of mother-only families in the United States increased from 6.7% in 1940, to about 10% in 1970, to 20% in 1990, and to 23% in 2002 (see Fields, 2003; Hernandez, 1994, pp. 9–10). This proportion has held steady recently and was 22.8% in 2008 (U.S. Census Bureau, 2009). Father-only families have also increased from a proportion of around 1% in 1970, to 5% in 2000, and then to 3.5% in 2008. The reasons for these trends are complex and vary significantly by race for American families, but they relate primarily to divorce and to out-of-wedlock births. The primary effect of this trend on children and childhood is often negative; a large proportion of children in the United States have been thrust into poverty in the past 20 years, and the poverty rates are much higher for children from mother-only families than they are for other family structures (Cancian & Reed, 2001; Hernandez, 1994; Rainwater & Smeeding, 1995). Although the topic is subject to much debate, there are negative social and psychological consequences for children born out of wedlock and for those from divorced families as well. Still many single-parent families are highly stable, and many children show strong resilience in dealing with divorce and the challenges of poverty. We will discuss the debate regarding these issues in Chapters 10 and 11, where we consider the social problems of children.

Patterns in Child Population by Race and Ethnicity

A final important trend related to children in families is related to changes in the overall makeup of the child population in the United States and changes in terms of race and ethnicity. In 2001, children younger than 18 made up 25% of the total population, a decrease from 36% in 1960, which was the end of the baby boom. Projections by the U.S. Census Bureau predict that this proportion will drop to 24% by 2010 and remain near that level through 2020 (U.S. Census Bureau, 2003).

A major change has occurred in the racial and ethnic diversity of the child population since 1980, as we can see in Exhibit 5.4. In 1980 White, non-Hispanic children were a sizable majority, constituting nearly three quarters of the child population. However, a decrease of nearly 20 percentage points is predicted by 2020 when this group will represent 55% of the total child population.

The overwhelming majority of this change is due to a large increase in the percentage of Hispanic children from just 9% of the child population in 1980, to 16% in 2000, to a projected 23% in 2020. As we see in Exhibit 5.4 the proportions of other racial and ethnic groups have remained relatively stable (Black, non-Hispanic and American Indian/Alaska Native) along with a slight increase in the proportion of Asian/Pacific Islander children.

These changes in the ethnic diversity of the child population will certainly affect educational policy and processes as well as cultural differences in children's lives both in their peer cultures and in their relationships with adults. Hernandez, Denton, & Macartney (2007b) noted that many young Hispanic children are not enrolled in preschool programs and also have limited English proficiency. This combination is clearly unfortunate as preschool provides needed experience and opportunities for second language learning that are often not available in the homes of Hispanic children. Given that young Hispanic children will in the near future comprise nearly 20% of the labor

Exhibit 5.4   Percentage of Children Younger than 18, by Race and Ethnicity, 1980–2020

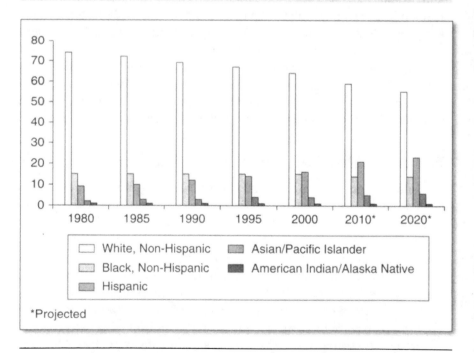

*Projected

Source: Adapted from *Trends in the Well-Being of America's Children and Youth. Section 1: Population, Family, and Neighborhood* (2003; http://usa.usembassy.de/etexts/soc/childtrends03 pop.pdf).

force and be supporting the predominately White, non-Hispanic baby boomers during their retirement, it is important for all of us in American society to invest in these children. As Hernandez and colleagues convincingly argued, these children need to "be afforded the opportunities to experience success in pursuing the American Dream that drew their parents to this country and that it is the birthright of all Americans" (2007a, p. 228). Similar changes in the diversity of childhood populations are also occurring in other Western societies as the result of immigration and fertility trends. Documenting the nature and effect of these changes is an important task for researchers in the sociology of childhood in the future.

The Effects of Recent Socioeconomic Changes on Children and Childhood in Developing Societies

Industrialization and modernization in the developing world have been both rapid and uneven. Although industrialization brought economic growth and an improved quality of life to some developing countries in the 1970s, a range of social, economic, ecological, and epidemic problems (especially ethnic violence, external indebtedness, drought, and AIDS) have more than reversed these gains in the past 30 years. How have these problems affected the lives of children? As York Bradshaw has noted, most international development research has "either ignored children or relegated them to a secondary status," which is highly "unfortunate because children represent one of the most vulnerable groups in most societies" (1993, p. 134). We will discuss Bradshaw's documentation of this neglect, and the negative effects modernization has wrought for many Third World children, in Chapter 11. Here we briefly consider how the disruption of traditional family structure, along with the indigenous family processes and practices brought on by modernization, affect the everyday lives of children.

Let's consider the work lives of the Poomkara youth of a rural Kerala village in South India, where changes regarding educational expectations for children often clash with traditional views of children's labor. Anthropologist Olga Nieuwenhuys (1993) noted that schooling has become popular in Kerala (and among members of the lower castes in general) because it is believed to be a way of escaping caste discrimination (by obtaining certification for government service). However, the underlying assumption of Kerala's educational policies is that while attending school "rural children would continue to work in support of themselves and their families in their spare time" (p. 105). In fact, both the state and parents see education "as a matter of personal endurance, gift and luck of the child, that is, as a child's frontier" (p. 105). This frontier is clearly challenging for Indian secondary school children because adults assume little responsibility for helping with school expenses such as transportation, food, supplies, and clothing. Children must pay for these expenses from meager allowances and from wages they earn from parents and other adults for their work. Furthermore, parents still consider it to be the children's primary duty to assist in daily work routines.

Although Nieuwenhuys pointed to some positive aspects of this difficult combination of schooling and work for the Indian youth (for example, increased independence and self-reliance), there are many negative aspects. Schooling has increased competition among children, a factor that threatens the solidarity of the communities. Also, many children fail at school, which generates feelings of inferiority. However, as Nieuwenhuys argued, "the most insidious and ill-understood effect may very well be the high level of drudgery" the children face in dealing with demands of school and work, which leaves them with little time for play and leisure (1993, p. 108). It is easy to see how Poomkara youth would come to appreciate Qvortrup's (1991) contention that education "is another type of work for children."

Let's return now to our earlier consideration of African families. In Cameroon, modernization and sociopolitical changes have affected the indigenous practice of collective child care by siblings and peers. Many contemporary Cameroonian adults and children "spend a greater part of their waking lives in schools, offices, farms, or marketplaces, [as well as] remote places, pursuing careers or performing a variety of activities and services that were previously unavailable" (Nsamenang, 1992a, p. 437). These changes make it very difficult for Cameroonians "to be their brother's keepers as they were during the old order" (p. 437).

Both mothers and children in Cameroon must make difficult adjustments. As was the case for the Poomkara youth previously discussed, Cameroonian children must accommodate their new school demands with their traditional work and caretaking responsibilities. Such accommodation can be extremely demanding. In some cases, preadolescent children are temporarily withdrawn from school to care for younger siblings; they return when their siblings reach school age. In other cases,

> some elementary school pupils bring along their younger siblings to school, while busy parents in the Bamenda Grassfields sometimes encourage their toddlers to sneak into classrooms in their neighborhoods in order to have the watchful attention of teachers and peers. (Nsamenang, 1992a, p. 433)

Similar problems of accommodation to modernization and to Western economic and educational practices have been reported for African families (see Bass, 2003; Harkness & Super, 1992). Recognition of these difficulties, especially for children, has led to a questioning by some African social scientists of a too rapid acceptance of Western practices (Nsamenang, 2006, 2010; Serpell, 1992). Such recognition has led many to argue that Africans may best aspire "to become more modern by being less Western" (Wober, 1975).

SUMMARY

In this chapter we built on our earlier discussion of the new history of childhood by examining how recent economic, social, and cultural changes have affected families and children. Our goal has been to better understand these changes from the perspectives of the children themselves. We addressed this goal in two ways: (a) by examining children's everyday lives in families, and (b) by considering how childhood as a structural form (that is, how the general experiences of children as a social group) has been affected by recent social and economic changes in families. In both cases we placed our analysis in a comparative perspective by including consideration of children, families, and childhood in both Western and developing societies.

In our review of studies of children's experiences in families in Western societies, we saw the utility of conceptualizing families as local cultures in which young children actively participate, contribute to their own social development, and affect the participation of all other family members. Studies of children's family lives in developing societies demonstrate a similar pattern of children's active participation, but these studies challenge many Western assumptions about the nature of parent-child and sibling relations. In many non-Western families, care of young children is seen as much more of a collective or community concern than an individual responsibility. Although parents (especially mothers) are always primary caregivers in these societies, kin, siblings, and older children play major roles. In African societies we saw that these collective child care practices, which entail giving responsibilities to older siblings and peers, serve as an apprenticeship system in which women and men are trained for parental roles.

Our analysis of the effects of recent socioeconomic changes on childhood examined a series of changes in families in Western societies from the middle of the 19th century to the present, including the rapid decline of the two-parent farm family, the decline of family size, the rise of mothers' labor force participation, and an increase in mother-only families. The decline in two-parent farm families means that children no longer work side by side with parents and siblings, contributing to the family subsistence. Rather, fathers spend their workdays away from home while mothers (at least 30 or 40 years ago) remain at home to care for children and to perform domestic work. Children continue to work, but the nature of their jobs centers on family chores and, in the teen years, outside employment in a narrow range of service and sales jobs. The decline in family size has meant fewer siblings available for companionship and for integration in neighborhood peer cultures, which are themselves less extensive than in the past. As a result of these changes, children find they must rely more on parents. However, parental work demands also increased in the period between the 1940s and the present. With many mothers working, there has been an increase in the general institutionalization of children in a range of child care programs, after-school programs, and sports, music, and art programs. The increase of mothers' labor force participation also means that children (especially preadolescent and adolescent females) are expected to contribute more to work in the home. Finally, the marked increase in mother-only families resulting from divorce and out-of-wedlock births since the 1950s has had negative effects on a large proportion of children in the United States in that many of these children have been thrust into poverty.

When looking at the nature of socioeconomic changes on childhood in the developing countries, we concentrated primarily on the effects of modernization on the indigenous practice of collective child care by siblings and peers and on the tension it creates between education and work for children. Child care now becomes more of a social problem as collective care is less viable in increasingly industrial and service economies (compared to traditional agricultural subsistence economies). Preadolescent and adolescent children feel the loss of their childhoods as they struggle to meet new educational demands and continue to perform their child care duties and other work in families and villages.

Many of the recent socioeconomic changes in Western and developing societies have resulted in children's increased separation from adults and their increased dependence on each other. This trend has brought about the development of extensive and complex peer cultures, which play a major role in the everyday lives of young children and preadolescents. It is to an examination of these peer cultures that we turn in the next part of the book.

PART THREE

Children's Cultures

As I noted in Chapter 3, my acceptance into the peer culture of Italian preschool children early in my career was related to my limited competence in Italian. In fact, given my struggling hold on the language at the time and my general lack of knowledge of the local school and peer cultures, I was in many ways like the 3-year-old Italian children who enter preschool for the first time. Over time, like the younger children in the mixed-age group of 3- to 5-year-olds, I developed as a participating member of the local culture.

After a month or so in the school, I started to feel that I had some of the everyday routines and activities down. But I was still on the periphery of things, still an outsider. Then something important happened. I was sitting on the floor with two boys, Felice and Roberto, racing some toy cars around in circles. Felice was talking about an Italian race car driver as we played, but because he was talking so fast I could understand only part of what he was saying. At one point, however, I clearly heard the phrase "*Lui é morto*," and I knew this meant "He's dead." I guessed that Felice must be recounting a tragic accident in some past grand prix event. At that moment I remembered a particular phrase that I had learned in my first Italian course: "*Che peccato!*" (What a pity!) Hearing me produce the expression, the two boys looked up in amazement, and Felice said, "Bill! Bill! *Ha ragione! Bravo* Bill!" (Bill! Bill! He's right! Way to go, Bill!) "Bravo Bill!" Roberto chimed in, and then I heard Felice calling out to other children in the school. Several of the children came over and listened attentively as Felice repeated the story of the tragic accident and then added, "and Bill said, 'Che peccato!'" The small group cheered, and some even clapped at this news. Not in the least embarrassed by all the attention, I felt good—like one of the group. I was no longer an outsider trying to gain membership. I was doing it. I was part of the action (Corsaro, 2003)!

In this part of the book, I want to try to capture what it is like to be a part of children's cultures. I want to take you beyond cognitive awareness to a deep emotional appreciation of children's memberships in their peer cultures. Chapter 6 defines the notion of children's peer culture and considers its main elements in detail. Until recently, much of the research on peer relations and culture has focused on the outcomes (both positive and negative) of peer interaction for individual development. The orientation of much of this work was either functionalist (in which culture is defined as shared values, beliefs, and artifacts) or cognitive (in which culture is a set of organizing principles that people keep in their heads and that guide behavior). Chapter 6 breaks from this tradition by viewing children's peer cultures as worthy of study in their own right and as essential components of cultural reproduction more generally. The approach to children's culture is interpretive, with an emphasis not only on shared values and concerns but also on public, collective, and performative aspects of social life. Chapter 6 also addresses the importance of children's early exposure to symbolic and material aspects of peer cultures in the family. This chapter is expanded from earlier editions to closely examine children's negotiations with parents about, and their own consumption of, new, more complex forms of media such as the Internet, video games, iPods, and cell phones. This discussion focuses on general trends in children's exposure to the media, debates about media influence, and children's use of media as symbolic and material aspects of peer culture. Later, Chapter 9 considers the consumption of and the importance of media generally defined in the lives of preadolescents and adolescents.

Chapters 7 and 8 examine basic features of the initial peer cultures of preschool and early elementary school children. Chapter 7 examines the basic themes of communal sharing and control in initial peer cultures as children develop a sense of group identity. Chapter 8 charts how children's negotiations and conflicts bring about social differentiation in initial peer cultures and also the elaboration of those cultures.

Chapter 9 examines how peer groups provide a secure base for older preadolescents as they attempt to make sense of and deal with new demands regarding personal relations, sexuality, and identity development. Everyday activities in peer cultures enable these youth to explore collectively a wide range of confusions and uncertainties that accompany their growing autonomy and individual responsibilities. In this new edition this chapter also discusses in some depth the importance of media generally defined in the family lives and peer cultures of preadolescents and adolescents.

6

Children's Peer Cultures and Interpretive Reproduction

Examining Peer Culture From Children's Perspective

As we discussed in Chapter 1, a major change in children's lives is their move outside the family. As we have seen, the timing and nature of children's movement from the family into a society of peers varies over time and across cultures. In discussing these issues, I am using the term _peers_ specifically to refer to that cohort or group of children who spend time together on an everyday basis. My focus is on local peer cultures that are produced and shared primarily through face-to-face interaction. (Of course, such local cultures are part of more general groups of children, which can be defined in terms of age or geographical boundaries—for example, all 3- to 6-year-olds in the United States.) Children produce a series of local peer cultures that become part of, and contribute to, the wider cultures of other children and adults within which they are embedded. These processes vary over time and across cultures, and the documentation and understanding of these variations should be a central topic in the new sociology of childhood.

Much of the traditional work on peer culture has focused on the outcomes (positive and negative) of experiences with peers on individual development. Most of this work has a functionalist view of culture; that is, culture is viewed as consisting of internalized shared values and norms that guide behavior. In line with the notion of interpretive reproduction, we need to break away from this traditional view of peer culture. First, although the study of individual development (or how the child becomes an adult) is important, children and their peer cultures are worthy of documentation and study in their own right. In simple terms, kids are deserving of study as kids. Second, children's culture is not something kids carry around in their heads to guide their behavior. Peer culture is public, collective, and performative (Geertz, 1973; Goffman, 1974). Therefore, in line with our interpretive approach, I define children's peer culture as a stable set of activities or routines, artifacts, values, and concerns that children produce and share in interaction with peers (Corsaro, 2003; Corsaro & Eder, 1990).

In this chapter, we'll discuss the importance of peer cultures for interpretive reproduction. We'll begin by considering how children's peer cultures fit into the general model of interpretive reproduction. We'll then go on to discuss the importance of children's experiences in their families to their transitions into initial peer cultures. Finally, we'll consider symbolic and material aspects of children's cultures.

Central Importance of Peer Culture in Interpretive Reproduction

In Chapters 1 and 2, we noted that from the perspective of interpretive reproduction, the focus is on children's place and participation in cultural production and reproduction rather than on children's private internalization of adult skills and knowledge. Central to this view is children's participation in cultural routines. Routines, rather than individuals, are analyzed. It is through collective production of and participation in routines that children's evolving memberships in both their peer cultures and the adult world are situated. Children's participation in adult-child routines often generates disturbances or uncertainties in their lives. Such disturbances (including confusion, ambiguities, fears, and conflicts) are a natural outcome of adult-child interaction, given the power of adults and the cognitive and emotional immaturity of children. Although children play an active role in the production of cultural routines with adults, they most often occupy subordinate positions and are exposed to much more cultural information than they can process and understand. Surely, many confusions, fears, and uncertainties are addressed as they arise in adult-child interaction. However, it is an important assumption of the interpretive approach that key features of peer cultures arise and develop as a result of children's attempts to make sense of, and to a certain extent to resist, the adult world.

From the perspective of interpretive reproduction, children's activities with peers and their collective production of a series of peer cultures are just as important as their interaction with adults. Furthermore, certain elements of peer culture also affect adult-child routines in the family and other cultural settings. We see, then, that children's participation in adult-child routines in the family and other settings and their participation in the routines of peer cultures both influence their evolving membership in their children's culture and in the adult world.

Parental Versus Peer Effects on Children's Development

Recently, research on parental effects on children's development has come under attack for its mixed and generally weak findings of parental influence, its failure to take genetic effects into account, and its underestimation of the influence of peers (Gladwell, 1998; Harris, 1998). Judith Harris, in her book *The Nurture Assumption*, reviewed research on parental effects on children's personality and was especially critical of the failure of this research to take genetic effects into account. For example, she pointed to work in behavioral genetics, which claims that about 50% of personality outcomes can be linked to genetic factors and the remaining 50% to the environment. The surprising finding from this work is that when behavior geneticists went on to study the effects of shared (in the family) and nonshared environments (outside the family), they consistently found that growing up in the same home and being reared by the same parents had little or no effect on adult personalities of siblings (Harris, 1998: Plomin & Daniels, 1987); nor did birth order have any significant effects (Dunn & Plomin, 1990; Harris, 1998; also see work by sociologists such as Freese, Powell, & Steelman, 1999).)

Given the findings from behavioral genetics, anthropology, and sociology on the importance of peer group interaction for children's development, Harris claimed that peers are more important than parents in regard to children's developmental outcomes. She did, however, qualify that parents have an important effect on their children's behavior within the family. Overall, Harris's argument and her group socialization theory, most especially its emphasis on the importance of social context, is quite similar to the theory of interpretive reproduction that we discussed in Chapters 1 and 2.

Children's Transition to Initial Peer Cultures

Although, like Harris, I believe peers and peer culture are central to children's evolving membership in their culture, this does not mean that parents and families are not important. Families play a key role in the development of peer culture in interpretive reproduction. Young children do not individually experience input from the adult world; rather, they participate in cultural routines in which information is first mediated by adults. In children's early years, most of these adult-child cultural routines take place in families. Thus, initial peer cultures do not arise from children's direct confrontations of the adult world. As children venture out from the family, they are aimed in specific directions, are prepared for interaction with distinct interpersonal and emotional orientations, and are armed with particular cultural resources that are all derived from earlier experiences in their families. Let's take a look at some of these family influences.

Family Influences on Children's Entry Into Initial Peer Cultures

Decisions about children's initial interactions with peers, including the nature of these interactions, are first made within families. Parents normally decide when children first move outside families and what types of peer settings and institutions their children will enter (for example, neighborhood playgroups, day care centers, or early education programs). The nature and timing of these decisions relate to cultural conditions, values, and practices; they vary across cultures and within cultures over time. We saw in Chapter 5, for example, that in many non-Western societies, children move as toddlers into multiage peer care groups or are cared for primarily by older siblings. As we saw in our discussion of Nasaw's (1985) *Children of the City* in Chapter 4, young sibling care by "little mothers" was the norm among the working class of major cities in turn-of-the-20th-century America. Sibling care probably was still common in the United States, especially in lower- and working-class families, at least into the 1950s, and it still exists today (Cicirelli, 1995; Y. Lee, Schneider, & Waite, 2003).

Beginning in the 1960s, the need for out-of-home care increased dramatically in Western societies as more and more women entered the workforce. Most countries in western Europe were quick to respond to the demands for needed child care. Child care and early education programs expanded dramatically in western Europe, especially for 3- to 5-year-olds. In Italy, for example, nearly 90% of all 3- to 5-year-olds attended government-supported early education programs in 1986, and more than 96% attend today (Corsaro & Emiliani, 1992; Corsaro and Molinari, 2005). In the United States, on the other hand, most parents believed until recently that preschool children are better cared for at home (Mason & Kuhlthau, 1989). Such values now, however, clearly conflict with the reality of the American economy; by 1990, the majority of 3- to 5-year-old children of working mothers were cared for outside the home (Hofferth, Brayfield, Deich, & Holcomb, 1991). Still, both the government and parents remain ambivalent about young children's moving outside the family before they reach the age when formal schooling begins.

Children's participation in decisions about nonparental care or early education in preschool programs is limited. Once children enter child care or early education settings, however, their experiences in those settings and in routines with parents who evaluate their performance and progress can prepare them for coming transitions to formal schooling. For example, in our interviews with Head Start parents, Katherine Rosier and I found that mothers frequently drew their children's attention to coming changes in their lives. One mother reported a story about her son, whom she had constantly reminded, "You're doing great in Head Start this year and you'll be going to kindergarten when you're five years old." The day after his 5th birthday in May, the boy awoke, dressed, and announced to his mother, "Well I'm ready to go to kinnygarten, Momma, walk me to kinny-garten." When his mother said he had to wait until autumn, he protested, "But I don't wanna go to Head Start no more, I'm five years old!" (Corsaro & Rosier, 1994, p. 7; also see Corsaro & Rosier, 2002; Rosier, 2000).

Interpersonal and Emotional Influences

Young children's relations with adults (teachers, coaches, counselors, and others) and peers in settings where peer cultures emerge are, in many ways, affected by earlier parent-child interactional routines in families (Parke & Ladd, 1992). Children seek, in adult caretakers and peers, the emotional bonds and feelings of security they first established in families (Giddens, 1991; Ladd, 1992). It could be argued that this striving to maintain the sense of security first established in families is the basis of children's formation of peer cultures. It is most certainly a strong factor in children's valuing of participation and communal sharing in their peer cultures and friendship relations. We will examine the processes of sharing and friendship in initial peer cultures in Chapter 7. Here, it is useful to consider how children's transitions from families to peer groups affect their relationships with others and their developing conceptions of friendship.

When children first arrive in preschools, they realize that their conceptions of ownership, possession, and sharing, which are based on their earlier experiences in families, are often not compatible with the interactive demands of preschools. Ownership is more tangible at home; some things belong to young children, other things to their siblings, and still other things to their parents. Problems with sharing these possessions, especially in families with one or two children, are most likely to occur when the young child has a visitor. On these occasions, the child is expected to share her or his possessions with playmates. Although children may resist, they soon learn that such sharing is temporary. Actual ownership of the objects is never challenged.

In preschools, things are different because all the toys and educational materials are communally owned. Thus, use of the toys and materials depends on negotiations for their temporary possession. It is in the course of these negotiations that children attempt to establish joint ownership of objects and of the play itself within a small group as well as to protect their sharing of the play against the intrusions of others. We will examine children's tendency to protect their interactive space in the next chapter, but here let's consider its more general significance in terms of children's transitions from families to preschools.

In preschools, children are, in a sense, anchoring ownership to themselves and their playmates when they verbally mark off a specific area of play as shared and protected from others ("We're playing here. Nobody else can come in."). One result of these negotiations is a more advanced notion of ownership, one that goes beyond matching objects to individuals. Now children begin to see that some objects can be owned in common and shared with others in specific interactive events (Corsaro, 1988).

A second process in the protection of interactive space relates to children's conceptions of friendship. Although no ethnographic studies demonstrate how parents arrange and encourage interactions between their preschool children and their peers in homes, some observational studies and surveys of parents provide suggestive data about these processes (Ladd, Profilet, & Hart, 1992; Lollis, Ross, & Tate, 1992). We know from these studies that parents do arrange and supervise informal playgroups. We also know that parents use a number of strategies for encouraging play and discouraging conflict (Thompson, O'Neill, & Cohen, 2001). However, none of the research looks closely at how these strategies relate to parents' actual talk about friendship with their children in such situations. Therefore, we must rely on indirect evidence and on some of my own informal observations to speculate about parents' talk about friendship in these situations.

It would appear from experiences in families that children come to see friends as other children with whom they come into contact. Adults tend to associate friendship and sharing ("Anna is your friend who has come to play, and you should share your toys with her"). As a result, children's early conception of *friend* is primarily as a label for certain other children they know who have been designated as such by parents. In preschools, as we've discussed, sharing and friendship are often tied to children's attempts to generate and protect shared interactive events. The concept of friend is no longer simply a label that is applied to a specific child. Rather, the notion of friendship relates to observable shared activities—playing together in specific areas and protecting the play from other children. Thus, children tend to mark the shared experience with phrases such as "We're friends, right?" and to dissuade the access attempts of others with the words, "You can't play; you're not our friend" (Corsaro, 1979, 1985, 2003).

As we noted earlier, one outcome of children's involvement in adult-child routines is the generation of disturbances or uncertainties for children. One source of such uncertainty is the simple fact that children are exposed to much more cultural information than they can process and understand. Unfortunately, disturbances also arise from the stress, conflicts, and even violence young children experience in their families. As psychoanalytic theorists point out, such experiences are especially emotionally stressful for young children who cannot understand why those whom they love so much can act in such unreasonable ways (Bettelheim, 1976). In such situations, children will often turn inward and blame themselves for parental failings. The activities and routines of peer culture can serve as therapeutic havens for confronting and dealing with anxieties from negative experiences in the family. Fantasy play with peers is especially important in these cases because it enables children to gain control over disturbing events and anxieties (Garbarino, Dubrow, Kostelny, & Pardo, 1992).

Symbolic Aspects of Children's Cultures

By *childhood symbolic culture*, we mean various representations or expressive symbols of children's beliefs, concerns, and values (Griswold, 1994, p. 3). Three primary sources of childhood symbolic culture are children's media (television, films, and so on), children's literature (especially fairy tales), and mythical figures and legends (Santa Claus, the tooth fairy, and others). Information from these three sources is primarily mediated by adults in cultural routines in the family and other settings. Children, however, quickly appropriate, use, and transform symbolic culture as they produce and participate in peer culture. In this section of this chapter, we will consider primarily the characteristics of symbolic culture and children's exposure to it. We'll discuss children's transformation and use of symbolic culture capital (that is, the specific items of symbolic culture that children possess and share) in their peer cultures in Chapters 7 through 9.

The Media

Although there has long been concern about the effects of television and to some extent films on children, electronic media have become much more complex to include DVD videos, computer video games, the Internet, cell phones, and MP3 players, with growing intersections of these different technologies ever evolving. Given these developments' being in a state of flux and the recent huge increase in theoretical and empirical scholarship on this issue, my review in this section will focus on the extensiveness and what we know about the effects of electronic media in the lives of young children from birth to 6 years of age. I also will confine the discussion of effects to electronic media as related to children's symbolic culture (television and film including DVDs) and consider computer technology (primarily computer games) in the section on children's material culture. I consider the roles of children and adults in the children's consumer culture in the final section of this chapter. I return to these same topics for preadolescents and to some extent adolescents in Chapter 9.

Although there is a great deal of debate about the effects of electronic media on young children, there is no dispute about the fact that young children are growing up immersed in media in the United States and many other industrialized societies. A recent large representative survey by the Kaiser Family Foundation of families in the United States (Rideout, Vandewater, & Wartella, 2003) found that children 6 and younger spend an average of 2 hours a day using screen media (1 hour, 58 minutes), about equal to the amount of time they spend playing outside (2 hours, 1 second), and well more time than they spend reading or being read to (39 minutes). More than one third (36%) of children have their own TVs in their bedrooms, and 27% of the children have VCRs or DVDs in their rooms. Some other interesting findings from this study are that children are active consumers of media as more than 77% turn on the TV themselves, 67% ask for particular shows, 62% use the remote control to change stations, and 71% ask for their favorite videos or DVDs. The study also found that 65% of the children live in homes where the TV is on at least half the time and 36% live in "heavy" TV households where the television is always on or on most of the time. Despite these findings of regular exposure to the media, the survey found that reading or being read to was a constant in most of the children's lives, with 65% of the children reading or being read to every day and another 26% reading or being read to a few times a week.

What should we make of these findings? Are the media contributing to the disappearance of childhood (Postman, 1994; Winn, 1984), or worse, in their gradual encroachment on print literacy, will they lead to moral decline and self-destructive violence (Sanders, 1995)? Or should we be asking instead whether there is an overreaction to fears about the growing presence and complexity of electronic media? Karen Sternheimer, for example, argued that instead of media's being the culprit, other changes in childhood that are part of broader social changes have "made adults uneasy about their ability to control children and the experience of childhood" (2003, p. 22). In a similar vein the British media expert David Buckingham (2000, 2009) argued that it is necessary to situate children's relationships with the media in the context of broader social and historical changes. He argued further that the focus should not be on excluding or protecting children from the adult world but rather on developing strategies to better understand children's active role in media consumption, to increase their media literacy, and to protect their rights as citizens.

Most studies on the content of television programming involve criticism of its violence, lack of educational value, sexism, and appeal to hedonism (see Buckingham, 2000; Center on Media for Child Health, 2005; Seiter, 1993; Sternheimer, 2003, for reviews). Many studies, especially in the United States during the past 30 years, have focused on what Buckingham (2000) called "effects" research involving experimental studies often based on behaviorist or learning theories in line with the deterministic approach we discussed in Chapter 1. These studies have found both negative and positive effects of media on young children. There are numerous studies that document how media violence can contribute to anxiety, desensitization, and increased aggression in children in both the short and the long term (see Center on Media for Child Health, 2005, for a detailed review). On the other hand, the degree of these negative effects is debated regarding, for example, the way both violence and aggression are measured in these studies (see Buckingham, 2000; Sternheimer, 2003). Other negative health outcomes related to television viewing are less debated. Heavy television viewing and having a TV in one's bedroom were related to increased obesity in children (Center on Media for Child Health, 2005). On the positive side, effects research shows that educational television such as *Sesame Street* and more recent children's programs such as *Blue's Clues* and *Dora the Explorer* teach young children important skills for short- and long-term school success (D. R. Anderson, Huston, Schmitt, Linebarger, & Wright, 2001; Center on Media for Child Health, 2005).

We know little, however, about how children negotiate with parents for access to children's television and other media, how they communicate with parents and peers about what they see, and how they appropriate, use, and extend information from the media. As Bazalgette and Buckingham argued, many studies "seem to underestimate the diverse ways in which children themselves may actually make sense of the media and relate them to their own experiences" (1995, p. 3). More recent research increasingly views children as active consumers of the media with adults and peers (Fingerson, 1999; Gotz, Lemish, Moon, & Aidman, 2005; Hoover & Clark, 2008; Kinder, 1991; Lemish, 2008; Seiter, 1993, 1999; Tobin, 2000; Walkerdine, 1997, 1998; also see Livingstone & Drotner, 2008, for a review of studies in this vein). Ellen Seiter's (1993) analysis of toy-based videos for girls (*My Little Pony*) and boys (*Slimer and the Real Ghostbusters*) is a good example of this trend. She argued that such programs are much more complex than middle-class parents assume. Later in this chapter, we will discuss Seiter's analysis of the toys on which these programs are based when we consider adult contributions to children's material culture.

For most people, the mere mention of children brings to mind the Walt Disney Company and its vast empire of theme parks, movies, videotapes, and books. Yet the few studies by scholarly researchers who have examined the Disney Company and its products have focused primarily on the company's marketing strategies, vision of childhood, and repackaging of classic fairy tales for mass consumption (Bell, Haas, & Sells, 1995; Giroux, 1996; Hunt & Frankenberg, 1990; Kline, 1993; Sternheimer, 2003; also see Buckingham, 1997, for a review of some of this and related work on Disney movies and theme parks). Sternheimer contrasted how Disney is embraced by many because its films "serve as cheerleaders for the American Dream" and because of its primarily moderate-right political values whereas other, more subversive media such as *South Park* and *The Simpsons* are seen as inappropriate and threatening of the innocence of especially young children (2003, pp. 106–107). Disney's influence is seen as so great that some have voiced concern about its merger with ABC

Television Group and its growing control over the global media market (see Wasko, Phillips, & Meehan, 2001, for discussion of Disney from a global perspective). Yet the roles that Disney images, characters, and stories play in children's actual lives in families and peer groups remain relatively unexplored. A recent exception is a study of the perspectives on royalty in several Disney films of American immigrant girls from Korea (L. Lee, 2009). Lee found that the 5- to 8-year-old girls in the study had complex interpretations of being a ruler and a princess in the films that were at variance with certain critics of Disney in terms of gender and race. Lee noted that the

> girls were not simply passive receivers who unthinkingly absorbed every cultural message about the representation of royalty in Disney films. Instead, they often reframed and recreated a cultural text by actively selecting and organizing its elements according to their own experiences, assumptions, concerns, and desires. (2009, p. 211)

Literature and Fairy Tales

Numerous textual analyses of children's books and fairy tales from a number of theoretical perspectives exist. Perhaps the most well known is Bruno Bettelheim's (1976) *The Uses of Enchantment*, which presents a psychoanalytic interpretation of classic fairy tales. Maria Tatar (1992) relied on Stanley Fish's (1980) notion of interpretive communities to criticize Bettelheim, other scholars of children's literature, and much of children's literature itself. Interpretive communities are practices or strategies we share as members of a community for organizing our experiences. They, in turn, preconstrain our construction of the meaning of texts. Tatar noted that most children's literature and nearly every study of it address the interpretive communities of adults. Tatar and others (see Lurie, 1990) attempted to remedy this situation by focusing on subversive children's literature, staying close to the surface level of the story, and attempting to adopt a children's perspective. By "subversive children's literature," Tatar and Lurie meant stories in which children successfully challenge adult authority and in the process make adults look foolish (we made reference above to subversive media such as the television shows *South Park* and *The Simpsons*, which depict teenage alienation and well-intentioned flawed adults). A classic example of subversive literature is *Pippi Longstocking* by the Swedish author Astrid Lindgren. The *Harry Potter* series shares many elements of subversion and empowerment of children and youth. Tatar, Lurie, and others will always fall short in capturing children's perspectives, however, because their analyses do not include children (or adults and children) constructing their interpretive communities over time.

One exception is a case study of two young girls, Lindsey and Ashley, which "demonstrates the innumerable ways in which books and other written texts lay beneath much of the everyday life of their family" (Wolf & Heath, 1992, p. 195). The case study is the result of a collaboration between Shelby Wolf, social scientist, lover of literature, and the mother of the girls, and Shirley Heath, anthropologist, linguist, and longtime ethnographer of literacy in children's everyday lives (see Heath, 1983). Wolf was the ethnographer in this study, observing the role of literature in the lives of her girls from their birth until Lindsey was 9 and Ashley was 6. Beginning shortly after Lindsey's 3rd birthday, Wolf's ethnography became more focused and rigorous as part of her master's thesis, and she began to routinely tape record reading sessions with both girls and to take notes on the children's extension of their experiences with the texts into their daily lives.

Wolf and her husband read a wide range of books with their girls, from classic fairy tales to adult fiction such as *To Kill a Mockingbird*. What most interests us is the mediational processes in which children acquire symbolic culture and how they use such symbolic culture in their everyday lives. In this regard, Wolf and Heath's analysis of their materials is richly textured with many wonderful instances of the symbolic culture of this family. The authors point out that the children played an active part in the readings. Although fascinated by stories with giants, dragons, monsters, and evil queens, the girls would, for example, often admonish their mother to "talk the dragon in a normal voice" because it was too scary. Wolf reported a frequent routine that occurred after readings of frightful stories in which she and her husband would hear Lindsey rummaging about in her room.

> Her door would open and we would hear a loud clump. Then another and another. The door would close and we would hear her bedsprings squeak in final surrender. Curious, we would creep up the stairs, only to discover several of her "scariest" books lying abandoned outside her door. (Wolf & Heath, 1992, p. 138)

The longitudinal design of the case study allowed the authors to capture historical patterns in which information was first shared in reading sessions and then later reproduced, often in the voice and words of the original characters, in appropriate contexts. What children consider to be appropriate contexts, however, can at times be a revelation to adults because children often achieve "potential recognitions of their own understanding of some element of literature in a totally new and unpredictable way" (Wolf & Heath, 1992, p. 122). Furthermore, "children's visual, logical, musical, and linguistic insights can exceed those of adults, since children, when they read literature, may be motivated by their quest for transformative powers to make the external world conform more fully to their wishes" (Wolf & Heath, 1992, p. 122). This insight, which is clearly in line with our notion of interpretive reproduction, is nicely captured in numerous examples in which "Lindsey and Ashley transformed literature for their own purposes in negotiating attention, affection, and reason with adults and each other" (Wolf & Heath, 1992, p. 8). One memorable example of such transformation occurred as part of Lindsey's and Ashley's response to a deserved punishment. The two girls had been quarreling and three times interrupted their mother's writing. Having lost her temper, Wolf reported,

> I flung the dusty kitchen rug out the door and sent Lindsey up the stairs for the vacuum cleaner. I stationed Ashley at the sink to do the breakfast dishes. Both girls eyed me resentfully, but I ignored their pleas and went back to work. After a while, I realized that it was much too quiet and descended the stairs again, expecting the worst.
>
> Instead, they were both happily scrubbing the kitchen floor. "I'm Laura and Ashley is Mary," Lindsey explained. "We're playing Little House in the Big Woods, and we've got to get the cabin clean for our mom!" (Wolf & Heath, 1992, p. 156)

In this example, argued Wolf and Heath, the girls "made their tasks acceptable by moving into the rules of the . . . girls' world, where children obeyed their parents instantly and rarely squabbled" (1992, p. 156).

Although Wolf and Heath studied just one family and two children, their work provides a wealth of information about how children are exposed to and appropriate symbolic culture through literature. It also reminds us of the obvious but infrequently acted-on truth: Children are the best sources for understanding childhood.

Mythical Figures and Legends

A good part of the symbolic culture that children bring with them as they enter communal life with peers is drawn from cultural myths and legends.

Especially relevant are mythical figures such as Santa Claus, the tooth fairy, and the Easter bunny, who are central to childhood culture and lore. A virtual legion of other imaginary figures inhabits children's literature and media. Parents introduce these mythical characters to children and regularly interweave them into their childhoods through what are often deeply cherished rituals. Furthermore, the meanings of these family rituals are enhanced by the subroutines that make up their overall structure—subroutines that are ripe for embellishment in the local cultures of the families. For example, most American families produce the general Easter bunny ritual but often vary the subroutines of its production. Eggs may be colored in different ways and at different times, they may be hidden inside the home or outside in the yard on Easter morning, children may follow a variety of rules when hunting for the eggs, and so forth. Thus, when children come together in neighborhoods, preschools, and kindergarten and elementary school classrooms and playgrounds, their joy and wonder in the embracement of these mythical figures is doubly exalted. They discover not only shared and valued childhood symbolic culture capital but also myriad variations for expressing and appreciating their shared wealth.

We are all familiar with family rituals regarding Santa Claus, the tooth fairy, and the Easter bunny in American culture. Before turning to some recent and very interesting research on such myths and legends in our own culture, though, let's briefly look at the role such legends play in family rituals in two other societies. We begin with an example that is both geographically and culturally distant from our own society: Gaingeen, a bogey that appears among the Murik of Papua New Guinea. We then move closer to home to discuss La Befana, a witch from Italy.

Gaingeen. Anthropologist Kathleen Barlow studied the Murik, a fishing and trading society of Papua New Guinea. The Murik are, according to Barlow, "fervently animistic" in that they believe in a number of "spirits who display human-like tendencies toward mischief, deceit, and irritability" (1985, p. 2). One of these spirits is Gaingeen, who appears sporadically in the village to chase and beat children, "if he can catch them, which he seldom does" (p. 3). Gaingeen never speaks but rather conveys his intentions through threatening gestures such as kicking and shaking the spears and sticks he always carries with him.

Infants and toddlers first encounter Gaingeen when parents or older siblings carry them out to observe the bogey during one of his appearances in the village. The young children often are terrified and cling tightly to whomever is holding them. Some parents go right up to Gaingeen and hand him their children (see Exhibit 6.1).

Exhibit 6.1   Gaingeen Holding a Child

Source: Photo by David Lipset.

Gaingeen comes to play an important part in caretaker-child routines in Murik households. Murik caretakers prefer to use indirect tactics such as distraction to get young children to stop crying or to dissuade them from undesirable behaviors. Once Gaingeen has been introduced, he is frequently called on for this purpose.

> Mothers who want to wean a child call, "*Gaingeen* you come o! She/He wants to nurse again here." Older siblings hurry their dawdling juniors along the path saying, "Yeay! Hurry up! *Gaingeen* is coming!" Grandmothers recall wandering toddlers from doorways and windows, "Eeee! *Gaingeen, Gaingeen!*" (Barlow, 1985, p. 4)

As children grow older, they learn that Gaingeen usually does not come every time he is called. Still, he may appear, and the young child will always look around to see if Gaingeen is coming when caretakers call his name.

When children are about 4 years old, they normally venture outside the home to play in mixed-age groups in the village under the care of older siblings. In these instances they tag along with the older children, who sometimes make Gaingeen costumes and engage in a form of approach-avoidance play, which we will discuss in the next chapter. When the younger children see their older siblings wearing costumes, they realize that the real Gaingeen, the one they have seen in the village, may be someone in costume as well. They are still afraid of Gaingeen, but they now become suspicious. Could he also be an older child or an adult in a costume?

Eventually, when the children are 7 years old or so, the "secret of the mask figure is revealed and the children discover he is an adolescent boy wearing a costume" (Barlow, 1985, p. 1). Despite this demystification, Gaingeen remains an important figure in play and learning throughout childhood. As we will see in the next chapter, the children appropriate Gaingeen and create their own peer routines in which he plays a central role in their attempts to deal with more general fears and anxieties.

La Befana. In Italy, children are fascinated by the mythical character La Befana (see Exhibit 6.2). La Befana, who is believed to have originated in southern Italy, is a witch who flies about on a broom bringing presents to children on January 6, at Epiphany. (Epiphany, or Three Kings' Day in some cultures, is a church festival commemorating the coming of the Magi as the first manifestation of Christ to the Gentiles.) According to legend, the three wise men stopped to ask La Befana for directions on their way to Bethlehem. They also invited her to join them. La Befana told them she was too busy sweeping and sent them away. Afterward, she was filled with remorse and tried to follow. She couldn't catch them and has been flying around Italy ever since, looking for the Christ child. She leaves presents at the house of each child in case one of them is the Savior (see Corsaro, 2009a).

This legend seems to have been altered somewhat in contemporary times, with parents warning their children that La Befana does not leave presents for bad children. She is said to slide down chimneys on her broom, delivering presents to good children and filling their stockings with candy, whereas bad children get switches or a lump of coal. Some mothers even tell their naughty children to behave or La Befana will steal them away. Many children, however, come to see La Befana as more than a benevolent arbiter of good and bad behavior. They view her as someone

Exhibit 6.2   La Befana

who, like Babbo Natale (the Italian Santa Claus), always comes through in the end with presents for all children.

In my observations in northern Italy, I found that children look forward to receiving gifts at Christmas from Babbo Natale, but they are just as excited about La Befana's coming several days later. Parents often actively promote the legend by constructing images of the witch in their homes, yards, and neighborhood parks. Like Gaingeen's, some of La Befana's appeal to children is the fact that she is both mysterious and frightening. In fact, Italian preschool children frequently debate the power of various threatening figures such as witches. In one preschool I studied, children frequently talked about *la Strega* (the witch). One little girl, Antonia, explained to me that witches do not really exist, that they are *"per finta"* (for pretend). But she later pointed out that *"la Strega e il Dracula sono gli amici"* (the witch and Dracula are friends).

Antonia's view of witches such as La Befana symbolizes the children's attraction to monsters. Monsters do not really exist, but we can pretend they do. And this pretense often has a tinge of reality, especially if the threatening agents are introduced by parents and are part of cultural legends, like La Befana and Gaingeen. These fascinating and threatening figures are appropriated from the routines and rituals in the family and are reproduced as part of routines in peer culture by the Murik and Italian children. We will look at the nature of these routines and their importance in peer cultures in Chapter 7.

The Tooth Fairy. What of children's mythical and fantasy figures in the United States? How are they introduced to children in the family, and how do they become part of children's symbolic culture? In her book *Flights of Fancy, Leaps of Faith,* Cindy Dell Clark (1995) went directly to children and parents to explore the rituals and meanings of Santa Claus, the tooth fairy, and the Easter bunny.

Perhaps the central insight in Clark's analysis is that children actively participate in and contribute to the dynamics of these mythical legends and rituals. Clark argued that children influence the interactive process of culture in two ways: (a) "The symbolic association of children with certain cultural values (including nature, as well as the capacity for wonder and awe) gives them implicit influence within ritual practices," and (b) "children directly affect cultural practices through their own actions" (1995, p. 103). Let's look at how these cultural processes are demonstrated in one of the mythical figures Clark investigated, the tooth fairy.

Although many cultures have shed-tooth rituals, "the Tooth Fairy is largely a Western custom, having evolved in the cultural melting pot of the United States" (C. Clark, 1995, p. 10). The ritual surrounding the tooth fairy involves a rite of passage. In a traditional sense, it is a reward for the physical pain and mental anguish that can accompany losing baby teeth. Clark found that most of the children she studied placed their lost teeth in a special receptacle, a tooth fairy pouch, to wait for the tooth fairy to replace it with money. Such pouches are often handcrafted items that are embroidered or hand sewn. They call attention to the feminine aspect of the ritual, with the tooth fairy (always a female) representing the healing and therapeutic mother comforting and rewarding children for their loss. But the ritual is prospective as well as retrospective. In retrospectively celebrating the loss of the tooth shortly after it has occurred, the ritual also marks the beginning of an occurrence that will have many repetitions (the loss of additional teeth in exchange for money from the tooth fairy). In this way, the ritual encourages children's awareness of ongoing transitions in their lives and helps prepare them for these changes.

Tooth loss and the tooth fairy ritual coincide with another important change in children's lives—their entry into formal schooling during kindergarten or first grade. Children are now deeply embedded in an initial peer culture and are becoming aware of their movement during the next few years into middle childhood and preadolescence. With this transition will come more personal autonomy and more responsibility. Clark had no direct data on activities in peer culture, but she did point to children's valuing of the power and independence that money from the tooth fairy can provide. One child remarked how having money made him "feel like a new person," and another observed, "I like carrying around my own money. I feel more grown up and special" (C. Clark, 1995, p. 19).

Undoubtedly, children share similar observations with their friends and see their loss of teeth, participation in the ritual, and acquisition of money as signs of maturity. The ritual is especially appealing to children of this age because of its repetition or reoccurrence and because of the inevitable accumulation of wealth. Clark noted that when she talked to children about money from the tooth fairy, they "were prone to run and fetch their stash of cash and to finger through it, Scrooge-like, while showing it to me" (1995, p. 19). Finally, Clark's reference to kindergarten and first-grade teachers' practice of keeping charts marking the occasion when children lose teeth also supports the notion that the ritual is highly valued in peer culture.

Let's now return to Clark's argument regarding children's active participation in the production of the tooth fairy ritual. The beginning of second dentition occurs when children are 6 or 7, a period of transition marked by children's movement from families to formal schooling. Clark maintained that adults (especially mothers) actively support the magical fairy as a way to keep children young, to extend their belief in fantasy. As a result, the spotlight in the ritual is on children whose sense of wonder and awe is reassuring to parents who would prefer they not grow up too fast. Children, on the other hand, with their successive shedding of baby teeth and growing embeddedness in peer cultures, come to view the process through a different lens, with a "more mature focus" (C. Clark, 1995, p. 105). With the loss of baby teeth and the accumulation of material cash wealth, children feel older, more independent, and more like their peers.

As Clark suggested, the process also involves children's gradual understanding of the underlying essence of faith and trust as represented by the belief in mythical figures such as the tooth fairy and Santa Claus. These mythical figures serve as what British psychiatrist D. W. Winnicott (1951) called "transition objects" in children's growing separation from their parents, in whom they have invested blind faith and trust. In the end, children do not so much discover that the tooth fairy is really Mom and Dad as they come to realize that their firm belief in the tooth fairy has been an expression of their faith in the unconditional love of their parents. They also discover that the seeds of this faith can be passed on through their participation in the same cultural rituals with their own children.

Material Aspects of Children's Cultures

By *childhood material culture,* I mean clothing, books, artistic and literacy tools (crayons, pens, paper, paints, and so forth), and, most especially, toys. Children can, and often do, use some of these objects to produce other material artifacts of childhood cultures (for example, pictures, paintings, block structures, improvised games and routines, and so on). In addition to the more traditional dolls, blocks, cars, LEGOs, and other toys, more and more young children are now playing computer or video games. The Kaiser Family Foundation study discussed above found that 48% of children 6 and younger have used computers and 30% have played video games (14% of those 3 and younger and 50% of 4- to 6-year-olds; Rideout et al., 2003). There is a growing market in video games for younger children from the VTech and Techno Source toy companies that are modified versions of Sony's PlayStation 2, Microsoft's Xbox, and Nintendo's Game Cube, now available for preschoolers (Marriott, 2004). With these new types of toys available, at least for the middle-class and wealthy families who can afford them, children are entering electronic game playing at younger and younger ages. Also, many of these games are related to children's symbolic culture as they are tie-ins to movie themes and characters. Most of the games are educational in nature, and future electronic games that soon may be available to children are aimed at early literacy development. Some of these games, which involve touch-screen controls, can now be accessed through applications on parents' cell phones and will soon be available for young children on the iPad that has just been introduced as an extension of the iPhone as a touch-control or hands-on computer.

Much of the research related to children's material culture focuses exclusively on toys. Most of it is carried out by psychologists; it is quantitative (experimental and quasi-experimental) and is designed to test hypotheses regarding the effects of specific content or features of toys on children's individual development. For example, a great deal of research exists on toys and gender stereotyping and the effects of war toys on aggressive behavior (Carlsson-Paige & Levin, 1987; Goldstein, 1994). Such a focus is too narrow and too similar to that of the effects research on symbolic culture. Very little of this research examines children's actual play with toys. Some research examining play with objects such as LEGO and other building materials, toy animals, dolls, cars, and other toys finds it not only is fun for kids but can contribute positively to their mathematical, cognitive, social, and emotional development (Corsaro, 2003; Johannesen, 2004; Morgenthaler, 2006; Ness & Farenga, 2007; Sawyer, 2002). We will discuss several of these studies in Chapter 7. However, we now turn to the work of historians and marketing researchers, which has revealed a great deal about children's interest in and play with toys.

Studies by historians and marketing researchers show that as children develop as individuals, they collectively and creatively appropriate, use, and infuse toys with meaning, both in families and in their peer cultures. These findings are in line with the notion of interpretive reproduction in that they demonstrate the importance of children's collective actions and how these actions contribute to the productions of innovative peer cultures as well as to reproduction and change in adult society. The main reason historical and marketing studies identify the importance of the children's collective actions is because their research designs (which are more qualitative and interpretive in nature) do not close themselves off from such possibilities to test how toys affect individual development.

Historical Studies of Children's Material Culture

As Brian Sutton-Smith has argued, the "predominant nature of play throughout history has been play with others, not play with objects" (Sutton-Smith, 1986, p. 26; also see Chudacoff, 2007). Objects were often incorporated into play but were second in importance to the social aspects of play. As a result, almost any physical object that could enhance a play theme would do. These objects, sometimes referred to as "playthings," varied over time, from sticks and stones to tires, tin cans, and coat hangers. Such objects were transformed to fit the arising themes of play and did not have fixed meanings. According to Mergen (1992, p. 88), however, two new attitudes toward toys emerged in the 1870s. First, children began to develop a desire for the accumulation of toys for their own sake, with material possessions indicating the status of the owner. Second, toys began to be seen as defining the identity of the child and childhood culture.

Historical studies based primarily on the analysis of autobiographies capture how these two attitudes toward toys often overlap. An excellent example of such overlap is Formanek-Brunell's (1992) study of dolls and doll play in the 19th century in the United States. Doll play before the Civil War was infrequent and was linked to learning and developing sewing skills and other kinds of domestic training. In the decades after the war, things were quite different. Middle- and upper-class girls were "encouraged by adults to imbue their numerous dolls with affect, to indulge in fantasy, and to display their elaborately dressed dolls at ritual occasions such as tea parties and while visiting" (Formanek-Brunell, 1992, p. 108). Although girls certainly adopted this attitude toward their dolls to some degree, they did not simply internalize the adult values as part of feminine socialization. On the contrary, the girls often had a different agenda as they appropriated and used the dolls "for purposes other than training in the emotional and practical skills of mothering" (p. 108). In the autobiographical data, women reported rebelling against sedate tea parties as girls by sliding their dolls down banisters atop tea trays and, in another case, wreaking havoc on their tea party "by smashing their unsuspecting dolls to bits" (p. 123). In fact, the physical mistreatment and even torturing of dolls was commonly mentioned in the memoirs. Most of these accounts involved the acts of boys, usually brothers, with the girls often looking on more in fascination than in horror. One woman remembered, "When my brother proved my doll had no brains by slicing off her head, I felt I had been deluded; I watched him with stoicism and took no more interest in dolls" (p. 121). Still, girls themselves also carried out such mistreatment, often in response to imagined misbehavior on the part of their dolls. For example, an article in a girl's magazine on doll play in 1908 reported a "four-year-old girl disciplined her doll by forcing it to eat dirt, stones, and coal" (p. 122).

Such behavior was often seen by adults of the time as the expression of repressed anger. In fact, adults encouraged a form of play that many might find horrific or at least in bad taste today: the enactment of doll funerals. According to Formanek-Brunell, doll funerals were much more frequent than doll weddings among middle-class girls in the 1870s and

1880s. She pointed out that "mourning clothes were packed in the trunks of French lady dolls, and Fathers constructed doll-sized coffins for their daughters' dolls instead of the more usual doll houses" (1992, p. 117). One woman remembered, "No day was too short for a funeral, just so they [my friends] all got home for supper" (p. 123). Such play was not seen as morbid but was viewed as helping to develop the nurturing and comforting skills that often were needed in a time when many relatives and friends died young. Girls, however, did not simply imitate proper comforting behavior in their doll funerals. Girls often changed the emphasis from cathartic funerals to ritualized executions or harrowing accidents that led to death. (Again, the adult model was appropriated, not simply internalized.)

It is important to keep in mind that autobiographical data of this type have certain validity problems (such as the faulty or selective memory of the author) and that they allow for limited generalizability given the upper-class backgrounds of most of the authors. Regarding generalizability, many working- and lower-class girls could not afford store-bought dolls, let alone the luxury of destroying them. Still, these historical materials provide direct evidence and therefore lead to more valid conclusions than does simply inferring the nature of play from the mere existence or content of toys. As Mergen noted, "toys have meaning only when children play with them," and if toys "are meaningful to the child they will be reused and remembered" (1992, p. 106). It is the symbolic meaning and value that children attach to toys that most interests market researchers, whose main aim is to understand children as consumers of toys and other material goods. It is to this work that we now turn.

Marketing Studies of Children's Material Culture

Developmental and educational psychologists who study children's material culture normally focus on the effects of various play objects and toys on children's cognitive and social development. They rely most often on quantitative, quasi-experimental, or experimental studies to estimate the educational value of toys and how play with various toys might contribute to children's cognitive growth and structure. In this approach, less attention is paid to children's toy preference or to the actual processes of children's play with the toys. Market researchers, on the other hand, have little interest in scientifically documenting the effects of toys on children's development (except in cases where they aim their goods at parents; here they do not hesitate to cite scientific research). Their research, argued Kline, "is both pragmatic and proprietary, but that in itself hasn't prevented the cultural industries from gaining insight into contemporary children's everyday experiences of play, fiction and leisure" (1993, p. 18). Relying on more qualitative methods such as focus groups, informal interviews, and direct observation, these researchers "don't bother to observe comatose children in the classroom being battered with literacy; they study them at play, at home watching television or in groups on the streets and shops" (p. 18). What they discover is that aspects of children's symbolic and material culture, such as "daydreams, hero worship, absurdist humour and a keen sense of group identity"— which academic researchers (and most adults) may see as "meaningless distractions or artefacts of immaturity"—are important attributes of children's cultures (p. 18). As Kline noted, marketers make good use of these insights in their strategies for selling things to children, whom they see as highly informed and powerful consumers (p. 18). One thing market researchers have discovered is that one appeal of certain toys and media products is the very fact that children realize that adults will not like such products and even see them as schmaltzy or disgusting and gross. This point relates to our earlier discussion of how children desire to gain control over their lives and challenge the power of adults.

In her book about children's consumer culture, *Sold Separately*, Ellen Seiter (1993) developed many of these basic themes. Seiter rightly noted that in contemporary American society it is mothers who most often ultimately decide on their children's consumption of symbolic and material culture. Today's mothers "may object to children's consumer culture, but they often give in to it as well, largely because of the usefulness of television programs and toys as convenience goods for caretakers of children" (Seiter, 1993, p. 8). In doing so, mothers often feel guilty that they are relinquishing their children to a superficial and hedonistic consumer culture.

Like Kline (1993), Seiter did see a certain value in children's consumer culture. She stressed especially the communal nature of children's shared culture with friends and classmates and its "strong imagination of community." Here, Seiter extended Kline's argument to point out that adults too "invest intense feeling in objects and attribute a wealth of personal and idiosyncratic meanings [to] mass-produced goods" (1993, p. 9). After all, is a sweatshirt with a Los Angeles Lakers or Indiana Hoosiers logo any more educational (or less expensive) than one with Mickey Mouse or Tweety Bird?

Seiter's point about similarities between adult and child consumer culture relates to our earlier discussion regarding the tendency of adults to evaluate children's activities prospectively. In other words, we adults most often take a linear view of development; we are concerned with how the present experiences of children contribute to their futures as adults. But surely, in terms of symbolic and material culture, children have some right to enjoy their childhoods!

Children's consumer culture does, of course, have some negative attributes. Parents are rightly concerned about the effects of their children's preferences for repetitive play with toy guns or grossly disproportioned Barbie dolls. In fact, Seiter argued that many aspects of children's media and toys promote negative images in regard to class, race, and gender in American society. On the other hand, she also noted that educationally endorsed and politically correct toys are often very expensive and can be elitist. She pointed, for example, to European-produced toys such as Playmobil's Victorian Dollhouse. The dollhouse retailed at $185 in 1993 and came with a description that introduced the character Vicki,

> a little girl from a good home who lived during the turn of the century. . . . Vicki's family belonged to "high society," because after all her father was the Chancellor of Commerce. Naturally, you can understand that Vicki should be raised by a governess. (Seiter, 1993, p. 218)

Ouch! My daughter got one of these dollhouses for Christmas when she was seven; however, I never heard her talk about Vicki and the governess. Of course, my daughter also owned and played just as often with her inexpensive Gumby, Tweety Bird, and My Little Ponies.

Studies of children's consumer culture such as Kline's and Seiter's are important because they take children—their perspectives, preferences, and shared cultures—seriously. They also look at children's consumer behavior as embedded in a complex interactive system. In this system, children are dependent on parents (usually mothers), but they are active negotiators in decisions regarding the purchase of toys and their access to the media through television and movies. However, a glaring omission in this work is adults' and children's joint participation in children's consumer culture and how that participation is mediated by the nature of marketing strategies and the social class background of consumers. Here recent work by social scientists on children, parents, and consumer culture addresses these issues.

Children, Parents, and Consumer Culture

As Cook (2009) has noted, merchants, marketers, and advertisers have engaged with children as consumers for the better part of a century. This recognition of the child consumer, as often mediated through parents, can be seen in the advertising and marketing of a wide range of products including books, clothing, food, and most especially toys. In his book *The Commodification of Childhood*, Cook (2004) examined historical patterns in trade journals and other documentary sources. His work shows how conceptions of the consuming child were materialized in the creation of separate children's clothing departments, segmented by age and gender gradations. His analysis captures "how contemporary childhood and consumer culture have become interwoven, asking whether one can any longer exist without the other" (2004, p. 151).

In his book *Kids' Stuff*, Gary Cross (1997) presented a historical account of the marketing of toys and the roles of parents and children in their consumption. He noted that until the end of the 19th century parents gave children few toys and the toys they did provide reflected the tastes of adults more than the desires of children. This pattern changed in the early 1900s, and the idea of toys as a part of children's own material culture emerged. However, adults were still very much in control of the process. In this period most toys were designed to train or prepare children to be adults through imaginative play with, for example, erector sets and trains for boys (the engineers and scientists of the future) and dolls and dollhouses for girls (future mothers and homemakers). However, by the 1960s, with adult occupations becoming more complex, changing, and unpredictable, such toys became less popular, and giant toy companies such as Mattel and Hasbro marketed more directly to the imaginations of children. These companies began to advertise toys on television especially on shows aimed at children such as the *Mickey Mouse Club* and a wide variety of cartoon programs.

These advertisements provided scripts for how to play with toys, and Cross argued, "by the early 1980s, these companies and others turned cartoon TV programs into half-hour commercials featuring specific toys as the cartoon characters" (1997, p. 5). These changes led to other, more recent marketing strategies that linked toys to films and also to fast food restaurants, which provided toys such as action heroes, Barbie dolls, race cars, and later Pokémon cards (among many other such items) as part of special or "happy" meals for children. This process of what Spigel (1992, quoted in Cook, 2009, p. 339) referred to as "intertextuality" involves the extension of media characters and narratives beyond a single medium or genre. The purpose of this marketing strategy is to produce the characters, narratives, toys, and related products from the sellers' perspective. With intertextuality consumption is always multiple. As Cook noted,

> Watching the SpongeBob SquarePants show, for instance, *is* in itself a form of brand exposure, but having the Kraft Corporation's SpongeBob Macaroni and Cheese meal for lunch is exposure to a brand of another order. When a child eats the Kraft Corporation's macaroni with the character on the box, she also simultaneously ingests SpongeBob *and* Nickelodeon Network (its corporate owner) as a kind of semiotic fare which accompanies the carbohydrates, protein, fat and sodium. (2009, p. 339).

This type of intertextuality of marketing to children was attacked by consumer action groups such as Action for Children's Television. Such groups were successful to some extent in pressing for the passage of legislation to protect young children by forcing programmers to more clearly demarcate commercials from programming. However, many critics such as Julie Schor (2004) bemoan the power of marketers whom Schor argued have co-opted children, parents, and even schools into their strategies to create "commercialized children." Others (Buckingham, 2000; Cook 2008, 2009; Cross, 1997; Sternheimer, 2003, 2010; Wasko, 2008) acknowledged the power of marketers, the commodification of youth culture, and the complexity of today's media culture but also recognized the agency of parents and children to be insightful consumers. These authors, above all else, called for increased consumer literacy. Cross, for example, near the end of his book captured this position well when he argued that adults "must develop the skills to raise independent children in, rather than against, a culture of consumption" (1997, p. 237).

Although the work reviewed above tells us a great deal about children, parents, and consumer culture, it is told from a distance, relying on historical and archival materials. What are missing are actual parents and children participating in consumer culture with each other and with their peers. Some recent ethnographic studies address this gap. We will consider one here that involves mainly younger children and a second in Chapter 9 when we discuss the media and consumer culture among older preadolescents and adolescents.

In her book *Longing and Belonging: Parents, Children, and Consumer Culture*, Allison Pugh (2009) observed 5- to 9-year-old children attending three economically and ethnically diverse after-school programs in Oakland, California. She also interviewed many of their parents and parents of other children she observed from the areas of the city where the schools were located.

Pugh's analysis of consumerism on the part of the children and their families is not so much related to individual desires, wants, or needs but is rather primarily about children's collective belonging—fitting into their peer groups in the present and maintaining or improving their collective social status in the future. Right away we see how this type of ethnographic research differs from the effects studies of media and marketing that focus on individuals isolated from social and cultural context. In the local peer cultures in the three after-school programs, Pugh studied how the children created and participated in what she called "economies of dignity." These economies had "their own scrip, or meaningful tokens, their own norms about managing children's conversations, and their own processes of negotiating value" (Pugh, 2009, p. 52). Scrip could range from material consumer goods such as Game Boys, Pokémon and Magic cards, and Bratz and American Girl dolls. However, they also included shared experiences with families and friends that were consumer related such as birthday parties, visits to amusement parks, and vacations. Pugh did not find some competitive hierarchy related to the expense of scrip. Rather the children vied to lay claim to having similar scrip to that of their peers or to be able to do what the sociologist Erving Goffman (1967) termed the necessary facework to maintain dignity when ownership of the particularly valued scrip was lacking. It was in this facework that children were particularly innovative and creative. For example, one boy in a low-income after-school program was unable to name toys or special trips he had made to fill in a poster about what he was thankful for as some of his peers had done. Instead the boy, urged on by a supportive friend, said he was thankful for his ancestors, something clearly valued by his family. Pugh noted another example among wealthy children wherein one boy claimed to have as many as 600 Pokémon cards and then another boy countered saying he had been given $500 for his birthday from his grandmother. Taken aback by such extravagance, a third boy was speechless for a moment but then said, "I'm saving money for college." Such examples aptly illustrate the collective nature of peer culture and how consumer artifacts and experiences get embedded in myriad ways in the children's strong desire for a sense of belonging to the group—a key feature of peer culture that we will discuss at length in the next chapter.

Both the wealthy and low-income parents Pugh interviewed were attuned to the relation between consumerism and their children's economies of dignity. Therefore, fearing "differences that threatened their children's social belonging," parents generally reported being responsive to their children's consumer requests (2009, p. 90). Wealthy parents worried more about the influence of the media and the hedonistic aspects of consumer culture and set rules for the use of consumer goods. They also normally gave children allowances from which they could save to make their own purchases. The lower-income families worried more about how to afford things their children wanted than media influence or the objects' intrinsic value. However, in contrast to typical portrayals of reckless spending by the poor, the lower-class parents in Pugh's study planned carefully for purchases by saving or waiting for times of unexpected cash flows (also see E. Chin, 2001, for an insightful analysis of the complex practices in consumer culture of poor, Black, preadolescent children).

In a novel twist, Pugh also discussed evidence in her interview data of what she called "pathway consumption." This type of consumption involves "spending on the opportunities that shape children's trajectories" or "a combination of aspiration and uncertainty we might identify as hope" (2009, p. 178). Here much of what Pugh identified, like private lessons, summer camps, or changing residence to be in a neighborhood with better public schools, is in line with Annette Lareau's (2003) notion of a "concerted cultivation" that we discussed in Chapter 5. Unlike Lareau, however, Pugh found the desire for pathway consumption among lower-class families as well, but it was most often blocked by lack of resources or what Pugh called the luxury of difference that affluent families took for granted. As in Lareau's study, we see how insidiously social reproduction works.

SUMMARY

In this chapter, we explored the concept of children's peer culture and how it relates to interpretive reproduction. We defined peer culture as a stable set of activities or routines, artifacts, values, and concerns that children produce and share in interaction with peers. This view of peer culture is in line with interpretive reproduction in that it stresses children's collective actions, shared values, and place and participation in cultural production. Families play a key role in the development of peer culture in interpretive reproduction. Children do not individually experience input from the adult world; rather, they participate in cultural routines in which information is first mediated by adults. However, once children begin to move outside the family, their activities with peers and their collective production of a series of peer cultures become just as important as their interactions with adults. Furthermore, certain elements of peer cultures also affect adult-child routines in the family and other cultural settings.

We also focused on children's introduction to elements of peer culture in the family. Children's peer cultures are affected by adults, most especially in adult-child routines in families, in two ways. First, important features of peer cultures arise and develop as a result of children's attempts to make sense of and to a certain extent resist the adult world. Second, children's experiences in the family prepare them for entry into initial peer cultures in that parents arrange for and structure their children's early interactive experiences with peers, provide them with emotional support and foster interpersonal styles or orientations, and introduce them to both symbolic and material aspects of children's culture. We examined children's introduction to symbolic and material aspects of peer culture in the family in some detail. We saw that parents introduce children to symbolic culture (that is, various representations or expressive symbols of children's beliefs, concerns, and values) by the way they control and encourage their children's access to media, literature, and mythical figures and legends. Parents introduce children to material culture (that is, books, artistic tools, and toys) through their purchase of, and their encouragement of certain types of play with, such cultural objects. In line with interpretive reproduction, we reviewed studies that attempted to capture how parents and children collectively negotiate access to material culture and how they interpret and use symbolic and material culture in everyday routines and rituals in the family. In this review, we noted that children often extend and transform symbolic and material culture that they first attain in the family in their interactions with peers. We now move to a discussion of children's production of preschool and preadolescent peer cultures in Chapters 7 through 9.

7

Sharing and Control
in Initial Peer Cultures

How do peer cultures come about? How are their elements shared and passed on to other groups? How do individual children come to produce and participate in a series of peer cultures? Although children's sense of belonging to a peer culture extends to a wide range of socioecological settings, the direct study of peer interaction and children's peer cultures is relatively recent. Most studies have been confined to a single setting over a limited period of time (usually a year or so at the most). Very few studies have followed children as they make transitions from the family to the peer group or from one peer culture to another. Therefore, it's difficult to answer all of these questions. Still, some patterns have emerged that allow us to begin to address these issues.

We can conceptualize peer cultures as general subcultures of a wider culture or society such as the United States, Italy, or Kenya. Most work on peer subcultures, however, focuses on particular micro or local cultures that are part of a wider network. The advantage of the notion of local culture is that it allows us to focus on culture as something that is directly produced and shared in face-to-face interaction. As G. A. Fine (1987) argued, we can study children's peer cultures as shared universes of discourse rather than as groups defined simply in terms of age or geographical boundaries.

Children are introduced to elements of a more general peer culture and to particular local cultures in the family—through interaction with older siblings, from television and other media, and even from parents.

In Chapter 6, we discussed some of the priming activities in the family that prepare children for the transition to the peer group. However, children actively enter and become participants in and contributors to local peer cultures for the first time as they move outside the family into the surrounding community. This initial peer culture may take the form of loosely structured kin-and neighborhood groups. In Western societies (and more and more in developing countries), however, children are moving into organized child care and educational settings at earlier ages. Given the amount of time that young children normally spend there, and the intensity of the interactions, these settings often serve as a hub in an interlocking network of peer settings or localities. It is through intensive, everyday interaction in this hub that the first local peer culture develops and flourishes (Corsaro, 2003).

Except for a few recent studies of children's playgroups in neighborhood settings in Western societies (Christensen & O'Brien, 2003; Goodwin, 1990; Matthews, Limb, & Taylor, 2000; McKendrick, 2009; Rasmussen, 2004) and of communal, multiage child care and playgroups in non-Western countries (Harkness & Super, 1992; Martini, 1994; Nsamenang, 1992b, 2010; Punch, 2000), most research on children's peer cultures has occurred in settings such as preschools, playgrounds, and classrooms of elementary schools as well as baseball fields and other locales for organized sports and leisure activities. Although there is clearly a need for studies focusing on a wider range of cultures and settings within cultures, the available research serves as a highly valuable starting point for a better understanding of children's cultures. Recent research has identified specific peer processes, routines, concerns, and values. These studies suggest that peer cultures emerge, develop, and are maintained and refined across the various social settings that make up children's worlds.

 ## Central Themes in Children's Initial Peer Cultures

Although a wide range of features of the peer cultures of young children has been identified, two central themes consistently appear: (a) Children make persistent attempts to gain control of their lives, and (b) they always attempt to share that control with each other. In the preschool years, the overriding concerns are social participation and challenging and gaining control over adult authority. These two themes are illustrated by the way young children's routines relate to their concerns with physical size.

For young children, interactive settings are characterized by the children's looking up to those adults who have power and authority (see Corsaro, 1985; for a review and extended discussion of physical size and other aspects of the bodies of children and youth see Fingerson, 2009; Prout, 2000). As a result of this recurrent need to look up to the adult world, young children are deeply concerned with physical size. They come to value growing up and getting bigger. In fact, for young children the distinguishing characteristic between themselves and adults is that adults are bigger. This difference in size—the fact that I'm bigger than the young children I study—is something I have never completely overcome in many years of ethnographic work. As I noted in Chapter 3, it is the primary reason that many of the young children I have studied have labeled me "Big Bill"—someone who is not a typical adult but is too big to be a kid.

The best support for the claim that children value being bigger is their preference for and their routines of play in areas of nursery schools where they are, in a very real sense, bigger. When playing on climbing structures or in playhouses, children routinely climb to the top levels, where they can look down on others, especially adults. Another attraction of these climbing structures is that they are not easily entered by adults because they are scaled to the size of the children. A frequent play routine in the climbing bars in all the nursery schools I have observed is for children to race each other to the top, where they then look down and call out, "We are bigger than anybody else!" Such chanting is often aimed at adults. For example, in one instance I recorded, several children in an American preschool climbed to the highest level of a playhouse in the outside yard. One child, Dominic, yelled out to a teaching assistant, "Willy! Willy! Hi, Willy!" Willy looked up and waved to Dominic. Then Eva and Allen yelled out, "Willy! Willy! Willy!" Soon the three children were joined by two others, Beth and Brian, and all five children began to chant in unison: "Willy! Willy! Willy! We are bigger than you are!" This chanting continued for several minutes, and Willy seemed slightly uncomfortable with all the shouting. He laughed, shook his head, and moved inside the school. I had been standing near the climbing house during this episode, and I felt a great deal of sympathy for Willy. In fact, I began to worry that the children would begin taunting me next, so I moved slightly away from the climbing house to sit on the ground near the slide, where I greeted children as they descended.

The themes of control and communal sharing are evidenced in a wide range of routine activities in the peer cultures of young children. In this chapter we'll focus on children's sharing, on friendship play, and on routines related to children's communal attempts to gain control over adult authority. In Chapter 8 we'll consider routines that relate to conflict and differentiation in the peer culture of young children.

Friendship, Sharing, and Social Participation

We will begin our analysis of communal play routines by first examining young children's friendships, sharing, and social participation in peer culture. We'll then consider play routines related to children's attempts to gain control over adult authority. Let's first look at friendship and sharing among peers, beginning with the earliest of peer relations among toddlers.

Play Routines Among Toddlers

Until recently, most studies of peer relations among toddlers have involved observing children in laboratory settings or in small playgroups in homes. For example, Mueller (1972) documented how cooperative play with toys serves as a basis for the emergence of social interchanges during the 2nd year. With further language development, these interchanges are expanded to become shared routines among toddlers who have a history of interaction. They may serve as the beginnings of friendship and a peer culture (Budwig, Strage, & Bamberg, 1986; Løkken, 2000b; also see Göncü, Mistry, & Mosier, 2000, for a discussion of cultural variation in toddler play).

Studies of peer relations among toddlers in day care settings are rare and have been restricted primarily to recent work in Brazil and Europe (but see A. Honig & Thompson, 1993). In Brazil the research, guided by a cultural and ethological theoretical approach and fine-grained analysis of video data, has demonstrated that toddlers and even babies are capable of shared interactions and play routines (see Amorim, Anjos, & Rossetti-Ferreira, 2008; Carvalho, Império-Hamburger, & Pedrosa, 1998). Rossetti-Ferreira, Oliveira, Campos-de-Carvalho, and Amorim (2010) presented a review of research on infants and toddlers in Brazil that has been published in Portuguese. Many of the reviewed studies, through the detailed analysis of babies in the 1st year of life, revealed peer interaction at this early age in child care centers. The interactions were frequent (though often brief and easily interrupted) and clearly went far beyond simply doing things together or parallel play. The children demonstrated recip-rocal if not necessarily intentional regulation of each other's behaviors. The analysis of episodes showed dialogue and meanings emerging among babies, although they were not structured by verbal means but rather coordinated actions and gestures to achieve shared attention. The studies documented that by the end of the 1st year of life, infants demon-strated both empathy and shared pretend play behaviors.

Stamback and Verba (1986) have verified the existence of numerous and lengthy episodes of common activities among children from 13 to 26 months in French *créches* (child care and education centers). Although the overall organization of the episodes varied, there was a common structure in which shared meaning was established and then a theme elaborated. Tullia Mussati has documented stable peer relations in the Italian *asilo nido* (a child care program for children from 6 months to 3 years). In one study, Mussati and Panni (1981) described the initiation and solidification of ritual play and how the children share knowledge of the basic structure of the rituals and the pleasure of their shared enactment.

Building on the theoretical views of Merleau-Ponty (1967), Løkken (2000a) observed that "through intentional, bodily actions, the toddler immediately understands him/herself and the world he/she is in, without having to reflect or talk about it" (p. 531). Toddlers communi-cate and play based on expressive bodily actions, something Løkken (2000a) termed the "toddling style." Løkken provided examples of Norwegian toddlers making music together (a "glee concert") and a "bathroom society" in the toddling style. In the bathroom society, sev-eral toddlers bang plastic cups, boats, and their hands simultaneously on a bench in the bathroom. Then, when the banging stops, one girl, Linda, says "no," and all the other children say "no" while simultaneously smiling and laughing.

> During the "no"-ing, the children rock on the bench, bowing forward as they say "no." Later, two girls, Sandra and Lisa, hide under the bench. Then they rise to sit on the bench next to each other, looking at each other. They simul-taneously rest their chins in their hands, leaning forward on the bench. Sandra sings "yah-yah-yah yah yah." And then "Oh we are us" to the same tune. "We are us," Lisa sings, after a tiny pause, and to a different tune. Smiling at Sandra. (Løkken, 2000a, p. 540)

Løkken noted that although "the 'We' was uttered by Sandra and con-firmed by Lisa, the communal, playful actions, vocalizations, and smiles in general were part of this piece of 'music' performed by the four children, living through a 'We' in vivid present" (p. 540).

In our study of peer interaction in an asilo nido in Bologna, Italy, Luisa Molinari and I found that the children produced several play routines during the first 2 months of observation that were elaborated over the course of the school year. One routine that we call the "little chairs" nicely captures the flavor of play among toddlers. The routine occurred in a large room that contained a number of small chairs (*seggiolini*) for the children to sit on for various activities and during meetings and group projects. The routine begins with one or more of the children pushing the little chairs to the center of the room. Once the play is under way, other children join by bringing other chairs or using those already put in line. The following case study is a summary of a short segment of the seggiolini routine that Luisa Molinari videotaped in the asilo nido (see Exhibits 7.1 and 7.2).

THE LITTLE CHAIRS ROUTINE

Arianna and Giorgio approach the chairs, and Arianna says, "I'll take the white chairs." The two children then begin pushing the chairs to the middle of the room and are joined in the activity by Stella and Franca. Meanwhile, two other children, Tommaso and Marco, who were watching while standing near the window, take two chairs and push them into the long line created by the other children.

Soon several other children join the play. At one point Stella says, "This is not well done!" and she moves some chairs closer together in the line. The children now begin walking on the line of chairs, which prompts Stella to tell one of the teachers that their construction is "well done."

Now a number of children are walking on the chairs and moving onto a table, where they jump down and run to the other end of the line and start again. At one point Marco sways and says, "I'm falling, I'm falling," but then quickly rights himself and laughs at his pretend crisis. One child, Elvira, kicks at a chair and knocks it from the line. She is immediately reprimanded by Stella, who then returns the chair to its proper place. The children now begin walking in different directions on the structure, and as they cross paths Tommaso pushes Stella. Stella shouts, "Tommaso always pushes me" to Arianna, who is waiting for her at the end of the line. The play continues until one of the teachers announces that it is now time to begin a planned activity.

Exhibit 7.1   Children Arrange *Seggiolini*

Exhibit 7.2   Children Walk on *Seggiolini*

Source: Adapted from Corsaro and Molinari (1990, p. 218).

In this case study, we see that all of the children participate in the routine to some degree. During the routine the teachers often warn the children to be careful, but they intervene only if they fear an injury may occur. In interviews the teachers told us that although they had some misgivings about the play, they did not want to restrict it, noting how much the children enjoyed their innovative creation. Along these lines, it is noteworthy that Marco incorporates the adult concerns into the routine by pretending to fall and then carefully righting himself. In fact, the children were well aware of the teachers' concerns and often reassured them. We can see, for example, how Stella tells a teacher that the design of the chairs is well constructed and therefore not dangerous. Moreover, the children often comfort each other when minor injuries occur and avoid asking the teachers for help even when there are disagreements. We can see that the routine gives the children a sense of control over their physical environment and the authority of the teachers.

The little chairs routine took a slightly different form every day, but some rules were always followed. The children were careful to space the seggiolini to ensure that a child could easily step from one to another, and they avoided taking away chairs from the finished structure. Some of the younger children did not always respect these rules, however, and were frequently advised of violations by older children. Finally, we found that the older children began experimenting with the design somewhat near the end of the school term. These experiments involved modifications that made the structure more difficult and challenging to walk on.

An important feature of toddler play routines like the "little chairs" is their simple and primarily nonverbal participant structure, which consists of a series of orchestrated actions. This simple structure facilitates the involvement of a large number of children with a fairly wide range of communicative, cognitive, and motor skills. The structure incorporates the option of frequently recycling the main elements of the routines. Such recycling allows children to begin and end participation over a lengthy time frame and to embellish or extend certain features of the routines over time.

The simple participant structure of play routines corresponds to a central value of peer cultures: doing things together (Corsaro, 1985, 2003). As we noted earlier, adults tend to view children's activities from a "utility point of view," which focuses on learning and social and cognitive development (Strandell, 1994). Young children do not know the world from this point of view. "For them," noted Strandell, "the course of events of which they are part has an immediate impact on their existence as children here in space and now in time" (1994, p. 8). It is for this reason that we adults seldom truly appreciate the strong emotional satisfaction children get from producing and participating in what seems to us to be simple repetitive play.

The Protection of Interactive Space and Children's Early Friendships

The peer routines of preschool children (3- to 6-year-olds) go beyond the primary nonverbal coordinated actions of toddlers in that they normally involve highly sophisticated verbal productions. However, gaining access to playgroups, maintaining interaction, and making friends are still demanding tasks for preschool children. Gaining access to playgroups is particularly difficult in preschool settings because young children tend to protect shared space, objects, and ongoing play from the entry of others.

Protection of interactive space is the tendency on the part of preschool children to protect their ongoing play from the intrusion of others. In my work in preschools, I have found that this tendency is directly related to the fragility of peer interaction, the multiple possibilities of disruption in most preschool settings, and the children's desire to maintain control over shared activities. Consider the following sequence, recorded on videotape in one of my studies in an American preschool:

> Richard and Barbara have been playing in the block area for several minutes. They are both building things and are sitting near each other. They have not spoken to each other, however, and they do not appear to be playing together. Another child, Nancy, who entered the area with Barbara, is sitting nearby watching.
>
> Richard says to Barbara, "We're playing here by ourselves."
>
> "Just—ah—we friends, right?" Barbara agrees.
>
> Richard replies, "Right."
>
> Barbara and Richard now begin to coordinate their activity and build a house together. Nancy stays on the fringes of the activity for a while but then moves closer, indicating her intent to join the play. Barbara and Richard resist her entry bid, telling Nancy she cannot play. Nancy returns to her onlooker role for a few minutes but then gives up and moves to another area.

Resistance of access attempts seems uncooperative or selfish to adults, including parents and most teachers (see Corsaro, 2003), but it is not that the children are refusing to cooperate or are resisting the idea of sharing.

In fact, as we see in this example, the defenders of interactive space are often intensely involved in creating a sense of sharing during the actual course of playing together and often mark this discovery with references to affiliation ("We friends, right?"). In simple terms, the children want to keep sharing what they are already sharing and see others as a threat to the community they have established.

Children not involved in ongoing play desire entry and want to be a part of shared activities. Because their entry bids are continually resisted, they realize they must be persistent. Over time, most children meet the challenge of resistance and develop a complex set of access strategies. Consider the following case study involving three 4-year-old girls in an American preschool.

ACCESS RITUALS IN AN AMERICAN PRESCHOOL

Jenny and Betty are playing around a sandbox in the outside courtyard of the school. I am sitting on the ground near the sandbox watching. The girls are putting sand in pots, cupcake pans, and teapots. Occasionally the girls bring me a sand cake to pretend to eat. Debbie now comes up to the sandbox and stands near me, observing the other two girls. After watching for about 5 minutes she circles the sandbox three times and stops again and stands next to me. After a few more minutes of watching, Debbie moves to the sandbox and reaches for a teapot. Jenny takes the pot away from Debbie and mumbles, "No." Debbie backs away and again stands near me, observing the activity of Jenny and Betty. Then she walks over next to Betty, who is filling the cupcake pan with sand.

Debbie watches Betty for just a few seconds, then says, "We're friends, right, Betty?"

Betty, not looking up at Debbie, continues to place sand in the pan and says, "Right."

Debbie now moves alongside Betty, takes a pot and spoon, begins putting sand in the pot, and says, "I'm making coffee."

"I'm making cupcakes," Betty replies.

Betty now turns to Jenny and says, "We're mothers, right, Jenny?"

"Right," says Jenny.

The three "mothers" continue to play together for about 20 more minutes, until the teachers announce cleanup time.

Source: Adapted from Corsaro (1979, pp. 320–321).

In this example, Debbie's efforts to enter the play illustrate a variety of access strategies. First, she merely places herself in the area of play, a strategy I call *nonverbal entry*. Receiving no response, Debbie keeps watching the play but now physically circles the sandbox (what I term *encirclement*). Some researchers refer to Debbie's actions as "onlooker behavior" and argue that it is an indicator of timidity or immature social skills. However, it is important to observe access attempts within their social contexts. Observing entire episodes of interaction, I find that access attempts often involve a series of strategies that build on one another.

In this case, Debbie, when stationary and when on the move, carefully makes note of what the other children are doing. With this information she is able to enter the area and produce a variant of the ongoing play. Although normally a successful access strategy, it is initially met with resistance in this instance. Not giving up, however, Debbie watches some more, again enters the area, and makes a verbal reference to affiliation ("We're friends, right?"). Betty responds positively but does not explicitly invite Debbie to play. Debbie then repeats her earlier strategy, producing a variant of the play, this time verbally describing it ("I'm making coffee"). Betty now responds in a way that includes Debbie in the play, noting that she is also making something (cupcakes). She then goes on to further define the new situation by saying, "We're mothers," which is confirmed by Jenny. Debbie is now clearly part of the play.

Although Debbie is eventually successful, one might wonder why she simply did not go up and say "Hi," "What ya doing?" or "Can I play?" I have found that nursery school children rarely use such direct strategies. One reason is that such strategies call for a direct response, and this response is very often negative. Remember our earlier point about the protection of interactive space. Children fear that others may disrupt the cherished but fragile sharing they have developed. Direct entry bids such as "What ya doing?" "Can I play?" or the frequently heard "You have to share!" actually signal that one does not understand what kind of sharing is going on and therefore may cause trouble. Developmental psychologist Catherine Garvey (1984) characterized such requests for information as the three "Don't's" in her guidelines for successful play entry:

> Don't ask questions for information (if you can't tell what's going on, you shouldn't be bothering those who do); don't mention yourself or state your feelings about the group or its activity (they're not interested at the moment); don't disagree or criticize the proceedings (you have no right to do so, since you're an outsider). (p. 164)

what to do

The "do's" in Garvey's guidelines all revolve around demonstrating that you can play without messing things up: Watch what's going on, figure out the play theme, enter the area, and plug into the action by producing a variant of the play theme. As Garvey noted, it is also a good idea to "hold off on making suggestions or attempting to redirect until you are well into the group" (p. 187).

Again, we see why it is important for adults to take the children's perspective. What may seem like selfish behavior is really an attempt to keep sharing. Furthermore, by actively confronting resistance to their access attempts, children acquire complex strategies that allow them to enter and share in play. (For a fascinating study of access rituals and friendship in a bilingual school among immigrant and native Swedish children, see Cromdal, 2001.)

There is one more point. The access skills that children develop in this multiparty setting are clear precursors to adult skills that are used in similar settings. Picture yourself at a party. Let's say you have just arrived, gone off to get a drink, been to the bathroom, or some such thing. Now, like the children in the preschool, you do not want to remain alone. What do you do? Do you go up to a group and say "Hi," "What ya talking about?" or "Can I talk too?" Probably not. Instead, you probably stand near a group, listen, figure out what they are talking about, and make a relevant contribution to the conversation. In short, you do pretty much what Debbie did in the previous example. There is one difference, however. Adults are not likely to tell the guy who bursts in on a conversation that he "is not our friend" or to "beat it." We may want to, but we send more subtle signals—like ignoring what he has to say. As grown-ups, we have learned tact (although it does not always work as well as we might like).

Children's developing knowledge of friendship is closely tied to the social and contextual demands of their peer worlds. Children construct concepts of friendship while at the same time linking these concepts to specific organizational features of peer culture in preschools and other peer settings. Through their experience in preschool, children come to realize that interaction with peers is fragile, and acceptance into ongoing activities is often difficult. Therefore, rather than limiting their social contacts to one or two playmates, the children most often develop stable relations with several playmates as a way to maximize the probability of successful entry and satisfying peer interaction.

For preschool children, friendship primarily serves specific integrative functions (gaining access, building solidarity and mutual trust, and protecting interactive space). Friendships are seldom enduring and are rarely based on perceived personal characteristics of playmates (see Corsaro, 1985, pp. 168–169). (It is important, however, to remember the importance of context in this interpretation of my findings; the nature of friendship processes will vary across social and cultural context. We will consider a comparative analysis of friendship processes in three cultural groups in Chapter 8.) It may be that enduring friendships are more common among preschool children in homes and neighborhoods (Gottman, 1983). Clearly there is a need for long-term ethnographic studies of children's friendships in such settings.

As we've seen, friendship concepts and skills do not arise solely or even primarily as a result of cognitive development or children's individual reflections. Friendships are collectively constructed through children's active involvement in their social worlds and peer cultures, an idea that clearly ties in to the notion of interpretive reproduction. Our earlier discussion of children's transitions from the family to the initial peer culture in preschool settings in Chapter 6 is also relevant here. There we pointed out that parents often make the association between friendship and sharing for their children by designating the playmates with whom their children share things as friends. In this sense, 2- and 3-year-olds are most apt to see friends as those children who are labeled as such by their parents. With experience in initial peer cultures, however, the concept of friendship is transformed from something denoted by a label that is applied to a specific child to something involving observable shared activity (Corsaro, 2003; Dunn, 2004). Friendship means producing shared activity together in a specific area and protecting that play from the intrusions of others. Thus, children creatively appropriate and extend social knowledge that was first presented to them in adult-child routines. Finally, in protecting their interactive space, children come to realize that they can manage their own activities. In negotiating who is in and who is out, who is one of them and who is not, children begin to grasp their developing social identities. Such differentiation among peers becomes more important throughout the preschool years and is a central process in the peer culture of preadolescents (P. Barnes, 2003; Bukowski, Newcomb, & Hartup, 1996; Corsaro, Molinari, Hadley, & Sugioka, 2003; Dunn, 2004). We will return to this issue of social differentiation in peer cultures in Chapters 8 and 9.

Language, Sharing Routines, and Rituals

Although children's cultures are composed of a wide range of language and behavioral routines, none are perhaps more symbolic of childhood ethos than sharing rituals. These collective activities involve patterned, repetitive, and cooperative expressions of the shared values and concerns of childhood. They often involve stylized performances and "constitute ritualized moments which are distinctive to the childhood world in which they are embedded and which punctuate the flow of social exchanges in that world" (Katriel, 1987, p. 306). Sometimes, such stylized performances are embedded in more general peer activities, as seen in Goodwin's (1985, 2006) study of African girls' negotiations during a game of jump rope and Mishler's (1979) analysis of "trading and bargaining" among middle-class American 6-year-olds at lunchtime (see Evaldsson, 2009, for a review of language play and rituals). A fascinating example of the power of Taiwanese children's language play routines can be seen in the work of Hadley (2003). Hadley found that through word play (such as manipulating teachers' and class names, Taiwanese kindergartners "both resisted and accommodated the Confucian values that the teachers aimed to instill in them" (p. 205).

Here, however, let us concentrate on ritual performances of Italian children whose overriding purpose of production is to mark communal sharing within peer culture. The art of verbal negotiation and debate is deeply valued in Italian society. Public discussion and debate (or what Italians refer to as *discussione*) are an integral part of everyday life and occur in bars, public squares, and shopping areas. Children also engage in discussione with adults and peers from an early age, and the activity is an important element of peer culture (Corsaro & Molinari, 2005; Corsaro & Rizzo, 1988, 1990; New, 1994). We will consider discussione among Italian children in the next chapter, when we discuss the importance of conflict in peer culture. For now, let's look at a particular verbal routine, the *cantilena*, which frequently arises in the course of children's discussions in the *scuola dell'infanzia* (a government-supported preschool program for 3- to 6-year-olds).

The cantilena is a tonal device or singsong chant that children produce in a range of verbal activities. The chanting is often accompanied rhythmically with nonverbal gestures such as hitting one's fists or the sides of one's open hands together. Aside from these basic rhythmic features and except that verbalizations normally occur in alternating, nonoverlapping turns, there are no set rules to its production. However, the repetition of lexical items (words or sounds) within turns and key phrases over the course of several exchanges is common. Consider the following example: Several children between the ages of 4 and 6 are sitting around a table drawing pictures. One of the children, Nino, suddenly hits his hands together and chants, "*Chi mi da il nero, é per sempre mio amico. Chi mi da il nero, é per sempre mio amico*" (He who gives me black, is my friend forever. He who gives me black, is my friend forever). Two children sitting near Nino, Giovanna and Luigi, rummage through a pile of marking pens on the table. Giovanna finds a black one first and hands it to Nino. This routine is repeated several times, with the three children alternating the role of enunciator of the cantilena.

It is difficult to capture the effect of the cantilena without actually hearing it. In this example, there is falling intonation in the first part of the phrase (*He who gives me black*) ending at the lowest point with the naming of the color, and then rising intonation in the second part ending at the highest point with the word *forever*. The fall and rise are rather easily produced in this example because a stock phrase about friendship is used. The children, however, often spontaneously produce the cantilena in the course of debates in which they often cannot anticipate the topics of discussion, let alone exact words or phrases. Consider the following case study of Italian children's production of the cantilena in a peer discussion.

ITALIAN CHILDREN'S PRODUCTION OF THE CANTILENA IN *DISCUSSIONE*

Several children (Franco, Paolo, Sara, Nino, Giovanna, and Luigi), who are all about 5 years old, are sitting around a table drawing. They are in the middle of a *discussione* about the existence of *lupi* (wolves or werewolves) and *fantasmi* (ghosts). After several claims and counterclaims, two of the children, Franco and Paolo, suggest that ghosts do exist and that they live in abandoned houses under the sea. At this point a girl, Sara, initiates a multiturn cantilena.

Sara: *Nelle—le case buie. Stanno nelle buie.* (In the—the dark houses. They stay in the dark.) (See Exhibit 7.3.)

Paolo: *Eh, è vero.* (Yes, it's true.)

Franco: *E sotto mar—è buio!* (And under the sea—it's dark.)

Nino: *Eh, è vero.* (Yes, it's true.)

Sara: *E sotto—ci vanno loro.* (And under—they go there.)

Luigi: *No, ci vanno anche i granchi.* (No, also crabs go there.) (See Exhibit 7.4.)

          [Hitting his hand against marker]

Franco: *Ci vanno i sommergibli.* (Submarines go there.)

Nino: *E anche i pescecani. E anche i pescecani.* (And also sharks. And also sharks.)

(Continued)

(Continued)

In her production of the cantilena, Sara strings together several elements from the earlier discussion (ghosts, dark houses, ghosts under
water). Her turn is especially impressive because it involves three separate phrases all produced in the falling and rising pitch of the cantilena
and all containing new elements related to the discussion with only
minor repetition. Again, it is hard to appreciate the phonetic aspects of
the cantilena without hearing it. To preserve the singsong pitch, it is
necessary to produce a phrase with at least four syllables, and one
quickly has to think of something to say of this length that fits the ongoing discussion. Long turns with new information are especially difficult
to produce, and difficult productions like Sara's are appreciated by one's
peers. On the other hand, minimal participation is also valued, and
rather easily produced, as we see in Paolo's response to Sara (*Eh, è vero*).
The trick here is to add the *Eh* (or *Si* or *No*) before the *è vero* to have
enough syllables to work with. In all my attempts to participate in the
children's cantilena, I never got past this simple but appreciated contribution. After Paolo's response, Franco, Nino, and Luigi all contribute to

Exhibit 7.3   A Child Initiates the *Cantilena*

Exhibit 7.4   Other Children Respond in *Cantilena*

the cantilena. They signal either agreement or disagreement, refine pre-viously mentioned information (it's under the sea), or add new informa-tion (other underwater objects such as crabs, submarines, and sharks). In all of these turns, the children rely on the repetition of key phrases to ensure coherence and to maintain the basic singsong cadence and rhythm of the cantilena.

Source: Adapted from Corsaro and Rizzo (1990, pp. 58–62).

An important feature of the cantilena is that the routine is a con-sciously shared element of peer culture. That is, the children not only produce the routine but refer to it using the term *cantilena*. Additionally, the teachers and the children's parents are aware of the cantilena. In fact, the children's frequent chanting often irritates parents, who restrict usage of the cantilena in the home with the command *"Non far la can-tilena!"* (Don't do the cantilena!). Interestingly, in family role-play in the *scuola materna*, children in superordinate roles (mother, father, and older siblings) often use this same command when disciplining peers in sub-ordinate roles (babies and younger children) when the latter produce the cantilena in pretend quarrels. In this way, the children take the adults' disapproving reactions to their peer routine and embed them into their shared peer culture in role-play. We again see how many peer play routines directly (or, in this case, more subtly and creatively) challenge adult authority.

We now turn to a more detailed look at the importance of play routines for autonomy and control in peer culture.

Autonomy and Control in Peer Culture

Earlier I noted that a major theme of peer culture revolves around children's desire to achieve autonomy from the rules and authority of adult caretakers and to gain control over their lives. This issue of control is apparent not only in children's active challenges to adult control but also in a range of play routines in which children collectively confront curiosities, confusions, and fears from the adult world.

Sociodramatic Role-Play

Child researchers have long argued for the importance of dramatic role-play for children's social and emotional development. Like most adults, these researchers most often see role-play as the direct imitation of adult models. Kids do not, however, simply imitate adult models in their role-play; rather, they continually elaborate and embellish adult models to address their own concerns.

Children's appropriation and embellishment of adult models is primarily about status, power, and control. Children are empowered when they take on adult roles. They use the dramatic license of imaginary play to project to the future—a time when they will be in charge and in control of themselves and others.

Role-play also allows children to experiment with how different types of people in society act and how they relate to each other. Of great importance here for children is gender and expectations about how girls and boys should act and how roles in society are gender stereotyped. Here again we will see that young children do not accept, but challenge and refine, such stereotypes. Thus, gender role expectations are not simply inculcated into children by adults; rather, they are socially constructed by children in their interactions with adults and each other.

Role-Play and Social Power. Children begin role-play as young as age 2, and most role-play among 2- to 5-year-olds is about the expression of power. In my dissertation research I was interested in language use in the play of a brother and sister, Krister and Mia, and a second boy, Buddy (yes, the same Buddy who was talking to his mother about blood and going to Sesame Street in Chapter 1). In one play session, Mia (who was 4 and had been to preschool) and the two boys (both around 2 and a half years old and without preschool experience) began a role-play sequence when Mia suggested we play teacher. Krister wanted to be the teacher and pushed a chair to the front of a large blackboard in the room. Mia, Buddy, and I sat on the floor as students.

Krister took the chalk and said, "Now write this!" and drew several lines.

"Those aren't letters, but just a bunch of lines!" I responded teasingly.

"He can't write so good," Mia told me, a bit annoyed. "Just pretend they're letters."

But Krister did not allow his authority to be tested. He shouted out at me, "Bill, you are bad! You most go sit in the corner right now!" Krister pointed to the corner of the room, and I took my paper and went over there to sit. Buddy and Mia began to laugh, but Krister gave some more orders about what to write, and Mia, Buddy, and I did what we were told.

Here we see a young child who had not attended preschool but had information that teachers are powerful and tell kids what to do. Also, bad kids are made to sit in the corner. Did Krister learn this from Mia? Possibly, but not as a result of her own experiences in preschool. Their father assured me there was no sitting in the corner in Mia's school. Perhaps it was from something on television such as a cartoon or an adult joking about kids having to sit in the corner if they are bad in school. Where Krister picked up the information is less important than his desire to express the power one has in an adult or superordinate role (that is, a role with the most power or authority), a situation in which young children seldom find themselves.

In sociodramatic play children relish taking on and expressing power. It's fun. As we can see in the following case study of a complex role-play episode from my work in Berkeley, California, a small group of children (all around 4 years old) clearly expressed power and control while in superordinate roles, misbehaved and obeyed in subordinate roles, cooperated in roles of equal status, but became confused about the alignment and gender expectations of other roles.

TWO HUSBANDS

A boy, Bill, and a girl, Rita, entered the upstairs playhouse carrying purses and a suitcase. Before coming upstairs they had agreed on the roles of husband and wife. As they dropped the purses and suitcases to the floor they looked down at children playing below. They saw two boys, Charles and Denny, crawling around and meowing like cats.

"Hey, there are our kitties," said Bill.

"Yeah, there down in the backyard," replied Rita.

Bill and Rita now went about arranging things in the house. They picked up blankets from the bed and placed the purses and suitcase on the floor in front of the bed. Bill then picked up a baby crib and placed it alongside of the front of the bed, blocking off the area around the bed from the rest of the room.

"This is our special room, right?" said Bill.

"Right," responded Rita.

"This is our little room we sleep in, right?" added Bill. "Our little room. Our—"

"We're the kitty family," said Denny, cutting off Bill; he and Charles have climbed up the stairs and into the playhouse. They began crawling around the room meowing.

"Here kitty-kitty, here kitty-kitty," said Rita, reaching out to pet them. "Yeah, here's our two kitties," she announced to Bill.

"Kitty, you can't come into this room!" Bill commanded sternly. But one of the kitties, Charles, immediately crawled into the room and climbed on the bed. Meanwhile the other kitty knocked a plate from the table to the floor.

"No! No!" yelled Bill. He then shooed the kitties back toward the stairs. "Go on! Get down in the backyard!"

Rita came to Bill's aid and shouted, "Get down in the backyard, you two cats! Go down! Down! Down!"

The kitties headed toward the stairs, and Charles started crawling down. But Denny stopped at the head of the stairs and said, "No, I'm the kitty. I'm the kitty."

"Go back in the backyard!" commanded Bill.

"You get in the backyard. Ya! Ya!" yelled Rita, pushing at the remaining kitty with her hands.

Denny now gave up and also went down the stairs.

Bill looked down at the two cats and said, "Go in the backyard, we're busy!"

"They were rough on us," said Rita.

After the kitties left, the husband and wife decided that the house needed cleaning. In line with stereotyped gender roles, Bill moved the furniture while his wife, Rita, cleaned the floor.

Bill picked up the table and said, "Be careful, I'm gonna move our table."

"You're a handyman, a handyman," sang Rita.

"Next," said Bill as he pushed the stove near the door and then moved the table next to it.

"Bill? Bill?" called Rita.

"What?"

"You're a strong man," Rita praised him.

"I know it. I just moved this," said Bill, referring to the table.

As Rita pretended to mop the floor the kitties returned. Bill tried to block them off, but they scurried by, moving on the just cleaned floor. Bill attempted to shoo the kitties back to the stairs.

"Come on kitties, get out! Get out! Scat! Scat!"

Rita stopped cleaning to help her husband, "Come scat. Scat!" she yelled.

Charles crawled back down the stairs, but Denny remained and stood up, announcing, "I'm not—I'm not a kitty anymore."

"You're a husband?" Bill asked.

"Yeah," agreed Denny.

"Good. We need two husbands," said Bill.

Now Bill called out to Rita, "Hey, two husbands."

Rita was not pleased with this development and offered an alternative. "I can't catch two husbands 'cause I have a grandma."

"Well, I—then I'm the husband," said Denny.

"Yeah, husbands! Husbands!" chanted Denny and Bill as they danced around the room.

"Hold it, Bill," said Rita. "I can't have two husbands."

Rita held up two fingers and shook her head, "Not two. Not two." She then walked down the stairs.

Meanwhile Bill and Denny continued dancing around upstairs and chanting "Two husbands! Two husbands!"

(Continued)

(Continued)

Rita walked around in front of the downstairs playhouse shaking her head. She stopped near the stairs just as Bill and Denny came down, and said, "I can't marry 'em, two husbands. I can't marry two husbands because I love them."

Bill said to Rita, "Yeah, we do." He then turned to Denny and said, "We gonna marry ourselves, right?"

"Right," responded Denny.

The boys then went back upstairs and continued chanting, "Husbands!" They danced around and jumped on the bed. Later Rita came upstairs and said she was a kitty. The two husbands admonished her for scratching them and misbehaving and chased her down the stairs. Shortly after, the role-play was brought to an end with the teacher's announcement of "cleanup time."

Source: Adapted from Corsaro (2003, pp. 113–117).

In this sequence the role-play hit a snag, at least for Rita, when Denny decided he didn't want to be a kitty anymore. Perhaps he was getting tired of being shooed down the stairs. In any case, Bill suggested Denny also be a husband, and when Denny accepted Bill even said, "Good. We need two husbands." It is not clear why Bill made this offer. Most likely because Denny is a boy and because males are husbands, Bill thought that Denny should be a husband like him.

Rita, however, thought otherwise and saw a problem that goes beyond gender stereotypes: one wife and two husbands. While the boys danced around and celebrated being two husbands, Rita argued to no avail that she cannot catch, have, marry, or love two husbands. She knew that something was wrong with this relationship (at least among the adults in her culture). What was wrong has to do with her emerging knowledge that the roles of husband and wife not only are gender specific but are related to each other in particular ways. Wives and husbands love each other and get married. It is even assumed that is the case in her pretend relationship with Bill. But what was she to do with Denny?

She seemed to offer up the role of grandma for Denny: "I can't catch two husbands 'cause I have a grandma." But her phrasing is confusing, and a grandma is the wrong gender; grandpa might have worked. The contrast of the boys' glee with being two husbands—Bill even suggested they marry themselves, but no such ceremony occurred—and Rita's discomfort with the proposed arrangement is interesting. In the end, she solves the problem by becoming a kitty, and the play continues with a reversion to misbehavior and discipline. However, Rita had a glimpse into the complexity of role relationships. In Piaget's terms as we discussed in Chapter 1, she had a disequilibrium in her sense of her social world for which she will strive to compensate. So we see that role-play is fun, improvised, unpredictable, and ripe with opportunities for reflection and learning.

Plying the Frame in Role-Play. Role-play involves more than learning specific social knowledge; it also involves learning about the relationship between context and behavior. As the anthropologist Gregory Bateson (1956) argued, when the child plays a role she or he not only learns something about that role's specific social position but "also learns that there is such a thing as a role" (p. 148). According to Bateson, the child "acquires a new view, partly flexible and partly rigid" and learns "the fact of stylistic flexibility and the fact that choice of style or role is related to the frame or context of behavior" (p. 148). Children's recognition of the transformative power of play is an important element of peer culture. It is their use of this transformative power in role-play that I will, in line with Bateson and the sociologist Irving Goffman (1974), refer to as "plying the frame."

Let's consider another example also from my research in a preschool in Bologna, Italy. A girl, Emilia, made an ice cream shop with two of her friends. She came to where I was playing with three boys, Alberto, Alessio, and Stefano. I had a microphone in my hand because we were videotaping the play (Corsaro, 2003).

NON C'È *ZUPPA INGLESE*

"Bill, will you come to see our store?" she asks.

"I can't now because—ah—I'm here with this—" I struggle with my answer, not sure how to say what I need to in Italian.

"*Microfono,*" she finishes my reply.

"Yes. I can't ah—" I say, motioning that the microphone wire is not long enough to go to her store. "Will you bring the ice cream to me?" I try to say, but my grammar is incorrect and she does not understand.

(Continued)

(Continued)

"What?"

"Take the ice—" I blurt out, confusing the words for *bring* and *take*. But then I recover quickly: "Bring me the ice cream, to me."

"Yes. But we still have to—" she begins.

"Chocolate and—ah—chocolate and va—vanilla," I say. I had noticed earlier that Emilia and her friends were using dirt as pretend chocolate ice cream and sand for *crema* or vanilla.

"Yes," she says, "but we must finish the store, we still have to make it— the vanilla."

"Yes, that's fine."

"After I give it to you," she continues, "there's also strawberry. There is— I'll tell you all the flavors."

"Yes," I say.

Emilia gestures, counting off each flavor, "Eh, strawberry, chocolate, vanilla—"

"Lemon?" asks Stefano.

"No, there is none," Emilia tells him.

I say, "I like ah—vanilla and ah—strawberry."

"Okay."

"For Stefano," I say, "for Stefano vanilla."

But Stefano wants to make his own order. "For me strawberry and banana."

"There is no banana!" Emilia insists.

"Lemon," says Stefano, knowing full well there is none.

"There is none!" replies Emilia.

"There is no lemon," I remind Stefano.

"Chocolate," Stefano finally agrees.

"Chocolate," repeats Emilia as she heads toward her store to fetch the ice cream.

However, now Alberto places an order: "Hey, hey, for me, *zuppa inglese*—whipped cream and pistachio!"

"Zuppa inglese," Stefano and I say, laughing.

"They don't have it," I tell Alberto.

Emilia returns and bends over Alberto and says, "There is no zuppa inglese, there is no pistachio!"

"Okay, then, I'll take banana," says Alberto.

"There is none!" Emilia says with a big grin.

"Okay, then, I'll take whatever there is, chocolate," Alberto finally agrees.

"There's chocolate. There's vanilla, chocolate, strawberry, maybe pistachio."

"Orange soda?" asks Alberto.

"Well, I'll go see," says Emilia, and she returns to her store.

Source: Adapted from Corsaro (2003, pp. 119–121).

In this example, Emilia at first wants to stay in the confined frame of pretending to have a small ice cream store with flavors that can be represented by features on the playground: dirt, sand, leaves, and so on. Although I have trouble making my order because of my not-so-good Italian, I stay within the frame and accept—no, even volunteer—chocolate, a flavor I know she has. But first Stefano and then Alberto more or less say, "What's the fun of that!" They ply or stretch the frame by purposely ordering flavors they know Emilia doesn't have or doesn't want to pretend to have. Then the whole role-play becomes about "playing with the play."

This turn of events is most apparent when Alberto calls out after Emilia as she is leaving and orders zuppa inglese (a rare ice cream flavor that is related to the English dessert trifle). Now even I get what is going on and join in the laughter of the other boys at Alberto's request. Emilia, feigning disgust, clearly enjoys dealing with Alberto. She relishes the opportunity of denying the request, by responding, *"Non c'è zuppa inglese!"* But Alberto's response to this is to ask for banana! Later, however, Emilia gives in some and says there may be some pistachio and she will check into the orange soda.

The Possible Universality of Role-Play. Given the ubiquity of role-play in children's play across historical times and across cultures it can be argued that it is a universal aspect of children's play and peer cultures. In Chapter 4 we saw that historian Barbara Hanawalt, in her book *Growing Up in Medieval London* (1993), reported that children of medieval London engaged in types of dramatic role-play such as reproducing the celebration of religious ceremonies and marriages.

We also saw in Chapter 4 that role-play was reported in interviews with former slaves by Lester Alston (1992) and David Wiggins (1985). They reported that slave children in the pre–Civil War South of the United States engaged in a variety of types of role-play that included religious ceremonies such as baptisms and most especially slave auctions, which clearly helped children deal with strong emotions about being separated from their families in the slave community.

More recently, in her ethnographic work on the play and work activities of rural Sudanese children in the 1980s, Cindi Katz (2004) documented elaborate role-play that was tied closely to adult activities. Boys reproduced various activities related to agricultural work and commerce from the profits of such work. Central to the play was a toy tractor one of the boys made from a variety of discarded objects with the help of an older brother. The boys made a plow for the tractor and cooperatively and painstakingly reproduced all the various elements of agricultural work from plowing the fields, to planting and watering the crops, to irrigating and weeding, and finally to harvesting the crops and taking them to a pretend storehouse. They also reproduced the process of selling their harvest using artificial currency. Finally, they used their pretend profits to play store; they bought a range of goods represented by objects such as bits of metal and glass and battery tops (Katz, 2004, pp. 12–13).

Girls' role-play was also elaborate. Girls made dolls from straw; gave names to the dolls, who represented males and females of all ages; and played with the dolls in houses "they established with dividers made of shoes, mortars, bricks, and pieces of tins" (Katz, 2004, p. 17). The girls used these props to enact a wide range of domestic activities such as cooking, eating, going to the well to fetch water, and visiting. These activities, although staying close to the adult model, were highly innovative in that the children inventively made their toys from a variety of discarded and natural materials as compared to the toys of children from Western societies.

Overall, there is good evidence to support the contention that socio-dramatic role-play is a universal feature of children's peer cultures. However, more studies of children's play from a wide range of cultural groups is necessary to support this contention fully and to capture the diversity in the styles and nature of these important play routines in children's everyday lives.

Challenging Adult Authority

Another aspect of children's peer culture that may be universal is children's tendency to challenge adult authority (Corsaro, 2003; Schwartzman, 1978). In Chapter 4 we saw that role-reversal games such as the boy bishops ritual existed as long ago as medieval times and that the newsies and street hustlers of turn-of-the-20th-century American cities clearly enjoyed outwitting adults. Regarding cross-cultural studies, Brian Sutton-Smith (1976) pointed to "order-disorder games" that can be found in Western and non-Western societies. In these games—for example, the familiar ring-around-the-rosy—everyone cooperates to create order, only to destroy it by collapsing. Although some might accuse Sutton-Smith of reading too much into such games, others argue that the subtle aspects of inversion, challenge, and satire are what make these games so appealing to children.

Helen Schwartzman argued that children not only experiment with and refine aspects of the adult world in play but also use play as an "arena for comment and criticism" (1978, p. 126). As an example, she pointed to some of the play of the children of the !Kung Bushmen of southwest Africa as described by the anthropologist Lorna Marshall (1976). One of the games of the !Kung children that Marshall described is called Frogs, a reverse form of Mother, May I? The game begins with one child's being chosen "mother for all" and the remaining children sitting in a circle. When the mother taps a child with a stick, the child pretends to sleep. While all the children are sleeping, the mother pulls hairs from her head and places them in an imaginary fire to cook. The hairs are frogs that have been gathered for food. When the frogs are cooked, the mother wakes her children one by one and asks each one to go and get her mortar and pestle so she can finish preparing the frogs. But each child refuses, so the angry mother goes to get the mortar and pestle herself. While she is away, the children steal the frogs and run off to hide with them. When the mother returns she pretends to be very angry and chases after the children.

> When she finds one, she strikes him/her on the head with her forefinger. This action "breaks the head" so that the child's "brains run out," and she then pretends to drink the "brains." The final part of the game frequently ends in chaos and pandemonium as the children try to dart away from mother's grasp. Soon everyone is chasing everyone else, shrieking and laughing and whacking each other on the head. (Schwartzman, 1978, p. 131)

Westerners might cringe at the references to drinking brains and the aggressiveness of the play. On the other hand, the !Kung would see our competitive games such as football and even hopscotch as similarly distasteful. In fact, Marshall pointed out that the !Kung do not play any competitive games (except tug-of-war) because the idea of winners and losers is not accepted in their culture, which values the group over the individual (Schwartzman, 1978, p. 130).

In a study in a Finnish preschool, Harriet Strandell (1997) showed how the children used language and playful mocking of the teachers to take control of the social arena and push the teachers' definition of the situation to the background. During lunch in the preschool, a group of 3-year-olds had just sat down to eat when older children were returning from an outing. A teacher suggested, "Let's show the big ones how nicely we can eat." The children began to eat but then called out names of the older children and a teacher they saw ("I saw Rita," "I saw Janne"). Then the verbal play was extended to fantasy as one child said, "I saw a lion," and another said, "I saw its tail." The teachers, sensing they were losing control of the situation, quieted the children. Later, after the children had finished eating, they ran into the hall, but a teacher called back to them, saying, "How about saying thank you!" One girl, Pia, stood by the dining room door and shouted, "Thank you so much, ladies!" All the other children started laughing and shouting, "Thanks, ladies!" A teacher said, "That's enough now," but the laughter and the kids' chorus of "Thanks, ladies! Thanks, ladies!" continued for some while longer until a teacher repeated, "That's enough now," in a calm voice, only to have one of the children shout, "Enough!" to more laughter (Strandell, 1997, pp. 459–460). The teachers were clearly put in a difficult situation here because of the children's clever use of language as they did what they were told (thanked the teachers) but in a way that clearly put them in control of the situation and created a great sense of fun and control among the children.

We explored children's secondary adjustments to adult rules in Chapter 2. Children's secondary adjustments in preschool settings contribute to a group identity and provide children with a tool for addressing personal interests and goals. Over the course of a year in a particular preschool, children's creation of and participation in a wide range of secondary adjustments leads to the development of what I have termed an "underlife" in preschools (Goffman, 1961). An underlife is a set of behaviors or activities that contradict, challenge, or violate the official norms or rules of a specific social organization or institution. The underlife exists alongside and in reaction to those organizational rules of preschools that impinge on the autonomy of the children. In this sense, the underlife is an essential part of the children's group identity.

The underlife is perhaps most apparent in secondary adjustments carried out through the active cooperation of several children. These secondary adjustments normally involve using legitimate resources in devious ways to get around rules and achieve personal or private needs or wants—what Goffman called "working the system" (1961, p. 210). Children frequently work the system to avoid helping at cleanup time. In preschools I have studied in the United States and Italy, cleanup usually occurs at transition points in the day (before snacks or meals, meeting times, and so on). There is a general rule that children stop play when cleanup time is announced and help teachers put things back in order. Children soon question the necessity and logic of cleanup time. I once overheard a child argue against putting toys away during cleanup time because "we'll just have to take 'em out all over again!"

Children often come up with strategies to evade cleanup time: relocation (immediately moving to another area of play upon hearing the announcement of cleanup); pretending not to hear the announcement (simply ignoring, for as long as possible, the command to obey the rule); and using personal-problem delay (claiming they cannot help clean up because of personal problems). This last strategy is particularly interesting. Children report a plethora of problems, such as feigned injury ("I hurt my foot"), pressing business ("I have to go to the bathroom"), or role-play demands ("I have to finish feeding the baby").

Once in Italy, a child named Franca told one of the teachers that she could not help clean up because I was in the process of teaching her English. There was some truth to this because children often asked me how to say certain words in English, and Franca had made such a request earlier in the day, but we clearly were not involved in this activity when cleanup time ensued. Fortunately, I was not brought into the dispute because the teacher rejected Franca's excuse out of hand. Nevertheless, during the course of this debate a good deal of the cleanup work was performed by other children. In fact,

identifying peer-adult roles and boundaries

all of the strategies to avoid cleanup are at least partially successful for this reason. Due to organizational constraints—teachers' need to get the children to lunch, to begin a meeting, and so on—any delaying tactic is somewhat effective. It does not take long for children to learn this and to "work the system" accordingly (Corsaro, 1990, p. 20). For example, one of my colleagues, Kathryn Hadley, has volunteered in many preschools and tells the story of a boy who upon the announcement of cleanup time went around the school asking teachers and other kids for a "big hug." What a friendly fellow this little "hugger" was at cleanup times. This strategy worked for quite a while before the teachers caught on (Corsaro, 2003, p. 150).

Children's secondary adjustments are innovative and collective responses to the adult world. Furthermore, by sharing a communal spirit as members of peer cultures, children come to experience how being a member of a group affects both themselves as individuals and how they relate to others. Through secondary adjustments, children come to see themselves as part of a group (a peer group of students), which is in some instances aligned with other groups and in other instances opposed to other groups (teachers and adult culture). At the same time, children begin to develop an awareness of how communal values can be used to address personal interests and goals (Löfdahl & Hägglund, 2006). Clear evidence of this can be seen in children's attempts to control the behavior of their peers by offering them the opportunity to share collectively in secondary adjustments. For example, on one occasion in an Italian preschool, I saw an older boy, Roberto, fail repeatedly to get a younger child, Fabrizio, to play a board game the "correct" way. Although exasperated with Fabrizio's refusal to follow directions, Roberto did not give up. He decided to abandon the game momentarily and took a small car from his pocket. He then rolled the car toward Fabrizio, who picked it up, looked it over, and rolled it back. After playing with the car for several minutes, Roberto put it back in his pocket and suggested that they play with the board game. This time the younger child played "correctly." After a few minutes, however, Fabrizio asked to see the car again, but this time Roberto said, "*Basta cosí!*" (Enough of this!) and left Fabrizio sitting alone at the table.

Confronting Confusions, Fears, and Conflicts in Fantasy Play

In Chapter 6 we explored how children's interactions with the adult world often generate disturbances or uncertainties for them. Children address some of these disturbances as they arise with parents and other adults, but they attempt to resolve many others in imaginary worlds that they create and share with peers. In these "as-if" worlds, "familiar activities may be carried out in different ways: inanimate objects may be treated as animate, one object (or gesture) may be substituted for another, and children may perform an activity usually carried out by adults" (Fein, 1981, p. 1096). This as-if quality does not mean, however, that there are no rules in imaginative play. Vygotsky argued that the very organization and coordination of pretend play demands attention to real-life rules and also the invention of new rules, which define and redefine the behavior of imaginary characters such as monsters, fairies, and ghosts (1978, p. 95).

Numerous studies document the complexity of young children's fantasy play throughout the world. Children's fantasy play is emotion laden and helps children deal with various concerns and fears such as being lost, facing a variety of dangers, and death (Corsaro, 1985, 2003; Edwards, 2000; Fromberg & Bergen, 2006; Goldman, 2000; Göncü, 1993; Göncü & Gaskins, 2006; Löfdahl, 2005). Sawyer (1997) impressively identified the poetic nature of American children's fantasy play. These poetic performances in children's fantasy play are part of a shared peer culture in that they are created in an improvised fashion that Sawyer called "collaborative emergence" (Sawyer, 2002). By *collaborative emergence* Sawyer meant that children's improvised play is unpredictable and contingent on the ongoing turn-by-turn production of play narrative. Thus, one child "proposes a new development for the play, and other children respond by modifying or embellishing the proposal" (Sawyer, 2002, p. 340). Sawyer argued, however, that the researcher can interpret the particular episode of fantasy play by assuming that the play narrative ceases with the end of a particular play episode.

Johannesen (2004; also see Corsaro & Johannesen, 2007), in her study of children's fantasy play with LEGOs, extended Sawyer's work by entering the practice of family play in terms of the practice itself. She did this by considering the play frame reality as voiced by the LEGO play characters as a real world and the voices as expressing real experiences. Given that her work is longitudinal, with the study of play with LEGOs by the same children over a long period of time, Johannesen demonstrated that the LEGO characters remain intact even when they, as embodied in play artifacts, are stacked away from one day or week to the next. Over time the children's play reality persists and becomes increasingly complex as the characters, as orchestrated by the children, plan and experience recurring episodes of danger-rescue and other themes. These recurrent experiences materialize in the enduring relational identities, artifacts, and participants in the play. Thus, we see many of the aspects of peer culture as we defined it in Chapter 1 (play routines, values and concerns, and artifacts) in the shared production of fantasy play over time (Corsaro & Johannesen, 2007).

In her work on "doing reality with play" based on observations of Finnish preschool children, Strandell (1997) made a similar point, maintaining that play in the peer culture should not be seen only as a means of reaching adult competence. Rather, she argued that play is a resource children use in their everyday life activities in the peer culture. Interestingly these and other studies of fantasy play demonstrate language and improvisational skills among the young children that can be seen as surpassing those of the majority of older children and adults.

Some fantasy play routines are only loosely connected to models from the adult world. Such routines are not well documented and in some cases seem to be acquired spontaneously in local peer cultures, whereas others seem to be passed along from older to younger children. Let's look at one such routine, which I refer to as *approach-avoidance play*.

Approach-avoidance play is a primarily nonverbal pretend play routine in the peer culture of preschool children in which children identify, approach, and then avoid a threatening agent or monster. The best way to get a feel for approach-avoidance play is to examine an enactment of the routine. Like many routines in peer culture, approach-avoidance is hard to appreciate outside its natural context. Furthermore, the routine is primarily nonverbal, making it even harder to capture on paper. I try to bring to life a videotaped enactment of the routine in the following case study.

THE WALKING BUCKET

Three children from an American preschool (Beth, Brian, and Mark), who are all about 5 years old, are playing on a rocking boat in the outside yard of the school. Suddenly, Beth notices another boy (Steven, 6 years old) walking some distance from the boat, with a large trash can over his head.

"Hey, a walking bucket! See the walking bucket!" shouts Beth.

"What?" says Brian. Beth, pointing to where Steven is walking, repeats, "A walking bucket. Look!" Brian and Mark turn, look, and see Steven. "Yeah!" says Brian, "Let's get off."

Brian, Mark, and Beth jump off the boat and slowly approach Steven. When they reach him, Mark and Brian push the bucket and start to lift it up.

Steven responds by lifting the bucket off his head. Brian yells, "Whoa!" and the three children pretend to be afraid of Steven and race back to the rocking boat. Steven pursues them, flailing his arms in a threatening manner. Brian, Mark, and Beth all hop onto the far side of the boat. Steven stops at the vacant side and rocks the boat by pushing down on the edge of it with his hands. Steven does not climb onto the boat, nor does he directly try to get at the other children.

Steven then returns to the dropped bucket and places it back over his head. Brian, Mark, and Beth watch from the boat, giggling and laughing.

This routine continues with Brian, Mark, Beth, and later another child, Frank, approaching Steven every time he replaces the bucket on his head. Each time he removes the bucket, the children flee back to home base with Steven in pursuit. With each approach, the group of children becomes more confident and aggressive. They taunt Steven (calling him a "big fat poop butt") and kick at his legs under the bucket without actually making contact. During a fourth approach, Steven flips off the bucket a bit prematurely and finds himself face-to-face with Mark. The two begin to push one another, and a teacher standing nearby intervenes, ending the play.

This example is typical of the approach-avoidance play that occurred spontaneously in the American and Italian preschools I studied. The routine is composed of three phases: identification, approach, and avoidance (see Exhibit 7.5). In this case study, the identification phase begins when Beth sees and refers to Steven as a walking bucket. Steven had never placed a bucket on his head before. Beth just happens to see Steven and spontaneously identifies him as a walking bucket. In approach-avoidance play, children often are thrust into the role of a threatening agent in this way. Beth's playmates confirm her identification when they turn to look at Steven and Brian responds, "Yeah." Although behaviorally very simple (it involves a call for attention, shared attention, labeling, and confirmation), identification provides an interpretive frame for Steven's behavior that is in line with the shared routine of approach-avoidance. Once the identification is offered and ratified, the routine literally clicks into operation.

Exhibit 7.5   Phases in Approach-Avoidance Play

The approach phase begins with Brian's suggestion, "Let's get off." The three children then jump to the ground and move slowly toward Steven. Although Steven seems aware of the approach, he does not react until Mark and Brian push the bucket and attempt to lift it. Steven then lifts the bucket from his head, enabling himself to see and chase the other children. The three children screech loudly in mock fear and race back to the boat. Several things are important here. It is clear that the three children are in this together. The approach is communally orchestrated, moving from Brian's proposal, to the slow advance toward Steven, to the pushing of the bucket, and finally to the feigned fear in reaction to Steven's taking the bucket from his head. A building tension occurs in the approach phase, which the children create and share.

Steven's participation to this point has been minimal. He is thrust into the role of threatening agent by the others. He is not even aware of this assignment until they push the bucket and he removes it. Steven actually begins to replace the bucket on his head but then notices the other children running away from him toward the boat.

The children's fleeing initiates the avoidance phase. This phase can proceed only with the threatening agent's active participation. Steven flails his arms in a threatening manner as he pursues the other children back to the boat. He does not, however, move onto the boat, signaling the limits to his power as a threatening agent. The boat thus becomes a home base for the threatened children. Steven returns to the bucket and replaces it on his head. The threatening agent is now again disabled, and the first cycle of the routine is complete.

Before pursuing further discussion of the importance of approach-avoidance in peer culture, let's look at a more formalized version of the routine Italian preschoolers refer to as *la Strega* (the Witch).

LA STREGA

Cristina, Luisa, and Rosa (all about 4 years old) are playing in the outside yard of the preschool. Rosa points to Cristina and says, "She is the witch." Luisa then asks Cristina, "Will you be the witch?" and Cristina agrees. Cristina now closes her eyes, and Luisa and Rosa move closer and closer toward her, almost touching her. As they approach, Cristina repeats, "*Colore! Colore! Colore!*" (Color! Color! Color!). Luisa and Rosa move closer with each repetition, and then Cristina shouts, "*Viola!*" (Violet!). Luisa and Rosa run off screeching, and Cristina, with her arms and hands outstretched in a threatening manner, chases after them. Luisa and Rosa now run in different directions, and Cristina chases after Rosa. Just as la Strega is about to catch her, Rosa touches a violet object (a toy on the ground that serves as home base). Cristina now turns to look for Luisa and sees that she also has found a violet object (the dress of another child). Cristina now again closes her eyes and repeats, "Colore! Colore! Colore!" The other two girls begin a second approach, and the routine is repeated, this time with gray as the announced color. Rosa and Luisa again find the correctly colored objects before Cristina can capture them. At this point, Cristina suggests that Rosa be the witch, and she agrees. The routine is repeated three more times with the colors yellow, green, and blue. Each time the witch chases but does not capture the fleeing children.

The la Strega routine highlights some additional implications of approach-avoidance play for children's peer culture. First, it allows for the personification of the feared (but fascinating) figure la Strega in the person of a fellow playmate. The fact that la Strega is now embodied in the actions of a living person is tempered by the fact that the animator is, after all, just Cristina (another child). The feared figure is now part of immediate reality, but this personification is both created and controlled by the children in their joint production of the routine.

A second thing to note is that the structure of the routine leads to both a buildup and a release of tension and excitement. In the approach phase, the witch relinquishes power by closing her eyes as the children draw near to her. The tension builds, however, as the witch repeats the word *colore* because she decides what the color will be and when it will be announced. This announcement signals the beginning of the witch's attempt to capture the children and the avoidance phase of the routine. Although the fleeing children may seem to be afraid in the avoidance phase, the fear is clearly feigned because objects of any color can easily be found and touched. Thus, the witch seldom actually captures a fleeing child. In fact, threatened children often prolong the avoidance phase by overlooking many potential objects of the appropriate color before selecting one.

We see in these examples that the threatened children have a great deal of control. They initiate and recycle the routine through their approach, and they have a reliable means of escape (home base) in the avoidance phase. These cross-cultural data nicely demonstrate how children cope with real fears by incorporating them into peer routines that they produce and control (Corsaro, 1988).

Variants of approach-avoidance play have been reported in many cross-cultural studies of children's play (see Schwartzman, 1978; Sutton-Smith, 1976, for reviews). In Chapter 6 we talked about Gaingeen, a bogey described by Barlow (1985) in her study of the Murik of Papua New Guinea. In her analysis, Barlow described and analyzed a strikingly similar type of approach-avoidance play among children of the Murik in response to Gaingeen. Barlow noted that although Gaingeen is "initially terrifying and strange, early in children's experience the secret of the masked figure is revealed" and the children discover he is an adolescent boy wearing a costume (1985, p. 1). Barlow pointed out, however, that Gaingeen loses none of his fascination after this demystification. Rather, children incorporate Gaingeen into the routines of peer culture. For preadolescents, there is a pattern in which Gaingeen himself is approached and avoided when he appears.

For the younger children, Gaingeen is created by one or several children who make costumes (see Exhibit 7.6) and take on the role of Gaingeen while the other children approach and avoid.

Exhibit 7.6   Young Children Make Gaingeen Costumes

Source: Photo by David Lipset.

SUMMARY

The concepts of sharing and gaining control are important to children's production of and participation in initial peer cultures. In the preschool and early elementary school years, children immensely enjoy simply doing things together. However, generating shared meaning and coordinating play are challenging tasks for young children. Thus, children spend a good deal of time creating, protecting, and gaining access to basic activities and routines in their peer culture.

We saw, for example, that once preschool children initiate a play activity, they tend to protect their interactive space from the intrusions of other children. Although the protection of interactive space seems uncooperative to adults, it is seen as just the opposite for the children. Given their developing cognitive and communicative skills, children have to work hard to establish shared play. Once shared play is initiated, children want to keep sharing what they are already sharing, and they see others as a threat to the community they have established. What about the children seen as intruders? They wish to enter and to become part of shared play. Thus, over time, by confronting resistance to their access attempts, children acquire complex access strategies that allow them to enter and share in play. These access strategies are clear precursors to adult skills for becoming part of interaction in similar multiparty settings.

Once children establish shared play, they produce a wide range of behavioral routines. None is perhaps more symbolic of childhood cultures than sharing rituals: collective activities that involve patterned, repetitive, and cooperative expressions of the shared values and concerns of peer culture. In this chapter, we discussed one such activity, Italian children's production of the cantilena, a tonal device or singsong chant that the children regularly produce in peer discussions and debates. Children's production of sharing routines like the cantilena reflects a range of concerns in the peer culture. Most important, it provides young children with a sense of excitement and emotional security.

Children attempt to gain control over their lives in a number of ways. One way children gain a sense of agency or control is in their sociodramatic role-play. As we saw, children are empowered when they take on adult roles. They use the dramatic license of imaginary play to project to the future—a time when they will be in charge and in control of themselves and others. Another way of gaining a sense of control in peer culture is by directly resisting and challenging adult rules and authority. Children challenge adult rules in the family from the 1st year of life. Such activity becomes more widespread and sophisticated when children discover common interests in preschool settings. In these settings, children produce a wide set of practices in which they both mock and evade adult authority. In fact, many of these secondary adjustments to adult rules are more complex (structurally and interactively) than the rules themselves.

Children attempt to deal with confusions, concerns, fears, and conflicts in their daily lives by creating and participating in various routines of their peer cultures. Young children are frequently warned of dangers by parents and other adult caretakers and, more indirectly, through their exposure to movies and fairy tales. Children, in turn, frequently incorporate a wide range of fears and dangers (from threatening agents such as monsters and witches to dangerous events such as fires, floods, and becoming lost) into their peer cultures. We saw examples of such incorporation in preschool children's pretend fantasy play and their production of the approach-avoidance routine. Approach-avoidance play—a pretend play routine in which children identify, approach, and avoid a threatening agent or monster—is especially interesting because its production has been documented in several cultures, which indicates its possible universality. Overall, by engaging in shared fantasy play and by producing games, routines, and rituals, children more firmly grasp and deal with social representations of evil and the unknown in the security of their peer cultures.

We turn now to Chapter 8, wherein we consider conflict and differentiation in children's peer cultures.

8

Conflict and Differentiation in the Initial Peer Culture

I n Chapter 7, we focused primarily on communal aspects of children's peer cultures. We saw that children do, at times, actively oppose adult control but that such conflict often increases the cohesion of and commitment to group identity. Peer cultures are not always the picture of peace, joy, and community spirit, however. Young children argue, fight, push, kick, and sometimes even bite. Although physical aggression is rare, verbal conflicts and disputes are common features of children's cultures. In this chapter we will examine disputes, conflict, and social differentiation in early childhood peer culture.

Conflict and Peer Relations

Recent studies of children's friendships have documented what at first glance seems to be a contradictory fact: conflicts frequently emerge in friendship relations. This finding seems surprising, noted Carolyn Shantz (1987), because much of the work on conflict by developmental psychologists does not carefully distinguish social conflict from individual acts of aggression and thus tends to focus on individual (rather than interpersonal and cultural) features of conflict. When we look closely at conflict in children's peer interaction, most especially verbal debates and arguments, we find that such conflict often serves to strengthen interpersonal

Conflict = creates peer cultures [handwritten]

— Digressing from subject to subject. Deviate [handwritten, left margin]

alliances and to organize social groups (Goodwin, 1990; Kyratzis, 2004; but see Stein & Albro, 2001, for a discussion of the relation between argumentative skills, compromise, and constructive social relations). In my research in preschools in the United States and Italy, I have found that children's social relations and friendships are embodied in the everyday discursive practices—that is, the talk that goes on—in the peer cultures and in the larger communities. Let's look at talk, disputes, and friendship in two Italian preschools, in an American Head Start program, and in an American upper-middle-class private preschool.

Discussion, Debate, and Peace in Italian Preschools

Discussion and Debate Among Italian Preschool Children. Italian preschool children, much like adults in their communities, frequently engage in highly stylized and dramatic discussions and debates. As we noted in Chapter 7, *discussione* is a central element of Italian everyday life. Having been exposed to and included in discussione by parents, teachers, and other adults in their community, preschool children generate and value this activity in their peer cultures.

In Chapter 7 we looked at an example of Italian children in a Bologna preschool using the *cantilena* and how the cantilena energized and added dramatic flair to their debates. Let's return to that example and pick up the debate at its beginning.

BAD WOLVES DO NOT EXIST

A group of kids (Sara, Franco, Luigi, Giovanna, and Nino, all about 5 years old) are sitting around a table drawing. It is *disegno libero* (free drawing) time, so the kids can draw whatever they like (as opposed to drawing for a school project). Franco draws a picture of what he says is an "extraterrestrial tree." Sara immediately shakes her head and says, "They don't exist." Franco insists that they do. A little later Franco draws what he says is a werewolf or bad wolf. Sara again challenges Franco, claiming, "Wolves do not exist."

"Yes, wolves exist," says Giovanna.

"They don't exist," counters Sara, "only their bones."

"It's not true," protests Franco. "Wolves do exist!"

"Yes," agrees Luigi, supporting Franco.

"But they do not exist," Sara insists, "only in the mountains."

At this point a boy, Paolo, who was painting at another table, comes over and, waving his paintbrush, says, "It's true. They exist!"

Sara waves Paolo away with her hand, saying, "You're not in this."

Franco, now visibly upset, pokes his finger at Sara's chest and says, "You're not in this because—"

Sara pokes back and interrupts Franco, "You—"

"You say that I'm not in this." Franco interrupts right back as he pushes Sara's hand away. "Wolves exist!"

"No, it's not true," denies Sara.

Paolo, not put off by Sara, leans forward between her and Franco and says, "Not even ghosts."

"It's true," says Franco.

"The ghosts—" starts Luigi.

"Yah!" Franco interrupts. "They don't exist."

"No, No. Those no," Sara agrees.

"Yes," says Franco, now changing his mind probably to spite Sara. "Yes, they exist. Ghosts, however, exist—"

"They're in the woods," Nino interrupts.

"Eh, it's not true," says Franco. "Ghost exist under the sea in houses—"

"In—in abandoned houses," says Paolo, finishing Franco's sentence.

"It's true," says Franco, "underwater houses."

Source: Adapted from Corsaro (2003, pp. 185–186).

In this sequence, several children debate the existence of supernatural phenomena (bad wolves or werewolves and ghosts), which are of much interest to young children. The debate begins with Sara's claim that wolves do not exist. Giovanna challenges Sara, claiming that wolves do indeed exist. Sara, then, gives in a bit by saying that only their bones exist. At this point, several other children join the dispute, including Paolo, who was not originally involved in the main activity. Paolo comes over, paintbrush in hand, to stand next to Sara and argue, "It's true. They exist!" Third-party entry of this type is interesting because although it was common among the Italian children, it never occurred in peer disputes I observed in American schools. In this instance, Sara tries to exclude Paolo ("You're not in this"), but Franco immediately challenges her action by throwing the same phrase back at her. In this way, Franco is implicitly challenging Sara's attempt to be the boss, which is a violation of a basic rule in Italian children's peer cultures: everyone has a right to be a part of any discussion. After Sara's attempted rebuttal, Franco says in essence, who are you to say I'm (or anyone is) not in this, and then he goes on to argue again that wolves do exist.

Paolo, now a full participant, adds a new element by arguing that ghosts do not exist. Franco first agrees with this claim but then changes his mind, probably to keep his dispute with Sara going. At this point there is a general discussion, with different children adding (and often arguing about) new information regarding where ghosts live if they do exist (in the woods, in abandoned houses, and finally in abandoned houses under the sea). As we saw earlier in Chapter 7, the children take turns continuing the debate in the singsong cadence of the cantilena.

Discussione is highly valued in Italian children's peer cultures for several reasons. First, it provides an arena for participation in and sharing of peer culture. The children debate things that are important to them (friendship, play activities, ghosts, werewolves, and so on) and in the process develop a shared sense of control over their social world. Second, discussione is a highly communal activity. It has a participant structure that has relatively easy entry requirements (for example, simple agreements, denials, or repetition), but it also has the attraction of multiple opportunities for embellishment and individual creativity (for example, Paolo's introduction of ghosts). Because of its communal nature, discussione is not restricted to the original participants, and third-party entry is common. In fact, Sara's attempt to exclude Paolo was inappropriate and was responded to as such by Franco. Third, discussione often accompanies and, at times, even takes over teacher-directed activities such as drawing, playing with materials, and eating at snack time and lunchtime. In this way, the initiation and continuation of a discussion of their choosing gives the children a sense of power and control over their environment and caretakers. This aspect of the routine is especially powerful and satisfying for the Italian children because the general activity of discussione is so highly valued in adult culture (Pontecorvo, Fasulo, & Sterponi, 2001; Pontecorvo & Sterponi, 2002).

Conflict Resolution and Achieving Peace in Italian Preschools. Sociologist M. P. Baumgartner (1992) has argued that children seldom negotiate compromises in their conflicts because they have ceded control of their disputes to adults, who have greater power and authority. Children's conflicts and disputes across cultural and subcultural groups vary considerably, however, and in groups in which kids are given more opportunity to settle their own conflicts, complex negotiated settlements occur. Such was the case in Italian preschools where teachers were slow to intervene in children's disputes. In my research in a preschool in Modena, the kids often worked hard to bring settlements or peace to their disputes (Corsaro, 2003; Corsaro & Molinari, 2005).

In one example I was brought into the dispute, but strictly because of my size and not for my perceived intelligence or negotiation skills. In this dispute, Mariana and Sandra are playing with dolls and Sandra insists that one of the dolls (an infant) with little hair must be a boy because it has short hair. Mariana disagrees and says that babies, both boys and girls, often have short hair. Other children playing nearby join the discussion, some siding with Mariana, some with Sandra. Mariana then points to the shelf where the children's personal books (which document the children's lives and time in the preschool) are stored. She asks me to reach up to get her book down because she can't reach it. I do so, and Mariana says, "*Grazie*, Bill," as I hand her the book. She then turns to a page with a picture of her when she was about 1 year old. (Each child's book has a baby picture.) Sandra and several others gather round to look at the picture. We all see that Mariana had little hair in her baby picture. "See," Mariana says to Sandra, "This is me, and I had short hair then." Sandra now says, "*Hai ragione*" (You're right), and the issue is settled.

The example shows how the children take an element of their collective experience in the school culture—the existence of the personal books that they have created about their experiences during the 3 years that they have been in the school—and use it to address a dispute in the peer culture. In doing so, they feel empowered to solve their own problems without adult intervention or assistance.

Here's a final example from the Modena preschool. Several children are sitting around a table with workbooks, which the teachers encourage the children to work on at their own pace to develop their literacy skills. Luciano makes a negative remark about the quality of Viviana's drawing while she works in her workbook. Viviana becomes upset, and the dispute escalates, with Viviana telling Luciano to mind his own business and commenting that his drawings are not perfect. The two go back and forth about this, and several other kids try to appease them. None of the kids calls a teacher to help, however. The teachers overhear the dispute but do not intervene. At one point, having grown weary of the arguing, another girl at the table, Michela, says, "*Adesso basta. Pace!*" (Now enough. Peace!). Viviana and Luciano agree to end their argument and a little later are laughing and joking. They even produce a rhyme: *"Pace, pace, carote, patate!"* (Peace, peace, carrots, potatoes; see Corsaro, 2003, pp. 190–191).

Oppositional Talk in a Head Start Center

Head Start is a federally sponsored compensatory preschool education program for economically disadvantaged children in the United States. The program emphasizes the development of cognitive and social skills. Parents must meet income eligibility criteria to enroll their children in this free program. The center I observed in a large Midwestern city reflected the population of its inner-city location in that the overwhelming majority of the children, teachers, and employees were African Americans.

The Head Start children constructed social identities, cultivated friendships, and both maintained and transformed the social order of the peer culture through opposition and confrontation. Peer interaction and play routines often contained oppositional talk. This is playful teasing and confrontational talk that some African American children frequently use to construct social identities, cultivate friendships, and both maintain and transform the social order of their peer cultures. "Why you following me like that for?" and "What you think you're doing, boy?" are examples of oppositional talk. Consider the following exchange, which took place while two girls were playing in the sandbox.

Pam: Hey, girl, don't use that little ol' thing [scoop]; use this big one.

Brenda: [Takes the bigger scoop] OK.

Brenda: What's a matter with you, girl; that's too much sugar in that cake!

Pam: No, it ain't.

Brenda: I said it is, girl.

The children seldom reacted negatively to oppositional talk of this type or ran to complain to the teachers. In fact, oppositional talk and teasing were valued (much like the Italian children's discussione) as part of the verbal enrichment of everyday play. Particularly clever oppositions or retorts were often marked as such with appreciative laughter and comments like "good one" or "you sure told her" by the audience and, at times, by the target child. Overall, the Head Start children explored, tested out, and developed friendship skills and knowledge in the general frame of oppositional talk and teasing (see Corsaro, 1994).

In addition to producing stylized oppositional talk in brief exchanges, the African American kids also engaged in extended group debates. Like the debates of the Italian kids we discussed earlier, these debates often grew out of one or more kids' opposing the stated beliefs or opinions of another kid.

Although the source of these group debates was often related to competitive relations among the African American children, the debates revealed much about their knowledge of the world and served as arenas for displaying self and building group solidarity.

In the Head Start center I observed, several kids (Roger, Jerome, Daren, Andre, Ryan, Alysha, and Zena) were at the same table eating lunch one day. I was sitting with them, and the teacher was sitting nearby at the serving table. The rest of the class was having lunch at two nearby tables. Roger and Jerome are good friends and value competitive talk about their knowledge, skills, and possessions.

On this particular day, the two boys are debating about programs they watch on television. Jerome claims he has watched a particular show, but Roger denies the show is on television. He challenges Jerome to name the station on which the show appeared, and the following discussion emerges.

"It comes on cable," says Jerome.

"We got cable," declares Roger.

"We got cable too. For real," Zena says.

"We do too," says Ryan.

"We do too," adds Darren.

competitive?

The mention of cable moves the competitive talk between Roger and Jerome to a group discussion. Several children (Zena, Ryan, and Darren) now enter the talk, and all note that they have cable. Zena's entry into the discussion is especially interesting because she says, "We got cable too. For real." Zena is from a very poor family, so poor in fact that she, her mother, and her sisters were living in a homeless shelter. However, the shelter had a hookup to cable television, which is probably why Zena thought it necessary to add "for real" to her claim. Here we see how the children's personal experiences become part of group debates. The discussion now continues with a debate about who has the biggest cable.

"I got the biggest cable. I got the biggest cable," claims Roger.

"I thought all cable was the same," says the teacher.

"So do I," I say, laughing.

"They ain't either," says Jerome. He then puts one of his hands under the table and the other up above his head and says, "My cable's this big!"

"Un-uh," denies Zena.

"My cable's 'bout this big," says Roger, as he holds his hands about 2 feet apart.

"Jesus is bigger than everybody," Alysha says, very softly.

"My—my cable's like this big," says Darren, holding his hand about 2 feet above the table.

"Marvin's head is bigger than anybody's," says Zena, teasing a boy at another table.

"I'm bigger than Jesus," says Jerome, responding to Alysha.

"Nah-uh," says Alysha. "Jesus is bigger than everybody!"

"My cousin's bigger than Jesus. My cousin is that big," says Jerome, as he holds his hands far apart.

"But he don't do—this," says Alysha, as she reaches her hand up as far as she can from the table. "He's [Jesus is] this big."

"My cousin's this big," says Jerome, as he raises his hand higher than Alysha's.

"Alysha," says the teacher, "get through so you drink your milk today."

"He's this big," says Andre, speaking for the first time. He holds his hand up higher than Jerome did.

"Who? Who?" asks Jerome.

"Jesus," Andre answers.

The talk about cable television leads Roger to claim that he has the "biggest cable," prompting the teacher and me to remark that cables are all the same size. However, Jerome denies our adult contention, and the talk about the size of cable continues, with the kids in firm control of their debate. After Jerome and Roger say and demonstrate with their hands how big their cable is, Alysha speaks for the first time. She builds on the competitive talk about cable size to argue that "Jesus is bigger than everybody."

Alysha comes from a very poor family, and they do not have cable television. However, Alysha's family is very religious, and they attend religious services several times a week. So, when the discussion came up about what is the biggest, Alysha, relying on her religious training, said softly but firmly, "Jesus is bigger than everybody."

Several other children were talking at the same time Alysha made her claim. Darren, responding to Jerome and Roger, moved his hand above the table and said his cable "is like this big." Zena tried to use the talk about things being big to tease Marvin, who was eating at the next table, saying that his "head is bigger than anybody's." This type of banter across tables was frequent during lunch, but Marvin ignored Zena and the playful teasing stopped there. At this point, things quieted down and Jerome challenged Alysha, saying "I'm bigger than Jesus." This challenge confirmed Alysha's entry into the debate, and Alysha immediately repeated her earlier assertion that Jesus is bigger than everybody.

Alysha's claim was related to her religious beliefs that Jesus is all knowing and all powerful. At this point, the mainly jocular discussion about the size of cable became more serious. However, Jerome's assertion that his cousin is bigger than Jesus was clearly presented in a nonserious way. Alysha stayed in the more serious vein and was wisely doubtful about Jerome's cousin, arguing that the cousin could not reach up as high as Jesus is tall.

The teacher then demanded that Alysha make progress with her lunch and thus drew her away from the discussion. However, Andre, speaking for the first time, took up Alysha's position, asserting that Jesus is indeed the biggest. The discussion ended soon thereafter, when the teacher told the children to begin to clean up their places and get ready to brush their teeth (see Corsaro, 1994, 2003).

The African American children's oppositional style in peer interactions often seems aggressive to middle-class White Americans. In fact, anthropologists, folklorists, and linguists have contrasted the oppositional style of African American speech with communicative practices of most European Americans, who tend to minimize antagonism and direct confrontation (Abrahams, 1975; Goodwin, 1990; Heath, 1983, 1990). Among African Americans, opposition and conflict, according to Abrahams, "tend to be viewed as constant contrarieties, antagonisms that cannot be eliminated and in fact may be used to effect a larger sense of cultural affirmation of community through a dramatization of opposing forces" (1975, p. 63).

The oppositions and challenges among the Head Start children were normally reacted to in kind, and the overall tenor of exchanges was one of playful banter. This verbal dueling sent dual messages that (a) a particular child could hold his or her own ground and (b) participation in oppositional talk signified allegiance to the values and concerns of the peer culture. Ultimately what emerged among the often-vying voices of the Head Start children were assertive and competitive friendship relationships that led to a mutual respect and group solidarity.

Conflict and Friendship in an American Upper-Middle-Class Preschool

In a private upper-middle-class preschool that I studied, emphasis was on individual expression and recognition of the uniqueness and rights of others. The teachers' interactions and style of discourse reflected a great deal of patience and respect for the children's individual needs. Although the teachers encouraged children to attempt to solve their own problems and disputes through talk and reflection, they also were open and comforting to children who came to them with complaints about the behavior of peers. The teachers' language style and suggestions for how to handle conflict affected the nature of peer and friendship relations in the preschool.

I observed a classroom of younger children (3-and-a-half- to 4-year-olds) and another of older children (4-and-a-half- to 5-year-olds) in the private preschool. The younger children used the word *friend* to attempt to gain access to play, to protect shared activities from intruders, to build solidarity and mutual trust in the playgroup, and to attempt to control the activity of playmates. Conflict frequently developed regarding the nature of play. In such instances, the children often used friendship in attempts to get their way. Consider the following example: Helen, Eric, and several other children are playing with toy dinosaurs in a sandbox. Eric hops his dinosaur close to Helen's and then flips it around so that its tail hits against Helen's toy. "Stop that!" says Helen. Eric repeats the action, and Helen says, "I won't be your buddy!" Eric says, "OK," and begins to bury his dinosaur in the sand.

The "denial of friendship" strategy that Helen uses here was often effective at this preschool. The children took such threats very seriously, often giving in immediately or becoming upset and going to a teacher for comfort. The use of the strategy was, however, a double-edged sword. Children on the receiving end in one instance could quickly turn things around and issue threats of their own in the next instance.

In the classroom of older children, several overlapping small groups or cliques of close friends developed over the course of the school term. There were also boys and girls who played with a number of peers but who did not belong to any particular friendship group. The interaction in the friendship groups was similar to the social relations of close friendships described in Thomas Rizzo's (1989) study of middle-class American first-grade children. Rizzo found that when the first graders noticed shortcomings or problems in their friends' behavior, they insisted that their friends make the necessary changes to set things right. This insistence often led to disagreements and disputes.

In the friendship groups of the older children I observed, such disputes were intense and, at times, persisted over the course of an entire day or even several days. In one instance a girl, Shirley, became very upset when her best friend, Megan, refused to allow her to enter a game Megan was playing with two other girls in their friendship group (Mary and Veronica). Mary and Veronica were pretending to be pet ponies under the direction of their owner, Megan. After Megan said Shirley could not play, Shirley began to cry and threatened Megan, saying they would not be "best buddies" anymore. She also said Megan would not be invited to her birthday party. Megan would not give in, however, so Shirley went off to complain to a teacher. The teacher suggested that Shirley "talk it over" with Megan or play with someone else. Shirley returned to plead her case, but to no avail. In the end, the two girls got into a shoving match, and both began to cry. At that point, we all went back inside the school, and a teacher sat the two girls down and talked to them about the problem. After the talk, Megan and Shirley sat alone, still sobbing, in their cubbies until lunchtime. Later in the day, after lunch and naptime, however, I saw the two girls sitting together and holding hands while watching a circus video.

In his work with first-grade children, Rizzo described numerous friendship disputes of this type. He argued that such disputes not only helped the children obtain a better understanding of what they could expect from each other as friends but also brought about intrapersonal reflection, resulting in the children's development of unique insight into their own actions and roles as friends.

The Contextual Nature of Conflict and Community

Overall, the studies discussed above capture the complex relationship of conflict and friendship in peer cultures. We see that peer relations and friendships are, in many ways, a reflection of the values and practices of the local and more general communities and cultures in which they emerge (see Cromdal, 2004; Kyratzis, 2004; Poveda, 2001, for discussions of comparative studies of children's conflicts). Comparative analysis demonstrates the importance of viewing friendship as a collective and cultural process. In this view, culture is not simply a force or variable that affects how children come to be or have friends. Rather, friendship processes are seen as deeply embedded in children's collective, interpretive reproduction of their cultures.

Social Differentiation in Initial Peer Cultures

Although social participation and friendship are central processes in the peer cultures of young children, differentiation in peer relations begins in early childhood and increases dramatically as children move into preadolescence. Social differentiation in young children's peer cultures is related primarily to gender and status. We shall discuss each in turn.

Gender Differentiation

The first sign of social differentiation in young children's peer relations is increasing gender separation, with children as young as age 3 showing preference for play with other children of the same sex (Maccoby, 1999). Gender separation or segregation becomes so dramatic in elementary school that "it is meaningful to speak of separate girls' and boys' worlds" (Thorne, 1986, p. 167). In one of the first ethnographies of preschool children, anthropologist Sigrid Berentzen (1984) observed peer interaction and culture among 5- to 7-year-old children in a Norwegian preschool in 1967. Berentzen found that the children constructed their peer cultures primarily around gender contrast. Both boys and girls followed the self-imposed rule that "girls/boys don't play with boys/girls," with few exceptions (p. 158). Girls and boys also organized their activities around different concerns. The boys valued competition and toughness, whereas the girls were concerned mostly with affiliation or establishing best friends.

Later studies in American, British, and Australian preschools and elementary schools, as well as on children's sports teams, reported similar findings (R. Best, 1983; Cahill, 1986; Davies, 1989; K. Martin, 1998; Messner, 2000; Paley, 1984; Thorne, 1993; Walkerdine, 1990). Vivian Paley's (1984)

Boys and Girls: Superheroes in the Doll Corner, which is based on observations in the author's kindergarten classroom, nicely captures the play themes of boys and girls. As boys in the guise of Darth Vader and Luke Skywalker lay claim on the block area and roam the outside play yard, girls gather in the doll corner to devise "dramatic plots that eliminate boys and bring in more sisters and princesses" (p. xi). When the boys come around the dollhouse to put out a fire, capture robbers, or have some dinner (even superheroes eat!), the girls resist this intrusion in their space. The boys are just as protective of their play, scoffing at the girls' attempts to build castles, houses, or zoos in the block area. Bothered by such conflicts and the gender polarity it symbolizes, Paley at first encouraged compromise, primarily through attempts at the partial domestication of the boys to make them more acceptable to the girls. In the end, however, Paley decided that indeed the robbers should stay out of the dollhouse, not because boys behave badly but because the story lines of the fantasy play of the boys and girls do not mesh. As a reflective teacher, she learned from the children that the "integrity of fantasy must be preserved" (p. 90).

In her work, Karin Martin (1998) also looked at how teachers affected the construction of gender in preschools. Unlike Paley's attempt to try to change difference in gender play and concepts, Martin discovered a "hidden curriculum" in the schools she studied that controlled children's bodily practices in line with gender differences and stereotypes. For example, the teachers were more likely to permit boys more relaxed as opposed to formal play compared to girls, and teachers were more likely to give girls rather than boys specific instructions about how to play and how to use their bodies (boys were normally told to stop doing something negative and rarely received instructions about alternative behaviors, whereas girls were told to sit up straight and speak softly). Martin's study is important because it focuses on how children use and are told to use their bodies, which is often overlooked in theories and research on the construction of gender and the nature of childhood more generally (also see Simpson, 2000).

Is gender differentiation among young children always this dramatic? Is it universal? As Thorne (1993) has pointed out, much of the work has a tendency to exaggerate gender differences and ignore similarities. Boys and girls do play and work together in educational settings, especially in more structured and group projects. Also, although instances of boys and girls playing together in free play are rare, they do occur and merit careful analysis. Features of group composition and setting are important. In a review of cross-cultural studies of children's worlds, Whiting and

Edwards found strong support for the emergence of gender segregation at about age 6, but they noted that segregation "seems to be a feature of same-age, not the mixed-age, social interaction" (1988, p. 80).

Recent comparative research shows that children of various cultures differ in their construction of gender concepts and behaviors. Goodwin (1990, 2003) found that African American boys and girls often engaged in playful, cross-sex debates and teasing when in each other's presence. Kyratzis and Guo (2001) found cross-cultural differences in the gendered speech patterns of preschoolers in the United States and China. They found that among American children, boys tend to be more assertive than girls in same-sex interactions, but in China girls are more assertive with one another than boys are. Context is important in determining who dominates cross-sex interaction, however. Chinese boys take the lead in discussions regarding work, but Chinese girls dominate when relationships and courtship are the themes. Both Chinese girls and American boys freely used bold, directive speech when they disagreed with their classmates, whereas American girls used mitigated, "double-voice" discourse (for example, the use of *please*, requests instead of commands, and the use of conditional tense) during disputes (see Sheldon, 1997).

In my research in the United States and Italy, I have found, in line with the general findings previously noted, much more gender segregation among older children (5- to 6-year-olds) as compared to younger children (3- to 5-year-olds). However, gender segregation and different activity preferences by gender were greater for American upper-middle-class children than for African American or Italian children, regardless of age. These findings may be related to the communal orientation and age composition of the programs. In line with the communal orientation of Italian preschools, the curricula of the preschools I studied often involved small groups of four or five children (mixed by age and gender) working on different aspects of elaborate group projects that lasted for several weeks (see Corsaro & Emiliani, 1992; Edwards, Gandini, & Forman, 1993, for a discussion of the communal orientation). There was also a communal orientation in the Head Start center, and the African American girls were, on the whole, more assertive and independent in their relationships with each other and with boys than were the upper-middle-class White girls I studied.

The differences regarding gender behavior and concepts in the different preschools I studied were complex and fascinating (Aydt & Corsaro, 2003). In the American preschools there was a high degree of gender difference in playgroups once the children reached the age of 5. However, the kids often spoke and joked about gender in same- and mixed-sex groups during structured play activities, meals, and snacks. When the children spoke about gender, they often did so in the context of discussions about adult relationships such as marriage. Indeed, they seemed fascinated by the idea of marriage and related topics such as sex and babies. Consider the following example of three girls around 5 years old.

> Ruth, Mary, and Anita are sitting at a table with me. While working on her portfolio, Ruth says, "Oh, I remember this [a writing page]. I really loved doing this!" Anita says, "Well, if you love it so much, why don't you marry it?" All of the children laugh at this joke. Anita says she saw that on a commercial. Mary agrees, saying it was a commercial for Cap'n Crunch. There is more talk about marrying it, and Ruth says, "Why don't you kiss it and have babies with it?" (Aydt & Corsaro, 2003, p. 1315)

In this episode, the kids display knowledge of how love, marriage, and sex are connected, and they are eager to talk about such matters. Furthermore, at least some of this knowledge has been taken from the media, in this case a commercial for a popular children's cereal. Ruth further expands the initial joke by using the other girls' familiarity with the connection among marriage, kissing, and babies to amuse her playmates. Joking and teasing about getting married and having babies were a frequent theme in this preschool. Once, at morning snack time, a girl, Veronica, said that she and Martin were going to get married. Martin agreed and said they were going to be doctors. "And live in New York," added Veronica. "Are you going to kiss and do sex?" asked Mark.

The others laughed at this, and then meeting time was announced.

Although the children enjoy joking about subjects they find titillating, it becomes apparent from this particular discussion that marriage is considered important, if not inevitable, by the kids. In another episode at snack time, Sean says he will not get married when he grows up. "You have to," says Mark, "or you will live alone and be lonely!" Mark was surprised to hear Sean dispute the idea that people must marry when they become adults, and he pointed out the problems Sean would have with a solitary life. Although this exchange is brief, such discussions among peers are important because they represent peer-culture knowledge about what constitutes proper relations between men and women. The marriage talk is significant in that it provides a script for what a close relationship between a male and female entails. This script changes the way kids look at their opposite-sex peers, and it encourages kids to think about relationships between people of the opposite sex as fundamentally different than relationships between people of the same sex. Because there is no well-defined model of what a close platonic friendship between a boy and a girl might look like, cross-sex relationships are likely to be coded by the children as romantic and emotionally charged. Consider the following example of some 5-year-olds in an American preschool.

> Anita, Ruth, and Sarah are chasing Sean and David who come over to a big rock where I am sitting and claim it as home base. Once when Anita and Sarah chase Sean and David they start to pull up their shirts and say, "You want to see my bra?" Anita says, "I have a bra for my belly button" and holds up her shirt to show her belly button. (Aydt & Corsaro, 2003, p. 1316)

Although the girls are far too young to actually have breasts, they are aware that women develop breasts and wear bras. Furthermore, they seem to grasp that displaying breasts intimidates the boys in some way, and they use this knowledge to enhance their run-and-chase play.

In my research at a Head Start center, I found that there was a good bit of gender separation among the predominately African American kids, but there was more cross-gender play than in the private middle- and upper-middle-class preschools I studied. Both cross- and same-sex play themes at the Head Start center were interesting because of their variety and their differences from gender stereotypes. The boys were not hesitant to engage in family role-play either with girls or on their own. It was not unusual for groups of four or five boys to enter the family play area, take out dishes, set the table, and pretend to prepare and eat meals. They also enjoyed sweeping the floor, getting the house in order, and making phone calls (see Corsaro, 2003).

The girls also liked family role-play and other activities such as arts and crafts that the boys seldom engaged in without prodding from the teachers. However, the girls relished competing with and challenging the boys. Such competition often occurred in the gym. One day, after an organized game in which the teachers would throw a large red ball in a random order to help build the kids' motor skills, several ran to a climbing house, and I followed behind them. Once in the house, one of the girls said, "This is the girls' clubhouse!" They chased out two boys who resisted at first but then ran off. Eventually seven girls occupied their clubhouse. It was clear that there was a history to this competition over the clubhouse, and the girls clearly relished running the boys off.

The assertiveness of the girls in the Head Start program was also apparent in particular personal interactions and relationships. For example, several of the girls in the class actively teased boys and other girls. One girl, Delia, frequently stood up to boys and delighted in taking them on in verbal disputes.

"Gender — what is expected to be of commonality" "Roles"

One day Delia asked to print her name in my notebook when she saw me taking notes in jail (where I had been locked up by several boys playing police). I handed her the notebook and pen, but as she started to print her name Dominic came over and said, "Give me that notebook." Delia told him, "Get out of my face while I write this name!"

"You're talking to the police," I reminded Delia.

Delia then said, "Get out of my face, police!" She finished printing her name, handed me back the notebook, and walked off.

Delia's assertiveness could also be seen in her relationship with Ramone, who had a crush on her. He told several of the other children and me that Delia was his girlfriend and that he visited her house. Delia denied both claims. Still, Ramone did not give up and continued to pursue her attention.

One day Delia and Alysha were putting together a large puzzle of a school bus on the floor near the circle area. They worked together to fit the pieces properly. When they were about to finish the puzzle, Ramone came over and asked to play. Delia said, "You play with girls, then you are a tomgirl!" Ramone took this as a rejection and moved away briefly but then came back and picked up a piece of the puzzle. Delia took it away and said that when she plays with boys she is called a tomboy, so if Ramone plays with them he is a tomgirl. She also said that they did not want Ramone to play anyway, and Alysha agreed. Ramone then gave up and moved to another part of the classroom.

What is fascinating about this exchange is Delia's invention of the term *tomgirl* to discourage Ramone from playing with the girls. Not only is this term an interesting adaptation of the *tomboy* label, but it also changes the nature of the rejection from "Don't play with me" to "Don't play with girls." Furthermore, when Delia explains the novel term *tomgirl* she reveals that she herself has been teased for playing with boys, and she now enjoys turning the tables on Ramone. Overall, from these examples, we see the complexity of the Head Start children's construction and use of gender in their peer play (Corsaro, 2003).

Earlier we discussed how the communal nature of Italian preschools encouraged cross-gender play. Another factor that contributed to the lack of differentiation by gender in the peer culture was the popularity of certain play routines. Although the Italian kids participated in traditional gender-typed activities, such as physical play and games (riding bikes, superhero play, and especially soccer) for boys and playing with dolls for girls, another typical gender-typed activity, dramatic role-play, had a more complex pattern. Although mainly girls engaged in domestic role-play, both girls and boys often participated in types of role-play that blurred and stretched gender stereotypes.

The most common was animal family role-play wherein both boys and girls pretended to be wild dogs, lions, or tigers. In most cases, the mother of this pack of wild animals was a girl who was very rough in disciplining her charges (both girls and boys) who went around growling and scratching each other and other children in the school (see Evaldsson & Corsaro, 1998).

In addition to animal role-play, the Italian children often re-created variety or game show television programs, which are very popular in Italy. One program that was very popular at the time of my research in a preschool in Modena had two central characters, a male host and a female gypsy fortune-teller, along with two couples (usually married) who competed for prize money. The show also featured elaborate sets and singers and dancers in colorful costumes. In their play, the kids focused primarily on a part of the game show in which each of the two couples selected a card from a set of seven laid out by the gypsy. The object was to correctly answer questions related to the various cards and win money while avoiding the *Luna Nera* (Black Moon) card; if this card was selected, the couple was eliminated from the contest and lost any money previously won. All of this occurred as the gypsy flipped the cards with suspenseful flair to a catchy musical refrain.

The show was popular among all the kids at the school, but one boy, Dario, especially liked it. He frequently organized other boys and girls to play the game using a regular deck of cards with the ace of spades serving as the Luna Nera. He also sometimes brought a toy version of the television game show from home. Perhaps because the gypsy was the central character, both girls and boys wanted to repeat the game several times with each having a turn in this glamorous and desired role. Thus, the kids shared the fun of reproducing the show in mixed-gender play, without having the girls or boys solely embodying its obvious gender-typed features (a boy as the host and a girl as the gypsy; see Corsaro, 2003).

What do these diverse findings on gender segregation and integration suggest regarding the formation of gender identity among young children? Traditional developmental theories—with their emphasis on biological factors, reinforcement contingencies, or stages of cognitive development—fall short in that they all focus on gender development as a process of individual change or adjustment to societal roles. The focus is on outcomes or developmental paths rather than on children's active construction and involvement in their social worlds. In the past 20 years or so, a number of theorists have linked gender directly to social action and collective practices (Connell, 1987; Davies, 1989; Thorne, 1993; Walkerdine, 1986).

Perhaps the best example of this general theoretical approach as applied to preschool children and gender can be seen in the work of Bronwyn Davies (1989; also see Fernie, Davies, Kantor, & McMurray, 1993). Her work stresses children's active role in their construction of gender identities and is a clear break from traditional functionalist notions of socialization and gender. Davies argued that masculinity and femininity are not inherent properties of individuals but rather structural properties of society. Social actors are constrained but not determined by these properties. Through our use of discursive practices (how we speak and act), we contribute to reproduction and change in society. Therefore, "as children learn the discursive practices of their society, they learn to position themselves correctly as male or female, since that is what is required of them to have a recognizable identity within the existing social order" (Davies, 1989, p. 13). The rigidity of such positioning, however, can often be problematic and constraining, and children soon realize that minor refinements and even genuinely different positionings are possible and desirable.

Davies and her colleagues provided examples that demonstrate the creativity and flexibility of preschool children "in their reinvention and maintenance of the rigid structure" of traditional gender roles (Fernie et al., 1993, p. 103). They presented the positioning strategies of a young girl, Lisa, as an example of the breaking of nontraditional gender frames. Over the course of the year, Lisa aligned herself with a high-status, core group of five boys in the preschool, boys who frequently engaged in superhero role-play. In both peer play and teacher-directed activity, Lisa embraced the male superhero role of Batman rather than the female alternative, Batgirl. Furthermore, it was clear that Lisa did not take the role just to gain entry to the boys' core group; she assumed the role even when the boys were not present. In one instance, Lisa persuaded one of the youngest girls in the class to come to her Batman house, wear a cape, and hold a stick for a gun. Happy with her new recruit, Lisa put her hands on her hips and announced, "We're bad. Stay out. This is our house" (Fernie et al., 1993, p. 102).

In this and the earlier examples we discussed from my work in the United States and Italy, we see children resisting dichotomized gender roles and displaying an openness to multiple positionings or ways of being male or female. These examples also suggest some possibilities of breaking down strict gender segregation among preschool children in free-play activities. As Davies noted, encouraging "home corner behavior" among boys and more "macho"-type play among girls is seldom successful (1989, p. 133). Children are confused by the purpose of such pressures and see them as arbitrarily restrictive of their play. Instead, Davies recommended encouraging a wide range of positionings in play. As a result, children are free to develop new positionings and to "find ways of thinking about and describing their own and other's behavior independently of what we currently think of as 'masculine' and 'feminine'" (pp. 133–134).

Race and Race Differentiation

Race is a much more complex construct than gender because racial and ethnic categories are not as clear-cut. Many researchers assume that children have temporary or native views about race and ethnicity until at least age 7 or 8, and thus they argue that racial issues are not relevant to the peer cultures of young children (Sacks, 2001; Tynes, 2001). Using an ethnographic approach as opposed to more traditional experimental or clinical interview methods, Holmes (1995) discovered that children construct race in their own language and interactions. She found that skin color is a dominant feature in how kindergartners see themselves. In particular, she found that "White" is the default race, even among children, as White children rarely mention skin color whereas Black children clearly stress their black skin.

Based on their interpretive research on preschool children aged 3 to 5, Van Ausdale and Feagin (2001) found that even very young children use race and ethnicity as identifying and stratifying markers and that they are salient features of children's cultures. The children they observed used racial and ethnic concepts to structure their play as a means to exclude and/or include children and as a means of controlling peer interactions. Van Ausdale and Feagin found that rather than using an adult-based understanding of race, children develop, through social interaction, their own intricate constructions and uses of race and ethnicity based on the color of their skin, the languages they speak, and how they understand their parents' color and race. Unlike Holmes (1995), who concluded that kindergartners' racial categories are fixed and unconditional, Van Ausdale and Feagin found that among preschoolers, ideas of race are more fluid and flexible and the children try to understand not only single race markers but also their peers of "mixed" heritage. Not all children fit into one category or the other; rather, there are multiple categories, and children move from one to another depending on the situation.

For example, one 4-year-old girl in Van Ausdale and Feagin's study was born in Africa of a White father and a Black African mother. Corinne was very aware of her mixed ancestry and stressed both her American and African heritage to other children and adults. Her fellow students often challenged Corinne. One White boy denied the fact that Corrine's father was White even when the father came to the school and verified that he was Corinne's father and that her mother was African. Adults also frequently challenged Corinne. New teachers and visitors to the school often corrected Corinne when she claimed to be African and would say, "Your mommy and daddy's ancestors came from Africa, but you are African American." At one point, Corinne got so frustrated that she retorted, "No, you don't get it, I'm from Africa. My daddy is from here" (Van Ausdale & Feagin, 2001, p. 85).

Van Ausdale and Feagin also found that adults did not believe that the children had made the negative racial remarks and slurs that the researchers had recorded, and they denied that children had any real understanding of such speech. Van Ausdale and Feagin argued that many adults misunderstand and underestimate young children's understanding and use of racial attitudes because they believe that children cannot be racist. However, seeing children as simply racist misses the point. Given the pervasive racism that exists in American society, it is not surprising that young children—in line with an interpretive approach to childhood socialization—observe, experience, and absorb racial thinking, discourse, and behavior and use such knowledge in their everyday lives (Van Ausdale & Feagin, 2001; also see Corsaro & Fingerson, 2003).

Status Differentiation

Earlier we saw that young children's resistance to adult rules leads them to develop a sense of "we-ness" or a group identity, which is a central feature of peer cultures. Emerging after and existing alongside this dynamic of affiliation, however, is another more contentious, competitive one (Fernie, Kantor, & Whaley, 1995). This competitive dynamic leads to the emergence of subgroups and status hierarchies within subgroups of peers, especially during kindergarten and the early elementary grades.

Formation of Status Hierarchies. A number of researchers have examined processes of status differentiation in peer groups. One group of researchers has identified dominance hierarchies in which higher ranked children consistently win out over those at lower ranks in aggressive conflicts (LaFrenier & Charlesworth, 1983; see also Strayer & Strayer, 1976).

Such findings must be evaluated with caution, however, given their strict focus on aggression and given certain ecological features of the settings and groups studied (Connolly & Smith, 1978). Group size is important because the larger the group is the more opportunities children have to avoid the aggressive behavior of some children and seek affiliation with others. More important, differentiation within groups of children is highly complex and cannot be understood by focusing only on physical dominance. Children frequently compete with and attempt to control one another using a wide range of interpersonal and communicative skills, and status hierarchies are often fluid and constantly changing. Such fluidity and complexity is increased when competition itself (through physical contests, verbal dueling, and narrative skills) is valued more than actually winning (see Goodwin, 1990).

Some researchers have found clear status hierarchies among preschool and elementary school boys (Berentzen, 1984; R. Best, 1983). Berentzen reported that the Norwegian preschool boys he studied constantly engaged in competition, made note of rankings, and acted in accordance with them (1984, pp. 107–108). In R. Best's study, elementary school boys often negotiated rank in advance of activities. Such ranking was based on perceived toughness and resulted in a designated chain of command (first, second, third captains). The boys referred to rank in structuring play and settling disputes (1983, p. 75).

Resistance of Status Hierarchies. Although Berentzen and Best found clear patterns of ranking among the boys, girls in these studies resisted explicit rankings and relied on more subtle methods for controlling one another. I, however, found no pattern of clear and stable status hierarchies among either boys or girls in my observations of American and Italian preschool children. Age may be a factor in the difference in these findings, especially given that most of the children in Berentzen's study were between the ages of 6 and 7 years old. In general, I found frequent competitive behavior among underdeveloped or highly fluid status hierarchies. This pattern was apparent in our earlier discussion of conflict in the peer relations of these children. The findings are also very similar to those of Goodwin (1990), whose research with preadolescent African American children we shall discuss in Chapter 9.

The lack of stable rankings in my studies relates to the children's preoccupation with process over structure in peer relations. That is, the American and Italian children were most interested in debating and negotiating where they stood with one another rather than in establishing and maintaining rankings. Attempts to be leader or boss usually were quickly challenged and were often thwarted. The older girls in the Italian preschool, for example, frequently debated about who should or should not be *il capo* (the boss or leader). In instances where a leader was agreed on, the chosen girl would offer up plans of action, and things would go fine for a while. Then minor violations of the leader's instructions would occur. The leader would soon become upset, but the other girls would appease her and promise to obey. Soon thereafter, however, the violations would grow more serious, and the leader's rules would be mocked with laughter and derision. The leader would then stomp off, refusing to play anymore. In most cases, the other girls would run after her, promising to straighten up if given one more chance. The leader would usually return, only to have the whole thing happen all over again!

I found similar resistance to girls' attempts to be the boss in my American data (also see D. Maynard, 1985, 1986; Rizzo, 1989). In one such instance, three girls (Ruth, Shirley, and Vickie, all about 5 and a half years old) are looking through department store catalogs and selecting items to cut out and paste on paper to make a collage. The girls are concentrating on what they call "girls' stuff" and refer to some of the other items as "yucky boys' stuff." After they have been playing for 10 minutes or so, another girl, Peggy, comes over and stands near Shirley.

Shirley points to a picture of a couch in a catalog. "We don't want that couch; that's dumb." "All we want is the pretty stuff," says Ruth.

Peggy now announces, "If you are going to come to my birthday, you have to obey my orders."

"Oh, we don't care," responds Ruth. Ignoring Ruth, Peggy continues, "And every girl in the whole school is invited. . . . Shirley, every girl."

Vickie now says, "Every girl, Shirley called every girl?"

"I'm going to put a sign up," continues Peggy, "that says, 'No boys allowed!'" "Oh good, good, good," says Vickie. "I hate boys."

Peggy now adds further information about her party, noting, "And the girls can't do whatever they do—they gotta obey my rules."

Shirley quickly rejects these restrictions, declaring, "Then we're not coming."

"Yeah, but the point is," adds Ruth, "we're cutting out all these for, for presents for your birthday, but we'll forget about it. We're not coming!"

Although the other girls seem to take Peggy's proposal about her birthday party seriously in this example, they probably do not believe that a birthday party only for girls would ever take place. It was a common practice in the preschool for all of the members of the class to be invited to birthday parties. Here Peggy's aim seems to be to insert herself into the ongoing activity and to take charge of it with the negative references to boys. The other girls seem open to the notion of excluding boys but are quick to reject Peggy's attempt to set proposed rules that would put her in charge of their behavior. In this example, all of the girls except Ruth are part of a friendship clique composed of six of the older girls in the class. There is a clear resistance in this group to any girl's setting herself up as leader or boss (see Corsaro, 1994, pp. 18–20). Berentzen found a similar pattern for the Norwegian preschool girls he studied, noting that their "cultural premises and criteria of rank lead to their constantly denying each other's rank" (1984, p. 108).

Mary Martini's (1994) study of mixed-age and mixed-gender playgroups of Polynesian children of the Marquesas Islands adds further insight into complex processes of status negotiations among young children. Polynesian children learn early in life that there are different rules for interacting with those of higher status (parents and other adults) and with those of equal status (peers in the same age range). Children are required to be restrained and compliant when dealing with adults, but peer relations are based on reciprocity (Martini, 1994). This reciprocity is based on both "a continual willingness to share what one has with others" and status rivalry (Howard, 1974, p. 206; Martini, 1994, p. 77). For example, Martini discovered a complex dominance hierarchy of (usually) older children (6- and 7-year-olds) in the roles of noisy and quiet leaders, 3- to 5-year-olds in the role of initiate members, and toddlers as peripheral members of the group. The use of the term *dominance hierarchy* can be misleading here because the children worked together in the specialized roles to coordinate group activity.

Noisy leaders introduce activities, direct group play, and keep players on track. Quiet leaders invent new play, monitor the bossiness of noisy leaders, and care for peripheral toddlers. Initiate members follow the leaders and support each other as they go through the process of hazing. They also care for peripheral toddlers and generally hold the group together from the inside. Peripheral toddlers are interested observers. Their incompetence highlights the skills of the older children. Older children gain status by helping and teaching dependent toddlers (Martini, 1994, p. 98).

This coordination of roles, argued Martini, "leads to [the] children generally avoiding danger, caring for their own needs, settling disputes efficiently, and distributing goods fairly" (1994, p. 99).

Martini's research and other comparative studies remind us of the Western bias that is evident in much of the research on children (also see Harkness & Super, 1992; Nsamenang, 1992b, 2006; Schildkrout, 1975/2002; Weisner & Gallimore, 1977; Whiting & Edwards, 1988). In the mixed-age and mixed-gender groups of children in many non-Western societies, attempts to control other children are most often prosocial rather than egoistic. That is, the goal is to maintain group cohesiveness rather than to attain individual desires (see Whiting & Edwards, 1988, p. 182). Martini contrasted this preference for prosocial versus egoistic control to peer interactions among middle-class American children who learn to value goal-directedness and individual achievement early in life. Such values clearly affect the nature of their peer relations as they move from preschool settings into kindergarten and the early grades.

Core Groups and Rejected, Neglected, and Controversial Children. A number of researchers have noted the emergence of higher status or core groups in the peer cultures of preschool, kindergarten, and elementary school children (R. Best, 1983; Fernie et al., 1995; Paley, 1992; Thorne, 1993). Members of these core groups often work together to resist the entry of new members. Here the resistance goes beyond the tendency to protect interactive space, an idea we discussed in Chapter 7. The protection of interactive space involves children's attempts to maintain control over specific play events that they have worked very hard to create. When stable core groups emerge in peer cultures, children are most often rejected simply because they are not members of the group; the rejection often has nothing to do with the protection of interactive space. The actual process of restricting membership often serves to solidify the core group. Most children do not accept rejection from core groups without a struggle. They may eventually gain acceptance by adopting core group values and play preferences, or they may work with other rejected children to develop their own core groups (Fernie et al., 1995).

Some children may play at the periphery of these core groups yet remain active participants in peer culture. Other children, however, are continually rejected; still others make little effort to enter peer play. Many clinical psychologists and educators argue that isolation from the peer group can have serious long-term effects on emotional development. Three types of low-status children have been identified in the research literature: rejected, neglected, and controversial children (see Ramsey, 1991, pp. 91–93).

Rejected children usually fall into two main groups: aggressive-rejected children, whose aggressive behavior leads others to resist their inclusion in play, and withdrawn-rejected children, who withdraw when they fail in their attempts to gain access to playgroups (Asher & Coie, 1990; Hatch, 1986; Ramsey, 1991). Neglected children are not consistently rejected, but they fail to become active participants in peer culture. They are often loners or "the quiet children who are content in their roles as minor players in the social arena" (Ramsey, 1991, p. 86). Controversial children are what some might call "characters." As Ramsey noted, these active, enthusiastic, and humorous children "have a major impact on the social life of the classroom, but their peers do not agree about what that effect is" (Ramsey, 1991, p. 87; also see Coie & Dodge, 1988). As a result, controversial children are seldom fully integrated into peer cultures.

I have encountered at least one such controversial child (it was usually a boy) in each of the several preschool classrooms I have studied. The children's humor and enthusiasm can be infectious, but at the same time their peers often come to see them as overbearing. In one of the American classrooms I studied, a boy (Daniel) spent a lot of time telling jokes and riddles and concocting very elaborate play plots. Consider the following example of Daniel's riddles.

The head teacher, Mary, is in the playhouse with several children, pretending to have dinner. Daniel is one of the children, and he says, "Mary, I want to tell you a riddle."

"OK," replies Mary.

Daniel asks, "How can a man fall into the ocean and not get his hair wet?"

"I don't know," says Mary. "Maybe he had a hat on."

"No," yells Daniel. "He was bald-headed!"

All the children and Mary laugh, but Daniel laughs the loudest and continually repeats the word *bald-headed*. Daniel then leaves the playhouse and runs around the school calling out to different children: "You're bald-headed!" Some children protest, saying they are not bald-headed, whereas others laugh gleefully and join Daniel in the name-calling. Eventually, the teachers respond to the ongoing disruption and put an end to the "bald-headed" episode.

Reactions to Daniel's complex plots were also mixed. He would sometimes gain the initial cooperation of several children and would propose complex lines of action as if he were a movie director. On one occasion, he had me and several children pretend to be the audience for a proposed puppet show. He gave each of us two wooden blocks (one representing a bar of candy and the other a flashlight to find our seats) and instructed us to "sit down and get ready for the show!" Then he and another boy, Tony, went behind a bookcase and began banging away with hammers, ostensibly building the set for the show. After about 10 minutes of banging, he reappeared and said the show was about to begin. Then there was more banging, and the audience began to dwindle. Meanwhile, I sat and waited patiently with Sue, Sheila, and Christopher. Finally, Daniel and Tony pushed two chairs up behind the bookcase, climbed onto the chairs, and called for our attention. We thought the show was about to begin, but Daniel announced that Tony "messed everything up" by not letting him use the good hammer and that "the puppet show was canceled." Tony denied this accusation and began pushing Daniel, and the two fell from the chairs. Tony hurt his leg and began to cry, and a teacher ran over to help. I remained seated, but the other children got up to leave, with Sheila dropping her candy and flashlight to the floor and declaring: "What a gyp!"

"You Can't Say, You Can't Play": Sharing and Exclusion Among Peers. In her book *You Can't Say, You Can't Play,* Vivian Paley (1992) presented her viewpoint regarding children's attempts to exclude peers from play. Rather than taking the view that children's attempts to exclude peers derive from a need to protect interactive space, she viewed such attempts as examples of rejection and considered them hurtful. In her book, Paley described how she first proposed the general rule, "You Can't Say, You Can't Play," discussed it with her kindergarten class and with first-through fifth-graders in her school, and then instituted the rule. (The meaning of the rule of course is, you can't tell another child that he or she can't join in and play.) As Paley explained, most of the children were against the rule, protesting that they wanted to play with their friends or that some kids didn't play right. Other children, especially those frequently rejected, generally supported the rule, saying it hurt their feelings to be left out. In the midst of all this discussion Paley realized that an essential part of her curriculum (placing disruptive children in time-out) was a violation of the rule, and she terminated the time-out procedure. Eventually, the You Can't Say, You Can't Play rule was established, and despite some rough spots, it worked pretty well. There was less exclusion, and the kids were generally nicer to one another.

In Paley's study, the teacher (Paley), most of the students, and the rule itself (at least on its surface) were clearly middle-class American. The children frequently complained about their peers being mean and hurting their feelings. The teacher was responsive to such complaints, and she developed a rule to address exclusion and meanness. When talking over the rule with the children after its institution, Paley traced its origin from another cultural context, the book of Leviticus from the Old Testament. She supplied the appropriate quotation: "The stranger that sojourneth with you shall be unto you as the homeborn among you" (1992, p. 102). The quotation seemed to bring about a recognition on her part. "You see, lately, I've come to understand," she wrote, "that although we all begin school as strangers, some children never learn to feel at home, to feel they really belong." "They are not made welcome enough," she concluded (1992, p. 103). Thus, Paley hoped that the institution of the rule would bring about a more humane and communal classroom.

Paley, however, overlooked the importance of the predominately White, middle-class cultural context in which she attempted to articulate the rule. In this and other middle-class American schools, there is, as we saw earlier, an emphasis on individual expression and a recognition of the uniqueness and rights of others. In such a cultural context, the rule seems restrictive of the individual rights of the majority of the children, and therefore it is resisted. Paley also failed to consider why that very cultural context creates the need for such a rule. Let's return to the work of Martini and to my research in the Italian *scuola materna* and in an American Head Start center. In these groups of children, there was a great deal of conflict, opposition, and debate in peer interaction and culture. Yet a general group ethos existed in which the children competed individually to collaborate collectively (Corsaro & Maynard, 1996). In these groups, the continual exclusion of particular children was rare, children seldom complained to teachers about hurt feelings, and time-out was not a routine part of the curricula. To the eyes and ears of many middle-class Americans, however, these groups of children seem threatening. Their debates and competitions seem too rough and intense, and the teachers seem a bit authoritarian. Viewed in this way, a rule may seem necessary for maintaining fairness. In evaluating these different responses to the practice of excluding children from play, we must remove our cultural blinders and remember that peer cultures are affected by and contribute to the reproduction of and changes in adult cultures within which they are embedded.

What then of Paley's rule? I think it is a good one. But it may take more than the proscription, You can't say, you can't play, to create a group ethos that echoes young Franco's attitude when he reprimanded Sara's attempt to exclude Paolo in the discussione: Who are you to say that I am or anyone is not in this?!

SUMMARY

Conflict and social differentiation are central elements of peer culture. Developmental psychologists have long stressed the importance of conflict for creating disequilibriums and providing clues for the elaboration of new cognitive structures and skills. More recently, psychologists, anthropologists, and sociologists have argued that conflicts are not merely cognitive but are relational in that they naturally emerge in children's interactions with adults and peers. In our comparative analysis of conflict, discussion, and friendship processes in three culturally different preschools, we saw how these processes constitute and bring about changes in peer cultures. We saw, for example, that Italian children frequently engaged in discussione, highly stylized and dramatic public debates in peer interaction. Such debates are highly communal activities in which the children address concerns that are important to them and, in the process, develop a shared sense of control over their social world. African American children produced a similar communal activity: oppositional talk. In this activity, the children playfully tease and challenge one another in peer play. The verbal dueling that makes up oppositional talk sends a dual message that (a) a particular child can hold his or her own ground and (b) participation in oppositional talk signifies allegiance to the values and concerns of the peer culture. In contrast to the Italian and African American children, we saw that American upper-middle-class preschool children took conflicts much more seriously. Their disputes were much more emotionally intense and were often related to attempts to control the behavior of other children they saw as friends. Overall, these comparative research findings demonstrate that conflict contributes to the social organization of peer groups, the reaffirmation of cultural values, and the individual development and display of self.

Conflict also contributes to the structural complexity of and differentiation in peer cultures. Processes of differentiation by gender, race, and status emerge in the peer cultures of young children. Although a general tendency toward increased differentiation by gender, race, and status in peer cultures may be universal, cross-cultural comparative research cautions us against assuming that these processes work themselves out in the same fashion. We must especially guard against the general acceptance of patterns discovered in the peer relations of White, middle-class children in the United States as models for understanding children's cultures.

We will continue to take comparative studies into account in Chapter 9, where we examine peer cultures and identity formation as children move from early childhood to preadolescence.

9

Preadolescent Peer Cultures

W hen does childhood end? That is a hard question to answer. Defining the boundaries of childhood (and deciding on the range and limits of our consideration of the sociology of childhood) is a difficult task. Childhood is a social construction that is clearly related to, but not determined by, physical maturation, cultural beliefs about age, and institutional age grading.

For the purposes of this book, childhood includes preadolescence, which is generally defined as the period from 7 to 13 years of age. Given the scope of this book, we will not be able to discuss the transition to adolescence or adolescent peer culture in detail. In the field of sociology, however, adolescence has received much more attention than childhood, and some excellent recent studies look specifically at the transition to adolescence (see Corsaro & Eder, 1990; Eder & Nenga, 2003). In this chapter we will consider adolescents and adolescent peer culture in regard to the role electronic media play in adolescents' lives. We will also include adolescence in our discussion, in Chapters 10 through 12, of the social problems of children and youth.

In Chapters 7 and 8 we identified two basic themes in children's peer cultures: (a) communal sharing, the strong desire for sharing and social participation, and (b) control, children's persistent attempts to actively gain control over their lives. In this chapter, we will discuss how these themes are produced and extended in the peer cultures of preadolescent children. The chapter is especially concerned with how the extensions of these patterns are related to children's development of unique social selves or identities as they make the transition from childhood to preadolescent peer cultures. The chapter also examines patterns and processes in the rapidly changing nature of electronic media in the lives of preadolescents and adolescents.

Peer Cultures in Preadolescence

Most of our knowledge of the peer cultures of preadolescent children is the result of research done in Western societies. We know from the research discussed in Chapters 6 through 8, however, that children's groups are much less age segregated in non-Western societies. Children in these societies who are 7 to 10 years old spend much of their lives in mixed-age groups caring for and playing with younger siblings and other younger children in their local communities. These preadolescents have much less time for peer play in general, as they take on a range of tasks to help support their families. Furthermore, as we will see later in this chapter, research across racial, ethnic, and social class groups in the United States challenges some of the well-documented patterns in the peer cultures of White, middle- and upper-class children. Therefore, we must be careful to keep these differences in mind as we explore the basic themes of sharing and control in the peer cultures of preadolescent children.

Friendship Processes in Preadolescent Peer Cultures

As we saw in Chapter 7, preschool children immensely enjoy the simple act of being with one another and doing things together. They often signal recognition of their ability to carry out joint actions with verbal references to friendship such as "We're friends, right?" (Corsaro, 2003). However, generating shared meaning and coordinating play are often difficult tasks for young children. Thus, preschoolers spend a great deal of time creating and protecting the shared play and peer routines that provide them with a sense of excitement and emotional security.

Things are different for preadolescents. Children 7 to 10 years of age easily generate and sustain peer activities, but they now collectively produce a set of stratified groups, and issues of acceptance, popularity, and group solidarity become very important. We will explore the importance and complexity of this increasing differentiation in peer relations by examining social participation and friendship processes, the nature and structure of differentiated friendship groups, and friendship, differentiation, gender, and race in preadolescence.

Social Participation and Friendships

In preadolescence, the primarily nonverbal play routines of early child-hood (for example, approach-avoidance and other play routines) are gradually replaced by verbal activities that involve planning and reflec-tive evaluation. It is for this reason that T. Chin and Phillips (2003) argued that in the study of preadolescents' play, we need to determine the inten-sity of children's involvement in their activities and not just identify their various activities. In short, Chin and Phillips argued that kids don't just play; they are collectively involved in their activities, from being absorbed in watching television to the point of knowing and talking about complex plot structures in soap operas, to being engaged in complex sociodramatic play, to exploring novel interactive settings with peers and adults. Chin and Phillips's research is especially interesting because the authors stud-ied children outside of the school setting—in their homes and neighbor-hoods during the summer months. These settings can challenge children's imaginations and interactive skills because there are often no structured activities to turn to as there are in schools or after-school programs. The authors presented a vivid example of two preadolescent girls, Jane and April, who spent much of the summer together. They often pretended that they were sisters and that the scooters they liked to ride were horses. In the following example, they talk to the researcher about a play scenario in which they pursue husbands on their horses (scooters) but make sure the play does not violate the rules of the church they attend.

> Jane said, "Yesterday we were playing that she [April] was dating the sheriff and I was dating the sheriff's brother." I [the researcher] didn't know what to say, so I said that dating the sheriff sounded like fun. Jane added, "*And* the sheriff's brother. . . ." I nodded and laughed. They started discussing dating the sheriff and whether or not they should play that game today. They decided to and then debated how old they should pretend to be [they had already chosen to be 13 and 17 for their previous game]. Jane said, "Well you can't if you're 13—you can't date one person until you're 18. It's against church standards." April sighed but nodded and they decided to be 18 and 19. (T. Chin & Phillips, 2003, p. 165)

This example shows how preadolescent children reflect on the nature of their play and how it relates to their futures and presents. The example also nicely captures the intensity of the play of children who are often together and consider themselves best friends.

Rizzo (1989), in his work in a first-grade classroom, found that devel-oping best friends was a key aspect of peer culture. He reported that first-grade children appeared to have an internalized concept of friendship that serves multiple functions in peer relations. Specifically, in his yearlong ethnography of first graders, Rizzo found that the children

> attempted to determine the existence of friendship by comparing the internal concept with specific features of interactions with frequent playmates, to act in accordance with this concept when with friends, and to object when their friends failed to live up to their expectations. (p. 105)

In short, the children had the beginnings of a reflective awareness of what a friend should be, and they realized that they did not have to wait until they found themselves playing with a peer to have a friend. They could try to control who their friends would be!

Many times, however, the children found that their friendship bids (asking to be one's friend or being nice to someone) were not accepted and were at times actively rejected. Having a better awareness of what being a friend involves did not ensure that they could develop close friendships. In fact, in Rizzo's study the most enduring friendships were the result of what could best be termed "local circumstances" of play and peer relations. Children became involved in types of play they enjoyed, and like the preschoolers we discussed earlier, they verbally marked and agreed that they were friends. Unlike the younger children, however, the first graders would maintain these patterns of shared play with certain children over time and come to mark the relationships as special—by considering themselves to be best friends.

Best friends, then, often tried both to protect their friendships from the possible intrusions of others and to expand their friendship groups. It is not surprising that these two processes came into conflict in a variety of ways. First, even though best friends wanted to expand their groups beyond their two-person dyads, they were very sensitive to the possible disruption of the fragile, dyadic best-friend relationships. Therefore, they often displayed jealousy when their best friends played with others without them, and they quarreled with their best friends about the general nature of their play with others.

Rizzo and others see these disputes and conflicts as serving many positive functions, which I will address in the section on disputes, conflict, friendship, and gender. Here, I want to discuss another process in peer relations that develops shortly after best friendships are formed: the increasing differentiation of friendship groups.

Social Differentiation and Friendships

Preadolescent children's alliances are often linked to changes of positions in friendship groups, providing the children with opportunities to test a series of social identities. Children's social identities "are thus oriented towards alliances with other children in activities that also separate the children" (Evaldsson, 1993, p. 258). In Rizzo's study, for example, best friends often tried to expand their groups by constructing clubs, with membership offered to other kids they liked. The children would sometimes give names to these clubs, but the clubs seldom had any real purpose except to provide a way of expanding the friendship group. Some children were not offered membership, and others were rejected, resulting in the beginning of the development of stratified groups.

In Rizzo's study these groups were rather loosely bound and often broke down and then re-formed. In Evaldsson's study of the play of Swedish 7- to 10-year-olds in after-school centers, the children formed more stable friendship groups that were centered on different activities in the two centers. In one center, the children highly valued possession of things, skills in acquiring these possessions, and competence in disputes and discussions about these valued objects. In this center the children frequently engaged in physical games, especially marbles, but competence in debating who was good at these games, in disputing issues of fair play, and in discussing who had the best possessions (marbles) was valued as much as competence in actually playing marbles. In the second center, the children's identities and friendship processes were more relational and emotional. Instead of centering on physical activities, skills, and talk about such activities and skills, the children in the second center were more concerned with appearances, romances, and involvements in secret activities. These values were displayed "in intimate alliances, where comparisons, guessing, teasing and joint laughter support social differentiation" (Evaldsson, 1993, p. 259).

We will return to Evaldsson's study to look more closely at the nature of these play activities and games in the next section because they nicely illustrate how children address ambiguities, concerns, fears, and conflicts in peer culture. What is of particular interest here, however, is that gender was not a central factor in the differentiation of friendship groups at the two centers she studied. This finding is quite different from the findings of studies of friendship processes among American White, middle- and upper-class preadolescents.

Social Differentiation, Friendships, Gender, Race, and Ethnicity

Gender and Peer Relations. As we saw in Chapter 8, many studies have documented increasing gender differentiation in children's peer interactions beginning at around 5 or 6 years of age and reaching a peak in the early elementary school years (Adler & Adler, 1998; Gottman, 1986; Maccoby, 1999; Oswald, Krappman, Chowdhuri, & von Salisch, 1987; Thorne, 1993). Although there is extensive gender segregation in peer relations in this period, it is rarely complete; most studies show consistent mixed-sex grouping and cross-sex interaction (usually on the order of 10% to 20%) even in the preadolescent period (Thorne, 1993). What is more important for our understanding of peer cultures is not simply the gender segregation that surely occurs in the preadolescent period but the nature of interactive patterns and interpersonal processes within the segregated groups. There is a growing debate about whether girls and boys have different peer cultures.

Thorne argued that a familiar story line runs through the literature on children and gender. "The story opens," noted Thorne, "by emphasizing patterns of mutual avoidance between boys and girls and then asserts that this daily separation results in, and is perpetuated by, deep and dichotomous gender differences" (1993, p. 89). These differences are seen as both affecting and being affected by the structure and nature of activities in gender-segregated groups. For example, several studies have found that boys interact in larger groups (Lever, 1978), engage in more aggressive and competitive play (Adler & Adler, 1998; R. Best, 1983), and frequently organize their activities and relations around organized sports (Adler & Adler, 1998; Eder & Parker, 1987; G. A. Fine, 1987; Lever, 1978; Thorne, 1993).

In their book *Peer Power*, a study of children's peer relations in and out of school in a primarily middle- and upper-middle-class community of about 90,000 people, Adler and Adler (1998) discussed how the nature of these different activities contributes to popularity within the peer cultures of preadolescent boys and girls. They defined popular children as those who are the most influential in setting group opinions and who have the greatest impact on determining the boundaries of membership in the most exclusive social groups.

They found that boys' and girls' popularity or rank in the status hierarchy was influenced by several factors. Boys' popularity revolved around athletic ability, a cult of masculinity or being tough, sophistication in social and interpersonal skills, a culture of coolness or detachment, and in later preadolescence, success in their relations with girls. Girls' popularity centered on family background, physical appearance, social skills, precocity or adult-like concerns and style, and good academic performance.

Adler and Adler also identified a rigid clique structure in each age and gender group they studied, with four main strata: the high, wannabe, middle, and low ranks (social isolates). Adler and Adler found the kids in the highest strata to be extremely manipulative and controlling in their relations with peers. The leaders of these popular cliques maintained their power and control by manipulating dynamics of membership inclusion, stigmatizing those in lower groups, and reminding subordinates of their tenuous group membership. Through practices of inclusion and exclusion, the popular cliques held group members, and those wanting to join the group (the wannabes), to stringent and often capricious norms of behavior. For example, one girl, Diane, recalled her inclusion in the popular group and its aftermath:

> In fifth grade I came into a new class and I knew nobody. None of my friends from the year before were in my class. So I get to school, a week late, and Tiffany comes up to me and she was like, "Hi Diane, how are you? Where were you? You look so pretty." And I was like, wow, she's so nice. And she was being nice for like two weeks, kiss-ass major. And then she started pulling her bitch moves. Maybe it was for a month that she was nice. And so then she had clawed me into her clique and her group, and so she won me over that way, but then she was a bitch to me once I was inside it, and I couldn't get out because I had no other friends. 'Cause I'd gone in there and already been accepted into the popular clique, so everyone else in the class didn't like me, so I had nowhere else to go. (Adler & Adler, 1998, p. 59)

Diane's experiences in the popular group were common, but things were quite different in middle-level friendship groups. These groups had lower prestige, but they also had more secure friendships without the manipulations that characterized the popular groups. Also, the middle groups made up a larger percentage of the school, so the manipulative behavior of the popular kids was not the norm. Still, the popular kids were more visible and had more power in the school and also received more attention from the Adlers in their documentation of peer power.

Popular boys were just as controlling and manipulative as girls within their groups and even more likely to make fun of and tease kids in lower groups, especially the social isolates. The Adlers' identification of mean girls is somewhat surprising but not unique given recent studies (see Simmons, 2002; Wiseman, 2002). Girls' aggression, although often indirect, is often very hurtful to peers and more prevalent than once thought.

These findings raise problems for claims by psychologist Carol Gilligan (1982). Gilligan argued that girls have a "different voice" in that they value relationships and caring as opposed to boys' concerns with individual rights and abstract notions of justice. Girls are so concerned with maintaining personal relationships that they strive to avoid conflict and negotiate problems indirectly for fear of seeming uncooperative.

Gilligan's work has led to the general acceptance of the "two-cultures" view of children's gender socialization, differences in men's and women's styles of talk, and the nature of social relationships across gender groups more generally (M. M. Barnes & Vangelisti, 1995; Gilligan, 1982; Tannen, 1990). We should not be too quick to accept this view of children's gender relations, however, as we saw from the Adlers' work. This view has recently been called into question for several other reasons.

First, most studies have been of White, middle- and upper-class American children. African American and Latino boys and girls are much less separated in their play than White, middle-class children. Also, the nature of peer activities, concerns, and values of African American and Latina girls is different from that of White, middle- and upper-class American girls (Goodwin, 2003; Schofield, 1982; Thorne, 1993). Goodwin, for example, found that African American and Latina girls engage in highly complex physical games and play in which competition and verbal conflict are recurrent and highly valued (1990, 1998). The important point here is not simply that the studies on which the two-cultures view is based have limited generalizability. Rather, the issue is that findings and interpretations in line with the "separate-cultures" view implies that there is something about the very nature of being male or female that leads to these differing values and social relations by gender. The implication is, therefore, that the pattern should be universal. There is little support for such a claim.

It is important to note that the issue runs deeper than possible class and cultural differences in gender relations among children. There is also the problem of interpreting data only in line with the two-cultures view, which stresses very clear-cut, almost dichotomous, sexual differences and perspectives. In many of the studies, exceptions to the general pattern are pushed aside and seldom pursued. Rarely, if ever, is there a search for negative cases. How might things be done differently? How might we go about identifying and interpreting exceptions to the separate-cultures view? Thorne (1993) has argued for the importance of grounding observations in a wider range of social contexts (focusing on the less visible and peripheral as well as on the most conspicuous and dominant groups and settings). We need to study both the core groups of the leaders and the more peripheral groups of less popular children. Goodwin has championed the intensive microanalysis of naturally occurring events—how children actually go about playing games such as jump rope, discussing friendships, and gossiping in their everyday lives. Goodwin's point is especially well taken. Even with the recent increase in ethnographic studies of peer relations, there is still a common reliance on reports of children's activities rather than on direct study of the activities themselves. In the next section we will focus on what preadolescents do in a range of social settings. We will discuss gender relations, and we will explore more generally how children's activities help them to gain control over their lives and further develop a sense of self and identity.

Goodwin's work is also important because it sheds light on the importance of race and ethnicity in children's peer relations. Until recently there have been few studies of children's friendships and peer relations across racial and ethnic groups. Work by Kimberly Scott (2002, 2003) and Valerie Moore (2001, 2002) has begun to address this neglect. Scott studied peer relations among first- to third-grade children in a middle-class, ethnically diverse elementary school and a poor, predominately African American elementary school. In her research, Scott focused on girls and found that in the middle-class school they played and made friends primarily during lunch periods and recesses. The girls' friendship groups were primarily segregated by color, with Black and Hispanic girls playing together and White girls playing together, with the exception of one group (a high-status club) of which all the girls aspired to be members. Membership in the club was based primarily on adherence to rules set by club leaders who were always White girls. The leaders decided who could be in the club and set the rules: Don't be too aggressive, always follow the leader's directives, and don't play with boys. To maintain their power, leaders frequently stigmatized one member (or more) of the group as "out girl" (usually for playing with boys but sometimes for arbitrary reasons that were not clearly explained). Furthermore, the out girl was almost always a girl of color. Scott found, through observations and interviews with girls of color, that they often disliked the leaders and their wielding of power but seldom challenged them. Thus, the prestige of belonging to the exclusive club overshadowed the loyalty of the girls to individual friends and the more egalitarian play in their more segregated groups.

Play and friendship at the poor, predominately African American school was communal and egalitarian in that there was little if any exclusion, the girls showed concern for the welfare of their playmates, and they enjoyed sharing toys and food. Nonetheless, as in the middle-class school, a club did exist. However, this club was inclusive and primarily reflected the structuring of relationships across age groups. Scott noted that the club was not always operative, and when it was not in action club members readily played with nonclub girls. When in action, the main goal of the club seemed to be one of older girls' socializing younger ones. The club had a "boss" and a leader, and "only second or third grade girls can be leaders because it is believed that older girls 'know what they doin' while first grade girls 'only be runnin' around'" (K. Scott, 2003, p. 198). Overall, Scott's study is fascinating in that we see that the tendency to form hierarchies through clubs existed in both groups but that the nature of the hierarchies varied greatly from exclusion to inclusion, given the overall racial, ethnic, and class makeup of the two schools studied.

Moore's (2001, 2002) research blends nicely with that of Scott in that Moore studied somewhat older children (6- to 12-year-olds) in summer camps. She labeled one camp typical in that it was similar to many summer camps in orientation and activities, whereas the other was a "cultural awareness" camp in that, in addition to typical camp activities, it had a goal of helping to foster respect and appreciation for cultural diversity. Moore found a good bit of segregation in both camps by age, gender, and especially race and ethnicity. When the White kids at the typical camp did engage kids of color, it was usually to ask them questions about "who they were" in a sense as being different from Whites and White culture. In the "culturally aware" camp, there was a powerful clique of primarily older Black kids (both boys and girls). In this camp, however, there were more instances of kids' struggling with challenging race-category membership as a legitimate way to establish in- and out-group membership. As a result, there was more instability in and questioning of clique membership as well as some shifting in the clique structure as a result.

Overall, Scott's and Moore's research adds race as an important dimension to studies of clique structure and dynamics among preadolescents as seen in the work of Adler and Adler (1998) and others. As Moore noted, her findings suggest

> that the peer cultures that kids create in multiracial settings encompass different "lessons" about power and conformity than do those in white settings. Not only does the presence of children of color introduce a wider range of power dynamics into clique structure, but the instability and fluidity regarding conceptions of race that kids of color bring to a setting disrupt easy definitions of "in-group" and "out-group," thus affecting the social negotiation of identity in that setting. (Moore, 2002, p. 76)

In one of the few studies of race and ethnicity in preadolescent peer culture that looks at Asian children, Nukaga (2008) studied school lunchtime interactions of Korean children at two elementary schools where Asian children were in the majority. She found that Korean children viewed their ethnic food as a symbol of the Korean identity or self and negotiated its meaning and value in interaction with peers. Different forms of food exchange had distinct relevance for marking, maintaining, and muting ethnic boundaries. Gift giving of wet or dry food was used to mark strong friendships and make new friends primarily within the same ethnic and gender group. Sharing of wet food was used to mark weaker friendships of mostly the same ethnic and gender group, whereas sharing of dry food could involve anyone at the school regardless of gender or ethnicity. Trading of wet food never occurred, but trading of dry food was used to mark power relations mainly across ethnicity and gender. At these predominately Korean schools certain kinds of Korean foods (especially dry seaweed) became popular mediums of exchange, which gave a certain degree of power to the Korean children over children of other races or ethnicities given their access to such foods. In fact, Latino and African American children, many of whom qualified for free lunches, had far fewer cultural resources to construct boundaries in ethnic terms.

These findings on peer relations and race and ethnicity are generally in line with other work on race in preadolescence that focuses more on teacher perceptions and school structure and processes that reinforce racial stereotypes, most especially of African American children (Ferguson, 2000; A. Lewis, 2003). Finally, recent research in Europe on interaction among immigrant and majority children (see Evaldsson, 2003; Hall, 2002; Poveda & Marcos, 2005; Rampton, 1995) demonstrates the importance of comparative research on peer relations across racial and ethnic groups.

Autonomy and Identity in Preadolescent Peer Cultures

Everyday activities in peer cultures enable preadolescents to negotiate and explore a wide range of norms regarding friendship processes, personal appearance, self-presentation, heterosexual relations, personal aspirations, and relations with adult authority figures. By participating in organized and informal games, verbal play routines, and collaborative storytelling, preadolescents explore developing norms and expectations about themselves and their place in peer and adult culture without the risk of direct confrontation and embarrassment. Let's explore these activities, looking at how they relate to friendship relations, conflicts and disputes, and the challenging of adult control and authority.

Verbal Routines, Games, and Heterosexual Relations

Like preschool children, preadolescents often engage in play routines that involve communal sharing. However, preadolescents with increased language and cognitive skills have more control over when and how such routines might occur. Thus, in addition to more loosely structured play routines, preadolescents often participate in formal games both spontaneously and in organized settings. Children of this age also talk about their play and games in a reflective way, and they can appreciate the subtle and symbolic aspects of play routines both during and after their enactments. Finally, preadolescent children often address concerns about appearance, self-presentation, and heterosexual relations within play routines and games. In this sense, they use the "as-if" or pretend frame of play and games as a secure base for addressing sensitive and potentially embarrassing concerns, desires, and ambiguities.

Routines, Verbal Play, and Humor. Preadolescent children often mark allegiance to friendship bonds through participation in sharing routines. These routines are similar to the general celebration of simply playing together that we saw among preschool children. Here, though, the very nature of participation in the routines forces children to think about their relationship to one another and their place as individuals in a group.

Consider the Israeli sharing routine *xibùdim*, documented by anthropologist Tamar Katriel (1987). Katriel conducted naturalistic observations of the sharing routine and also interviewed 20 preadolescents (ages 9 to 12) and 10 younger children (ages 5 to 7). Xibùdim usually occurred on the way home from school:

> A group of five children approaches the falafel stand. One exclaims "I'm buying." Another counters, *"Bexibùdim! Bexibùdim!"* in a melodious chant. He gets a falafel portion, holds it in his hands, and all take a bite in turn, with a gay clamor. After the third one has eaten, the buyer mutters, "Hey, *beraxmanut"* (with pity) and offers it to the last child. He then eats his falafel, walking along with his friends. (Katriel, 1987, p. 309)

As we can see, this routine has a definite structure: (a) the opening or announcement of an intention to buy a treat by a particular child; (b) the acknowledgment by other children, usually involving the exclamation *Bexibùdim! Bexibùdim!* uttered in a melodious chant; (c) the purchase of the treat by the proposer; (d) the offering and sharing of the treat, with each accompanying child taking a small bite; and (e) the optional recycling of a second round of sharing. The routine involves delicate negotiation in that, as Katriel has noted, the bite size has to be regulated so that everybody gets a share and about half the treat is left for the owner. (This is illustrated by the owner's request for pity before offering the last bite.) According to Katriel, the sharing of treats in xibùdim "can be viewed as a ritualized gesture that functions to express and regulate social relationships within the peer group" (1987, p. 307). A key element here is the concept of the individual's respect for others in her or his group of friends; *xibùdim* is derived from the verb *lexabed*, whose literal meaning is "to respect." In an interview, an 11-year-old girl explained her insistence on getting a bit of her friend's treat in this way: "It's not that I will die if I don't get a bite of the popsicle, that I will die a day earlier or something, but it is simply . . . respect, as the word says" (p. 307). This statement, along with the main features of the routine, support Katriel's insightful interpretation of the routine as a "symbolic sacrifice in which one's self-interest and primordial greed are controlled and subordinated to an idea of sociality shaped by particular cultural values, such as equality and generalized reciprocity" (p. 318). Finally, on a more concrete level, sharing routines such as xibùdim are fun. Their production "serves to reassert the very existence of children's peer group culture" as a "celebration of childhood" (p. 318).

Routines like xibùdim also are interesting because they simultaneously assert individual rights and creativity and collective solidarity. Many other activities in preadolescents' peer cultures possess this characteristic, especially those related to verbal games and humor. For example, preadolescents produce and embellish a wide range of children's lore—games, jokes, chants, rhymes, riddles, songs, and other verbal routines that are created and transmitted by children over time and across societies. Such lore has been well documented by child folklorists (McDowell, 1979; Opie & Opie, 1959, 1969). These activities are rich with laughter, which serves as a communicative marker. It both signals that the activity at hand is not serious and "also signifies support; others with you" (Frønes, 1995, p. 223).

We saw examples of children's lore in our earlier discussion of humor among preschool children, as well as in the Italian children's chanting routine or *cantilena*. However, the humor and verbal play rituals of preadolescents are often more complex, reflective, and portable than those of preschoolers. Merely saying the words *pee-pee* or *poo-poo* can generate laughter anywhere or anytime among preschoolers. This joke provides little opportunity for reflective awareness or embellishment, however, and its expression in play and games often disrupts the activity at hand. Preadolescent children collect jokes and riddles and practice and embellish their presentations, often embedding the joking and laughter in other peer activities. They try out jokes on older siblings and parents and discover that this audience also can be the source of new additions to their developing repertoires. These jokes and riddles often have a two-step, set-up-and-punch-line structure, which demands a certain level of cognitive decentering (the punch line or solution must be inferred from the set up) and language skills (questions must be asked, words phrased or voiced in a certain way, and so on).

My daughter constantly tried out new jokes on me when she was in elementary school. Here is an example of one she told when she was about 6 years old: "What do you call a train filled with bubble gum?" "I don't know." "A Chew-Chew Train!" From an adult point of view, the jokes get better as the child ages. When she was 8, my daughter's jokes contained elements of indirectness, involving a play on words or some other type of deception in the setup. She learned many of these from other kids but also several from her uncle. Here are two examples:

1. "If there are 20 sick sheep [sounds like '26 sheep'] and 1 dies, how many are left?" "25." "No, 19. I said '20 sick sheep!'"

2. "If a plane crashed right on the border between Canada and the United States, where would they bury the survivors?" "I don't know, probably in their hometowns." "No, silly, they don't bury survivors!"

Like the preschool children who laugh over and over again at the mere mention of certain bodily functions, preadolescents like to repeat their jokes again and again and laugh uproariously at the punch line. They are often unconcerned when the joke's recipient gets the right answer and laugh just as loud at his or her statement of the punch line. Adults, on the other hand, tire of these types of jokes pretty quickly and would rather not hear them even a second time. However, such adult reactions often make repeating the jokes more fun for the children and give them a sense of control over their elders. My daughter would preface many of her jokes (especially several she had heard from her uncle) by saying, "Daddy, pretend you didn't hear the one about—." She did this so often that at one point I threatened to strangle my brother for telling her the jokes. Not fully appreciative of my teasing, she said, "Daddy, you're not really going to strangle Uncle Joe, are you?"

Games, Secrets, Self, and Interpersonal Relations. Preadolescent children like to play games. They play a variety of games in a wide range of informal and formal settings. Although a great deal of work has documented such games and how children's participation influences their cognitive, emotional, and social development, studies of children actually playing games are rare. Several fairly recent studies have addressed this neglect.

One example is G. A. Fine's (1987) study of Little League baseball teams. This work is important because it shows how preadolescent boys' participation in organized sports over an extended period of time provides them with a number of interactive settings and occasions for the production and maintenance of a local peer culture. During a Little League season, the boys do much more than learn and practice baseball skills and develop a competitive ethos. Interwoven within the culture of baseball is a local peer culture in which the boys develop a strong sense of male bonding and address a wide range of concerns about identity and their perceptions and relations with girls. The boys also use the activities of baseball practice and games as a backdrop for producing, sharing, and acquiring the language, jokes, and lore of preadolescent cultures.

Perhaps some of the best work on children's games as situated activities is that of Goodwin (1985, 1990) and Evaldsson (1993). By *situated activities,* these researchers mean games that are produced in real settings with real children who often have long interactional histories. Research that is based on verbal reports of children's participation in games or that relies on analysis of the form and structure of games abstracted from the actual performances misses this situated aspect. Such research is bloodless, so to speak. It surely tells us something about how children spend their time and about the developmental implications of participating in games with various physical, cognitive, language, and emotional demands. But if one really wants to capture the rich social world of children's lives and peer cultures, it is necessary to enter their play, to be willing to get your pants dirty and shoes muddy.

This is just what Goodwin and Evaldsson have done. Goodwin has studied the play and games of African American and Latino children in the United States for many years. She has observed, audiovisually recorded, and analyzed these children participating in a wide range of play and games (dramatic role-play, team sports, jump rope, hopscotch, racing, pitching pennies, and more) in their neighborhoods and in nearby playgrounds. Goodwin has found that the children's play and games are marked by complex verbal negotiations, disputes, and conflicts through which the children display and develop social identities and organize their peer cultures. We will return to look at Goodwin's work in detail in the next section, where we consider the importance of conflict and disputes in children's peer culture. Here, we want to look more carefully at Evaldsson's study of children's participation in games in Swedish after-school programs.

Evaldsson studied two programs for 6- to 10-year-old children over an 8-month period. She found that the children repeated games day after day. The children in the Panda center preferred to play and trade marbles, whereas the children at the Bumblebee center often engaged in jump rope. Marbles is a highly complex game. Piaget (1932) analyzed in some depth the game's contributions to children's negotiation strategies and their moral development. Evaldsson, on the other hand, focused on how children relied on repeated performances of the game to create a locally shared peer culture and to display and evaluate selves and identities in that culture.

Marbles involves skills in playing the game—that is, aiming and shooting marbles at a hole or at another player's marbles, quickly anticipating the flow of play, and shouting various restrictions regarding shooting. Evaluating the value of marbles from a competition and trading standpoint is also important. Although the children in the study played marbles in dyads, there was always an audience of nonplayers who observed and often participated in arranging matches, evaluating the play, and negotiating marble trading. Evaldsson found that boys primarily played the games, with girls more actively involved in evaluating the play and trading.

The games and trades had natural histories in that they occurred during the school term, and during this period of time the children came to assess each other in terms of these various skills. In her documentation of the history of marble play as a complex series of situated activities, Evaldsson found that the children's selves were intimately related to status, which was linked to the possession and negotiated value of marbles as things. In other words, as the children increased and decreased their status in relation to their possession of the valued objects, they used talk to negotiate the value of the objects (1993, p. 133). The whole process was made even more complex by shifting alliances of children in judgments and negotiations during both the playing and the trading of marbles.

Thus, we see the developing notion of identity or self embedded in the collectively produced peer culture.

Jump rope, like marbles, is rule governed, and participants are expected to have a particular orientation to one another during play (Evaldsson, 1993; Goodwin, 1985). Although there is a good bit of variation, the general pattern in jump rope is for two children to hold opposite ends of a rope and turn it for a third child, who jumps when the rope hits the ground. The child who jumps is normally entitled to continue until she misses. When this occurs, the jumper exchanges places with one of the turners, who now has the opportunity to jump. Legitimate misses are the fault of the jumper and not the turner. Therefore, misses are sometimes negotiated to assign fault, and these negotiations can become very heated and complex. Jump rope is competitive because successful jumpers earn high status and often obtain the valued position of "first jumper" in initial rounds of play. However, a most interesting fact of jump rope is that children must cooperate to compete. There is a built-in motivation to turn the rope fairly for jumpers because if one turns too fast or not in synchrony with the beat, there is a chance that when the jumper next becomes a turner, he or she will do the same for the previous offender (Evaldsson, 1993; Goodwin, 1985).

We can see from this description that jump rope is much more complex than some previous studies, like that of Lever (1978), suggest. Lever argued that girls' games such as jump rope or hopscotch are eventless turn-taking games with much less complex structures than boys' competitive sports games. Such a misperception is the result of not observing, recording, and carefully analyzing the play of the games themselves. However, the complexity and significance of the games are even more apparent when their production and place in peer culture are examined over long periods of time. For example, in a recent study of the game Four Square among immigrant and native Swedish children, Evaldsson (2003) found that many of the games were gender integrated, and several of the girls were active participants who could play as well as or better than the boys. In her analysis, Evaldsson presented descriptions and visual data that clearly challenge the notion of "throwing like a girl."

But let's return to girls' games and consider a typical game of jump rope in Evaldsson's (1993) study. She found that in the Bumblebee after-school center, both boys and girls engaged in jump rope activities on a regular basis. The most frequent game was Cradle of Love. This variant of jump rope can be played a number of ways, but the most common variety at Bumblebee was this: A jumper jumps as turners and members of an audience call out the letters of the alphabet. If the jumper misses on a particular letter, others call out the name of another child or of some media character, who then becomes the potential (or pretend) love interest of the jumper. For example, if Amy misses at the letter *P*, someone may call out "Paul!" Then Amy jumps to the rhyme, "Paul do you love me? Tell me truly aye or nay." Then the speed of turning is increased and the rhyme continues: "Yes-No Yes-No Yes-No," with the romantic link confirmed or denied according to when a miss occurs. If a jumper succeeds in moving through the entire alphabet, she can propose the name of the love interest without the constraint of the initial letter. In this case, however, other children quickly offer up potential names for the jumper to evaluate.

We can see that repetitions of this game among boys and girls who spend a lot of time together take on characteristics that have as much to do with their developing relationships toward the opposite sex as they do with their competitive skill in jumping. Let's look at a more extended example from Evaldsson's work.

CRADLE OF LOVE

Sara has just successfully jumped through the alphabet. She gets to pick a name, and two children suggest Dag (Dan in Swedish), who is one of the most popular boys with girls in first grade. Sara seems a bit embarrassed and quietly says "no." Then the children suggest comic book characters such as Batman and Superman, and Sara responds "no" to all these suggestions. The children then return to offering names of children in the group.

Ania: Leif?

Sara: No.

Paul: Paul?

Fred: Someone in your class?

Paul: Axel?

Ania: Paul?

Fred: Paul?

Sara: Nope.

Axel: Per-Ola?

Paul:	We've already had Per-Ola.
Sara:	Dag [very quietly]. I'll take Dag then. Yes, Dag then.
Mona:	Dag in our class?
Sara:	Nope.
Ania:	Dag sitting over there in the green cap?
Paul:	Is that him?
Sara:	Tuuurn!
Paul:	Him [pointing].
Fred:	Wowww! Wooowie!
All:	Dag Do You Love Me
	Tell Me Truly Aye or Nay [turning faster now]
	Yes-No Yes-No Yes-No Yes-No [turning stops]
	Yeeeessss!
Flera:	Yeesss ho ho ho [laughing]
Fred:	Dag! [Calling to Dag]
Flera:	Ha ha ho ho ho ho [laughing]
Rick:	Dag, well that doesn't necessarily mean Dag.
Fred:	But she said Dag.
Ania:	Congrats, Dag!

Source: Adapted from Evaldsson (1993, pp. 117–119).

Evaldsson suggested that Sara was probably too shy to reveal her true preference for Dag when the name was first suggested. Also, because there was more than one Dag in the group, the matter was somewhat ambiguous. However, Sara clears up the ambiguity later and takes the game seriously when she chooses the boy she is fond of in real life. Now this ordinary, everyday game of jump rope is intensified or transformed as the pretend versus real frame is blurred. This transformation is nicely signaled with the children's laughing, shouts of "Wooowie," and teasing of Dag and Sara. In this way, in the midst of the jump rope game, love becomes a public topic that can engage nearly all the children at that center. Sara takes a chance by addressing her real concerns, feelings, and uncertainties about boys, but she is "protected" by the safety of the play frame, which in this case she dares to stretch.

In addition to participating in organized games, preadolescent children also create their own cultural artifacts to organize and share their activities. For example, children at this age often separate themselves from others through the sharing of secrets. Sharing secrets involves activities ranging from verbal whispering to the writing and passing of notes, the establishment of secret clubs, and the production of complex texts and artifacts. The whispering talk and control of space marks the fact that members of a secret club are part of an exclusive group.

The children in Evaldsson's study produced a number of artifacts related to secrets in their peer culture. These included "love lists" and "fortune-tellers." Both boys and girls constructed love lists on which they wrote the names of best friends in order of preference. These lists were then shared with selected friends and often became the topic of discussions, teasing, and sometimes disputes. Children created fortune-tellers by folding a sheet of paper into four parts, then folding the corners into the center, and finally folding the paper into four parts again. The folded paper was then arranged to fit two fingers from each hand for opening and closing (Evaldsson, 1993, p. 196; see Exhibit 9.1).

After constructing the fortune-tellers, children painted the different parts various colors and wrote messages in the corners that were concealed by the folds. They often talked together as they decided which messages to write. They then played with the fortune-tellers in dyads, with other children observing. In play, the owner of the fortune-teller asks the other player to choose a number and then counts it out, opening and closing the folds. Then the owner asks for a color and upon hearing the response folds back the corner of that color and reads the message aloud. Most messages either tease or insult the recipient, saying, for example, that he or she looks like a monkey or is in love with a particular child. The children were fascinated with the magic quality of fortune-tellers and greatly appreciated that these artifacts were of their own creation. The creation of and play with fortune-tellers is not restricted to Sweden, of course, as they also have been documented among American children (Knapp & Knapp, 1976). Many readers may have constructed them in their youth. They are similar, of course, to toys such as the Magic Eight Ball and decoder rings.

Exhibit 9.1   Making a "Fortune-Teller"

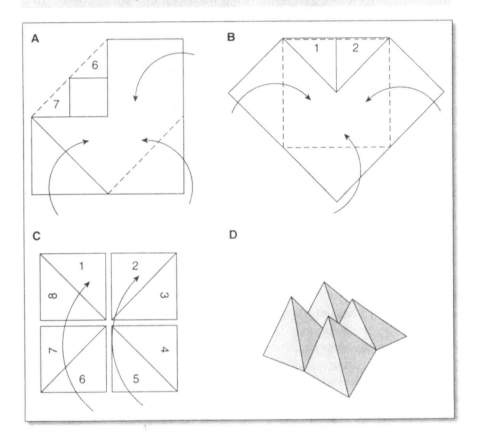

An important point about both love lists and fortune-tellers is that they are durable creations of peer culture. They not only conceal private information and secrets but make them last longer and allow for their transformation outside the situation of actual use. This transformation often generates a traceable history of their use, which can make them subjects of teasing, debates, and conflicts among peers.

Disputes, Conflict, Friendships, and Gender

Many activities that bring preadolescent children together and build friendships are often the source of disputes and conflicts. Rizzo (1989), for example, found that as first graders developed best friendships they set higher expectations for their friends' behaviors. These expectations often led to disagreements and arguments. In fact, it is a common lament of many kindergarten, first-, and second-grade teachers that so-called best friends seem to be fighting all the time! We have to be careful, however, not to accept the adult perspective regarding conflict among young children too readily—most especially the middle-class American adult perspective. Middle-class adults in the United States are often uncomfortable with disputes and conflicts among children. As we saw in our earlier discussion of the peer cultures of preschool children, there is wide variation in the nature and evaluation of conflict and argumentation across cultures and across subcultural groups within American society. Furthermore, recent research documents the positive aspects of conflict and disputes in children's everyday lives. Let's look at some of this research, examining first verbal conflicts and disputes in peer relations and then behavioral routines involving cross-gender conflict.

Verbal Disputes and Conflict in Peer Relations

What are some of the causes of conflict and disputes among preadolescents? How are conflicts important in their daily activities and peer cultures? The chief cause may be the increased differentiation in friendship groups in preadolescence, but conflict, especially arguments and teasing, can also bring children together and help organize their activities. In this sense, cooperation and competition are not mutually exclusive and often coexist within the same activities (Goodwin, 1990, p. 84). Research on peer conflict among elementary school children shows how disputes are a basic means for constructing social order; cultivating, testing, and maintaining friendships; and developing and displaying social identity (Davies, 1982; Goodwin, 1990, 1998; Katriel, 1985; D. Maynard, 1985; Rizzo, 1989).

Goodwin's work on preadolescent children's play and games in neighborhood settings clearly demonstrates the important role of conflict in the organization of peer activities. For example, Goodwin found that the African American children she studied organized their talk to build and highlight opposition. Boys engaged in arguments and ritual insults as a way of dramatizing their play and to construct and display character. Conflicts and disputes seldom reached clear resolution, as disagreements between individual children often expanded into group debates. In short, conflict was enjoyed, even relished, and the children actually cooperated to embellish and extend rounds of arguments and insults.

Furthermore, the children never complained to adults about peer teasing and insults, rarely excluded peers from play, and did not produce rigid status hierarchies.

Let's take a closer look at Goodwin's work on conflict among preadolescent African American and Latina girls to capture the tenor of her work. The research is especially important because the everyday lives of these children are seldom carefully studied and are often misunderstood in American social science.

An especially impressive example of research on children's dispute routines is Goodwin's (1990) analysis of gossip disputes among Black female preadolescents. Unlike males, in their direct competitive disputes (Goodwin, 1990; Labov, 1972), Black females frequently engage in gossip disputes during which absent parties are evaluated. The airing of such grievances frequently culminates into he-said-she-said confrontations. A *he-said-she- said confrontation* can be defined as a type of gossip routine that is brought about when one party to a dispute gossips about the other party in his or her absence. The confrontation comes about when the absent party challenges his or her antagonist at a later time. Consider the following example: "In the midst of play, Annette confronts Benita saying: 'And Arthur said that you said that I was showing off just because I had that blouse on'" (Goodwin, 1990, p. 195).

Annette is speaking to Benita in the present about what Arthur told her in the recent past about what Benita said about Annette in the more remote past. This complex temporal structure is crucial to he-said-she-said exchanges because the accusation locates the statement made by the defendant about the speaker as having been made in the speaker's absence. Such talking behind one's back is considered a serious offense in the peer culture. In her analysis, Goodwin specified the complex linguistic structures that the children use in such confrontations to order a field of events, to negotiate identities, and to construct social order. The gossip routine is important because it is inappropriate to insult, command, or accuse others openly in the girls' peer culture.

Goodwin (1998, 2006) has also carried out comparative studies of disputes and conflicts in preadolescent girls' games of hopscotch. On the surface, hopscotch seems to be a simple turn-taking game, demanding a fair amount of physical coordination. One person jumps at a time through a grid of squares usually numbered from one to nine. The object is to be the first player to advance a token (rock or bean bag) from the lowest to the highest square and back again. At the start, a player tosses her token from below square one into a square and, while standing on one leg, jumps from one end of the grid and back again on one foot, avoiding squares where other tokens have been tossed. Where there are two unoccupied squares next to each other, the jumper's feet should land in the two adjacent blocks. If a player falls down, steps on a line, or steps outside the correct square, she loses her turn.

Hopscotch can involve a great deal of negotiation about the rules. In the hopscotch play of the African American and Latina girls that Goodwin studied, nonjumpers intensely scrutinized the body movements of jumpers and were quick to call out infractions and enforce the rules. Consider the following example:

Lucianda takes her turn, jumping twice in square two and possibly putting her foot on the line of square one. Joy sees the violation and yells, "You out."

Lucianda shakes her head no, "No, I'm not!"

"You hit the line," counters Joy. Now Crystal comes over in support of Joy and says, "Yes, you did. You hit the line. You hit the line," as she points to the line.

Lucianda leans towards Crystal. "I ain't hit no line!"

"Yes, you did," shouts Alisha, who has now come over to the group. Crystal supports Alisha, smiling and shaking her head as she points to the spot of the violation, "You did. You s—"

"No, I didn't," interrupts Lucianda.

"Yes, you did," counters Alisha again.

"Didn't she go like this?" Crystal asks the others. And then looking at Lucianda she says, "You did like this," as she steps on the line in an imitation of Lucianda's jump. "You did like that."

Joy now walks up to the grid and rubs her foot across the line, "Yeah, you hit that line." Then she taps the line twice with her foot and says, "Right there, honey!"

Finally, another nonjumper, Vanessa, comes over and says to Lucianda, "You out now!" (Adapted from Goodwin, 1998, pp. 35–36)

In this example, we see that the girls negotiate and enforce the rules with a great deal of teasing and dramatic flair. In fact, in many cases the stylized disputes and arguments over misses or what were labeled "attempts to cheat" became more important than the actual play of hopscotch. Rather than simply following the rules or ignoring them, the girls work and play with them, often purposely highlighting opposition (Goodwin, 1998, p. 38).

Things were quite different in the hopscotch play of the middle-class White girls Goodwin observed. Instead of closely observing and evaluating the play, the children paid less attention to misses and mitigated their responses to them. Consider this example:

MAKE LESS SEVERE, SERIOUS, OR PAINFUL.

Linsey, Liz, Kendrick, and Cathleen are playing. Linsey throws her stone and hits a line. Linsey then begins jumping. "Oh! Good job, Linsey! You got it all the way on the 7," says Liz.

Kendrick clearly sees that Linsey has hit a line with her foot. She shakes her head, "That's—I think that's sort of on the line though." "Uh," says Liz to Linsey, "your foot's in the wrong spot."

"Sorry," says Kendrick, "that was a good try."

Later Linsey is jumping again and she makes it through several squares. "You did it!" shouts Cathleen. "Yes!" says Linsey. She then hits a line as she nears the end of her turn.

"Whoa," says Cathleen softly. Kendrick then laughing a bit says encouragingly, "You accidentally jumped on that. But that's okay." (Adapted from Goodwin, 1998, p. 37)

Some feminist scholars see the mitigated nature of children's speech of this type as positive, arguing that it demonstrates concern for affiliation and promotes relational solidarity (M. M. Barnes & Vangelisti, 1995; Gilligan, 1982). Goodwin, however, noted that group solidarity can be achieved in a variety of ways. Furthermore, she pointed to a "lack of accountability for one's action" in the mitigated language style of the middle-class White girls in this example. She argued that interpersonal conflict is often the heart of social life. In fact, conflicts seldom disrupted play in her data; rather, they added spice and flair. In this view, conflict and cooperation are not opposites but overlapping processes that are embedded in the larger ethos of playfulness. Disputes, teasing, and conflict can add a creative tension that increases its enjoyment (Goodwin, 1998).

In her recent book *The Hidden Life of Girls*, Goodwin (2006) has developed these points even further, which expands her earlier work with

ETHOS
CHARACTERISTIC OF CULTURE, ERA, OR COMMUNITY AS MANIFESTED IN ITS BELIEFS & ASPIRATIONS

African American boys and girls from Philadelphia and African American and Latina girls from South Carolina. In the latest work she studied the play of girls and boys from a wide range of ethnicities (Korean, Chinese, and Vietnamese in a working-class area of Los Angeles and immigrant children of similar backgrounds from Saudi Arabia, Mexico, Puerto Rico, and Azerbaijan living in South Carolina) as well as racially and ethnically mixed, primarily middle-class girls and boys from a Southern California elementary school. As Goodwin found in earlier work, both boys and girls show a preference for disagreement in the play of hopscotch and other games. She noted,

> Emotion is conveyed through affective intensity, vowel lengthening and raised volume. Unlike delayed disagreement observable in adult conversation, the girls, through their intonation and gestures (such as extended finger points) display in a forceful, integrated manner that opposition is occurring, thus countering many of the stereotypical views of female language use. (2006, p. 43)

In the Southern California primary school she studied, Goodwin found that the girls she studied arranged themselves in cliques that were composed of asymmetrical relations on the playground. In maintaining these relations they made use of bald imperatives, accusatory statements invoking age and gender, and pejorative descriptions, and they "generally demonstrated their ability to artfully collaborate to present a position and debate it through clever, appropriate, and forceful comebacks" (2006, p. 119). These findings fly in the face of girls as cooperative and supportive in their peer relations. She also found that the clique of girls she studied challenged the right of boys to control an area of the playground (the soccer field) and negotiated sharing the space with the boys and playground aides who at first resisted such a solution.

Goodwin also added to her earlier work on children's play of jump rope. In this latest work she again demonstrated the complexity of the game, that both boys and girls played, and that girls were better performers and controlled boys' participation in cross-gender play. She also found that the girls in the fifth- and sixth-grade clique she studied competed for status through storytelling, verbal assessments of one another, and bragging. Assessments and types of bragging were as direct and competitive as what has been found in boys' groups but in some ways were more complex as girls who tried to place themselves too far above the group were open to sanction.

We can make one final point about the relationship between conflict and cooperation in children's play: When children who have spent most of their time in different sociocultural groups come together for play, they often misinterpret each other's styles. Middle-class White girls, for example, often find the teasing, oppositional style of Latina and African American girls to be threatening, bossy, and mean, whereas African American and Latina girls see the mitigated and polite style of middle-class White girls as patronizing (Rosier, 2000; Schofield, 1982). These findings show the value of research on differences in interpersonal interaction and play styles across sociocultural groups. The identification of sources of misinterpretations can be a first step in improving cross-cultural relations.

Borderwork in Cross-Gender Relations

The relationship among teasing, conflict, and tension in peer relations is probably nowhere more apparent than in cross-gender relations among preadolescents. Girls and boys are often apart at this age, but for certain activities they do work and play together with little obvious attention paid to gender. For example, a number of researchers have found that children often play in mixed-gender groups in neighborhoods, most especially if the playgroups are also mixed in age (Ellis, Rogoff, & Cromer, 1981; Thorne, 1993; Whiting & Edwards, 1988). Others have found consistent cross-gender interaction in schools, but it occurs primarily in settings that are not controlled by peer groups such as in classrooms and in extracurricular activities (Thorne, 1993). However, it is in peer-dominated and highly public settings in schools—such as cafeterias and playgrounds—that gender separation is most complete. In fact, many activities and routines of preadolescent children's peer cultures in these settings seem to be all about gender. In these activities and routines, girls and boys try to make sense of and deal with ambiguities and concerns related to gender differences and relations. Many of these activities involve conflict, disputes, and teasing. Thorne (1993) has captured the complexity of such activities with her discussion and analysis of borderwork.

Borderwork refers to activities that mark and strengthen boundaries between groups. When gender boundaries are activated, "other social definitions get squeezed out by heightened awareness of gender as a dichotomy and of 'the girls' and 'the boys' as opposite and even antagonistic sides"

DICHOTOMY—A DIFFERENCE BETWEEN TWO OPPOSITE THINGS

(Thorne, 1993, p. 66; also see Boyle, Marshall, & Robeson, 2003; Voss, 1997). In her work in elementary schools, Thorne identified several types of borderwork. The first type is contests between groups of girls and boys. Among the groups Thorne studied, contests were initiated by both children and teachers. Sometimes teachers pitted boys and girls against each other in math and spelling competitions. On one occasion a teacher named the two teams "Beastly Boys" and "Gossipy Girls," thereby supporting such contests and gender stereotypes (Thorne, 1993, p. 67). Boys and girls would at times play cooperatively in sports games on the playground, but these games were often transformed into boy-girl competitions full of taunts, teasing, and insults usually aimed at the girls.

Another type of borderwork, chasing, is also competitive, but this activity is more symbolic in its affirmation of boundaries between girls and boys. Cross-gender chasing is very similar in structure to the approach-avoidance routines of preschool children that we discussed in Chapter 6. In fact, I observed several instances of cross-gender approach-avoidance play in my work with preschoolers. Among preadolescents, chasing routines usually begin when a child from one gender group taunts members of the other group. These taunts lead to chases that are often accompanied by threats that are seldom carried out. For example, boys may taunt and tease girls, leading the girls to run after the boys and threaten to catch and kiss them. These routines are generally referred to as "chase-and-kiss," "kiss-chase," and "kissers and chasers" (Richert, 1990; Thorne, 1993). In her work, Thorne found that the chases had a long history, with children talking about them for days afterward with friends and even parents (1993, p. 69). Children talk about cross-gender chases because this type of borderwork gives rise to lots of tension. Children are experimenting with their growing concerns and desires regarding the opposite sex. In fact, like approach-avoidance play among preschoolers, chasing routines include the children's marking and acceptance of safety or free zones where children find relief from mounting tensions of the chase. Among the preadolescents, however, safety zones are more than geographical spaces to which children flee to escape threatening agents. For preadolescents, the areas serve as both physical and psychological havens where the children reflect on and talk about the meaning of their experiences. In this way, the preadolescents have more direct control over the meaning of the play and collectively create shared histories of the events.

Thorne found that episodes of chasing sometimes become entwined with rituals of pollution in playground activities. Rituals of pollution are play routines or rituals in which specific individuals or groups are treated as contaminated (as in "having cooties"). Pollution games have been observed in many parts of the world (Opie & Opie, 1969). Thorne found that variants of "cootie games" were very much a part of cross-gender conflict and teasing in that although "girls and boys may transfer cooties to one another, and girls may give cooties to girls, boys do not generally give cooties to boys" (1993, p. 74). Thus, girls are central to pollution games that contribute to boys' power and control over them. In fact, boys sometimes treat objects associated with girls as polluting and threatening to their status in all-boy groups.

Although Thorne stressed the power of boys over girls in such pollution games, girls do reflect on the significance of these games and their images of boys. Consider the following example drawn from an Internet chat between two girls about their favorite country and western singer, Bryan White, using the girls' own writing and punctuation (spelling as well as use of uppercase and lowercase).

BOYS AND COOTIES

Posted by GIRL on January 08,
    Hi Jen, or jennifer, hahahaha.
    arent I funny/I thought so.
    sometimes I snort when I laugh isnt that so funny. hahahahahaha, im 10 and i like bryan. well, not like but you know what I mean. Boyz usually have cooties so I know if bryan does or not.
    GIRL thats 10
    Reply to GIRL on January 9
    Haven't you learned anything by now? Bry doesn't have cooties. There is no such thing as cooties.
    Reply to Bryan White Fan (Jennifer)
    Posted by GIRL on January 9,
    how do you know they don't have cooties??
    the boys at my school do, they eat bugs and pick their nose.
    girl
    Reply to GIRL, Posted by Bryan White Fan on January 9,
    Okay. THEY do have something wrong but very sickening and worse.

This example shows that many preadolescent girls find boys, even those they admire, to possess many negative characteristics; it also displays these unacquainted girls' appropriation and use of the new technology of the Internet to share their experiences, interests, and beliefs in very creative ways.

Like pollution games, the final type of borderwork, invasions, have much to do with power and dominance of boys over girls. Thorne found a pattern, which has been observed repeatedly in similar studies of preadolescent children's activities on playgrounds. The boys in Thorne's study would, individually or in groups, deliberately disrupt the activities of groups of girls (Thorne, 1993, p. 76; also see Grant, 1984; Voss, 1997). Boys ran under girls' jump ropes, kicked their markers from hopscotch grids, and taunted and teased the girls in attempts to disrupt their play. Although boys much more frequently invaded girls' space, there were some interesting exceptions to this pattern. First, although some boys specialized in disruptive behavior, the majority of the boys were not drawn to the activity. Thorne suggested that the frequent disrupters may have acted like bullies in their behaviors with peers more generally. Second, Thorne described a small number of fifth- and sixth-grade girls who organized themselves into what she called "troupes" and roamed the playground in search of action. These girls would often chase boys. The leaders of these troupes were often tall, well-developed girls who somewhat intimidated the boys.

These exceptions are important because they draw our attention to the complexity of interpreting the importance of borderwork. Borderwork, like the jump rope activities among the Swedish preadolescents in Evaldsson's study, is play, but in the play children address issues that are of serious concern. In this way, the key feature of these types of play is ambiguity and tension. However, tension is what makes the activities so appealing to children. In fact, this very tension and ambiguity led Kelle (2000) to challenge Thorne's assumption that heterosexual desire or interest is a precondition for borderwork. Kelle, on the other hand, found in her study of German preadolescents that information about heterosexual desire and interest was collectively produced in the gender games themselves. Thus, concerns about sexuality are a product of, not a precondition for, borderwork.

Thorne rightly pointed out that a good deal of borderwork tips the balance of power to boys because they are frequently the aggressors, control more space, and seem not to suffer from any negative implications that might be associated with engaging in such rituals. Furthermore, borderwork often supports gender stereotypes and exaggerates gender differences. As a result, girls are clearly more apt to be adversely affected by the negative elements of borderwork than boys. However, Thorne argued that borderwork does create a space where preadolescent girls and boys can come together to experiment and reflect on how to relate to one another. The trick is how to encourage changes in or set limits to some types of borderwork to preserve that space and the delicate play frame while evening the balance of power, which more often than not now tilts in the boys' direction.

Challenging Adult Authority and Norms

Preadolescents, like preschoolers, see adults as having ultimate power over their everyday lives. Possessed of increased autonomy on the one hand and a lack of adult status on the other, preadolescents continually find themselves at odds with adults. Their challenges to adult authority are at once more subtle and more direct than those of preschoolers, and these challenges are shared and evaluated more reflectively in their peer cultures.

Consider some findings from an innovative study of the hallway behavior of elementary school children by Don Ratcliff (1994). He found that the children most frequently moved about hallways in phalanxes. He defined a phalanx as two or more people side by side, usually facing the same direction and moving at least temporarily toward some presumed destination. Members of phalanxes normally engage in communication as they move.

The general rule in the elementary school was for children to move as quietly as possible in the halls in files, or lines. As a result, moving in phalanxes in hallways was valued in the peer culture because it gave children control of their interactive space, enabled them to talk and be with friends, and allowed them to challenge the authority of teachers all at the same time. Ratcliff found that "kids like phalanxes." Some children noted that they felt happy, cool, bad, excited, and "as good as anybody else when they were in the phalanx" (1994). In interviews with teachers, Ratcliff found that some teachers saw phalanxes as disruptive but seldom enforced the rule against them. One teacher admitted talking to other teachers in hallway phalanxes and therefore saw it as hypocritical to forbid them. The children were probably well aware of the teachers' double bind in this situation, and this may have made the behavior even more meaningful and enjoyable for them.

Most preadolescents enjoy getting the upper hand with teachers and parents. They often mock adult rules and imitate and exaggerate adults' communicative styles in rule enforcement. For example, Parker (1991) talked about middle school basketball players who complained about their coaches' strict adherence to practice drills. During a practice drill, the players were expected to practice only fundamental basketball moves. As they gathered before practice, the boys would violate this philosophy by dribbling through their legs, throwing passes behind their backs, and taking 30-foot jump shots. Preadolescents also enjoy creating dramas in which they recall past events involving teachers' and parents' disciplining them for misbehavior. In these narratives, children often act out the roles of adult authority figures, taking care to precisely capture and mock their voices, expressions, and gestures (Davies, 1982; Eder, 1988; G. A. Fine, 1987). Often, certain children become widely known and popular in peer culture for their ability to impersonate, mock, and make fun of adults.

Unlike preschoolers, who sometimes balk at adult authority and rules but eventually give in, preadolescents are much more likely to stand their ground against adult rules. Preadolescents are especially sensitive to what they see as adult hypocrisy and injustice and band together to demand their rights. In Chapter 4 we saw an example of such resistance in our discussion of the newsboys' strike in turn-of-the-20th-century America. Several researchers of contemporary preadolescent peer cultures report similar findings (Davies, 1982; Evaldsson, 1993; Thorne, 1993). For some preadolescents the challenging of adult authority goes beyond talking back, arguing, or pointing out injustices. In fact, actively defying adult authority, challenging adult rules, and receiving disciplinary action often comes to be valued among preadolescents. Thus, earning a reputation as a troublemaker can result in higher status in the peer group (Adler & Adler, 1998). Although challenging adult authority and being in trouble was more highly valued among males, Adler and Adler (1998) also found that girls who participated in taboo activities or who belonged to a wild or fast crowd were highly popular in their peer culture.

Finally, as children in contemporary society advance into preadolescence and adolescence they become more immersed in the electronic and digital world of computer games, cell phones, and the Internet. In fact today's preadolescents and adolescents are the digital generation and can be very intimidating to adults who have fewer digital or electronic skills and less knowledge in this area. This digital divide between youth and adults raises fears and concerns among many parents, even those who are highly skilled in the electronic media. We next turn to a consideration of the role electronic media and related consumer culture play in the lives of preadolescents and adolescents.

Generation M: Electronic Media in the Lives of Preadolescents and Adolescents

In a recent entry from the comic strip *Blondie*, Dagwood's young neighbor Elmo is playing with a fire truck when he gets a call on his cell phone. Dagwood remarks that Elmo has "some slick gadgets." Elmo responds, "I guess so, Mr. B, but this one doesn't even download movies," and he adds, "I feel like I'm going backwards these days." Dagwood, who is watching TV and does not have a slick cell phone, tells Elmo "to hang in there." The comic is instructive in several ways. Elmo, a young preadolescent, seems more interested in his truck than the television program that Dagwood is watching, illustrating that children still like to play with toys even if the TV is on. More interesting is the digital divide we see in the generations. Elmo has a slick new cell phone that he can use to make and take calls, send text messages, play music, take pictures, and probably also record movies. However, he bemoans the fact that his phone cannot download movies and that he is going backward in the new technology. It is indeed hard to keep up, but preadolescents and adolescents are in the forefront of staying abreast of the constantly changing digital technology.

Patterns in Media Use

A recent report by the Kaiser Family Foundation (Rideout, Foehr, & Roberts, 2010) examines media in the lives of a nationally representative sample of 2,032 third- through twelfth-grade students, ages 8 through 18. It also includes a subsample of 694 respondents who volunteered to complete 7-day media use diaries. The study was conducted from October 2008 until May 2009. It covers a wide variety of types of media use including computers, movies, music, print, television content, and video games. The study focuses on the children's use of media for entertainment or pleasure and does not include the use of these various sources for activities directly related to schoolwork. The findings are primarily descriptive and involve comparison with earlier findings from a 2004 study. Though descriptive, the findings are diverse and complex, and I summarize some of the main patterns here. I then consider other studies of media use that address the effects of various types of media use on children and youth and directly examine the role of media use in the lives of children and youth in the family and with peers.

Rideout et al. noted that during the 5 years between the two studies, "young people have increased the amount of time they spend consuming media by an hour and seventeen minutes daily, from 6:21 to 7:38" (2010, p. 2). When multitasking (using more than one medium at a time) is taken into account, the amount of media use or exposure increases to 10 hours and 45 minutes a day. If we assume children and youth sleep 7 to 8 hours a day, these findings indicate they are linked to electronic media in some way or another more than 65% of their waking hours each day! Although watching television content and listening to music are the most frequent forms of media use, it must be remembered that with changing technologies both of these types of use can be and are accomplished from multiple platforms (televisions, radios, computers, cell phones, and MP3 players). One of the most interesting findings from the study is the increased possession of new technology platforms. During the 5 years between the two studies, the proportion of 8- to 18-year-olds who own their own cell phones has grown from 39% to 66%, whereas the proportion with iPods or other MP3 players increased even more dramatically, jumping from 18% to 76% (p. 3).

Let's take a brief look at the findings from the study for each type of media, remembering that with multitasking they are often intertwined. The report finds that children and youth view some form of TV content 4 and a half hours each day. The majority is live TV (59%); 12% is viewed via DVDs, 12% is viewed on cell phones or iPods, 9% is viewed via the Internet, and 8% is viewed via On Demand or recordings from TiVo or some other type of video recorder. Younger children, 8- to 14-year-olds, watch more TV than 15- to 18-year-olds, and many children, especially 7th to 12th graders, multitask (use a computer, read, play video games, send text messages, or listen to music) most or some of the time while watching TV. Not surprisingly, parental restrictions about program content and viewing time decrease with age, with the most restrictions being placed on 8- to 10-year-olds. As noted earlier, there has been a big increase in ownership of cell phones, with 66% of children and youth owning their own phones. The proportion varies by age, from 31% of 8- to 10-year-olds, to 69% of 11- to 14-year-olds, to 85% of 15- to 18-year-olds. Younger children

(8- to 10-year-olds) report using cell phones less frequently and primarily for talking or for listening to music, playing games, or watching TV, with little text messaging. In contrast, older children do more texting than talking. On average, 7th to 12th graders report spending about an hour and a half engaged in sending and receiving texts a day, and all those who text send an average of 118 messages in a typical day! Although not discussed as such in the report, these findings regarding texting imply that children have transformed the use of this new technology originally primarily designed for verbal communication to communication primarily via text. However, we know it is a highly abbreviated form of text often invented by youth and infused with their own meanings in line with their friendships and identities. Clearly, there is a need for in-depth research on this phenomenon. We will consider several studies on youth and texting below.

The study finds that on a typical day, 64% of 8- to 18-year-olds use a computer for entertainment purposes (with 11- to 18-year-olds spending 1 hour and 45 minutes a day on computers, about an hour more than 8- to 10-year-olds). All age groups spend a considerable amount of time playing computer games and visiting websites on the Internet, especially the video website YouTube. However, older children (especially 11- to 14-year-olds) spend nearly a half hour each day social networking on sites such as MySpace and Facebook. Among the older children who engage in social networking, there are no gender differences, but girls remain and participate at such sites for longer amounts of time.

Children's video game playing is found to have increased in the study, but most of the increase is away from console players, which are still the most popular, to play on handheld games and on cell phones (49% play on consoles such as Wii, PlayStation, or Xbox; 29% play on handheld players; and 23% play on cell phones). Here again we see how cell phone technology affects much of the media use among children and youth. Video game playing peaks among 11- to 14-year-olds (1 hour and 25 minutes per day, compared to about 1 hour a day for 8- to 10-year-olds and 15- to 18-year-olds). Boys spend considerably more time playing video games than girls (1 hour and 37 minutes a day compared to 49 minutes a day). However, almost all of this difference is in regard to play on console games, whereas boys and girls play generally an equal amount of time on handheld games or cell phones. There is a great deal of controversy about violence in video games, which we will discuss more below. The study finds that a large percentage of children and youth (primarily boys) have played the most notorious of violent video games, *Grand Theft Auto*, despite its M (Mature Audience) rating. Play of this game is more frequent for older compared to younger children (72% of 15- to 18-year-olds, 60% of 11- to 14-year-olds, and 25% of 8- to 10-year-olds report playing the game). The number of younger children having access to and playing the game is surprising and worrisome. However, it is doubtful they are regular players, and it is much like watching an R-rated movie. Thus, playing the game once might be both an act of rebellion against adult rules and a way to impress peers. Not surprisingly, a much higher percentage of boys than girls report playing the game. On the positive side, the study finds that many more young people play music and sports games. New music games such as *Guitar Hero* and *Rock Band* show how new technology can bring together different types of media. With these games children and youth have another platform to experience music, but here it is in a more active way of performing rather than just listening.

Children are, however, still avid listeners to music. The study finds that listening to music increases by age from a little more than an hour a day for 8- to 10-year-olds, to 2 hours and 22 minutes for 11- to 14-year-olds, to a little more than 3 hours for 15- to 18-year-olds. Children and youth still listen to music on the radio, but most now listen on iPods and MP3 players. Also more and more, especially older teens, listen on cell phones and computers. Girls listen to music more than boys, but the difference is negligible for listening on iPods and MP3 players, cell phones, and computers. Finally, of all electronic media use, listening to music is most often involved with multitasking. This finding is especially true for 7th to 12th graders. Of this group 73% report that they are most of the time or some of the time involved with other media activities while listening to music.

Finally, the study reports on the more traditional types of media activities, watching movies in theatres and reading. Despite new technologies for watching movies at home (such as HDTV, On Demand, and Blu-ray as well as easier access via Netflix), children and teens report spending the same amount of time watching films in theatres as they did in a study 5 years earlier and more than they did in a study 10 years earlier. The study finds that on a given day about 12% of all children and youth report watching a film in a theatre, and there are few differences by age and gender. Regarding reading for pleasure in terms of types of reading (magazines, newspapers, and books), percentage of those who read, and the amount of time reading, the study finds a major decrease from the last study done 5 years ago. For all print reading the percentage who report reading of any type for pleasure dropped from 73% to 66%, and the amount of time reading per day dropped from 43 minutes to 38 minutes. Children and youth are, of course, doing some reading online, but that amount raises total reading only about 2 minutes. The report notes that reading for pleasure continues to be the only media activity that decreases with age. It finds that 8- to 10-year-olds spend an average of 46 minutes a day reading print media, compared to 33 minutes for 15- to 18-year-olds. The difference is entirely accounted for by the fact that younger children spend more time reading books than do their older counterparts. The study offers the explanation that it "may well be that as reading assignments for school become more demanding, the amount of time young people choose to devote to reading *outside* of school work decreases" (Rideout et al., 2010, p. 31). This explanation is certainly viable, but it could be that reading is still a relatively new skill for young children and they enjoy appropriating something taught to them by adults in school to their own activities in the family and with peers. This may also explain the appeal of many books (for example, the *Harry Potter* series) that are marketed to younger readers.

Before leaving the study, it is useful to point out some demographic and other patterns regarding most of the media use data. First, for all types of media use (except for print media) the study finds that Black and Hispanic children and youth (controlling for other factors such as age, parent education, and whether the child is from a single- or two-parent family) are heavier users than White children and youth. The difference by race and ethnicity is the greatest for watching television and listening to music. It should also be pointed out that although Blacks and Hispanics read less than Whites, the difference is significant only for reading books. These findings are somewhat surprising as there is a digital divide by class, race, and ethnicity, with more wealthy White children and youth having greater access to computers and cell phones than do lower income minority children and youth (Lenhart, Arafeh, Smith, & McGill, 2008). It could be that the findings are related to sampling techniques in the study. Finally, the study finds that children who spend more time with media ("heavy users") report lower grades and lower levels of personal contentment compared to moderate and light users. However, it should be noted that the study "cannot establish whether there is a cause and effect relationship between media use and grades, or between media use and personal contentment. And if there are such relationships, they could well run in both directions simultaneously" (Rideout et al., 2010, p. 4).

Effects and Process of Media Use in the Lives of Preadolescents and Adolescents

The descriptive findings reviewed above give us a fascinating look into the fast-changing nature of media use by preadolescents and adolescents. However, outside of reference to some negative effects on academic and psychological health on heavy users of media, the findings tell us little about overall effects of media use and, more important, how media use is integrated into the lives of preadolescents and adolescents. Finally, the Kaiser Family Foundation study focuses only on American children and youth. We know that the increased media use of children and youth is global in nature, and much important research on this issue has taken place in other parts of the world. In this section I review research on media use as part of the lives of children and youth in their families and peer cultures.

Livingstone (2007), in an important article, laid out two differing positions in most theorizing and research on media and children and youth. On one side there are those who see the media as a social problem negatively affecting children in various ways (leading to aggression and violence, early sexuality, obesity, and so on) and set out to identify these effects. This position is in line with the "effects" literature related to children's symbolic and material culture that we discussed in Chapter 6. On the other side there are those who do not begin with the assumption that a grave social problem exists. Instead these process theorists and researchers (who take a constructivist or cultural studies approach much in line with interpretive reproduction) stress the agency of children and argue that media use must be evaluated in social and cultural context. From this view electronic media can and often do have a positive side in which children and youth enjoy media, use them, and can gain from them.

Results from research based on the social problem or effects model are mixed and generally inconclusive. They are nicely summarized in an article by British scholars Browne and Hamilton-Giachritsis (2005, quoted in Livingstone, 2007):

> There is consistent evidence that violent imagery in television, film and video, and computer games has substantial short-term effects on arousal, thoughts, and emotions, increasing the likelihood of aggressive or fearful behaviour in younger children, especially in boys. The evidence becomes inconsistent when considering older children and teenagers, and long-term outcomes for all ages. The multifactorial nature of aggression is emphasised,

together with the methodological difficulties of showing causation. Nevertheless, a small but significant association is shown in the research, with an effect size that has a substantial effect on public health. By contrast, only weak evidence from correlation studies links media violence directly to crime. (pp. 6–7)

Results from process studies on electronic media and children and youth based on constructivist or cultural studies approaches, and often using qualitative methods, cannot be so easily summarized (but see Buckingham, 2009; Drotner, 2009; Drotner & Livingstone, 2008; Ito et al., 2010). I will touch on some things we know from studies using this approach for different types of media use in the family and peer group.

Adult family members (most especially parents and particularly mothers; see Horst, 2010, p. 173) have most direct involvement with preadolescents' and adolescents' viewing of televisio.. or films on DVDs in the family. Such involvement involves both collaborative viewing with children and youth and the control over viewing through rules regarding the types of programming and amount of time viewing can occur. In an observation and interview study of 269 parents and children in 62 families in the United States, Hoover, Clark, Alters, Champ, and Hood (2004; also see Hoover & Clark, 2008) found different themes of media engagement. One theme is distinction in which families use rules about and viewing of media with their children as a way for placing or charting their families compared to others. Some families set themselves apart from what they see as the mainstream culture with regard to media viewing, whereas other families more or less embrace their practices as being a part of mainstream culture. A second theme running through all the families was an acceptance of the inevitability of media; even with controls and negotiation their children would consume and be affected by the media to different degrees. A third theme had to do with the difficulty of establishing a normative definition of "good media" in which families often fell back on defining good media as media seen as inoffensive. However, where some families could easily agree that programs such as *Home Improvement* met the criteria, there was disagreement among the families regarding edgier or subversive programming such as *The Simpsons*, which had a great deal of appeal to their children and youth. These themes were in line with another general principle that was generally embraced in the families, and that was "that parenting should involve *pedagogy rather than prohibition;* that good parenting should involve training children to become active media consumers" (Hoover & Clark, 2008, p. 117).

Results from smaller intensive ethnographies of adolescents' use of media in the family are reported in Ito et al. (2010). One ethnography focuses on a single-parent, low-income Latino family in which Maxwel, a 14-year-old seventh grader, lives in a studio apartment with his mother Lydia and two older sisters in Los Angeles (Martínez, 2010, pp. 158–162). The family's media possessions include two televisions (one for broadcast TV and a DVD player and another linked to a Nintendo 64 for video game play) and a digital camera. The family has a computer that was given to them as a gift from a relative, but it has been nonfunctional and in need of repair for some time. Maxwel must negotiate his TV viewing with his mother and sisters but is not unhappy about this and especially enjoys watching Spanish-language soap operas with his mother, who speaks little English. His mother in turn watches sitcoms with her son as she can enjoy the physical humor and improve her English. The digital camera, which is a possession of one of the older daughters, is useful for documenting areas of the house in need of repair (especially the bathroom and kitchen ceilings) to negotiate lower rent. The camera is also highly valued for taking photos of family events and of the family's participation in an immigrants' rights march. Here we see a relational approach to media use in the family where there is a positive synergy among family members that makes the most of only minimal electronic resources.

What we know about television viewing among peers is more indirect as it is based primarily on focus group interviews of children and youth rather than ethnographic observations. These interview studies reveal that children and youth have clear notions about what is seen as appropriate content for them by adults (for example, in terms of sex and violence). Preadolescents (7- to 11-year-olds) are more accepting of such views, whereas adolescents are more likely to challenge them as they see themselves as more mature and ready to view such content (see Buckingham, 2009; Kelly, Buckingham, & Davies, 1999). For both preadolescents and adolescents there is an interest in more adult content on television as a sort of forbidden fruit or for the purpose of testing boundaries even if they do not watch such material on a regular basis. The testing of boundaries can be tied directly to peer culture in the sense that viewing adult-oriented television shows or rented DVDs of R-rated movies can be something to brag about or a sign of being "cool" (Adler & Adler, 1998; Olesen, 1999). Also, watching violent or horror movies is a sort of risk management for children and youth in which they challenge themselves emotionally and deal with fears. Here we see a parallel to our discussion in Chapter 7 of the approach-avoidance play of younger children.

Also in line with this theme of testing fears, interview studies of preadolescent and adolescent children show that they distinguish between real and fictional violence and show more concern with being victims of real crime they see perpetrated on news programs than with violence of fictionalized evil characters on television or in movies (Buckingham, 1996; Livingstone, 2007; Nightingale, Dickenson, & Griff, 2000). I encountered an example of this phenomenon in my own work with much younger children in a Head Start program. Several of the children sometimes played a type of approach-avoidance game they called "Nightmare Freddy" based on the horror film series *Nightmare on Elm Street* featuring the evil mass murder Freddy Kruger. I told two of the children, Ramone and Zena, that they should not watch such "scary" movies. Both children scoffed at my concern, noting that these shows are "not scary" because they are "not real." Ramone explained to me that Freddy has "just got on a costume that makes people scared." When I asked if these films caused them to have bad dreams, Zena dismissed the notion by explaining that her bad dreams related to real-life concerns: She didn't have bad dreams about Freddy; she had bad dreams about a mean dog that chased and tried to bite her. Zena and Ramone left little doubt about their ability to distinguish make-believe from real threats, and they displayed highly sophisticated reasoning that was very impressive for children of this age (see Rosier, 2000, p. 104, for a discussion of these data).

Many scholars who do work on electronic media and children and youth point to what they call "moral panics" (Buckingham, 2000; Critcher, 2008). Such panics center on the belief that media expose and corrupt youth with their violent content. These panics are often spurred on by extensive news coverage of violent acts by children and youth such as the Columbine High School shootings. In this discourse about negative effects of media on youth, the argument goes beyond issues of desensitization to violence and increased aggression to one of inciting youth to violent acts. Such moral panics are particularly part of concerns about video games given that the content of the most popular games involves a great deal of violent action.

There are a number of responses to moral panic. Some are sociological, pointing to other structural causes of violence such as inequality and poverty, the wide availability of guns, youth gangs, and drug trafficking, to name just a few. Here authors such as Sternheimer (2003) pointed to the fact that as video game play among children and youth increased dramatically in the 1990s, rates of violent crime decreased. It is interesting, however, that in arguing it is not the media that are the cause of violence in this case (or at least not video games or films), Sternheimer did feel the news and television media contribute to these moral panics through their sensationalized reporting of high school shootings and the wide coverage they give to research on youth and the media that suggests a connection. We will return to this issue of moral panics when we discuss children as social problems and the social problems of children later in the book. But here I want to focus on what we know about video games and negative effects such as violence and about recent research on the playing of video games by children and youth in cultural context. This latter research shows the many positive and creative aspects of video game play.

In their book *Grand Theft Childhood: The Surprising Truth About Violent Video Games,* Lawrence Kutner and Cheryl Olson (2008) reviewed the literature on gaming, violence, and aggression and reported results from their own study on the subject. Kutner and Olson found some indications that high levels of play with Mature Audience–rated video games is correlated with aggression. However, they found there is no conclusive evidence of a causal relation or that game play is correlated with violent crime. In fact, Kutner and Olson concluded, "The strong link between video games violence and real world violence, and the conclusion that video games lead to social isolation and poor interpersonal skills, are drawn from bad or irrelevant research, muddle-headed thinking and unfounded, simplistic news reports" (p. 8).

Kutner and Olson's book surely does not put an end to the debate about video games and violence, but it does suggest that a more nuanced look at video games in the lives of children and youth is in order. For video games a key is to focus on the lived culture of gaming. As De Castell and Jenson (2003) argued, in "gaming culture, games are not just played, they are talked about, read about, 'cheated,' fantasized about, altered, and become models for everyday life and for the formation of subjectivity and intersubjectivity" (p. 651). Although there is an image of video games' being the domain of preadolescent and adolescent boys, both the types of games played and who plays them has been diversifying in the United States. Ito and Bittanti (2010), for example, pointed to data from the Entertainment Software Association that "reports that 38 percent of game players are women" (p. 196). They also noted that women "age eighteen or older represent a significantly greater share of the game playing population (30 percent) than boys age seventeen or younger (23 percent)" (p. 196). Still, boys are more likely to have video game consoles in their rooms and play what are termed "first-person shooter" games such as *Halo.* Girls play these games as well but more often play a wider variety of games both on consoles and handheld devices and on cell phones. Girls also play the first-person shooter types of games differently than boys, often using a strategy of trying to avoid death or elimination rather than destroying or killing adversaries (Walkerdine, 2009). Walkerdine argued that shooter games are in their design, strategies, and goals much in line with action-hero masculinity, making the task of becoming masculine more straightforward in terms of self-management practices. Girls, on the other hand, "have to pursue the demands of contemporary femininity which blend together traditional masculinity and femininity. Trying to do this while playing games is a very complex and difficult task" (2004, p. 28). Using a relational model of gender and documenting variations in girls' negotiations and styles while playing video games, Walkerdine's (2004, 2009) research is highly insightful not only regarding our conceptualization of gender and video games but also about women and new technologies more generally.

Focusing on children actually playing video games in social context, many researchers in the 1980s and 1990s found educational elements (Ito, 2009). More recently, educational researchers have argued that simulation and state-of-the-art games provide important avenues for the development of cognitive skills and literacy development (Gee, 2003, 2008; Shaffer, 2006). Gee argued for

the importance of video games as "action-and-goal directed preparations for, and simulations of, embodied experience." They are the new technological arena—just as were literacy and computers earlier—around which we can study the mind and externalize some of its most important features to improve human thinking and learning. (2008, p. 203)

Others have investigated the social nature of gaming of different types among preadolescents and adolescents. For example, Horst, Herr-Stephenson, and Robinson (2010) described three genres of children's and youth's participation in new media activities: "hanging out," "messing around," and "geeking out." Hanging out is a collaborative and friendship-driven engagement with media, whereas messing around involves more intensive engagement and experimentation in media use. Finally, *geeking out* refers to an intense commitment or engagement with media technology, often involving considerable expertise in a particular media property, genre, or type of technology (Horst et al., 2010, pp. 35–75).

Regarding video games, hanging out entails emphasis on the social enjoyment of playing games together and is similar in nature to playing traditional board games. Ito and Bittanti (2010) pointed to the Nitendo Wii as the "emblematic platform for hanging out as gaming practice" along with music games such as *Rock Band* and *Guitar Hero* as well as other types of music, dance, and sports games (p. 207). Messing around involves more competitive and committed recreational gaming. This type of gaming is favored by adolescent and young adult males. Although deeply social, it is unlike the hanging out genre in that "game play itself is the impetus and focus for getting together" (Ito & Bittanti, 2010, p. 211). Here gamers often organize intense and lengthy parties for playing a particular game such as *Halo*. A 14-year-old boy described how he participated in such a party with 16 kids. A local area network was set up with four Xboxes and four TVs. The boy recounted,

> It was for five hours straight. After the second hour, I couldn't take it anymore. I had to go out with me and my friend, Josh, just kind of went out and skateboarded a little bit while everybody was playing 'cause my eyes started to hurt. (Ito & Bittanti, 2010, p. 212)

Geeking out involves even more investment in play, with structured kinds of social arrangements such as guilds, teams, clans, clubs, and so on. This type of gaming is more common among older teens and young adults developing out of competitive game playing. It also involves what is called "augmented game play" or engagement with the wide range of secondary productions that are part of the knowledge networks surrounding play (for example, cheats, fan sites, modifications, hacks, walkthroughs, game guides, and various websites and blogs; see Ito & Bittanti, 2010, p. 220). Overall, we see the great complexity of video game culture in these examples and the agency and creativity of youth involved in their participation with this new medium.

In a recent article in the *New York Times* (Holson, 2008), Russell Hampton, president of Walt Disney Company's children's book and magazine publishing unit, recounted an incident that occurred while he was driving his 14-year-old daughter and two of her friends to a play in Los Angeles. The girls were discussing the movie actor Orlando Bloom, and Hampton, whose company produced films in which Bloom had starred, made a comment about him to join in the conversation. In return he heard dismissive sighs from the girls and noticed his daughter rolling her eyes "as if to say, 'Oh Dad, you are so out of it.'" Shortly after this retort the talking among the girls stopped. Hampton looked in his rearview mirror to see his daughter sending a text message on her phone. He admonished her for being rude and texting while with her friends. His daughter rolled her eyes again and said, "But, Dad, we're texting each other and I don't want you to hear what I'm saying."

Teens are the consummate mobile telephone users, and most of their use of these devices involves texting rather than talking (Ling & Haddon, 2008; Rideout et al., 2010). Although mobile phones were first purchased by parents for both preadolescents and teens for security purposes, youth soon appropriated these devices to emancipate themselves from parents (in the above example even while being chauffeured in the family car) and to create new and diverse practices in their own peer cultures. Ling and Haddon noted that it is not "an overstatement to say that texting has been a phenomenon that was developed among teens" (2008, p. 140). Teens discovered the advantages of texting when it was free to use and quickly developed creative ways to communicate through the medium they appropriated. Teens' texting is a global phenomenon, and much of the research on teens and texting has been conducted outside the United States (Ling & Haddon, 2008). As Ling has noted,

Teens have made text messaging into a common form of interaction. They have learned how to coordinate and indeed microcoordinate interaction via the mobile telephone. They use the camera to share photos of enticing members of the opposite sex and to gather peer opinion on the color of potential clothes purchases. (2007, p. 60).

The mobile phone itself, with its various styles and ring tones, is a fashion statement for teens. Additionally, teens' use of various lingo, jargon, and emoticons is another way of expressing their identity and style in peer cultures as well as exploring new and intimate relationships (boyd, 2010; Pascoe, 2010). These positive and creative aspects of mobile phone use have been accompanied by more negative elements such as gossiping, bullying, and sexting (Lenhart, 2009; Ling, 2007; Ling & Haddon, 2008). Sexting, or sending sexually suggestive nude or near nude images via text, has raised both adult concern and debate about the legal rights of youth as some teens have been prosecuted for child pornography for sending or having nude images of themselves or peers on cell phones (Lenhart, 2009; "Prosecutors Gone Wild," 2010).

A study by the Pew Research Center (Lenhart, 2009) reports that 4% of cell-owning teens say they have sent sexually suggestive (nude or nearly nude images) of themselves to someone else via text messaging, whereas 15% have received a sexually suggestive image or video of someone they know. Sexting is usually a part of early courtship among teens as a way of exploring possible romantic and sexual relationships or can be an integral part of ongoing romantic relationships. The study finds that teens' attitudes about sexting vary widely. Some say it is inappropriate, "slutty," and possibly illegal. A number of females also feel they were pressured into sharing sexual images by boyfriends. On the other hand, many teens view sexting as a safe alternative to real-life sexual activity and see it as common and not a big deal. It is doubtful that parents see sexting as no big deal. However, adults do not share in the everyday peer culture that has appropriated this technology. Still, adults are better able to anticipate the possible legal aspects and how a nude photo or suggestive message sent in confidence can be shared with others or even be used in purposefully negative ways as a result of an acrimonious breakup. Overall, as Ling and Haddon argued, the use of cell phones and text messaging among youth can be seen as "the best and most widespread contemporary example of unanticipated innovation from users" (2008, p. 147).

Although both late preadolescents and teens frequently use text messaging in their social relations, primarily older teens are involved with Internet social networking sites such as Facebook and MySpace. These sites limit access to those older than 13, but studies have found that children as young as 8 or 9 years old use such sites. These sites (especially Facebook) are also widely used by adults. The use of the sites by teens is primarily driven by peer and friendship relations. Much of what occurs on these sites regarding friendship parallels what we know about teen friendship practices in peer groups in schools (Eder & Nenga, 2003; Kinney, 1993; Milner, 2004). In fact, danah boyd, who has intensively studied peer relations on online sites, argued that despite the perception

> that online media are enabling teens to reach out to a new set of social relations online, we have found that for the vast majority of teens, the relations fostered in school are by far the most dominant in how they define their peers and friendships. (2010, p. 82)

Still, social networking sites provide new ways to build on and amplify friendships and intimate relationships that primarily exist off-site (boyd, 2010; Pascoe, 2010). Here again we see children and youth appropriating aspects of the adult world to use in ways that meet their peer concerns. In doing so, children and youth are affected by features of this new technology but also gain a certain amount of control over it.

In her work, boyd (2010) found that teens avoid contact with strangers for the most part, but there were exceptions. For example, teens who feel marginalized or ostracized in school seek out new connections on social networking sites with peers who share their interests (for example, in gaming or creative production) or their isolation and discrimination (such as lesbian, gay, bisexual, and transgender youth; see boyd, 2010, p. 90). Most teens, however, use features such as address books and friend or buddy lists to enact and expand friendships. Facebook and MySpace offer incentives for adding people other than close friends, but privacy features can be used to limit those who are not close friends from viewing profiles, leaving comments, and even sending messages. Teens develop general strategies of accepting requests from peers they do not know well to avoid offending them but then limiting their involvement. Teens do monitor each others' practices when it comes to friend or buddy lists. Those who accept large numbers of requests to be seen as popular are criticized and even labeled as, for example, "MySpace whores" (boyd, 2010, p. 96). Certain features such as the MySpace feature of top friends lead to the public display of friendship hierarchies as teens rank their best friends. For those teens using this feature (usually girls) there is often a great deal of competition, jealousy, and hurt feelings. Some youth use the features but get around this problem by listing family and relatives as best friends or use rotating lists of best friends related to shared activities and interests. boyd found that friendship features of social networking sites force teens to navigate their social lives in new ways, but their overall practices and norms mirror how they go about relating to friends offline. However, when teens choose to perform friendships online these often similar processes become more explicit and public, "providing a broader set of contexts for observing these informal forms of social-evaluation learning" (boyd, 2010, p. 100), thus making "peer negotiations visible in new ways, leading to heightened stakes as well as opportunities to observe and learn about social norms from their peers" (boyd, 2010, p. 100).

Other activities on social networking sites involve gossip and rumors, which could lead to harassment or bullying. Social networking sites lead to gossip and rumors often spreading further and faster than they do in off-site peer and friendship relations, thereby increasing tensions and drama. One 17-year-old male in boyd's (2010) study noted,

MySpace is a huge drama maker, but when you stick a lot of people in one thing, then it's . . . it always causes drama. 'Cause, like . . . Myspace is, like, a really big school . . . school's filled with drama. Myspace is filled with drama. It's just when you get people together like that, that's just how life works and stuff. (p. 105)

Many teens choose to opt out of such gossip and drama by using privacy settings. Others actively participate but do not see the drama created as bullying because it is not physical, premeditated, or persistent. Still, some youth do see such activities as hurtful and a form of bullying, but not as commonplace. In fact, as boyd noted, although drama is common, "teens actually spend much more time and effort trying to preserve harmony, reassure friends, and reaffirm relationships" (p. 110). Overall, boyd believed social media mirror and magnify teen friendship practices. She concluded,

> Teens who are growing older together with social media are coconstructing new sets of social norms with their peers and through the efforts of technology developers. The dynamics of social reciprocity and negotiations over popularity and status all are being supported by participation in publics of the networked variety as formative influences in teen life. While we see no indication that social media are changing the fundamental nature of these friendship practices, we do see differences in the intensity of engagement among peers, and conversely, in the relative alienation of parents and teachers from these social worlds. (boyd, 2010, p. 114)

Here again we see the importance of peer culture in line with the orb web model we discussed in Chapter 2. For example, we can see how intergenerational relations are clearly affected by social change related to processes (here in technology and communication) of social reproduction.

SUMMARY

In this chapter we examined the peer cultures of preadolescent children and defined preadolescence as the period from 7 to 13 years of age. Given the lack of research on preadolescent culture in non-Western societies, and because children in these societies often take on adult responsibilities in preadolescence, our discussion focused primarily on Western societies. We were, however, careful to consider racial, ethnic, and social class differences in our review.

We first considered the relationship among friendship, social differentiation, gender, race, and ethnicity. Preadolescents, compared to preschool children, have developed more stable concepts of friendship, and they strive to make their interactions with peers fit their developing conceptions of how best friends should behave with one another.

One result of these attempts to link cognitive concepts and behavior is increasing social differentiation in the peer culture. As preadolescents forge social alliances and secure friendship relations with peers, they also separate themselves from others. These processes of separation are most apparent in gender differentiation in peer interaction, which reaches its peak in preadolescence. Many theorists argue that gender differentiation affects and is affected by deep, dichotomous, and universal gender differences (that is, by the very nature of being male or female). According to this view, women have a different voice in that they value relationships and caring for others, whereas men are concerned about individual rights and notions of justice. These differences have been found among preadolescents, where studies show that girls' concerns center on the valuing of compliance and conformity, romantic love, and an ideology of domesticity, whereas boys' concerns revolve around a cult of masculinity, physical contests, autonomy, and self-reliance. Other theorists challenge this separate-cultures view of peer relations. They argue that the examination of naturally occurring peer interaction in a wide range of social settings and groups reveals a good deal of gender mixing in preadolescent peer relations. Furthermore, these studies of children's situated activities (activities produced in diverse settings by children who have long interactional histories) document a greater complexity in gender relations in preadolescence, which challenges the separate-cultures view. We also saw in recent studies that children frequently separate themselves by race and ethnicity as well as gender. Much research still needs to be done in this area as it is extremely important for raising awareness about diversity in children' peer relations in and out of school.

Studies of situated activities also provide important information about preadolescent children's lore (games, jokes, riddles, songs, and verbal and behavioral routines) and how children in the process of engaging in these activities address issues related to self, identity, and autonomy from adult control. Our discussion of situated activities focused most specifically on children's games, verbal dispute routines, and cross-gender play and rituals. Evaldsson's and Goodwin's studies of the actual play of jump rope and hopscotch within children's peer cultures over time reveal that these games are much more complex than earlier studies—which focus only on the rules and structures of the games—claim. Evaldsson found that preadolescents not only develop certain physical, communicative, and cognitive skills in playing jump rope but also use the game as an arena for addressing personal concerns, feelings, and uncertainties regarding gender relations. Goodwin's research demonstrated the importance of cultural variation in the play of games. She found that African American and Latina girls take the rules of hopscotch very seriously, engage in highly complex and dramatic debates about rule enforcement, and tease each other regarding poor performances. This style of play contrasts with that of middle-class White girls, who often overlook rule violations and mitigate their responses to their peers' miscues. These findings, along with those from Goodwin's documentation of the complex linguistic structure and importance of conflict rituals such as the he-said-she-said dispute routine, show how conflict and cooperation are often overlapping processes that are embedded in the larger ethos of playfulness. Goodwin's work also demonstrates the importance of comparative work for documenting differences in preadolescent peer cultures across sociocultural groups.

How conflict can sometimes contribute to the social organization of preadolescent peer relations and can generate creative tension in preadolescent peer relations also is evident in Thorne's work on borderwork. *Borderwork* refers to activities that mark and strengthen boundaries between groups. In her study of cross-gender relations among preadolescents, Thorne identified three types of borderwork (contests, chases, and invasions) that heighten the awareness of gender and gender differences. Contests are initiated by children and teachers and transform classroom lessons and peer games into competitions of boys against girls. Chases, like contests, are competitive, but they are more symbolic in their affirmation of boundaries between boys and girls. In chases, boys often taunt and tease girls in line with the aggressive nature of boys' peer culture, whereas the girls threaten the boys with kissing or affection, resulting in "chase-and-kiss" games. Chases are often intertwined with rituals of pollution, wherein specific groups are treated as contaminated (as in having cooties). It is girls who are normally seen as contaminated in cross-gender chases, and in this way the borderwork often contributes to boys' power over girls. The final type of borderwork, invasions, also has much to do with power and dominance of boys over girls. Thorne found that some boys invade girls' space and purposely disrupt their play and taunt and tease them. Despite some exceptions, Thorne concluded that girls are clearly more apt to be adversely affected by the negative elements of borderwork than are boys. Nonetheless, she argued that there are creative elements in borderwork and suggested that it does create a space where preadolescent girls and boys can come together and reflect on how to relate to one another.

Preadolescence is a time when children struggle to gain stable identities, and their peer cultures provide both a sense of autonomy from adults and an arena for dealing with the uncertainties of an increasingly complex world. The many positive features of their peer cultures (for example, verbal routines, games, and enduring friendships) allow preadolescents to hold on to their childhoods a little longer while simultaneously preparing themselves for the transition to adolescence. A crucial factor in preadolescent peer culture is children's ability to reflect on and evaluate the meaning of their changing worlds in talk with each other and with adults. In this sense, preadolescents become aware of themselves as individual actors in the collective production of their peer cultures. They also come to recognize how their peer cultures affect and are affected by the more general adult world.

Finally, in this chapter we considered what has been termed "Generation M," or the role of electronic media in the lives of preadolescents and adolescents. We first reviewed recent descriptive studies of patterns in media use by preadolescents and adolescents. We saw that there has been a major increase in the time that children and youth spend in using a variety of media products and platforms in their lives. We also saw that media use is highly complex and rapidly changing with almost constant innovation. Children and youth are clearly media literate, inventive, and savvy. We also examined many recent studies of the effects and processes of media use in the lives of preadolescents and adolescents. These studies capture the complex debates regarding both the positive and the negative effects of electronic media on children's lives. Perhaps more important, the studies demonstrate how youth actively engage, appropriate, and embellish the new media and make it their own, much in line with the notion of interpretive reproduction.

PART FOUR

Children, Social Problems, and the Future of Childhood

In the United States and many other Western societies, we have come to see children and social problems in two interrelated ways: children as social problems and the social problems of children. Seeing children as social problems occurs in several ways. The first relates to viewing children as what Penelope Leach called an "out-group." By this Leach meant that children are not seen as adults in the making but as inferior and not worthy of the same respect as adults (1994, p. 204). Here, children are often seen as a nuisance and disruptive to respectable adult life. Such a view leads to discrimination against children as a group that would not be tolerated or legal if directed toward other groups. For example, in the United States children can be banned from certain forms of housing and even from whole communities. Recently, I received an advertisement for an adults-only cruise. The ad pictured a young red-headed boy sticking out his tongue and making a face. Under the photo, the text assured me that this boy was someone I would not run into on the cruise because the ships were "kid-free" throughout. The advertisement also had pictures of adults enjoying themselves, and underneath the pictures the caption read, *"Smoke-Free and Kid-Free Throughout."* Kids were actually equated with smoke (see Corsaro, 2003)! Can you imagine the reaction if any other group in society was discriminated against and portrayed in such a negative way?

Another way we see children as a social problem is through our extreme worry and anxiety about their safety. Richard Louv (1990) has labeled this tendency the "bogeyman syndrome," the general fear of the victimization of children in contemporary industrialized societies, most especially the United States (pp. 28–41). These excessive fears for children have been fueled by extensive media coverage of childhood abductions and school shootings like the one at Columbine High School in Littleton, Colorado, where two teenage boys shot and killed a teacher and 12 of their classmates. Although such tragedies are rare (school violence has actually decreased during the past several years), adult anxiety and fears for their children have increased (Newman, Fox, Roth, Mehta, & Harding, 2004). Sociologist Joel Best (1990, 1994) has argued that such fears are related to the sentimentalization of children that evolved gradually in the 18th and 19th centuries and to claims-making processes (processes by which different groups make various claims regarding the extent or severity of various social problems such as child abuse, teenage pregnancy, and so on) that occur in the construction of social problems in modern societies (also see Rosier, 2009). These two factors are related as the sentimentalization of children often leads to rhetorical processes and movements about children's safety. For example, Zelizer (1985) documented how certain safety campaigns in the 1920s and 1930s led to a reduction in accidental deaths for children. However, these same campaigns also promoted the domestication of children—their movement from the streets and their increased isolation from the adult world (Zelizer, 1985, pp. 49–55).

Best pointed to similar claims-making processes related to childhood abduction. After several notorious cases of children's being abducted and killed by strangers in the late 1970s, sweeping claims were made about the number of such abductions. One of the most controversial claims was that 1.8 million children were reported missing in the United States each year (J. Best, 1990, p. 46). Others then remarked that these claims were overstated because they included runaway children, who made up the majority of the cases. According to these counterclaims, the exaggerated claims of the first group were leading to increased anxiety among parents and children that was in some ways worse than the actual small chance of an occurrence of abduction. Although the abduction of even one child is a tragic event, the press coverage and claims-making processes that follow such crimes can draw attention away from the more frequent and everyday problems of children. For example, the large number of runaway children was part of the debate but was not seen as a major social problem. Many of these children come from dysfunctional families in which they have been neglected and physically, sexually, and emotionally abused. Most of these children find their lives on the streets even more dangerous as they fall victim to sexual predators and other criminals. Why do their problems receive less media attention? Why are their problems less appealing than those of abducted children? Amber alerts would be shown in the background of television shows 24 hours a day if we considered runaway children a major problem in the United States.

This discussion of runaway children brings us to a final way of viewing children as social problems—blaming the victim. *Blaming the victim* refers to the tendency to hold certain children personally responsible for the complex social and economic forces and problems that so dramatically affect their lives (see Rosier, 2009). For example, runaway children make the decision to run away; if they have been mistreated, that decision to run away can be seen as their parents' fault for failing to live up to their responsibilities in caring for the children they decided to bring into the world. Here the notion of personal responsibility and family values enters the picture. This rhetoric is most evident in debates about teenage pregnancies and what some term "illegitimate children." But the term *illegitimate child* is itself a prime example of blaming the victim because there is no such thing as an illegitimate child as children have no control over their parentage. Yet many are quick to label teen mothers and their children as the cause of a range of social problems in the United States (Murray, 1984). We will discuss teen pregnancies and births at length in Chapter 11 (especially their relation to poverty). Here, I want to note that the rate of teen pregnancies is decreasing, but not the rhetoric that surrounds the problem. Although it is certainly true that many young girls who have become pregnant should have been more responsible, a sizable proportion of these girls were impregnated by older, adult men (see Males, 1999, pp. 189–194). Many of these girls (especially those 16 and younger) were coerced into sex or raped by older males, many of them adults. Clearly, holding such girls responsible for being victims fails to address the many complex factors behind this and other social problems of children and youth.

In Chapters 10 and 11 we'll look directly at the nature and extent of social problems of children and youth: first those most directly related to their lives in the family (Chapter 10) and then those related to their social

— LANGUAGE INTENDED TO INFLUENCE PEOPLE + THAT MAY NOT BE HONEST OR REASONABLE.

positions in society (Chapter 11). We'll examine disturbing global trends in family instability, poverty, and violence, all of which have contributed to a decline in the quality of life of many of the world's children. We'll also note some improvement in these problems in recent years and discuss why and how such progress has been made. Finally, in Chapter 12, we'll revisit and summarize some of the main themes in the book and discuss the future of childhood by focusing on some major challenges facing the world's children. And we consider the wide range of things we all can do right now to enrich children's lives.

10

Children, Social Problems, and the Family

To explore and discuss the social problems of children in detail would take us beyond the scope of this book. Instead, in this chapter and in Chapter 11 we'll examine the general state of the world's children, identify positive trends and setbacks in our attempts to improve the quality of children's lives, and consider some real-life examples, which put a human face on the difficult challenges many children encounter every day. In this chapter we will focus on social problems of children related to their being members of families. We will examine the effects of socioeconomic change and accompanying changes in family structure and children's lives, the effects of divorce on children, and child abuse.

Changing Family Structures and Children's Lives

In Chapter 5 we discussed recent structural changes in families in industrialized and developing societies and how such changes affect the lives of children. Here we want to consider these changes in the family as social problems of children; that is, we want to estimate how the various changes may or may not negatively affect children's lives and the nature of their childhoods. We concentrate on Western industrialized societies because there has been a good deal of social research on how children in these societies are affected by changes in family structure, as well as much

275

political debate and some policy formation related to these changes. Three types of structural changes in the family are seen as the most potentially harmful to children: (a) the increase in the number of families in which both parents are working, (b) the dramatic rise in divorce, and (c) the growing number of single-parent families.

Work, Families, and Childhood

In looking at work, families, and childhood in the United States, we first consider the possible effects that the dramatic increase in the number of working mothers of young children has on the children themselves. We then discuss what the United States and other industrialized countries are doing to support working families and their children.

Working Mothers and Young Children

In 2008, 64% of American women with children younger than 6 years old were working outside the home (Bureau of Labor Statistics, 2009). There has been a similar increase in working mothers in most industrialized countries. The major result of this structural change in families for children is that they spend increasingly more time in nonparental care.

A series of studies in the 1980s raised questions about the effects of infant child care on the security of children's attachments. In these studies, in what has been called the "strange situation experiment," secure attachment was measured by children's responses to their mothers' return after brief separations. In this experiment, an infant is brought by her mother to a playroom setting in a laboratory. The mother engages the child in play with some toys and then leaves her alone with a female researcher. The infant's responses to her mother's brief absence and then to her return are seen as indicators of the child's attachment to the mother. Attached children are expected to show anxiety during the mother's absence and relief upon her return. The reunion behavior turned out to be most important in the original use of the strange situation experiment by Ainsworth, Blehar, Waters, and Wall (1978), who found that children who either ignored, avoided, or actively resisted their mothers upon reunion had problems with emotional security later in life. (The original study investigated the relationship between attachment and children's psychological development.) None of the children in the original study had attended infant day care, but later studies found that infants of full-time working mothers were 1.6 times more likely (Belsky & Rovine, 1988) or 1.2 times more likely (K. A. Clarke-Stewart, 1989) to be classified as insecure in their relationships with their mothers (Clerkx & Van Ijzendoorn, 1992, p. 72).

These results, although alarming, were questioned on many grounds, most especially that of whether the child's behavior upon reunion could be considered a valid measure of secure attachment. It was pointed out, for example, that it was hardly surprising that a child who had a great deal of experience in day care might ignore her mother and continue to play with toys after the mother returned following a brief absence. In fact, many would see this behavior as quite normal and indicative of security and independence on the part of the child (K. A. Clarke-Stewart, 1989; Eyer, 1993). Later research on this issue, sponsored by the National Institute of Child Health and Human Development, found that

> the sense of trust felt by fifteen-month-old children in their mothers was not affected by whether the children were in day care, by how many hours they spent there, by the age they entered day care, by the quality or type of care, or by how many times care arrangements were changed. (Chira, 1996, p. 1)

The thing that did affect an infant's trust was a mother's sensitivity and responsiveness. For mothers who are lacking in these skills, the troubled mother-infant bond can be increased by poor-quality child care.

Finally, the very latest research on the effects of child care raises concerns for parents. This study followed up on the earlier National Institute of Child Health and Human Development study when the original children were 4 and a half years of age and again when they were in kindergarten. The researchers found that regardless of the quality and type of child care, the more time children spent in any nonmaternal care arrangements during the first 4 and a half years of life, the more externalizing problems (i.e., acting out) and conflict with adults they manifested at 54 months of age and in kindergarten. These negative behaviors were reported by parents, caregivers, and teachers (National Institute of Child Health and Human Development Early Child Care Research Network, 2003). These effects were only modestly significant, and no such negative effects were reported by trained observers of the children in preschool and kindergarten. Although these findings are cause for some concern, they clearly need to be put into context. First, as noted, they were statistically modest. Second, the fact that trained observers

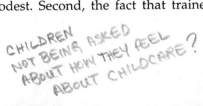
CHILDREN ASKED NOT BEING ASKED ABOUT HOW THEY FEEL ABOUT CHILDCARE?

who were not involved in actual child care did not report the negative behaviors raises questions about the validity of the parent and teacher reports. Finally, even if these modest negative effects were valid and reliable, one must raise the question of how much time in child care is too much. Could it be that the real problem is spending a great deal of time in day care during the 1st year of life because many families in the United States lack paid maternity leave? The findings may simply reflect this lack of paid leave, which forces many parents to put their children in child care during their 1st year; this is not the case in Europe, where there is paid maternity leave. This last point is especially important because European countries, which provide government-supported paid maternity leave, child care, and early education, report very positive outcomes for children. Furthermore, several researchers commenting on the study raised important issues related to the types and quality of care the children experienced at different ages (Greenspan, 2003; Maccoby & Lewis, 2003; also see Vandell, 2004). More than anything else, these findings and their interpretations suggest that providing paid family leave, quality child care, and quality early educational programs is the most important way we can support families in our contemporary global economy.

Social Policy Regarding Maternity and Family Leave

Debates about infant attachment and, in fact, most debates about the harmful effects of nonparental care for young children in the United States are counterproductive. The real issue regarding infant care centers is not day care but reasonable government policy regarding maternity and family leave. Until 1993, the United States was the only industrialized country in the world, except South Africa, with no formal policy for maternity leave. The Family and Medical Leave Act, which was passed in the initial months of the Clinton administration, mandates that employers of 50 or more employees provide up to 12 weeks of unpaid, job-protected leave to employees for certain family and medical reasons. Reasons for the leave include the birth of the employee's child, the employee's adoption of a child, or his or her taking in a foster child; the care of the employee's spouse, son, daughter, or parent with a serious health condition; or a serious health condition that renders the employee unable to perform his or her job. The length of the leave (up to the maximum 12 weeks) is at the discretion of the employee. Although the Family and Medical Leave Act was clearly a step in the right direction, especially because of its guarantee of job protection, the fact that the leave is unpaid is a major shortcoming. Most working-class and low-income families (especially single-parent families) cannot afford to take more than a week or so off work because of the lost income.

Other industrialized countries are far ahead of the United States on this issue. All west European countries provide maternity leave at 50% to 100% of earnings (most from 90% to 100%) for 6 weeks to 1 year. Most countries provide additional family leave time (normally during the child's 1st year) at some percentage of earnings or at a flat fee (Clearinghouse on International Developments in Child, Youth and Family Policies, 2010).

A brief look at three representative west European countries is instructive. Sweden has a highly complex and generous system of maternity and family leave. Families (mothers, fathers, or some combination) are entitled to full parental leave until the child is 18 months, at 80% of earnings, and up to 6 additional months at a low flat fee. The leave can be taken full- or part-time, from the child's birth until his eighth birthday. Fathers are also entitled to 10 days of paternity leave at full pay upon the birth of a child. In Italy, whose policies fall in the middle range of European countries, 20 weeks of maternity leave, at 80% of earnings, and up to 10 months of additional family leave (for the father or mother), at 30% of earnings, are provided. Finally, Greece, on the low end of the European scale, provides 17 weeks of maternity leave for mothers at 50% of earnings (see Kamerman, 2000).

Given these policies, one can see that debates about child attachment and infant care rarely arise in western Europe. There is clear recognition that families need support in a child's 1st year. Most European policies went into effect in the mid to late 1980s and usually do not take the form of simple government mandates to employers. Rather, the government (through general income or related taxes), employers, and employees all contribute in some way to the cost of such programs.

Social Policy Regarding Child Care and Early Childhood Education

Debates about child care in the United States seldom address the importance of distinguishing between nonparental child care and early education programs, and they do not properly focus on how to provide high-quality services in these areas. In the United States, all prekindergarten children are often lumped together, irrespective of age, in debates about nonparental care. Only 55% of kindergarten programs are full day, and thus a very sizable minority provide only limited child care and preparation for first grade (Vecchiotti, 2003). In western Europe, maternity and parental-leave policies address infants' needs in the 1st year, custodial care programs are available for toddlers between the ages of 1 and 3, and early education programs are normally provided for nearly all 3- to 6-year-olds. The cost and availability of programs for toddlers are similar to what we find in the United States. But even here, most programs are government subsidized to reduce costs for parents, and many have evolved from being mainly custodial to being more educational in approach (see Corsaro & Emiliani, 1992; Corsaro & Molinari, 2005; Gandini & Edwards, 2001).

The biggest difference between the United States and western Europe is the extensiveness and overall quality of early education programs for 3- to 6-year-olds. Almost all European countries offer quality programs at a low cost. Although early education teachers have generally less training and are normally paid somewhat less than elementary and secondary teachers, their incomes are much higher on average than those of early education teachers in the United States. There are also much lower rates of teacher turnover in west European preschool programs, compared to those in the United States (see Lamb, Sternberg, Hwang, & Broberg, 1992). In countries such as France and Italy, more than 97% of all 3- to 6-year-olds attend government-supported programs, and parents pay very low fees—primarily to cover the costs of meals (see Clawson & Gerstel, 2002; Corsaro & Molinari, 2005). Programs in these two countries are seen as exemplars of the best early education in the world (Bohlen, 1995; Edwards, Gandini, & Forman, 1998). They are based on carefully developed early childhood curricula that stress social and language skills and bridge the child's transition from the family to the community and formal schooling (Corsaro & Molinari, 2000, 2005). (In earlier chapters we saw how such programs in Italian preschools promote children's construction of peer cultures, which both enriches their childhoods and contributes to their development of social, language, and cognitive skills.)

In the United States, day care and early education policies have several general features: "parent responsibility for selecting and paying for care, local government and market forces for regulation, limited government financing, and market forces to regulate supply" (Haskins, 1992, p. 279). This does not mean that the U.S. government does not support child care and early education. Haskins (1992) believed the government does a lot by providing early education for poor children through Head Start programs, tax credits to help offset child care costs (including the Earned Income Tax Credit for low-income families), and various block grants to states, which can be used to support day care and before- and after-school programs. It should be pointed out, however, that many of these programs are now under serious threat of cutbacks intended to balance the federal and state budgets, and most are highly limited in meeting the needs of low-income and poor families. Head Start, for example, serves only about 42% of the very poor children who qualify for its program. Furthermore, in many states Head Start is a limited program, often serving only 4-year-olds with relatively few full-day programs. Although an important program, Head Start cannot be seen as providing consistent child care for working mothers with low incomes, and like many child care and early education programs in the United States, it suffers from incoherent educational goals and high levels of teacher turnover.

The biggest problem with Head Start and most other moderately priced private day care and early education programs is the quality of such programs. As we noted earlier, such programs in the United States are primarily market driven. Therefore, a case could be made that the overall supply of day care in the United States is sufficient; however, the contention that the quality of affordable day care is adequate is extremely hard to defend (cf. Haskins, 1992). Numerous studies have pointed to problems with minimal safety standards, limited educational curricula, low staff pay, and high staff turnover in both family day care in private homes and larger day care centers (see Helburn & Bergmann, 2002; Lamb, Sternberg, & Ketterlinus, 1992; Lewin, 1990; Pear, 1994). Moreover, the cost of enrolling children in even moderately priced programs is difficult for working-class and low-income families to meet (Polakow, 2007). Perhaps the biggest problem is low staff pay, especially in for-profit private centers with strong pressures to keep costs down. Recent studies report that child care workers and early education teachers make $18,970 to $22,120 a year, on average, which was barely above the poverty level in 2008 (Bureau of Labor Statistics, 2010). In fact, many early childhood teachers cannot afford to enroll their children in the programs in which they work! Not surprisingly, these low salaries are directly related to high teacher turnover, which is about 40% per year.

Overall, we see that the real issue is not so much how working parents and day care may be negatively affecting young children's lives but rather how creative and committed community and government programs can help families adapt to and minimize the negative effects of these changes (Corsaro & Molinari, 2005; Waldfogel, 2006). Again we see a pattern wherein the United States has developed some policies and programs to aid middle- and upper-class families in dealing with these problems. Such families are given a period of unpaid family leave and moderate support (mostly through tax credits)—enough to buy adequate- to high-quality child care and early education. Working-class and low-income families, on the other hand, face much more difficult challenges (National Research Council, 1995; Polakow, 2007). Mothers must quickly return to work after giving birth, and those child care and early education programs that are affordable are often of low quality.

Divorce and Its Effects on Children

In discussing divorce and its effects on children, we will look first at patterns in divorce rates in industrialized societies. We then will consider how laws regulating divorce and child support affect the economic security of women and children. Finally, we will review research on the social and psychological consequences of divorce for children and youth.

Patterns in Divorce and Economic Consequences for Women and Children

A major change in family structure in the industrialized world has resulted from the dramatic increase in the number of divorces during the period from the 1960s to the late 1980s. Nowhere has this increase been more apparent than in the United States, where the number of children directly experiencing divorce rose from 463,000 in 1960 to 1,174,000 in 1980 (U.S. Census Bureau, 1992). The divorce rate peaked in the 1980s and dipped slightly in the early 1990s, with the number of children experiencing divorce dropping to 985,000. This slow but steady decline in the divorce rate has continued—from a peak rate of 5.3 divorces per 1,000 population in 1980, to 4.7 in 1990, to 4.4 in 1995, to 4.0 in 2001, and to 3.6 in 2007 (Tejada-Vera & Sutton, 2008; U.S. Census Bureau, 2002). Although this decline is significant, divorce rates are still nearly double what they were in 1957, when there were 2.2 divorces per 1,000 population (U.S. Census Bureau, 2003).

Several factors have been attributed to the increase in the divorce rate in the period between 1960 and 1985, including the entrance of women into the workforce, changing values and increasing individualism, liberalization of attitudes and laws regarding divorce, and economic pressures and family stress (see Cherlin, 2009; Furstenberg & Cherlin, 1991). Because all of these factors are interrelated, it is doubtful that any one cause can be singled out as more important than another. Other factors have been offered to explain the recent decrease in the divorce rate in the United States. Wilcox (2009) pointed to three. First, the increase of age at first marriage has risen from 20.8 for women and 23.2 for men in 1970 to 25.6 for women and 27.5 for men in 2007. Wilcox argued that this "means that fewer Americans are marrying when they are too immature to forge successful marriages" (2009, p. 88). Another aspect of delayed marriage is related to a second factor, that being that many couples marry when they finish their educations and have more financial stability. Wilcox, citing S. Martin (2004), refers to this as the "divorce divide" in that college educated "Americans have seen their divorce rates drop by about 30% since the early 1980s, whereas Americans without college degrees have seen their divorce rates increase by about 6%" (Wilcox 2009, p. 90). A third factor offered by Wilcox is in line with his conservative stance on divorce and is more debatable. He argued that social science data about the consequences of divorce have moved many scholars across the political spectrum to warn against continuing what he called the "divorce revolution." However, there still is much debate among social scientists about divorce outcomes for spouses and their children, and it is hard to estimate the influence of warnings or any kind of advice of social scientists on the general public.

In any case, regardless of the recent decrease in divorce and possible factors contributing to it, the divorce rate in the United States is still much higher than those in other industrialized countries. Exhibit 10.1 presents divorce rates in selected industrialized countries for three time periods (1980, 2002, and 2006). We can see a number of patterns. First, the United States has a higher divorce rate than the other countries in all three time periods. However, this difference has decreased, as have the divorce rates in the United States during the latter two time periods. Second, the rate in the United States was much higher than that in the United Kingdom, around double those in Denmark and Sweden, and around 5 times as high as—or higher—than those in the other countries in 1980. Third, the divorce rate has increased (substantially in Japan and Germany) in all of the countries except for the United Kingdom and the United States, where there was a substantial decrease between 1980 and 2002. Although it is difficult to explain these differences, several of the countries with the lowest rates (France, Italy, and Japan) have religious or collectivist values that are not favorable to divorce. Furthermore, France and Italy have required waiting periods of several years to complete dissolution. Such waiting periods mean that couples cannot quickly enter into second marriages, which are often prone to divorce. The recent increase in Japan between

1980 and 2002 is a major change from previous periods. Some have tied the rise to an increase in women's rights in the country. It is interesting to see that the divorce rate decreased some in Japan between 2002 and 2006. The increase in Germany between 1980 and 2002 could have been affected by the inclusion of former East Germany in the 2002 data. Finally, there were decreases in all countries except for France and Italy between 2002 and 2006. However, in both cases the increases were relatively small.

Considering divorce rates alone is not enough to capture other important differences between the United States and other countries. There is a need to examine broader patterns in what the sociologist Andrew Cherlin (2009) called "The Marriage-Go-Round." Cherlin, comparing

Exhibit 10.1 Divorce Rates for Selected Countries (1980, 2002, 2006)

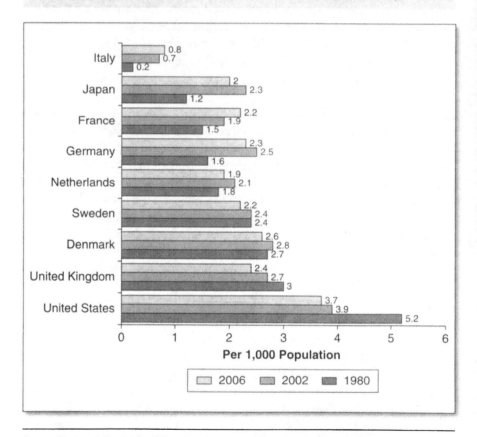

Source: National Center for Education Statistics (1996), Tejada-Vera & Sutton (2008), United Nations Statistics Division (2007), U.S. Census Bureau (2003).

the United States with several other Western nations (Australia, Austria, Canada, Finland, Belgium, France, West Germany, Great Britain, Italy, New Zealand, Norway, Spain, and Sweden) in the mid 1990s noted that Americans display different patterns in several respects. First, Americans marry and cohabit the first time sooner than people in most other Western countries. Second, a higher proportion of Americans marry at some point in their lives than do people in most other Western nations. Third, marriages and cohabiting relationships in the United States are far more fragile than elsewhere. Fourth, because of these fragile partnerships, American children born to married or cohabiting parents are more likely to see their parents' partnerships break up than are children in most other countries. Fifth, after their breakups, American parents are more likely to enter new relationships. Finally, American women become parents at an earlier age and are much more likely to spend time as lone parents in their teens and 20s than are women in other Western countries (Cherlin, 2009, pp. 16–18). What these patterns show, argued Cherlin, "is that family life in the United States involves more transitions than anywhere else" (2009, p. 19).

In the United States there is more marriage, more divorce, more lone parenting, and more repartnering. Cherlin (2009) reported estimates by Jeffery Timberlake of the percentage of women in several countries who have three or more live-in partners (married or cohabiting) by age 35. This pattern is very low in most countries:

> almost no one in Italy or Spain, less than 2 percent in France or Canada, and 3 percent in Germany. The highest figures elsewhere were 4.5 percent in Sweden and 4 percent in New Zealand. But in the United States, 10 percent of women had three or more husbands or live-in partners by age thirty-five, more than twice the percentage in Sweden and New Zealand and several times the percentage anywhere else. (Cherlin, 2009, p. 19)

We will discuss the often-negative consequences of all these complex family transitions on children later in this chapter.

Many commentators who see divorce as having strong negative effects on children point out the need to reconsider the liberalization of values and laws regarding divorce in the United States (Popenoe, 1992). We will return to this issue in Chapter 12. First, however, let's consider what we currently know about the economic effects of divorce on women and children. As we discussed in Chapter 5, separation and divorce often have severe negative economic consequences for women and children. The present system of child support in the United States often puts an enormous economic burden on women in the period of separation and following divorce. Women who were not employed before a divorce often find they must enter a job market for which they have limited skills or training. Most who are employed find that their meager incomes are not enough to maintain their own and their children's former economic well-being. Many women and their children must live near or below the poverty line following divorce, as mothers work longer hours or combine work and further education and job training. Many women choose to remarry soon after divorce in an attempt to regain economic security (Coontz, 1997; Furstenberg & Cherlin, 1991; Sidel, 1992). Children, of course, must share in and adapt to these economic difficulties. Children often have to relocate to smaller homes or rented apartments, have less money for their basic and leisure needs, and spend less time with both their fathers and their mothers.

A number of men in the United States pay little or no child support because they can get away with it. Lax enforcement of child support laws has been linked to traditional gender role ideology in the United States and to an overall reluctance in our society to face up to the consequences of divorce. Men, whether they pay support or not, often make out much better financially than their children and ex-wives following divorce. However, many men underestimate and rationalize such inequities because they usually have less interaction with their children and frequently enter into new relationships or marriages in which they have new children to help support. In this way, many American men exchange old obligations for new ones; from their point of view, they are not disregarding their family responsibilities but rather redefining them as they move from one marriage to the next (Furstenberg & Cherlin, 1991).

Things are quite different in western European countries, where child support laws are more strictly enforced and where government often takes up the slack for those who do not pay through assured child support policies. Some changes are beginning to appear in the United States; as we will discuss in Chapter 12, these changes, which involve new and stricter methods of enforcing child support, may have a real impact on the economic consequences of divorce for children.

Social and Psychological Effects of Divorce on Children

Social and psychological effects of divorce on children are much harder to measure, interpret, and understand than are the economic consequences. And although a good deal of research has been done in this area, the results are inconclusive. There are several interrelated challenges in estimating the social and psychological effects of divorce on children. First, most studies measure effects at one point in time; however, divorce and its consequences are processes that unfold during a long period of time (Furstenberg & Cherlin, 1991). For example, many studies estimate the short- and long-term consequences of divorce by way of interviews or surveys that estimate psychological well-being or through the collection of behavioral measures (school grades, drug use, sexual activity, criminal behavior) during separation or after divorce. As a result, it is hard to know if these outcome measures were affected by preexisting conditions such as the level of conflict in the family before separation and divorce or certain individual characteristics of the children (Skolnick, 1991). A second problem is that some studies include matched groups of children who have not experienced divorce but many studies do not. The issue here is that certain psychological and behavioral problems of the children may themselves have contributed to family instability, family conflict, and the eventual dissolution of the marriage. Without matched samples, there is no way to sort out such effects.

With these cautions in mind, we can turn to a summary of findings about the consequences of divorce for children. First we consider the findings reviewed in the book *Divided Families* by Furstenberg and Cherlin (1991). In terms of short-term psychological effects, Furstenberg and Cherlin pointed to two types of disorders that may result from divorce: externalizing disorders ("acting out" behaviors such as aggression, disobedience, and lying) and internalizing disorders (depression, anxiety, or withdrawal). Boys in high-conflict families (whether these conflicts lead to divorce or not) tend to show more aggressive and antisocial behavior. Aggressive behavior among boys during separation or after divorce is seen as possibly related to the fact that the boys most often live with the opposite-sex parent. Sometimes a pattern occurs in which acting out by boys is followed by overly harsh discipline or indulgence from mothers, which then leads to more acting out. For girls, the findings are less consistent. In studies of divorced families, girls seem to do better after marital disruption; however, they may develop internalizing disorders that become apparent several years later.

Furstenberg and Cherlin stressed the importance of having matched samples of children from intact families when drawing conclusions about long-term effects. They referred to one such study that found that 34% of children from disrupted families had problems in school some 8 years after the divorce, compared with 20% of children from intact families. Is this a significant finding? Yes and no, said Furstenberg and Cherlin. First, children from disrupted families clearly have more problems, but we do not know if (and certainly not how or why) these problems are related to family experiences. Second, the majority of children in the study from disrupted families (66%) did not have problems in school. Other research, which looked at high school graduation rates, reported similar findings. In a final study discussed by Furstenberg and Cherlin, children from intact families in which there was a great deal of conflict between parents were doing no better, and were often doing worse, than the children of divorce. A recent study by Li (2007) did not involve matched samples, but it is noteworthy because of its large sample (more than 6,000 children) and its longitudinal design. Li examined children's behavior before and after parents divorced. He relied on a 28-item checklist filled out by mothers measuring problem behaviors across several social and psychological dimensions such as crying, cheating, disobeying, being withdrawn, and so on. He found a slight post-divorce increase in bad behavior that was not statistically significant. Li argued that the trajectory of misbehavior that started before the divorce may have continued even if the parents had not divorced. He concluded that children of divorce in his study would have fared equally well or poor in terms of their emotional well-being if their parents had remained married.

Two other well-known books report on longitudinal, matched-sample studies that build on and expand the studies reviewed by Furstenberg and Cherlin. These two books, *For Better or for Worse* by E. Mavis Hetherington and John Kelly (2002) and *The Unexpected Legacy of Divorce* by Judith Wallerstein, Julia Lewis, and Sandra Blakeslee (2001), come to two quite different conclusions about the short- and long-term effects of divorce on children. First, we need to consider the methods of the two books. The Hetherington and Kelly work is based on several interrelated studies involving 1,400 families (the overwhelming majority of the families were White and middle class), roughly half divorced and half not divorced. For many of the families, data were collected several times over the course of 24 years. These studies relied primarily on standardized methods including structured interviews, observations of family interaction in the home, journal entries by participants, and standardized personality tests.

In the Wallerstein, Lewis, and Blakeslee study, Wallerstein, a clinical psychologist, and other clinicians carried out intensive interviews with children and parents of 59 divorced families during 25 years as well as interviews with 44 adults who had grown up in intact families. Like the participants in the Hetherington and Kelly study, the families were primarily White and middle class.

Both studies found that children from families who do not experience divorce do better in the short and long term than children from divorced families. In their intensive interviews of children of divorce, Wallerstein, Lewis, and Blakeslee found that there were often long-lasting negative effects that persisted well into adulthood. For example, many children from divorced families had trouble establishing satisfying relationships later in life, felt that they could not relate well to or trust their partners in the romantic relationships they did develop, and if they married, often reported dissatisfaction; many, like their parents, ended their marriages in divorce. Although Wallerstein, Lewis, and Blakeslee did find that some children of divorce in their sample were quite resilient, happily married, and living satisfying lives, these children were in the minority, and the authors acknowledged but did not explore these success stories in detail.

Resiliency was one of the big themes and even a primary lesson in Hetherington and Kelly's interpretation of their findings. The authors noted that about 20 to 25% of youth from divorced families, compared to 10% from nondivorced families, had serious social, emotional, or psychological problems. For this reason, the authors argued that divorce is a serious problem and couples should carefully consider the effects that ending their marriage might have on their children. On the other hand, as previously noted, the authors found that children and youth are very resilient and that 20 years after divorce the men and women in their study were coping reasonably well with their new situations. Many were in happy marriages and leading constructive lives. The authors concluded,

> It isn't a matter of whether the glass is half empty or half full. In the long run, after a divorce, the glass is three-quarters full of reasonably happy and competent adults and children, who have been resilient in coping with the challenge of divorce. (Hetherington & Kelly, 2002, p. 280)

Both of these studies are quite complex, and the brief review provided here does not do them justice. Both have their strengths and weaknesses. Hetherington and Kelly's study is much larger, and the sample more diverse, than that of Wallerstein, Lewis, and Blakeslee. In addition, the Wallerstein, Lewis, and Blakeslee study was not longitudinal for both groups, because the comparative group consisted of adults from nondivorced families. Still, with needed qualifications about generalizability, the intensive-interview method of the study is a key strength. The researchers developed good rapport with their respondents and were able to tap memories and emotions that were not easily captured in the more standardized methods used by Hetherington and Kelly. For example, many of the children from divorced families in the Wallerstein, Lewis, and Blakeslee study said that their parents (especially fathers) felt little obligation to them or concern about their welfare, most especially when they reached 18 years of age. Although some of the parents helped a lot or at least a little with college expenses, many did not help at all. Worse, parents often argued about who should be providing the support, whether the young adult should be more independent and work her or his way through college, and so on. We must remember that these families were predominately middle and upper middle class, so it was often not a matter of lack of resources but in a way, from the perspective of the children, an alienation from parental responsibility related to divorce. These findings contrast with those about the adults from nondivorced families in the Wallerstein, Lewis, and Blakeslee study, the overwhelming majority of whom received financial support for higher education from their parents.

Although these two studies contributed a great deal to what we know about the long-term effects of divorce, the debate continues with many new studies with varying results (see A. Clarke-Stewart & Brentano, 2006, for a review). In some ways the debate has grown into a cottage industry. Authors such as Constance Ahrons (1994, 2004) and Elizabeth Marquardt (2005) reported dramatically different findings and took radically different positions on divorce and children. Ahrons argued that there can be "good divorces" and found few if any long-term negative effects on children in her research. Marquardt, in contrast, maintained there is no such thing as a good divorce, and her research finds that children of divorced parents often struggle with challenges and negative emotions related to their parents' divorce from childhood into early adulthood. Both authors have their own webpages and frequently participate in public discourse about the issue in the media and through public lectures.

Finally, let us return to our earlier discussion of Cherlin's (2009) emphasis not just on divorce per se but on how the number of transitions or disruptions in their families' lives affect children's behavior and emotional well-being. It is important to focus on transitions and disruptions of this type because of the reality of the nature of marriage, family life, and divorce in American society. According to Cherlin, Americans hold two contradictory views of personal and family life. The first is a strong commitment to marriage and to sharing one's life with another, which is strongly attached to religious beliefs. The second is individualism, which stresses personal growth and development. It is the "mixture of these cultural themes of marriage and individualism," argued Cherlin, that "explains the American paradox of high rates of both marriage and divorce—and, by extension, the greater likelihood of having two, three, or more intimate partners, marital or cohabiting, during one's lifetime" (2009, pp. 182–183). Cherlin reported on a series of studies in the United States and Europe that find that children "who experience a series of transitions appear to have more difficulties than children raised in stable two-parent families and perhaps even more than children raised in stable lone-parent families" (2009, p. 20; also see Fromby & Cherlin, 2007). These findings are in line with our earlier discussion about the importance of stable cultural and family routines in children's lives. They also mesh with studies we discuss below about the negative effects of changes of residence for children, which often occur after divorce. It is for these reasons that Cherlin (2009) advised Americans to slow down what he calls the "Marriage-Go-Round" and the turbulence it creates in our family lives.

Overall, we see that there are many methodological challenges to studying the effects of divorce on children. We know much more than we did in the past, but the research is not conclusive. It is also clear that the debate will continue long into the future. Regardless of the debate about long-term outcomes, it is clear that children lose some of their childhood when dealing with the experience of divorce in their families. On the other hand, the stress of intense conflict in unhappy marriages also affects children's childhood in negative ways as they have to deal with the everyday tensions in their families.

The research indicates that there is no definite path down which children of divorce progress. Still, the research does suggest some important strategies in reducing the negative effects of divorce on children. First, how the custodial parent (usually the mother) functions as a parent in the first months after a separation is of crucial importance. This is a critical time for children, who are trying to come to terms with the fact that their lives are changing in highly troubling and confusing ways. Furthermore, some children tend to blame themselves for their parents' problems during this period. If the custodial parent can keep the family functioning in line with established and predictable routines, the children generally will do well.

Here again we see, as we have throughout this book, the importance of familiar, everyday routines for security in children's lives. Of course, maintaining such routines is no small task for a custodial parent whose life may seem to be crumbling all around her. Making matters worse, after a separation or divorce, economic demands often require a change of residence, and leaving behind the family home and everyday interactions with friends and teachers often has negative effects on children (McLanahan & Sandefur, 1994; Tucker, Marx, & Long, 1998). This is a time when both parents need to cooperate for the sake of the children—even though their partnership is coming apart. Such cooperation is an overwhelming challenge, and it is at this point in the divorce process that outside support from relatives, community organizations, and government agencies is most crucial.

A second key factor in minimizing the negative effects of separation and divorce on children is maintaining a low level of conflict between parents. Persistent, intense, and highly visible conflict during the separation and after divorce magnifies the negative impact of the disruption. Again, however, minimizing conflict while terminating a marriage is a tall order. Rather than lessening conflict, some divorcing couples become so caught up in anger and bitterness toward one another that they bring children into their disputes, at times even forcing them to take sides in bitter custody battles.

In a course I taught regularly on childhood and contemporary society, I asked my students to write papers in which they were to reflect on problems in their own childhoods. Many students wrote about experiencing divorce. Time and time again they referred to the level of conflict between parents throughout the divorce process. Unfortunately, many students whose parents could not escape cycles of hostility and resentment still displayed anxiety and distress in their accounts, even if the divorce occurred many years in the past. Students' reports were much more positive and heartening in those cases where parents managed to put their bitterness aside and cooperate as best they could for their children. Such students often noted that the experience was still stressful but manageable. Furthermore, they felt that over time, they developed a deeper respect for and understanding of their parents' commitment to them.

Child Abuse in the Family

Only one thing is worse than losing a child to tragic and unforeseen circumstances such as war, disease, or disaster. That is losing a child through willful, intentional, and preventable acts of abuse. All too often, such acts occur right in the sanctity of the child's home—the place where he or she ought to feel safe and protected from harm.

When children are abused by caretakers, they not only are physically and emotionally harmed but often blame themselves for the failings of those they trust and love. The consequences of abuse are thus doubly tragic and often long lasting. In some cases they even perpetuate more abuse; the abused child herself also becomes a child abuser.

Of course, no family is perfect. All families have their ups and downs. Most parents, excluding perhaps TV parents such as Ward and June Cleaver, lose patience with their children and yell at them now and then. At times, regrettably, most parents give their preschooler, preadolescent, or adolescent a shake or slap on the bottom or face. Does this constitute child abuse? I do not think the fact that parents may lose their patience once in a while is the same as child abuse, but I do think persistent striking, yelling, or belittling children is. Some parents may not think so. In fact, some may think any form of physical punishment is permissible if it is administered by a parent. I can understand this view of discipline because I got a few spankings in my time and probably deserved them. Yet to me it is a form of abuse. In our society we do not allow corporal punishment of adults; why should we allow it of children? A number of Scandinavian countries have passed laws against physical punishment in the home, and most countries in the industrialized world (except for Australia and the United States) now forbid it in schools. To me, this is a step in the right direction (for differing views on corporal punishment, see Dobson, 1996, and Straus & Donnelly, 2001).

It is clear that child abuse is not easily defined, nor is its prevalence easily estimated. This fact is due to the generally held value in most societies that children belong to their parents. As a result, any society's attempt to define and control child abuse immediately runs up against issues of family privacy and the belief that people have the right to bring up their own children without government interference or regulation. Most agree, however, that there are limits to parental authority, and most child abuse laws and regulations revolve around the determination of misuse of parental authority. Most laws are generally in line with a definition offered by Landau: "Parental authority and power are misused when they are employed to damage the child either physically or emotionally or administered in any manner that reduces or limits the child's opportunity for normal growth and development" (1994, p. 116). A big problem in dealing with child abuse, however, is in determining such misuses of power. Child neglect, the most common form of child abuse, is best defined as an omission or failure of the parents to meet their children's needs in regard to health, development, and physical safety.

What is the extent of child abuse? Is it increasing? Does it vary across societies, social classes, and cultural groups within societies? Such questions cannot be readily addressed because of the difficulty in defining and measuring abuse. Also, until recently most countries did not even keep accurate records of child abuse. Things are changing mainly because of the work of child health advocacy groups. One of the few comparative studies of child abuse relied on a measure developed by the World Health Organization. This measure focused on child abuse that resulted in deaths in infancy. Clearly the measure underestimates abuse, but we can at least be somewhat confident of its accuracy because statistics about death are normally carefully collected and reported in industrialized countries. The World Health Organization measure combined infant homicides with infant deaths from undetermined external causes. This measure was recently used to rank 23 countries in terms of the number of deaths per 100,000 live births between 1985 and 1990. Four countries (Denmark, the former Czechoslovakia, the United States, and the former Soviet Union) had rates between 8.1 and 10.1, with the United States's having a rate of 8.4 deaths per 100,000 births. This was an increase from 4.3 deaths per 100,000 live births in 1970 (Child Trends, 2003). Nine other European countries, along with Australia, New Zealand, and Japan, had rates between 3.1 and 7.4, and 7 countries (Canada, Poland, the Netherlands, Norway, Sweden, Italy, and Spain) had rates less than 3.0 (Belsey, 1993). More recent international data about infant homicides are not available, but information is available regarding recent trends in the United States. The rate of infant homicides remained high but stable in the 1990s but jumped to 8.7 in 1999 and then peaked at 9.2 per 100,000 before falling to 8.2 in 2001; it was 8.1 in 2006. These numbers are alarming, and most experts believe the rate is even higher because many such homicides occur on the day of birth and therefore may go undetected (that is, not reported on official death certificates; Child Trends, 2003; National Center for Health Statistics, 2010).

It was only fairly recently that child abuse statistics began to be recorded on the national level in the United States. Such records are now gathered by the National Child Abuse and Neglect Data System, which is part of the U.S. Department of Health and Human Services. Exhibit 10.2 presents the estimated number of child victims of abuse and neglect as well as the rates per 1,000 children from 1993 to 2007. We can see from the exhibit that the number of victims and the rate was highest in 1993 with 1,026,000 victims, which was a rate of 15.3 per 1,000 children in the population. These numbers remained relatively stable until 1997, when there began to be some substantial decline, with the lowest number of victims and rate of 11.8 per 1,000 children recorded in 1999. There was then a slight increase and a stable rate between 12 and 12.4 per 1,000 children

Exhibit 10.2 Estimated Number of Child Victims and Rate per 1,000 Children

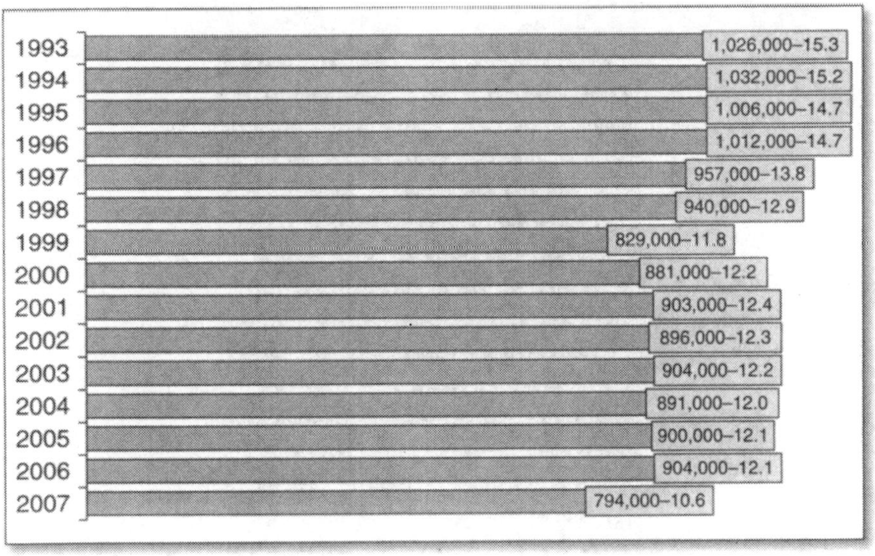

Year	
1993	1,026,000–15.3
1994	1,032,000–15.2
1995	1,006,000–14.7
1996	1,012,000–14.7
1997	957,000–13.8
1998	940,000–12.9
1999	829,000–11.8
2000	881,000–12.2
2001	903,000–12.4
2002	896,000–12.3
2003	904,000–12.2
2004	891,000–12.0
2005	900,000–12.1
2006	904,000–12.1
2007	794,000–10.6

Source: U.S. Department of Health and Human Services (2009).

during the next several years from 2000 to 2006. For 2007 there was an encouraging drop to 794,000 victims with a rate of 10.6 per 1,000 children. This decline is encouraging and has been attributed to a number of factors including increased economic prosperity during the period, increasing agents of social intervention, and improvement in the treatment of depression and related psychological disorders as a result of advance psychiatric pharmacology (see Finkelhor & Jones, 2006).

The fact that more than a million children were victims of abuse or neglect in the early 1990s is highly disturbing. The decline in the late 1990s is heartening as is the most recent drop to 10.6 per 1,000, but even though we are headed in the right direction the recent rate of 10.6 is still far too high. Also given the current deep recession we may very well see an increase when statistics for recent years become available. As sobering as these statistics are, we still need to be careful about how we interpret the problem and decide on ways to prevent it. First, it is important to keep in mind that there are various types of child abuse. Exhibit 10.3 presents the percentage of different types of child maltreatment in the United States in 2007. The fact that the overwhelming majority of cases were

Exhibit 10.3   Types of Child Maltreatment (2007)

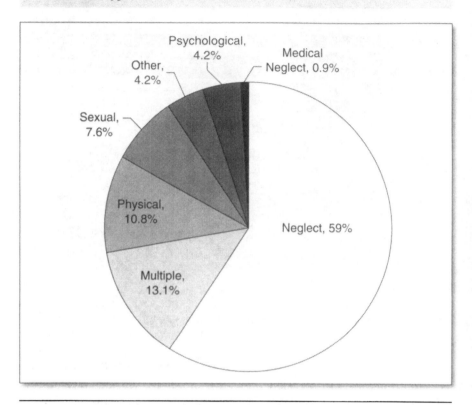

Source: U.S. Department of Health and Human Services (2009).

some form of neglect is somewhat heartening because this problem is more easily attacked by preventive programs such as family education, child safety laws, and so on. Still, the fact that more than 13% of the cases involve multiple types of abuse is worrisome. Further, the 4.2% of cases classified as "Other," including such things as "abandonment," "threats of harm to the child," and "congenital drug addiction," display the many ways especially infants and young children can be abused. We must also remember that other types of abuse, especially sexual and emotional abuse, are less likely to be reported. Overall, these statistics demonstrate how deeply rooted child abuse is in our society.

Numerous and interrelated factors contribute to child abuse and neglect, including poverty, parental substance abuse, social isolation, and a lack of experience in caring for young children. Although abuse occurs in families from all social classes, it occurs in a larger proportion of poor families, in which parents face a multitude of challenges and in which many have drug and other substance abuse problems. In February 1994, Chicago police who were conducting a drug raid entered an apartment in the inner city only to find two toddlers sharing a bone with a dog. As police moved through the filthy, two-room apartment, they found, "buried beneath blankets and dirty clothes on the floor or crammed on top of two soiled mattresses," 17 other children, ranging in age from 1 to 14 (Terry, 1994a, p. A1). The 19 children were the offspring of at least four sisters, all in their 20s, who lived in the apartment with the children. Three of the mothers had been investigated in the past when one of the children was born with drugs in his system. They also were investigated because of inadequate supervision of several of the children. On this day, as the children were being carried away through the cold toward a fleet of police cars, several asked for food, and one child pleaded with Officer Patricia Warner, "Would you be my mommy? Would you take me home?" (Terry, 1994a, p. A11).

City and state agencies that are supposed to care for and protect abused and neglected children are often overwhelmed by caseloads and lack of money. Many state welfare officials are concerned about the fact that state governments are almost totally responsible for administration of the child abuse programs. These concerns are related to the ups and downs of state economies and budgets. In the current severe recession of 2009–2010 many states have cut back on child welfare services. There is a clear need for the federal government to take on more of a leadership role in dealing with better social services for our children.

Some of the effects of child abuse and child neglect are fatal, some leave physical injuries from which it may take years to recover, and others leave permanent emotional scars that lead victims eventually to abuse their own children. Many such injuries may also have important developmental consequences that have not been investigated (Finkelhor & Dziuba-Leatherman, 1994). In 2007 an estimated 1,760 children died as a result of abuse or neglect—a rate of 2.35 deaths per 100,000 children in the population. Children younger than 1 year old accounted for 42.2% of fatalities, and 75.5% of fatalities were younger than 4 years of age (U.S. Department of Health and Human Services, 2009). It was found in 1995 that about 46% of the perpetrators of child abuse had current or prior contact with local child protective services (National Committee to Prevent Child Abuse,

1996). More recent data from 2002 show that male perpetrators of child maltreatment have a recidivist rate of 9% after 12 months compared with a recidivist rate of 12% after the same time period for female perpetrators (Shusterman & Fluke, 2005). From these statistics it is clear that identifying children at risk of repeated victimization should be a high priority of child welfare agencies in the United States.

Some research has been done on the short- and long-term effects of sexual abuse on children's mental health. It has been found that children who have been sexually victimized appear to be at a nearly fourfold increased lifetime risk for any psychiatric disorder and at a threefold risk for substance abuse (Finkelhor & Dziuba-Leatherman, 1994, p. 181). Finally, a great deal of evidence supports the contention that a history of victimization increases the chances that one will become a perpetrator of violence, abuse, or crime. As Finkelhor and Dziuba-Leatherman noted, an important qualification in this regard "is that victims are not necessarily prone to repeat their own form of victimization" (1994, p. 181).

Education, prevention programs, and harsher penalties for repeat offenders are the best methods for dealing with this problem. A great deal of headway has been made in education with help from private child advocacy organizations and individual volunteers. Needed comprehensive prevention programs are being implemented slowly, however, because of their expense at a time when state government budget constraints are severe. In fact, in the severe recession period of 2009–2010 there have been cutbacks to comprehensive programs at the state level. We will argue in Chapter 12 that a rethinking of priorities that balances short-term costs with long-term benefits is needed in dealing with this issue.

SUMMARY

In this chapter we reviewed social problems that affect children's lives in the family. We considered how changes in family structures affected children's lives in Western societies. As an increasing number of mothers with young children entered the workforce in the United States, some researchers questioned how the increasing need for child care affected the security of children's attachment to their mothers. One positive result of the debate about attachment has been an evaluation of the quality of affordable day care and an examination of governmental policy regarding maternity and family leave, day care, and early education in the United

States. The United States lags far behind almost all other industrialized countries regarding these issues. Many other countries have extensive programs of maternity and family leave as well as subsidized high-quality early education programs.

The divorce rate increased in all industrialized countries during the 1970s and 1980s, with a leveling off in some cases recently. The divorce rate and the number of children affected by divorce are much higher in some countries than in others, with the United States having the highest rates. Most of the best research on the effects of divorce on children has documented the negative economic consequences of divorce for women and children. Here again, the United States does poorly when compared to other industrialized countries primarily because the present system of child support in the United States puts an enormous economic burden on women in the periods during separation and following divorce. Social and psychological effects of divorce on children are much harder to measure, interpret, and understand than economic consequences, but there are important patterns in findings from the recent research. First, the studies show that in divorced families wherein there has been a great deal of conflict, boys are more likely to display externalizing disorders (acting-out behaviors such as aggression, disobedience, and lying) whereas girls are more apt to display internalizing disorders (depression, anxiety, or withdrawal). Second, studies using matched samples of children from intact families have found that whereas children from disrupted families were more likely to show long-term effects (such as problems in school), the majority of children from divorced families did not have such problems. Still, there is a great deal of debate about the long-term effects of divorce. Other studies have identified two key ways of minimizing the negative effects of divorce: (a) The custodial parent should keep the family functioning in line with established and predictable routines as much as possible, and (b) parents should maintain low levels of conflict in their dealings with each other in the presence of their children.

In the final section of this chapter we considered what constitutes child abuse, the various types of child abuse, and trends in the incidence of abuse in the family. Many abuse cases involve neglect, a problem that is more easily attacked through preventive programs such as family education and child safety laws than are other types of abuse. However, there is a great need for more extensive programs and a greater awareness of the extent of the problem. The growing body of evidence indicates that a history of abuse increases the chances that a child will become a perpetrator of violence, abuse, or crime.

11

Children, Social Problems, and Society

I n this chapter we'll examine social problems related to the quality of children's lives and their opportunities for the future as adults in the societies in which they live. We begin the discussion with a focus on poverty and its effects on children's lives in developed and developing societies. We then consider several problems related to poverty, teen pregnancy and births, and violence against children.

Poverty and the Quality of Children's Lives

Of all the factors that contribute to the social problems of children, poverty is the most pervasive and the most insidious. Poverty clearly steals the childhoods and often the very lives of many children in the developing world. In recent years, however, the proportion of children living in poverty in industrialized societies has increased dramatically, especially in the United States. Let's examine the effects of poverty on children's lives in developing countries and in the industrialized world.

Problems and Progress in Developing Countries

Most of us have a familiar and painful image of child poverty in the developing world. Starving children are affected by droughts or famine, or they suffer from diseases that are well in check in developed countries. Although problems of malnutrition, lack of vaccinations, and poor health care still plague many children in poor countries, improvements have been made in recent years. For example, the first United Nations World Summit for Children in 1990 set a number of goals for improving the quality of life of children in the developing world. These included a one-third reduction in child deaths, a halving of child malnutrition, immuniza-tion levels of 90%, control of the major childhood diseases, the eradication of polio, the elimination of micronutrient deficiencies, a halving of mater-nal mortality rates, primary school education for at least 80% of children, the provision of clean water and safe sanitation to all communities, and the universal ratification of the new Convention on the Rights of the Child (UNICEF, 1995b). The means used to measure progress in these areas are far from perfect, and several setbacks have occurred because of wars, new diseases such as AIDS, and major debt problems in the developing world. Still, UNICEF reported that more than 100 of the developing nations (including more than 90% of the developing world's children) are making significant practical progress toward meeting these goals. Malnutrition has been reduced, immunization levels are generally being maintained or increased, deaths from measles are down by 80%, and the incidence of many other diseases has been reduced significantly. In addition, progress in primary education has resumed, and the Convention on the Rights of the Child has been widely and rapidly ratified. In human terms, this progress means that approximately 2.5 million fewer children died in 1996 than died in 1990, and millions will be spared insidious impediments to their development due to malnutrition. It also means that at least three quarters of a million fewer children each year will be disabled, blinded, crippled, or born mentally retarded (UNICEF, 1995b). These are signifi-cant achievements that deserve high praise. They demonstrate that hard work and commitment to goals can pay off. More important, such progress makes it possible to counter charges that efforts such as these fail in the developing world and that organizations like the United Nations are ineffective.

More recently, actions in line with the Convention on the Rights of the Child have led to programs to improve the participation of children in political decisions and actions that affect their lives (UNICEF, 2009). In May 2002, 2 youth, 1 from Bolivia and 1 from Monaco, were selected by a larger group of 400 children to speak at a special session on children at the United Nations. They spoke to what they saw in a future world fit for chil-dren. They pointed out that in this future world they saw respect for the rights of the child; an end to exploitation, abuse, and violence; an end to war; the provision of health care; the eradication of HIV/AIDS; the protection of the environment; an end to the vicious cycle of poverty; the provision of education; and the active participation of children. The children closed their statement with the following points.

We pledge an equal partnership in this fight for children's rights. And while we promise to support the actions you take on behalf of children, we also ask for your commitment and support in the actions we are taking—because the children of the world are misunderstood.

We are not the sources of problems: we are the resources that are needed to solve them.

We are not expenses; we are investments.

We are not just young children; we are people and citizens of this world.

Until others accept their responsibility to us, we will fight for our rights.

We have the will, the knowledge, the sensitivity and the dedication.

We promise that as adults we will defend children's rights with the same passion that we have now as children.

We promise to treat each other with dignity and respect.

We promise to be open and sensitive to our differences.

We are the children of the world, and despite our different backgrounds, we share a common reality.

We are united by our struggle to make the world a better place for all.

You call us the future, but we are also the present. (UNICEF, 2003, pp. 66–67)

These are lofty but elegant goals, and they are especially forceful because they were formulated and stated by children themselves. Yet much work remains to be done, and the challenges are daunting (see Freeman, 2009, for a review of the contentious issues addressed in the drafting and adoption of the Convention on the Rights of the Child in 1989 and the challenges that remain in reaching its goals). Most of the children of the developing world are still greatly affected by poverty and the related problems it breeds. In fact, in some countries initial progress has been followed by continuing setbacks. These setbacks are all the more frustrating and threatening for children because they are occurring at a moment in history when traditional values, family organization, and economic structures are rapidly changing in the developing world. Let's consider two cases from South America and Africa.

Poverty and Street Children in Brazil. Many countries in Central and South America have experienced mass urbanization and its many related social problems. The country most well known for the plight of its street children is Brazil. The problems of Brazil's street children, however, must be placed in context. Deteriorating economic conditions persist; however, recent attempts have been made within the country to recognize and address the problem. Although there have always been wide disparities in the distribution of wealth in Brazil, the country experienced strong economic growth between 1960 and 1980. Annual growth rates of 10% during this period led to profound economic and social changes and to the development of a modern and diversified economic structure. Unfortunately, this period was followed by a severe recession in the 1980s, when the gross national product dropped more than 6%, the average minimum salary declined 33%, and inflation soared to a level of 50% per month. These changes were accompanied by rapid population growth: from 119 to 144 million in the 10 years from 1980 to 1990, with approximately 40% of the population under 17 years of age. Furthermore, since the early 1960s Brazil has become highly urbanized. By 1990 the populations of São Paulo and Rio de Janeiro exceeded, respectively, 17 million and 11 million, and 14 other cities had more than 1 million inhabitants (Rizzini, Rizzini, Munoz-Vargas, & Galeano, 1994, pp. 56–57). It is not surprising that these factors combined to severely worsen the situation of the poor, most especially children.

Most studies of economic growth and the physical quality of life have ignored children or treated them as faceless variables (Bradshaw, 1993). Children live and work on the streets for many reasons. Almost all are poor; some are orphans working to support themselves but also to contribute to the family. International reaction to the deplorable condition of Brazil's street children has drawn some direct attention to children, but think of what it took to get this attention. Children were being killed—executed—often because of the fact that they were poor! A study cited by Rizzini and colleagues (1994) found that 457 children were murdered on the streets of Rio, São Paulo, and Recife in one 6-month period in 1989.

> Most of the victims (390) were males and most (336) between 15 and 17; only 11 had police records, and 13, at the most, were suspected of drug trafficking. The overwhelming majority had known addresses and lived with their parents. None was known to have ever carried weapons. (Rizzini et al., 1994, p. 66)

The authors went on to note,

> These crimes, which resembled executions, are believed to have been committed by hired gunmen. Police are investigating drug traffickers and gangsters who are the prime suspects; individuals who take justice into their own hands ("vigilantes," "death or extermination squads"); and a third group, the military and civil police and private security guards. Few of these cases have been resolved. It is worth emphasizing that the victims are commonly perceived as a social evil *which should be suppressed* [italics added]. (p. 66)

The last line of this quote is especially chilling. Even if all of the victims were small-time drug traffickers or petty thieves, did they deserve to be summarily executed? And has this "common perception" of a social evil resulted in the summary execution of suspected adult drug traffickers and thieves? It is clear that young children—even those whose primary reason for being on the streets is the poverty of their families—are easy prey for such vigilantism. Fifty-four percent of Brazilian children live in households in which the monthly per capita income is half the minimum wage or less (Rizzini et al., 1994, p. 65).

In his study of the street children of Recife in northeast Brazil, Hecht (1998) captured the complexity of their local cultures and life on the street and its relation to global economic forces. Almost all of the children Hecht studied had some dedication to their mothers and homes but chose life on the streets for the independence and small economic rewards it offered through begging and small-time, street-level crime such as petty theft and violence. Almost all of the lives of the children Hecht studied turned out badly, and many were murdered on the street. However, Hecht argued that focusing only on these outcomes and the problem of street violence can miss the socioeconomic forces that create the street culture as the only alternative for many of these children (also see Gough & Franch, 2005, for a comparative study of wealthy and poor youth in Recife and differences in their neighborhoods and use of space in city life). According to Hecht, street children

> are a reminder, literally on the doorsteps of rich Brazilians and just outside the five-star hotels where the development consultants stay, of the contradictions of contemporary social life: the opulence of the few amid the poverty of the majority, the plethora of resources amid the squandering of opportunities. (1998, p. 214)

In this sense, argued Hecht, street children "embody the failure of an unacknowledged social apartheid to keep the poor out of view. At home in the street, they are painful reminders of the dangerous and endangered world in which we live" (p. 214).

As depressing and bleak as the situation of Brazil's street children is, negative reactions to the problem and cries of outrage (both internationally and domestically) have resulted in many new programs, many new policies, and much-needed legislation. Much of this action has been spurred by nongovernmental organizations (NGOs), organizations that have no government affiliation, promote change, and address various social and economic problems at the community or grassroots level. As Rizzini and colleagues noted, implementing these laws "to make a real difference in the everyday lives of all children in Brazil is the challenge that lies ahead" (1994, p. 98). Also we must not overlook the agency and resiliency of street children and must strive to understand their perceptions of their lives. Advocacy research shows that independence and freedom are important motivations for choosing street life, and street children report they often look out for one another and build strong group solidarity (Ataöv & Haider, 2006; Rizzini & Butler, 2003).

Progress and Setbacks in Kenya. More and more, children in many of the countries of sub-Saharan Africa find themselves on urban streets in a struggle for the economic survival of their families (Bass, 2004; Droz, 2006; Evans, 2006; Van Blerk, 2005). The causes of their poverty are similar to the causes of poverty in the countries of South America. The main culprit is the severe recession of the 1980s and the resulting debt crisis. Kenya is a good example of what is happening in many parts of Africa. After gaining political independence in 1963, and continuing until 1980, Kenya's national economy was one of the strongest in Africa. The annual total gross national product growth averaged 9.7%, with inflation and unemployment's remaining relatively low (Bradshaw, Buchmann, & Mbatia, 1994). However, economic growth then slowed and reached a point of nearly zero growth in the early 1990s. Inflation also increased dramatically to a rate of more than 40%, resulting in severe hardships for many citizens.

This economic downturn led the International Monetary Fund, the World Bank, and other global financial organizations to demand increasing debt and austerity programs (Bradshaw, 1993; Bradshaw, Noonan, Gash, & Sershen, 1993). In Kenya, as in most developing countries, a very large percentage of the population are children: 59% of the population are younger than 20, and more than 27% are younger than 5 years of age (Bradshaw et al., 1994). These children's lives were altered dramatically by these changes as nutrition, health, education, and other social service programs were cut back. One effect of child impoverishment has been the large increase in street children working as beggars, parking boys, or laborers in small business establishments. These children have, for the most part, abandoned their education and are often exploited by adults. Although most of the street children are boys, girls are often employed as housemaids, where they work for long hours doing housework and caring for young children. There also has been an alarming increase in child prostitution, with many young boys and girls' contracting sexually transmitted diseases, including HIV. One estimate is that 20% of children with AIDS are in the 5- to 14-year-old age range, an increase that is tied directly to street prostitution. This statistic is made even bleaker by the fact that 8 to 9% of the general population in Kenya are HIV positive and many more persons are expected to become so. This means that if children do not contract the virus and die before their parents, many of them will become AIDS orphans (Bradshaw et al., 1994). However, recently Meintjes and Giese (2006) have questioned the generally singular focus on orphanhood in the context of HIV/AIDS in Africa, most specifically in South Africa. They argued that local notions of vulnerability and orphanhood are often incongruous with international policy definitions. This mismatch leads to stereotypes and adversely affects local applications of the term. Meintjes and Giese maintained,

> Policy recommendations, service designs, implementation procedures and other forms of intervention that derive from orphan-centered thinking are unlikely to be sufficiently sensitive to local ways of understanding the word (and the consequences of the pandemic), and they may thereby inadvertently create new social inequities and increase the risk of harm for some of the very children whom these interventions are designed to assist. (2006, p. 426)

The authors pointed to the overwhelming complexity of the issue and argued that "we have yet to understand and articulate many aspects of the impact of HIV/AIDS on children's lives" (2006, p. 426).

Although the problems of children of sub-Saharan Africa may seem overwhelming, there are possible long-term solutions. The brightest rays of hope come from NGOs like those in Brazil, which have sprung up in local communities and can make a real difference in children's lives. Support of these organizations, especially by foreign donors and the international financial community, as well as government reform could bring about real change. However, these efforts must be carried out with a deep understanding of the culture, customs, and ways of life of those children and adults in need.

Poverty and Child Labor in Developing Countries

One area in which growing recognition of the plight of children in developing countries may be effecting change is in the area of child labor exploitation. But again as we saw in the Western conceptualizations of poverty, street children, and HIV/AIDS in the developing world, child labor is a complex issue. One reason for the routine exploitation of children's labor is the contradictions that exist between legislation and enforcement of child labor laws in many parts of the world. As Qvortrup noted, many countries "turn a blind eye" to the reality of extensive, full-time child labor despite child labor laws. Furthermore, because much of children's work is illegal, "they are rendered vulnerable to exploitation over conditions, hours, pay and safety standards—factors which for adult workers are regulated by their unions" (Qvortrup, 1991, p. 31; but also see Mizen, Pole, & Bolton, 2001, for discussions of the complexities of child labor in industrialized societies in North America, Europe, and the former Soviet Union and Nieuwenhuys, 2009, for an instructive discussion of the global nature of children's work and the importance of not just protecting children from exploitive work but also guaranteeing their rights as workers for work they desire to undertake for the livelihoods and those of their families). Two possible solutions to these problems are (a) international condemnation of the problem along with carefully developed economic actions against offending countries and (b) creative activism by NGOs within offending countries.

Exploitative child labor exists throughout the developing world, but it is most appalling in southeast Asia, where in countries such as India and Pakistan, children are often sold into indentured servitude or kidnapped to work on farms and in factories, mills, and sweatshops. Carpet factories especially value young children "because they can squat easily, and their nimble fingers can make the smallest, tightest knots" ("Pakistanis Silence Youthful Voice," 1995). Recent international outrage has led a German-Indian export-import association to form the Rugmark Foundation, which certifies carpets that are made in child-free factories. Because of the Indian government's general indifference to the problem, however, two bills under consideration in the United States would ban all Indian carpets. One supporter of the bill, Iowa senator Tom Harkin, asked, "Can we really afford the price that children pay to make these products?" ("The Young and the Damned," 1996). The Child Labor Deterrence Act was never passed into law, but several bills related to child labor are still under consideration.

Although condemnation and legislation from outside the offending countries is important, social movements and activism within the countries is most effective. A number of NGOs in India and Pakistan have organized child workers, lobbied their governments, and promoted mass demonstrations and rallies against the exploitation of child workers. Some groups and organizations go further and raid factories in search of children. Such raids have resulted in the rescue of many ill-treated child workers. One child, Iqbal Masih, was not so lucky.

THE ABRAHAM LINCOLN OF CHILD WORKERS

Not long ago, at the age of 10, Iqbal Masih sneaked away from a Pakistani carpet factory, where he had worked since he was 4 years old. (He was sold into indentured servitude by his parents for less than $16.) A labor organizer told Iqbal that he did not have to return to work because of new child labor laws. But Iqbal went back anyway to tell other child workers. During the next 2 years, Iqbal roamed the Pakistani countryside, entering factories and bringing the message of freedom to his peers ("Pakistanis Silence Youthful Voice," 1995, p. 6). His activism drew international attention, and Reebok International brought him to Boston, where he was presented with a human rights award. In a 7-minute acceptance speech, Iqbal said he wanted to become a lawyer "so he could be the Abraham Lincoln of his people" ("Pakistanis Silence Youthful Voice," 1995, p. 6). With the promise of a 4-year scholarship from Brandeis University, Iqbal began to attend school in India as he continued his labor activism. He received repeated death threats, however, and on Easter Sunday, 1995, Iqbal was shot to death while riding his bicycle with friends near his grandmother's house in the small village of Muritke, Pakistan. It is believed that he was killed by vengeful members of the carpet industry. In his short and tragic life, Iqbal Masih had accomplished much. "He was so brave...you can't imagine," said Ehsan Ullah Kahn, the labor organizer who had first told Iqbal he did not have to return to his oppressive bosses. "He also has managed to free thousands of children" ("Pakistanis Silence Youthful Voice," 1995, p. 6).

To ensure the sacrifice of Iqbal Masih we must remember his legacy not only as an exploited child worker but as a child activist for his own cause. As Nieuwenhuys (2005, 2009) has argued from a global and historical perspective, concern for the protection of children by adults in the developed world often blunts our understanding of the complexity of and need for children's labor in developing countries. In developing countries many children combine schooling and work, and their labor (directly for their families and for others) is an economic necessity. She argued that those who wish to protect children from exploitation must recognize working children's movements as organizing for the right to work in dignity and to fight for their rights. Here again, as we saw earlier when discussing street children in South America and Africa and HIV/AIDS orphans, developed countries' perceptions, beliefs, and understanding of childhood, children's problems, and children's rights should not be forced on the developing world. We must take care to understand the complexity of these issues from multiple points of view. It is necessary for us to work not only *for* or *in the name of* but *with* those children and the adults in their lives whom we want to help.

Child Poverty in Industrialized Countries

In the wealthy nations of the world, children are not shot on the streets for being poor, nor are they allowed to be sold into indentured servitude. The overwhelming majority of children in Western industrialized societies live in relative comfort and have high aspirations and bright futures. However, many poor children do live in the modern industrialized world, and a significant number live in impoverished and dangerous environments. Children's poverty varies across wealthy nations. The richest nation in the world, the United States, has one of the highest poverty rates. Worse, despite a growing awareness of the problem, the proportion of children living in poverty is on the rise in the United States and in several other Western countries and is much higher than it was 25 years ago. Let's examine this problem by considering recent trends in child poverty in the United States, looking at divergent poverty rates among children and the elderly, and comparing American child poverty to that in other industrialized countries.

Trends in Child Poverty in the United States. Poverty can be measured in a number of ways. In the United States, the official poverty rate provided by the Census Bureau reflects an absolute measure of poverty that is supposed to represent the dollar amount a family needs to achieve a "minimally adequate" standard of living (Bianchi, 1993). The absolute rate is misleading for several reasons. First, it is based on pretax rather than after-tax income and does not take into account access to resources such as food stamps and medical coverage. Poverty measures that take tax and income transfer resources into account are used to figure what is normally referred to as the *posttax and transfer poverty rate*. Second, many argue that poverty is a relative concept and that what is considered "minimally adequate" varies as average living standards increase or decrease (Bianchi, 1993, p. 94; Hernandez, 1994, p. 13; also see Hernandez, Denton, and Macartney, 2007a, for a discussion of various measures of child poverty in the United States especially as it pertains to minority and immigrant children). Those who believe in the importance of using relative measures of poverty normally set the poverty rate between 40 and 50% of the median income of all families in a particular community or country at a given time. For a variety of reasons, different reports of child poverty in the United States and other countries are based on different poverty measures. This leads to a great deal of confusion and distortion in political debates about the extent and causes of child poverty. In our discussion we will always be clear about the particular measure being used and why it is most relevant given a particular comparison.

In terms of absolute measures of poverty, the proportion of children who lived in poverty in the United States in the late 1930s was very high (nearly 70%) but declined dramatically in the 1940s and 1950s as the country emerged from the Great Depression and enjoyed an economic boom after World War II. The rate continued to drop in the 1960s, reaching a low of 14% in 1969. Child poverty increased in the 1970s and early 1980s as economic growth slowed and the country suffered through several recessions. After reaching a high of 22.3% in 1983, the child poverty rate dropped to 19.5% by 1988 as a result of sustained economic growth. This reduction, however, was much less than was expected and was in no way comparable to the major drop in child poverty during the economic boom of the 1950s. Furthermore, with the recession that began in late 1990, the proportion of children in poverty began to increase again and reached a level of 21.8% in 1991 (see Bianchi, 1993). These patterns of child poverty are not confined to the highly segregated inner-city neighborhoods of large metropolitan areas. Poverty rates are similar, if not higher, among nonmetropolitan children (Lichter & Eggebeen, 1992). Overall, as Bianchi noted, recent patterns indicate that "poor macroeconomic growth continues to move more children into poverty, but good macroeconomic performance seems less able to do the opposite" (1993, p. 95). This argument has by and large been sustained as childhood poverty dropped somewhat in the late 1990s when the economy improved and the child poverty rate fell to 16.7% in 2001 where it remained in 2002 (Proctor & Dalaker, 2003). This drop was noteworthy but not spectacular, given the good economic times, and this rate is still much higher than the rates of most other modern societies, as we will see below. However, as the economy again faltered and we entered a deep recession the absolute child poverty rate began to climb anew and reached 19% in 2008 (see Chau, 2009; U.S. Census Bureau, 2009; Wight, Chau, and Aratani, 2010). As the recession lingers and with unemployment near 10% in early 2010 we can expect even higher rates of child poverty until we pull fully out of the recession and see significant improvement in the economy in the United States.

Why has child poverty stayed at this consistently high level of between 15 and 20%? There are a number of interrelated reasons. Most often cited as the main cause is the dramatic structural changes in American families since the 1950s. A major increase in the divorce rate and in the number of nonmarital births (especially to young, poor women) has moved many women and children into poverty (Hernandez, 1994; Sidel, 1992). Many fathers of these children added to the problem by failing to take seriously the responsibility of providing for their offspring; state governments, until recently, have not passed and enforced child support laws to ensure that fathers meet their responsibilities. Some have argued that the federal government needs to become involved in the efficient collection of the $34 billion a year in unpaid child support (Skocpol & Wilson, 1994).

We will discuss the effects of changes in family structure on children's economic, social, and psychological well-being later in the chapter. Here, we need to look at another important factor in child poverty: the way social welfare policies in the United States affect children and the elderly.

Social Welfare Policy and Divergent Poverty Rates of Children and the Elderly. Although Americans advocate strict equality in the distribution of political and judicial rights, they are wary about supporting attempts to ensure economic equality that involve government redistribution (Burtless, 1994, p. 83). Unlike most western European countries, the United States is a highly market-oriented society and designs its social welfare programs accordingly. This fact is nowhere more evident than in the disparity between the poverty rate of children and that of the elderly.

As many Progressives like to point out, the Great Society programs (the expansion of social security and the institution of Medicare and Medicaid) in the 1960s substantially reduced poverty among the elderly. In calculating this change, using a posttax and transfer poverty rate—as previously mentioned, a measure that takes tax and income transfer resources into account—is crucial. Using such a measure, the poverty rate for persons 65 years and older in 1960 was around 30%, whereas by 1994 it was reduced to 12%; in 2002 it was 10.5%, and it was 9.7% in 2008 (Proctor & Dalaker, 2003; U.S. Census Bureau, 2009). The major reason for this reduction was government programs that supported the elderly. Similar government programs for children are much less generous. To estimate the difference, let's look at how government programs affected rates of poverty among the elderly and children in the United States in 1996. For the elderly (persons 65 and older), the poverty rate before taking government programs and tax credits into account was around 50%. After taking the programs and tax credits into account, the poverty rate was 12%, a reduction of 38%. Things were quite different for children 17 and under in 1986. The poverty rate was reduced from 23.6% to 16.1% when taking government programs and tax credits into account, a reduction of only 7.5% (Center on Budget and Policy Priorities, 1998). These differences in the poverty rates of the elderly and children have persisted since 1996, as we previously noted. In fact, social welfare policies and a number of other factors have contributed to a general trend in which the quality of the lives of the elderly and children have moved in different directions—up for the elderly and down for children (Preston, 1984; Sgritta, 1994, 1997). Do we care more for our elderly than for our children? Does it make sense to invest more in the elderly than in children?

Most Americans, young and old, would answer "no" to both questions. Yet we currently treat our elderly much better than our children. The reasons for this are complicated. Let's return to the nature of social welfare policy in the United States. The two largest social welfare programs for the elderly, social security and Medicare, are social insurance programs. These programs are financed by payroll taxes and are paid for by those currently employed and their employers, and the benefits are provided to the retired, dependents of deceased workers, and insured unemployed (Burtless, 1994, p. 54). Social insurance programs differ from other types of social welfare programs in that they are not means tested or restricted to only the poor. Means-tested programs distribute money and other types of resources to the poor and near poor (Burtless, 1994, p. 53). In theory, social insurance programs pay for themselves: People who work pay taxes, and these payroll taxes cover their social security and Medicare costs in their retirement years. Right away there is a problem with such thinking, however. Many people have entered into retirement (and therefore have been entitled to Medicare) after paying very little into the system. Furthermore, due to advances in medical technology and the success of the programs themselves, the elderly are living longer and longer. Thus, these programs become more and more expensive as the number of people covered increases. This economic problem is accelerated by the growing costs of medical care; new technologies such as heart transplants keep people alive longer but are very expensive.

Spending on programs for the elderly (social security, Medicare, and Medicaid—a large percentage of Medicaid spending is for nursing home care for the elderly) makes up a large percentage of the federal budget. In President Obama's proposed budget for 2011, spending on social security and Medicare and half the budget for Medicaid are estimated to be more than $1.3 trillion. This amount is a fair estimate of the budget to be devoted to people older than 65. It makes up more than 35.6% of the total budget (U.S. Office of Management and Budget, 2010). The amount is more than double all proposed nondefense discretionary spending. It is only $46 billion less than proposed total discretionary spending for both defense and nondefense programs. Furthermore, the budgets for social security, Medicare, and Medicaid have increased at a much higher rate than programs for poor children such as Temporary Assistance for Needy Families, food stamps through the Supplemental Nutrition Assistance Program, and Head Start.

Julia Isaacs (2009) of the Brookings Institution did research an all government spending (federal and local) on the children and the elderly in 2004. One would predict that with spending on education at the state level, government spending on children and the elderly would even out. However, Isaacs's estimates were that public "spending on children averaged $8,942 per child under age 19 in 2004" whereas in "the same year, public spending on the elderly was $21,904 per elderly person, or 2.4 times as high as that on children" (Isaacs, 2009, p. 1). In the same article Isaacs pointed to other studies (one carried out by the Congressional Budget Office finds an even higher ratio of spending on the elderly compared to children).

Do these differences mean we are spending too much on the elderly? No, actually these differences show the success of these programs, especially Medicare, as people are living longer lives because of advanced medical technology. Further, the elderly are deserving of social security pensions given their investments in society over their lives. However, the large inequity in government spending on the elderly compared to children does suggest we need to control the costs of Medicare and health care more generally in the United States. Aaron (2009), in response to Isaacs, argued that the main problem is the high and growing costs of health care in the United States, especially for the elderly; that these costs need to be better managed; and that any fraud in Medicare should be eliminated. He argued, however, that this inequity in spending is not unjust, because it is logical that there would be more need for health care spending on the elderly than on children. Children, he maintained, will be repaid for the present inequity when they reach old age and have greater need for health care. Aaron was surely correct that there are major needs to reduce the cost of health care in the United States and to make it more available for all citizens. However, the inequity in spending between the elderly and children cannot be so easily explained away through the balance of health care spending over time. This first assumes all children in the United States have equal access to health care compared to the elderly, but many American children are still without health care insurance. Also the major difference in poverty rates between children and the elderly shows that children are not on an even playing field except for differences in health care investment. The inequity in investment in children compared to the elderly in the United States is a major problem that has negative effects on children's quality of life as they live their childhoods. Reducing poverty and investing more in children will improve their childhoods and increase the likelihood of their becoming productive citizens in their futures, an outcome that benefits all Americans.

Yet some argue that even a small increase in any level of welfare spending for poor families with children is too much. Such an attitude is understandable in a country where most social welfare programs related to medical care, nutrition, and housing are means tested. Because only the truly impoverished are covered by most of these welfare programs, many working people who can barely make ends meet and who cannot afford health insurance come to resent those who receive basic benefits without working.

Variations in Child Poverty and Quality of Life in Industrialized Countries

Most other countries in the industrialized world do not make such sharp distinctions between entitlement programs such as old age pensions and other types of social welfare. In these countries, basic nutrition, medical care, family leave, child care, and preschool education are provided at a base level for all citizens. In short, other industrialized countries have attempted to deal with the very real demands of increasing social welfare costs of the elderly while at the same time maintaining investments in their children (Sgritta, 1994). These countries are less market oriented than the United States, and their citizens are willing to pay higher tax rates for the social benefits they receive.

This difference leads to a number of interesting patterns regarding the quality of life among children. Timothy Smeeding, Lee Rainwater, and Gary Burtless (2001) looked at overall child poverty rates of children in the United States and in 17 other industrialized nations. The authors used a relative measure of poverty (children younger than 18 living in households with incomes less than 40% of the national median) that was adjusted for family size and age of the head of the household. The survey studied the period from 1990 to 1997. Overall, they found the following:

> Higher [child] poverty rates in countries with a high level of overall inequality (the United States and Italy), in geographically large and diverse countries (the United States, Canada, Australia), and in countries with less-developed welfare states (Spain). Low poverty rates are more common in smaller, well-developed, and high spending welfare states (the European community, Scandinavia) and in countries where unemployment compensation is more generous, social policies provide more generous support to single mothers and working women (through paid leave, for example), and social assistance minimums are high. (Smeeding et al., 2001, pp. 171–172)

Exhibit 11.1 presents an update to the Smeeding et al. study of the 1990s with data from the Luxembourg Income Study files for 20 countries for the years 1999 to 2005. The overall pattern still fits the general conclusions found in the earlier study. Only 1 country, Israel, had a higher rate of child poverty than the United States (16.1% compared to 14.7%). Israel's rate has increased dramatically since the early 1990s, whereas the rate in the United States was the same in 2004 as it was in 1997. As we see in Exhibit 11.1, 3 other countries had high rates of child poverty at around 10% (Italy, Spain, and Canada), and again this pattern was the same as it was for the 1990s. The poverty rates were all less than 10% in most other European countries (except Ireland), and they were less than 5% in 11 of the countries, with the least child poverty in Finland, Denmark, and Sweden. Again we see the general pattern of lower child poverty rates in the Scandinavian countries, which Smeeding et al. found in the 1990s. Outside of Israel, the country with one of the biggest changes in child poverty was the United Kingdom, where child poverty rates dropped from 8.3% in 1995 to 5.7% in 2004. This reduction was due to an initiative by then prime minster Tony Blair to halve the child poverty rate during the 1997–2007 decade. The United Kingdom was not quite there by 2004 and is not likely to succeed given the present global recession. In fact, we should expect an increase in child poverty in all countries when the data are available for 2010. Yet the decrease in child poverty in the United Kingdom is significant because it was 1 of only 8 countries (along with

Exhibit 11.1   Child Poverty in 20 Countries

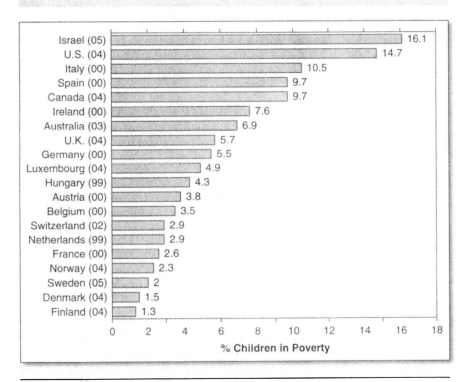

Source: Author's tabulations from the Luxembourg Income Study files.

Note: Poverty is measured at 40% of median income for individuals.

Australia, Denmark, Finland, Germany, Italy, the Netherlands, and Switzerland) that had decreases. Overall, it is clear that many industrialized countries need to decrease the amount of child poverty much more, most especially the United States.

Child poverty rates, however, do not tell the whole story. Rainwater and Smeeding (2003) also looked at the economic well-being of children across income levels of households in 18 countries in the 1990s. They found that "rich American children are much better off compared with advantaged children in other countries" (p. 42). Children from wealthy families in Switzerland and Canada are somewhat near children in the United States in terms of disposable income, whereas rich children in all the other countries studied have less spendable income than their counterparts in the United States by a wide margin. The pattern is quite different for low-income children. Rainwater and Smeeding found that in only 3 of the 14 comparison countries (the United Kingdom, Spain, and Italy) poor children were worse off than comparable poor children in the United States. They found further that in "five countries the average disadvantaged child has one-third or more real income as the average poor American child. In Norway and Switzerland the relatively disadvantaged child has more than half again the real income of the poor American child" (p. 45).

We must also remember that although most of the countries studied provide paid maternal or family leave, some form of government-supported child care, and early education programs, the United States either provides no such services or has very limited programs, such as Head Start. Therefore, the economic challenges that poor families and their children face are much greater in the United States than in any other country in the industrialized world. Overall, these data indicate a much greater level of commitment in other countries of the industrialized world to the well-being of all children, as compared to the United States.

The Human Face of Poverty: The Story of Nicholas

Given growing concern about the budget deficit, opposition to higher taxes, skepticism about welfare policy, and the political power of the elderly, it is unlikely that the United States will face up to its growing problem of child poverty anytime soon. Some things can be done right away, however, and we will consider several important first steps in the next chapter. For now, we close this section with an inspiring case study of an inner-city Chicago boy who is doing his best to make the most of his childhood in very difficult circumstances.

GROWING UP FAST: THE STORY OF NICHOLAS

In 1993, the *New York Times* published an important series of articles titled "Children of the Shadows," which captured the lives of 10 children growing up poor in American cities. The first article, written by Isabel Wilkerson (1993), told the inspiring story of Nicholas, an African American 10-year-old living with his family in the dangerous Englewood section of Chicago. The economic circumstances of Nicholas and his family can be expressed quite simply—they are very poor. However, his family structure and those of his mother and the other adults who care for him are very complex. Wilkerson describes a scene in which the boy is called from his fourth-grade classroom and asked to explain why no one has picked up his younger sister, Ishtar, from her morning kindergarten class. Nicholas has a hard time explaining that his mother, a welfare recipient rearing five young children, is in college trying to become a nurse and so is not home during the day; that Ishtar's father is separated from his mother and in a drug-and-alcohol haze most of the time; that the grandmother he used to live with is at work; and that, besides, he cannot possibly account for the man who is supposed to take his sister home—his mother's companion, the father of her youngest child (Wilkerson, 1993, p. 1). In the end, Nicholas simply says that his stepfather is supposed to pick up Ishtar, and he then gives the principal the phone number of his aunt.

Nicholas's mother, Angela, fits many of the stereotyped descriptions of welfare recipients. She is Black, a 10th-grade dropout who bore her first child, Nicholas, at age 16 and then had four more children with three different men. Angela also went through a very difficult period in which she was addicted to crack cocaine. Her mother cared for her children; Angela went through treatment and has stayed away from drugs ever since. She has been on and off welfare and has worked a long succession of jobs, from picking okra in Louisiana to waiting tables in downtown Chicago. She, like most of us, has made mistakes—the two biggest being her teenage pregnancy and her drug addiction. When the poor make mistakes, however, they seldom get a second chance, and the recovery process is long and hard.

Angela and her mother are deeply religious and attend services in a tiny storefront church, Faith Temple, several times a week. The deep spirituality of many inner-city African Americans is often overlooked in the stereotypes.

(Continued)

(Continued)

It is this spirituality, an Ethiopian-derived Christianity, that has kept Angela striving for her goal—a nursing degree that could pull her family out of poverty and into the working class. Spirituality also sustains her family against many of the dangers—crack houses, drive-by shootings, robberies—of their inner-city environment. (In Angela's neighborhood in 1992, 80 people were murdered; as Wilkerson, 1993, p. 16, pointed out, this is more than the number of murders in Omaha and Pittsburgh combined for that year.)

Every morning before her children go to school, Angela shakes an aerosol can containing a special religious oil and tells them to close their eyes tight as "she sprays them long and furious so they will come back to her, alive and safe, at day's end" (Wilkerson, 1993, p. 16). She has faith in the oil, but she also recites the rules to her children each morning: no playing on the way to and from school, and if you hear shooting—run! "Why do I say run?" the mother asks each day. "Because a bullet don't have no eyes," Nicholas and his brother Willie shout in reply. Once Willie almost got shot on the way home from school as he straggled along behind his brother—a sixth-grade boy pulled out a gun and started shooting. Willie heard the shots and ran, unhurt, to catch up with his brother. So far the rules and the oil have worked.

In many ways Nicholas is a typical 10-year-old. He gets only average grades, and he slides down banisters, shirttail out, hoping to become a fireman. But he has many of the responsibilities of a man. He must look after his younger siblings, often getting their breakfast in the morning and washing clothes at night because the children have so few things to wear. "I know my baby's running out of hands," Angela says low one night as Nicholas works on the laundry. She worries about him, and Nicholas, in turn, worries about her and about his siblings. He worries much too much for a young boy. He is worried the morning his mother has an early test and he has to take the little ones to day care before going to school himself. At the day care center, his youngest brother, John-John, begins to cry as Nicholas walks away. "Nicholas bent down and hugged him and kissed him. Everything, Nicholas assured him, was going to be O.K." (Wilkerson, 1993, p. 16).

In a follow-up story written by Isabel Wilkerson (2005) 12 years later we learn more about the lives of Nicholas and his family. Things have gotten better for some family members, worse for others. Angela and her younger children have fared the best. She met and married a Chicago police detective, finished her studies and became a registered nurse, found a steady job in the nursing profession, and joined the middle class. These successes positively affected the lives of her younger children (including a new son born after the original story was written) who are doing well in school, with Ishtar a recent high school graduate. However, Angela's turning around of her life came too late for Nicholas and his brother Willie. Both became involved in drug activities in preadolescence when the family still lived in a housing project. Both have spent short periods of time in jail, have struggled to stay out of trouble, and have barely made ends meet as they try to support children they fathered out of wedlock. Willie has had the toughest life, twice being shot in drug-related incidents. Nicholas, the boy who grew up too fast, now is a man with an uncertain future and the dream of becoming a rap artist. It seems like a long shot, but his mother Angela, after a troubled childhood and early adulthood turned her life around. She prays and hopes that Willie and Nicholas will be able to do the same.

Teen Pregnancy and Nonmarital Births

Perhaps no other change in family structure has been more controversial than the rising number of nonmarital births in Western industrialized societies. This issue seemed to reach its peak in the United States in 1992 when a fictional television character, Murphy Brown (an older than 40-year-old television investigative journalist), was criticized by then vice president Dan Quayle for deciding to have a child out of wedlock. Nonmarital births seem most disturbing to those who hold traditional values regarding family structure because they are seen as a rejection of the two-parent family (Luker, 2006). However, the issue was intensified in the 1980s and early 1990s by the increase of nonmarital births by adolescent girls, most especially poor minority youth. In this case, as we saw in Chapter 10, all the negative aspects of blaming the victim come to the fore. Debates about nonmarital births and what is best for the children and the children having the children become tinged with racism and stereotypes of the poor.

Let me be clear from the start. Teenage pregnancy, nonmarital births on the part of young girls, and abortion among youth are best avoided at all costs. They clearly are destructive of childhoods. That said, understanding the extent of the problem, interpreting its effects on children and youth, and doing something about it are indeed highly challenging tasks.

The Rise in Teen Nonmarital Births

What is the extent of the problem, and how has it grown? Teen sexuality and pregnancy are clearly a global problem, but here we will restrict our discussion to industrialized countries, primarily the United States. In the United States, measures of teen pregnancy over time are unreliable because of difficulties in obtaining data on abortion, most especially before its legalization in 1973. By looking at birth rates and available data on abortion after 1973, however, it does appear that the pregnancy rate among teenagers has not increased dramatically since the 1950s. The Alan Guttmacher Institute (2010) recently provided estimates of pregnancy and abortion rates for women ages 15 to 19 in the United States from 1986 until 2006. The institute estimated that the pregnancy rate has steadily declined from a high of 116.9 per 1,000 women in 1990, to 83.6 per 1,000 women in 2000, to 71.5 per 1,000 women in 2006. The institute also estimated a steady decline in the abortion rate from a high of 43.5 per 1,000 women in 1988, to 24.0 per 1,000 women in 2000, to 19.3 per 1,000 women in 2006 (p. 6).

Exhibit 11.2 presents information about the rate of births for women ages 15 to 19 in the United States from 1940 to 2006. We can see that the rate was 53.5 births per 1,000 women in 1940 but rose to 79.5 in 1950 before peaking at 91.0 births per 1,000 in 1960 as part of an overall baby boom. Teen births then began to decline. By 1980 they were back down to between 50 and 60 per 1,000 women, where they remained until 2000 when the rate was 47.7. They continued to decline in the first 5 years of the 21st century and reached a low of 40.5 per 1,000 women in 2005, only to rise slightly to 41.9 in 2006 (J. Martin et al., 2009; J. Martin, Park, & Sutton, 2002).

What has been increasing dramatically until recently in the United States is the percentage of out-of-wedlock teen births. The same pattern exists for teens as it does for all women 15 to 44 years of age between the period from 1950 to 1990: a steady increase from about 13 births per 1,000 women in 1950 to around 43 births per 1,000 women in 1990 (J. Martin et al., 2002). However, as we can see in Exhibit 11.3, the teen out-of-wedlock birth rate reached a peak in 1995 of 43.8 per 1,000 unmarried women and then steadily declined to a rate of 39.0 in 2000, to 34.5 in 2005, before increasing slightly to 36.2 in 2006.

However, underlying these overall rates are important racial and ethnic differences. As Exhibit 11.3 shows, the rate of out-of-wedlock births has been high for Black and Hispanic teens for many years. For Black teens, the rate rose from 87.9 births to 106.0 births per 1,000 women

Exhibit 11.2   Birth Rates Per 1,000 Women Aged 15 to 19, 1940–2006

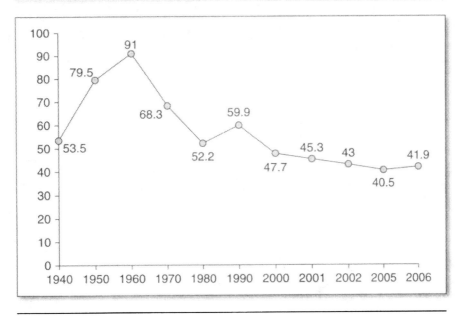

Source: Adapted from J. Martin, Park, and Sutton (2002) and J. Martin et al. (2009).

between 1980 and 1990. For Hispanic teens, data have been available since 1990; the rate rose from 65.9 to 73.2 nonmarital births per 1,000 women in 1994. The rate of out-of-wedlock births for White teens has been much lower than for non-White teens, but the rate has increased dramatically, rising from 16.5 births per 1,000 women in 1980 to 30.6 births per 1,000 women in 1990 (J. Martin et al., 2002).

Again, however, we have seen a decline in nonmarital births among all racial and ethnic groups since the mid 1990s, but the decrease has not been a steady one for Hispanic teens. The rate for Black teens has declined the most—from a peak of 106.0 births per 1,000 women in 1990, to 76.0 births per 1,000 women in 2000, to a low of 60.6 in 2005, with a slight increase to 63.5 in 2006. For White teens the drop has been less dramatic but has been fairly steady. For White teens, nonmarital births peaked at 35.0 births per 1,000 women in 1995 and dropped to 32.7 per 1,000 women in 2000. Since then there has been a steady decline to a low of around 30.0 per 1,000 women in 2005 and again as for all groups a slight increase in 2006. For Hispanic women the pattern is more complex; the rate dropped from 73.2 per 1,000 women in 1995 to a low of 66.1

Exhibit 11.3   Rates of Nonmarital Births per 1,000 Women Ages 15 to 19, 1980–2006

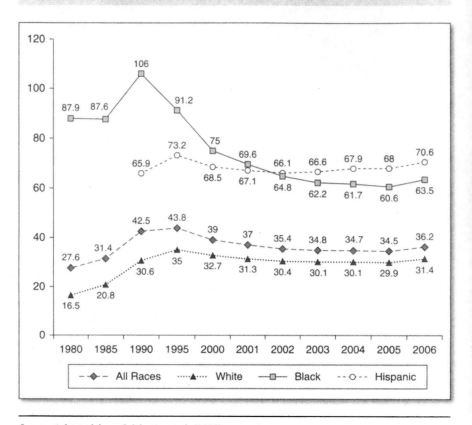

Source: Adapted from J. Martin et al. (2009).

per 1,000 women in 2002. However, then the nonmarital birth rate became higher for Hispanic teens compared to Black teens and began a steady increase, reaching 70.6 per 1,000 women in 2006 (J. Martin et al., 2009). Overall, even though there has been a decrease in nonmarital births in recent years, the overall rate is still high, and the increase for all racial and ethnic groups in 2006 is worrisome.

Before considering the possible factors underlying these changes and the consequences of teen births for both the young parents and their children, it is useful to consider comparative data from other industrialized countries. Exhibit 11.4 presents birth rates for 15- to 19-year-old women in 2006 for the United States and 15 other countries. We can see that the United States has the highest teen birth rate (at nearly 42 per 1,000 women)

Exhibit 11.4   Birth Rates for 15- to 19-Year-Olds in Selected Countries, 2006

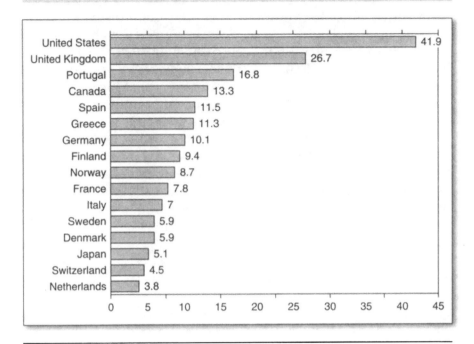

Source: Adapted from United Nations Statistics Division (2006) and National Campaign to Prevent Teen and Unplanned Pregnancy (2010).

compared to all the other countries. The rates in the United Kingdom and Portugal are relatively high, but nevertheless the teen birth rate in the United States is still substantially higher than in these two countries. For all the other countries, the teen birth rates are much lower than that of the United States, with Germany, Finland, Norway, France, Italy, Sweden, Denmark, and Japan all having birth rates lower than 10 whereas Switzerland and the Netherlands have rates lower than 5 per 1,000 for 15- to 19-year-olds.

Possible Cause of Trends in Teen Nonmarital Births

These comparative data put us in a better position for evaluating the many factors that most influence teen nonmarital births in the United States. One of the reasons offered for such increases among teens in all industrialized countries is that young women are delaying marriage but are becoming involved in sexual activity at younger ages than in the past.

One important factor here is the declining age of puberty due to nutritional and other changes. At the turn of the 20th century, the average age of menarche for adolescent females was 14.8 years, whereas in 1999 the average age was about 12.3 years. Some adolescent girls begin to menstruate as early as 10 years of age (Alan Guttmacher Institute, 1994; S. Anderson & Musi, 2005). Thus, contemporary youth in industrialized society will live on average nearly a decade of their lives as sexually mature and single (Luker, 1991). Therefore, given that teens were more sexually active (with more sexual partners) in the 1980s and 1990s than they were 20 years earlier, it is not surprising that we have seen some increase in nonmarital births. It is doubtful, however, that this increase in sexual activity over a longer period of time can in and of itself explain the dramatic rise in nonmarital births in the United States. Nor can it explain the differences we see between the nonmarital birth rates of the United States and most west European countries, where teens also face a long period of sexual maturity prior to marriage and where they report similar levels of sexual activity (Boonstra, 2002; Darroch, Singh, & Frost, 2001; E. Jones et al., 1985).

A second factor to consider is teens' knowledge about reproductive processes and contraception as well as their access to contraception and abortion services. Here, the United States seems far behind most west European countries, where extensive sex education programs in schools begin in the early grades and contraceptive devices and services are widely available in clinics and pharmacies. In general, there is more openness about and tolerance of teenage sexual activity in the European countries than there is in most of the United States and in parts of Canada (Weaver, Smith, & Kippax, 2005).

One reason for the more successful experience of the European countries may be that public attention is generally less focused on the morality of early sexual activity and more focused on the search for ways to prevent increased teenage pregnancy, abortions, and childbearing (Berne & Huberman, 1999; Schalet, 2004). In the United States, contentious debates arise about whether sex education and the availability of contraceptives will increase sexual activity among teens and result in even higher rates of teen pregnancy and births (Luker, 2006). But surely the dramatic differences we see in pregnancy, abortion, and birth rates when we compare the United States to west European countries do not support such beliefs (Santelli, Lindberg, Finer, & Singh, 2007). Furthermore, American teenagers seem to have inherited the worst of all possible worlds regarding their exposure to messages about sex. Movies, music, radio, and TV tell them that sex is romantic, exciting, and titillating; pre-marital sex and cohabitation are familiar ways of life among the adults around them; and their own parents or their parents' friends are often divorced or separated but involved in sexual relationships. In spite of this, adults continually send teens the message, "Good girls should just say no" to the expected sexual advances of boys and young adult males. Almost nothing that they see or hear about sex informs them about con-traception, the importance of avoiding pregnancy, and the responsibility of both females and males in sexual activity (Agnvall, 2006; E. Jones et al., 1985; Kisker, 1985).

Large numbers of American youth do manage to navigate successfully through what Luker referred to as the "reproductive minefield of extended adolescence" without experiencing (or causing) pregnancy, making deci-sions about abortion, or bearing children in or out of wedlock (1991, p. 79). How do these teens differ from those who are not successful? Although many who move through the period unscathed are less sexually active and in some cases even abstinent, many others are sexually active but take care to avoid pregnancy or, if they become pregnant, rely on abortion.

Let's return now to the issue of poverty, which is so often the central factor for the social problems of children. In the United States, teen birthrates are highest for those who have the greatest economic disad-vantages. Interestingly, in the current debate about teenage pregnancy, this general finding is often interpreted to mean that teenage childbearing causes poverty, rather than the other way around. The next step in this way of thinking is that many welfare programs that provide assistance for unmarried mothers create a financial incentive for young poor women to bear children outside of marriage. Thus, welfare policies themselves cause poverty (Murray, 1984).

Let's begin with the second part of the argument—that welfare policies contribute to high rates of teen pregnancy and births. First, such an argu-ment clearly is not supported by the comparative data we discussed ear-lier. Let's return to Exhibit 11.4. All of the other countries provide more extensive benefits to poor mothers (including child care, medical care, food supplements, housing, and family allowances) than those provided in the United States (Clearinghouse on International Developments in Child, Youth and Family Policies, 2010; E. Jones et al., 1985). Yet these countries all have substantially lower teen pregnancy, abortion, and mar-ital and nonmarital birth rates.

Many conservatives eschew such comparative data, arguing that what might work in the more collectivist welfare states of western Europe will not work in the United States. On the surface, such an argument may seem to have merit. For example, from 1976 to 1992, about 42% of all single women receiving Aid to Families With Dependent Children in the United States were, or had been, teenage mothers (American Psychological Association, 1995; General Accounting Office, 1994, p. 8). But is there evidence that specific U.S. welfare policies play a significant role in adolescents' fertility-related behavior? Although researchers on this question are not in complete agreement, reviews of the welfare incentive literature conclude that welfare benefits do not serve as a reasonable explanation for variations in pregnancy and childbearing rates among unmarried adolescents (American Psychological Association, 1995). What the research does find is that poverty, race and ethnicity, and education—not specific welfare policies—have the most significant effects on teenage childbearing. Luker nicely summarized the general findings of this research:

> First, since poor and minority youth tend to become sexually active at an earlier age than more advantaged youngsters, they are "at risk" for a longer period of time, including years when they are less cognitively mature. Young teens are also less likely to use contraceptives than older teenagers. Second, the use of contraception is more common among teens who are white, come from more affluent homes, have higher educational aspirations, and who are doing well in school. And, finally, among youngsters who become pregnant, abortions are more common if they are affluent, white, urban, of higher socio-economic status, get good grades, come from two-parent families, and aspire to higher education. Thus more advantaged youth get filtered out of the pool of young women at risk of teen parenthood. (1991, p. 76)

"But wait a minute!" say conservatives and also many Americans who view problems like teenage pregnancy individualistically rather than structurally. Why can't these disadvantaged teens act more responsibly and sensibly, more like their advantaged counterparts? In this view, noted Luker, the teenage pregnancy problem is cast as a universal: Everyone was a teenager once, and teenagers must control their impulses and be responsible about their futures (1991, p. 81). But here's the rub. Teenagers are not all the same. Many are not well prepared for the challenges of puberty, do not have support from caring adults when they make difficult decisions, and do not have parents who can or will bail them out when they make mistakes. In fact, as we discussed in Chapter 10, many economically disadvantaged girls not only lack supportive caring adults in their lives but also must often fight off adult sexual abuse and coercion. Finally, and perhaps most important, many poor youth are different from middle-class and wealthy teens in that they see little hope that their lives will improve—there are no bright horizons in their futures. As a result, they often drift into pregnancy and then into parenthood (Furstenberg, Brooks-Gunn, & Chase-Landale, 1989).

Given the Personal Responsibility and Work Opportunity Reconciliation Act, or what has become known as welfare reform, and the replacement of Aid to Families With Dependent Children with Temporary Assistance for Needy Families, the debate about welfare and teen pregnancy subsided. However, most recent research suggests that welfare reform has not reduced teenage fertility (Hao & Cherlin, 2004). In any case, with welfare reform and the decline in teen births there has been a shift to a new debate regarding the best programs of sex education for teens. Here social conservatives argue strongly for abstinence-only programs whereas Progressives stress the need for comprehensive sex education involving both abstinence and instruction about the types, availability, and use of contraception. In the George W. Bush administration the federal government promoted abstinence until marriage ("abstinence-only") programs and restricted federal funding to schools that used such programs. The requirements for abstinence-only programs specified "that these programs must have as their 'exclusive purpose' the promotion of abstinence outside of marriage and that they must not, in any way, advocate contraceptive use or discuss contraceptive methods other than to emphasize their failure rates" (Santelli et al., 2007, p. 150; also see Luker, 2006; Santelli et al., 2006). Some abstinence-only advocates bring great religious fervor to the debate, leading to the promotion of youth's making virginity pledges in some schools and even purity balls where preadolescent and teenage girls pledge virginity until marriage to their fathers at formal dances or balls (Gibbs, 2008; see Valenti, 2009, for an interpretation and critique of the practice). Progressives, including many health care specialists, agree that abstinence (especially for preadolescents and young teens) should be part of sex education in schools. However, they argue strongly that abstinence-plus programs, which provide information about the types, availability, and proper use of contraception, are essential. Santelli et al. argued that

> public policies and programs in the United States and elsewhere should vigorously promote provision of accurate information on contraception and on sexual behavior and relationships, support increased availability and accessibility of contraceptive services and supplies for adolescents, and promote the value of responsible and protective behaviors, including condom and contraceptive use and pregnancy planning. (2007, p. 155)

Such arguments have had effects as there has been a nationwide trend against abstinence-only sex education, with 43 states and the District of Columbia no longer accepting funds under the Title V abstinence-only education program (Boonstra, 2009).

Research studies comparing a range of sex education programs, including abstinence-only programs, virginity pledges, and more comprehensive programs (often called abstinence plus), have been mixed. They show that abstinence-only programs and virginity pledges do not generally increase the age at which youth initiate sexual behavior, reduce their number of sexual partners, or reduce their likelihood of contracting a sexually transmitted disease, becoming pregnant, or causing a pregnancy (see Santelli et al., 2006, for a review). Regarding virginity pledges, studies find that students who take such pledges are more likely to delay sexual activity longer compared to those who do not. However, once those who have pledged become sexually active they are less likely to use contraception than, and are equally likely to contract a sexually transmitted disease as, those who have not made such a pledge (Bearman & Brückner, 2001; Brückner & Bearman, 2005). The most comprehensive study to evaluate abstinence-only programs as precisely defined by Title V government finding is that of Trenholm et al. (2008). Unlike other studies, Trenholm et al.'s is based on an experimental design and examines students who were involved in four abstinence-only programs around the country as well as youth in control groups from the same communities who did not participate in such programs. The sample of 2,057 youth participating in the study came from big cities (Miami and Milwaukee) as well as rural communities (Powhatan, Virginia, and Clarksdale, Mississippi). The students were in late preadolescence or early adolescence at the time the study began, and the study continued for 42 to 78 months. Students who participated in abstinence-only programs were just as likely to have sex over the course of the study as those in the control groups. They reported having a similar number of sexual partners, and they first had sex on average at about the same age as those in the control group— 14 years, 9 months. However, unlike the students who took virginity pledges, students in abstinence-only programs in this study were no more likely to have unprotected sex than those in the control group (see Trenholm et al., 2008, for more detail).

These findings influenced President Obama recently to end the restriction of federal funding to abstinence-only sex education programs and to sponsor more comprehensive programs in his 2010 federal budget (Cohen, 2009). However, a very recent study (Jemmott & Jemmott, 2010) has reignited the debate. This study was based on the participation of 662 African American students in Grades 6 and 7 in schools in Philadelphia. Each participant was randomly assigned to one of four groups—an 8-hour abstinence-only program stressing the benefits of delaying intercourse, an 8-hour safer sex program stressing condom use, a comprehensive intervention that covered both abstinence and condoms, and a control group that offered health information unrelated to sexual behavior. Rivara and Joffe (2010) summarized the findings in an editorial accompanying the article. They noted that

> the abstinence-only curriculum appeared to be as effective as a combined curriculum and more effective than the safer sex–only curriculum in delaying sexual activity over the 24 month follow up. None of the curricula had any effect on the prevalence of unprotected sexual intercourse or consistent condom use. (p. 200; see Jemmott & Jemmot, 2010, for more detail)

These findings are important but do not generally support abstinence-only programs under the much more rigid requirements of abstinence until marriage of the former Bush administration. In fact, the study's recommendations are in line with most abstinence-plus programs in their emphasis on advising abstinence for 10- to 14-year-olds. However, the long battle over sex education is sure to continue with each side pointing to different studies to support its case for why abstinence-only or comprehensive programs first led to a decrease, but now a recent increase, in teenage births. Luker (2006) argued that these debates about sex education in the United States have always really been "about sex and marriage, and that debates about sex and marriage are also debates about gender, about how men and women (and boys and girls) should relate to one another, sexually and otherwise" (p. 238). If the debate is indeed about these broader values regarding sex, marriage, and gender, they seem bound to continue long into the future.

Consequences for Teen Parents and Their Children

Given the relationship between poverty and teen pregnancy, it should not be surprising that many researchers have found it difficult to "sort out the effects of early childbearing from the selective factors that lead some youth to become teen parents" (Furstenberg et al., 1989, p. 315). For most teen mothers, early childbearing immediately worsens their quality of life and often leads to a number of negative consequences as far as their educational, economic, and marital futures are concerned. Short-term studies have found that teen mothers are more likely to drop out of school, fail to find stable and remunerative employment, and enter into stable marriages than are women who begin childbearing in later life (Furstenberg et al., 1989; Hofferth & Hayes, 1987; R. Maynard, 1997). In a rare long-term study, however, Furstenberg and his colleagues found that although teen mothers did not do as well as later childbearers, most teen mothers managed to stage a recovery in later life (Furstenberg et al., 1989). The key to such recoveries was the women's successes in educational achievement, fertility control, and stable marriages. In a more recent study Hofferth, Reid, and Mott (2001) found that the effects on high school completion because of teen pregnancy declined in the 1980s and 1990s because young women completed high school or earned GEDs regardless of the timing of their first births. However, the gap between early and late childbearers in postsecondary school attendance widened nearly 20 percentage points between the early 1960s and the early 1990s. Given the increasing importance of college education, teen mothers today are at least as disadvantaged as those of past generations.

Elaine Bell Kaplan's (1997) ethnography of Black teenage motherhood challenges many stereotypes, especially the assumption that the African American community condones teen pregnancy. Using her experience as an African American teenage mother, Kaplan developed close relations with her informants and offered important proposals for rethinking and reassessing the class factors, gender relations, and racism that influence Black teenagers to become mothers.

What do we know about the lives of children of teen mothers? We have frequently discovered in our exploration of childhood in this book that many things are assumed about children's lives even though the detailed study and research required to really understand them or to do something about them is lacking. We see this pattern again when it comes to teenage pregnancy. As Furstenberg et al. noted, "it is commonly presumed that early childbearing adversely affects children, although only a limited amount of evidence has been marshaled to demonstrate this seemingly obvious proposition" (1989, p. 316). One wonders how much more we might know about the everyday lives of teen mothers and their offspring if we had invested as much research funding and time in direct studies of them as we have in trying to find a relationship between welfare spending and teenage pregnancy. More studies like the one done by Kaplan (1997) are clearly needed.

In any case, we do know some things. Generally, children born to teenage mothers are at a developmental disadvantage compared with children born to older mothers. For younger children, these differences are much more likely to be observed in sons than in daughters, with sons of teenage mothers being more aggressive and lacking self-control compared to sons of older mothers. In adolescence, school achievement is markedly lower among offspring of teenage mothers, and these youth display behavioral problems and a lack of interest in learning compared to the interest displayed by children of older mothers (Furstenberg et al., 1989). However, a wide range of factors are associated with having a teenage mother (for example, disadvantaged neighborhoods, low-quality schools, lower educational attainment of the mother, emotional problems of the mother, and so on), and it is not clear which of these factors may account for these differences.

Violence, Victimization, and the Loss of Childhood

In Chapter 10 we discussed the bogeyman syndrome or the general fear of the victimization of children in contemporary industrialized societies. These heightened fears about children's safety are, to a large degree, a reflection of our own adult anxieties about our lack of control in a rapidly changing world. Yet even if the world is a place no more dangerous (and perhaps even less dangerous) than it was in the past, violence and inhumanity do exist. Children, more than any other group, are the main victims of such evils—victims of anger, violence, and neglect in their societies, communities, and families. Recent revelations of child molestation in the Catholic Church have raised the already growing concern about child physical and sexual abuse outside the home. Many parents ask, Where can my children be safe?

Children are at a high risk of victimization for several reasons, including (a) their dependency on adults, (b) their relatively small physical stature, and (c) the legal toleration of victimization (Finkelhor & Dziuba-Leatherman, 1994). Furthermore, given their dependency on adults, children often have little choice regarding with whom they associate and where they live. These limited options are especially unfortunate for economically disadvantaged children who live in dangerous neighborhoods because they increase their "vulnerability to both intimate victimization and street crime" (Finkelhor & Dziuba-Leatherman, 1994, p. 177). In our review, we will concentrate primarily on child victimization in and outside the family in American society, with some comparison with other industrialized societies. We will not be able to address important work on children victimized by war and political violence (but see Carlton-Ford, 2004; Dodge & Raundalen, 1991; Garbarino, Kostelny, & Dubrow, 1991, for discussions of this issue).

As we saw in Chapter 10, the potential of victimization of young children is highest in the home and family. Yet as children grow older and spend more time outside the home, they encounter a whole new set of dangers. Loving and responsible parents often find they have less control over their children's security, whereas the dangers for children who grow up in unstable and threatening families increase dramatically. A much underestimated and understudied social problem for children is peer abuse. The topic of peer abuse usually calls to mind bullying and the general value in many societies that boys need to learn to stand up for themselves. One thinks of the memorable episode of the old *Andy Griffith Show* in which Opie is tormented by a bully who keeps taking his lunch money. Barney wants to intervene, but Andy indirectly pushes his son to stand his ground by telling him the story of how a bully had once tried to steal his favorite fishing hole. In the end Opie takes on the bully and gets a black eye for his efforts. The bully, however, backs off, and Opie keeps his lunch money.

The elements and message of this story are generally in line with what we know about the interpersonal nature of bullying and the individual characteristics of bullies and their victims from research done by clinical psychologists. Much of this research on bullying originated in Europe and Australia, but now there has been a good deal of research about bullying and the development of policies to deal with it in the United States as well (Nansel et al., 2001; Olweus, 1993; Pellegrini & Long, 2002; Rigby, 2002). Surely, such individual-level research is useful, but it tells us little about the sociocultural dimensions of peer abuse. Peer abuse, like peer interaction more generally, is socioculturally situated in children's lives. Peer abuse varies over time and place and is produced and resisted in various ways across cultural and social classes, ages, genders, and racial and ethnic groups (Ambert, 1995). Peer abuse can also take place in the family at the hands of siblings (Wiehe, 2002).

Let's consider three ways that a sociocultural approach captures the complexity of peer abuse in children's lives. First, recent research reveals that girls are the victims of peer abuse as frequently as (or perhaps even more frequently than) boys. The most frequent type of peer abuse is verbal harassment, but girls are often victims of physical and sexual assault by peers. Their tormentors are often boys. Some are classmates they do not even like and try to avoid, whereas others are their boyfriends with whom they are intimately involved (Ambert, 1995; Eder, 1995; Milner, 2004; Pascoe, 2007; Stein, 1993). A telephone interview study of 11- to 17-year-old children by the child advocacy group Children Now found that 40% of girls ages 14 to 17 said they had a friend in their age group who had been hit or beaten by a boyfriend (Lewin, 1995b). These findings are generally in line with earlier research on the issue and demonstrate its seriousness (Ambert, 1995; Henton & Cate, 1983).

Second, a sociocultural approach to peer abuse would take sexual orientation into account. Thorne pointed out that lesbian and gay adolescents, unlike heterosexual youth, have no public rituals to validate their desires: "There are no affirming markers about what they are feeling and thinking" (Gagon, 1972, p. 238, quoted in Thorne, 1993, p. 154). In fact, lesbian and gay youth witness markers to sexual orientation used in highly negative ways; terms such as *fag* and *queer* are highly insulting in the peer cultures of preadolescents and adolescents (Gray, 1999; Pascoe, 2007). Furthermore, in her study of peer interaction in middle schools, Eder found that social isolates were often labeled "queer" and "fag" because "they were perceived to lack the very social characteristics that represented the rigid gender and sexual roles" in the peer culture (1995, p. 155; also see Pascoe, 2007, for similar findings). Pascoe (2007), in her study of high school peer relations and masculinity, also found that males suspected of being gay were tormented and harassed by peers as a way of displaying and asserting masculinity. These findings capture the challenging circumstances lesbian and gay youth face in adolescent peer cultures. Such features of adolescent culture contribute to problems of low self-esteem among lesbian and gay youth, which in turn may be related to high rates of suicide among these youth. Much more research is needed in this area (see Dorais & Lajeunesse, 2004; Kulkin, Chauvin, & Percie, 2000; Remafedi, 1994). There is more public recognition of the problem, however, as evidenced in Massachusetts, for example, where former governor William Weld formed the Commission of Gay and Lesbian Youth to develop strategies to combat gay teen suicide (see Lindop, 2007).

Finally, a sociocultural approach to peer abuse also draws our attention to the importance of social class and minority status. The Children Now study finds that "minority children face a rougher world than white children do, reporting greater exposure to gangs and drugs and more fear of violence and crime" (Lewin, 1995b, p. A17). Other research on and statistics about the tremendous rise of violent crime during the 1980s and early

1990s in poor neighborhoods and schools in inner cities and even small towns are in line with this finding (Garofalo, Siegel, & Laub, 1987; Hagan, 1994; Morgan & Zedner, 1992). Much of this violence is related to crime and gang activity. The majority of children who live in impoverished environments do not engage in illegal activities. They do, however, despite their own best efforts and those of their parents, often find themselves caught up in violence perpetrated by other children.

Another story from Chicago captures the tragic nature of violence and poverty for children. One night in late August 1994, a member of a street gang stepped out of the shadows between two storefront churches on Chicago's far south side and started shooting wildly at a group of teenagers playing football. When the gunfire stopped, a 14-year-old girl lay dead, killed by a bullet apparently meant for someone else. At first, the shooting appeared to be another senseless, though increasingly common, story of innocents slaughtered in the streets (Terry, 1994b, p. A1). What sets this incident apart from other such shootings, though, is the neighborhood in which the shooting occurred and the age of the suspected assailant.

The neighborhood was in a working-class area of single-story homes with well-kept yards. There had been so much gang trouble in the neighborhood before the shooting that parents kept their children near their homes. A makeshift basketball backboard and hoop were erected on a curbside by parents to dissuade their children from playing at the local school, which they felt was too dangerous. In spite of this precaution, Shavon Dean was shot and killed, and another boy was seriously wounded. The police's prime suspect was an 11-year-old boy. The boy had many prior serious scrapes with the law (including arson, auto theft, and armed robbery), and police suspected he had been recruited by older gang members to carry out the shooting. He was living with his grandmother after having been taken away from his mother at age 3, when social workers discovered cigarette burns on his body and other signs of physical abuse. The Chicago police superintendent described the boy as dangerous but "still an eleven-year-old" (Terry, 1994b, p. A1) who fell through the cracks of the city's social services.

How did this tragic story end? The 11-year-old boy was never apprehended by police. He never had his day in juvenile court. He did not end up in prison. Five days after the shooting, on Friday, September 2, 1994, the headline in the Chicago Tribune read, "ROBERT . . . : EXECUTED AT 11." Although Robert's last name and that of his mother and grandmother made all the national papers and television news programs on that day, we'll use only his first name. Robert was found dead in a tunnel under the tracks of the South Shore Railroad with two bullets in the back of his head. He had been killed execution style. Two other gang members, a 14-year-old and a 16-year-old, were arrested for Robert's murder. Police believe their motive was to keep Robert from talking. At the news of her grandson's death, Robert's grandmother sobbed, "He's a baby. He's just a baby." Exactly the same words were uttered by the grief-stricken aunt of Shavon Dean upon her hearing the news about Robert. When Robert was found dead, he was wearing a T-shirt with the image of a cartoon character, the Tasmanian Devil, printed on it.

As sad as this story is, it is even more tragic when one realizes that more and more children are, like Shavon Dean, being caught up in the crossfire of violence in the United States. Some but certainly not all of this violence and crime is gang related; much of it is perpetrated on children by adults. Although poor and minority youth are much more likely to experience violence in their lives than White, middle- and upper-class children, the overall homicide rate for children in the United States is much higher than in any other industrialized country. In 1990 more than three thousand 15- to 19-year-olds were murdered in the United States, a rate of nearly 17.0 per 100,000 children. This rate is much higher than that of our nearest competitor among industrialized nations, Canada, where the rate was 2.3 per 100,000. In Italy, the land of the Mafia, 109 teenagers were murdered in 1990, a rate of 2.1 per 100,000. Japan and Norway had the lowest rates in the industrial world—0.3 per 100,000. In Norway, only 1 teenager between 15 and 19 was murdered in 1990 (UNICEF, 1995b). A more recent study by the World Health Organization (2002) shows a similar pattern but uses a much wider age category of 10 to 29 for children and youth. These differences are, of course, at least somewhat due to the wide availability of guns in the United States as compared to other countries. Yet the differences go well beyond differences in gun laws. The United States is a highly violent society.

There has, however, been a recent drop in violent crime in the United States. This decline has included crimes involving youth. For example, the homicide victim rate for 14- to 17-year-olds reached a high of 11.3 per 100,000 in 1993, and then the rate began to decline; in 2000, the rate was more than cut in half, to 4.7 per 100,000 14- to 17-year-olds.

We have seen a similar decline in the number of victims of violent crimes other than homicide. Although this trend is a positive one, it is shocking to see that in 2008 violent crime touched 12- to 15-year-old children more than any other age group. The data in Exhibit 11.5 are

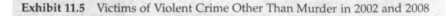

Exhibit 11.5   Victims of Violent Crime Other Than Murder in 2002 and 2008

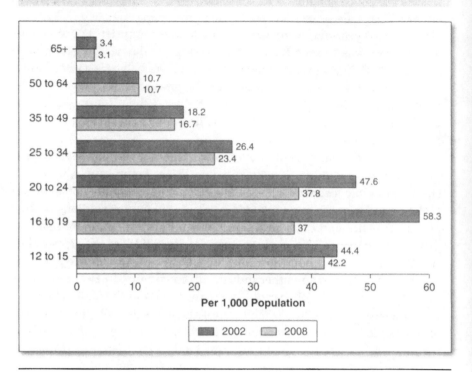

Source: Bureau of Justice Statistics (2009).

perhaps the most striking of any I have presented in this chapter. They show the number of victims of violent crimes other than murder by age group in the United States for 2002 and 2008. It is immediately clear that the odds of victimization are much higher in the lower age groups. The rates in the youngest three age groups do not vary substantially. Still, it is striking that the rate for 12- to 15-year-olds is now higher than the rates for 16- to 19-year-olds and 20- to 24-year-olds, who normally are thought of as most vulnerable to violence because of their high activity levels and risk taking. Finally, it is surprising how much higher the rates are for the youngest age group of 12- to 15-year-olds, compared to young and middle-aged adults. The rate for 12- to 15-year-olds in 2008 was nearly double that for 25- to 34-year-olds. The rate for the youngest age group was more than double that for 35- to 40-year-olds and more than 4 times that for 50- to 64-year-olds in 2008, even after the rates had dropped.

Although these statistics are somewhat heartening in that the overall level of violence has dropped, they again reinforce the extreme vulnerability and mistreatment of a significant proportion of children in our society. We can begin to understand why Nicholas's mother Angela sprays her children each morning with a religious oil and why Nicholas's younger brother Willie prefers the playground at McDonald's. "'There's a giant hamburger and you can go inside of it,' Willie said. 'And it's made out of steel, so no bullets can get through'" (Wilkerson, 1993, p. 16).

SUMMARY

In this chapter we reviewed social problems that affect children's lives outside the family. We examined trends in child poverty and looked at their effects from a global perspective. Although there has been some progress in reducing malnutrition, improving health care, and expanding educational opportunities of children in many countries in the developing world, there also have been setbacks due to uneven economic development and the resulting austerity programs, which were instituted to address the debt crisis. We looked at how these economic trends have resulted in violence against street children in Brazil, the exploitation of urban child workers in Kenya, and the kidnapping or sale of children to work on farms and in sweatshops in India and Pakistan. One encouraging factor we saw in all these case studies was the emergence of NGOs. These organizations, which are directed by caring adults and children with no government affiliation, promote change and address problems of child poverty and exploitation at the grassroots level.

Although the majority of children in Western industrialized countries live in secure economic circumstances and have bright futures, there is still a much-too-high proportion of children living in poverty in the United States and several other industrialized countries. In contrast, most of the other countries in the industrialized world have much lower rates of child poverty and have had reductions in child poverty in recent years.

There was a dramatic increase in teenage nonmarital births in the 1980s and early 1990s. The recent decrease in such births is a positive trend. Yet for most teen mothers, childrearing, most especially in the early teen years and among girls from economically disadvantaged families, almost always worsens their quality of life and limits their futures and those of their children. More research is needed on the effects of teenage childbearing on teen mothers and their children. We do know, however, that many teen mothers and their children who are adversely affected by the early childbearing overcome their problems later in life. Overall, these findings suggest a number of programs for combating the problem that are best aimed at specific groups. The programs should be both preventive (providing sex education, promoting abstinence, making youth aware of family planning services) and, in cases where childbearing has occurred, supportive or ameliorative (providing prenatal care, parenting classes, and child care).

In the final section of this chapter we looked at violence and the victimization of children outside the family. Although there has been some decrease in violence against children, child victimization is still high and is a national tragedy. Children are often caught up in violence in their schools, neighborhoods, and wider communities. Much of this violence is at the hands of other children, and especially in the 1980s and most of the 1990s, it became much more lethal given the wide availability of handguns. Although poor and minority children and youth are much more likely to experience violence in their lives than are White, middle- and upper-class children, violence has spread to middle-class schools and communities, as we have seen in cases such as the Columbine shootings. The United States is a violent country with rates of child homicide and violent crime that are much higher than those of any other industrialized country. We have seen some improvement in decreases in violent crime in the United States, but we still have a long way to go in protecting the lives of our children.

The range and severity of problems that young children face are depressing. Yet in this chapter we covered only some of the more serious challenges children face, and we restricted our discussion primarily to the United States. There are times when those of us who study, work with, or act as advocates for children feel overwhelmed and pessimistic about the future of children and childhood. Problems related to child care and early education, access to health care, teen pregnancy, child abuse, and violence in children's lives seem to grow as political rhetoric in support of "our children" or the motto "leave no child behind" seem hollow and there is no real political action. Yet there are reasons to be optimistic about childhood and its future. Change may be slow, but more individuals and groups are joining the debate, making financial contributions, and volunteering their time and energy to causes that help children. In the final chapter we will consider the future of childhood and discuss some major and many more modest proposals to improve children's lives.

12

The Future of Childhood

I began this book by recounting an everyday event in the life of some Italian preschool children, which involved their wonderful creation of a traveling bank. My point was to highlight the active participation of children in society and their creation of their own unique peer cultures. I followed this depiction with a brief summary of the 1995 bombing of the Alfred P. Murrah Federal Building in Oklahoma City, which killed 168 persons, 19 of them children who were attending a preschool in the building. The Oklahoma City bombing was a grim reminder that children are very much part of, and affected by, the adult world.

As I write the conclusion to this edition of the book, it has been 15 years since the bombing in Oklahoma City. After several years away from the field I started a new study on children in civil society in Norway. However, a few years ago I returned for a month to Modena, Italy, where I interviewed eight children whom I have followed as they moved from preschool, to elementary school, and then to middle school. The children were then in high school, and they and their families had become my great and probably lifelong friends. I think back again to when I was with the kids in preschool. The Modena preschool is in the province of Emilia-Romagna—arguably the best place in the world to be a preschool child. I worked in the preschool with a group of 5- to 6-year-olds and their teachers, who had been together for 3 years. The children and teachers were all so comfortable with each other, so confident about their places in the interrelated peer and school local cultures.

I think about the period of mid-June 1996, when the kids' time together in the preschool was coming to an end. It was a time of anticipation. We had made two visits to the elementary school that most of the children would attend in the fall. I started first grade with these kids and became very involved with them, their new teachers, and the school. I think about how we first met our prospective new teachers and their students. The teachers were then teaching fifth grade, but they moved back to first grade in the fall of 1996. The big fifth graders took us under their wings, gave us a glimpse of their everyday lives in the school, served us a great snack, and sang songs with us. It was all very exciting! I then think of the time when the kids in the group I studied did the same thing as fifth graders in the spring of 2001 (see Corsaro & Molinari, 2005).

I continue to think back about my time with the kids in the preschool, most especially the planning for and enjoyment of the wonderful *festa di nonni* (party for grandparents) at the preschool. Many grandparents who lived in the city attended. Some grandmothers worked with the boys and girls, making clothes for Barbie and other dolls, while other *nonne* went up to the kitchen with a group of kids to make dessert. Some grandfathers worked outside in the garden with one group, and one grandfather made kites. We later took these kites out into the yard, and the kids took turns flying them around. My job was fetching the wayward kites out of the trees without damaging them.

What I remember most, however, happened right before lunch. The kids sang several songs for their grandparents. They had been practicing and singing these songs all year; in fact, in the previous month they had sung them at a festival in the center of the city with other children from preschools all across town. I had heard these songs again and again. I knew them by heart. As the children sang the first two songs, I sang along with them, softly mouthing the words. In the middle of the third song, the children, who were sitting in small chairs, laid their arms over each other's shoulders and began to sway with the music. Their faces were beaming. I looked at the grandparents. They were misty eyed. So was I.

This story illustrates how the interweaving of the local cultures of the children's and adults' worlds clearly enriches the children's lives as well as the lives of the adults. I remember other events from children's lives that I have been fortunate enough to share during the past 35 years. I think about some upper-middle-class American kids who created a play scenario around a sandbox. In it, they were the owners of an ice cream store, and they decided to donate some of their profits to "sick kids" in the hospital. I remember some Head Start boys who transformed the family play area into a barber shop, pretended to trim my hair and beard, held up two mirrors so I could inspect my haircut, front and back, and then carefully brushed me off with a whisk broom. I also recall a pretend phone conversation between two Head Start girls. The girls were pretending to be their mothers and were having a conversation about the demands of parenting in poverty. They talked about the difficulties of shopping and responding to their children's demands to be taken to the park when they did not have a car and the public transportation system was expensive and inadequate. They also talked sadly of their domestic lives, with one pretend mother saying, "My man's been hitting on me!" The other little girl's response broke my heart. "You got one and I don't have one," she said. "My kids been askin' for 'my Daddy.' They say, 'I want my Daddy, I want my Daddy,' all day" (see Corsaro, 2003; Rosier, 2000).

Finally, I think of the children of Oklahoma City. I am sad but also surprisingly buoyed by this jumble of thoughts and emotions. The actions of confused, misguided, and cowardly adults took away the lives of those young children. Although those children are no longer with us, the spirit of their lives in their families, their schools, and their communities is not diminished.

Shortly after the Oklahoma City tragedy, columnist Bob Herbert recounted a television interview with a firefighter and police officer who tried to rescue 1-year-old Baylee Almon. Baylee died, but as Herbert noted, the effort to save her was typical of the response to the tragedy. In a television interview, the police officer who found her, Sergeant John Avera, said, "I heard a baby crying and we started moving bricks and rocks . . . and we found two babies. The officer I was with took one down one hallway and I took my baby out the other way." *My baby*, stressed Herbert. The thought leads him to quote Plutarch:

> Good fortunes will elevate even petty minds, and give them the appearance of a certain greatness and stateliness, as from their high place they look down upon the world; but the truly noble and resolved spirit raises itself; and becomes more conspicuous in times of disaster and ill fortune. (Herbert, 1995, p. 15)

The nature of the adult world has profound effects on childhood. Even in the most impoverished and threatening environments, however, children will appropriate and construct their own worlds. Children's actions in their peer cultures, families, schools, and other social institutions contribute much to the adult world. How can we enrich children's appropriations, constructions, and contributions? How can we make investments in children and their childhoods? How can we create a spirit of doing our best for our children, for their lives today as well as for their futures as adults? How can we sustain the noble and resolved spirit that was so evident in the aftermath of Oklahoma City, and channel it to address their needs every day of the year?

The Major Challenges

The major challenges to enriching the quality of children's lives are primarily economic. As we saw time and time again in Chapters 10 and 11, many of the social problems of children are linked to poverty. Which types of government policies and actions are needed in confronting child poverty? In addressing this question, we will focus primarily on American children, but we also will explore the responsibility of the United States and other industrialized countries for combating child poverty in the developing world.

Confronting Child Poverty in the United States

As we saw in Chapter 11, American middle- and high-income children are generally better off than their counterparts in other industrialized countries. In contrast, working-class and poor children in other Western nations enjoy living standards that are significantly above those of similar children in the United States. How can we do better for our working-class and poor children while maintaining the economic security of children from more wealthy families? Here we can learn from other countries and also build on and expand successful American economic initiatives. As Smeeding (2002) has pointed out, the United Kingdom recently found itself in a situation similar to that of the United States in regard to child poverty. Recognizing the problem, then prime minister Tony Blair set a national goal of improving living standards and halving child poverty in Britain during the 1997–2007 decade. Blair matched his rhetoric with action, with some large measure of real fiscal effort that has had impact. It is estimated "that the Blair government increased annual spending on families with children by .9 percent of GDP from 1997 to 2002, lowering absolute poverty from three to five percentage points and removing 1 million British children from poverty" (Smeeding, 2002, p. 22). Unfortunately, the United States under the George W. Bush administration of 2000–2008 was slow in following the model of the United Kingdom and other European countries in investing in children. The present Obama administration shows more commitment to helping children in poverty, but progress is slow in that we are just beginning to emerge from a very deep recession. However, this does not mean that we cannot do better as there are clear policies we can pursue to improve the quality of children's lives (see Garfinkel, Rainwater, & Smeeding, 2010).

Economic Investment in Families and Children. The United States is the most economically stratified country in the industrialized world, and the gap between rich and poor has been growing dramatically. Data from the Congressional Budget Office show that between 1979 and 2000, the average after-tax income of the top 1% of the United States population tripled, rising by $576,000. Average after-tax income of the top 1% rose from $286,000 in 1979 to $507,000 in 1989 and then to $863,000 in 2000, an increase of 201% during the 1979–2000 period, adjusted for inflation. By contrast, between 1979 and 2000, the average after-tax income of the middle fifth of the population rose 15% (or $5,500) to $41,900. The average after-tax income of the bottom fifth rose 9% (or $1,100) to $13,700 (Greenstein & Shapiro, 2004). This trend has continued in recent years. As Saez (2009) reported, in 2007, just before the great recession of 2008–2010, the average income per family grew by a solid 3.7%. However, the average real income for the top 1% grew 6.8%, increasing the top percentile share of all income from 22.8 to 23.5%. This made 2007 the "the second highest year on record since 1913 almost equaling 1928, the record year when the top percentile share reached 23.9 percent" (Saez, 2009, p. 1). Things were even better for the super rich as the top 0.01% of American earners took home 6% of total U.S. wages. This trend not only contributes to the growing rate of child poverty but also can have dire consequences for our society both economically and socially.

What can be done? Other countries have less disparity in income distribution than the United States because their citizens, especially the wealthy, pay more in taxes. Tax increases are not popular in the United States and are unlikely to be accepted. However, we already have some programs in place that could be expanded without big tax hikes. We also can make investments in human capital. What poor children need most are parents who have jobs that earn enough to keep their families out of poverty (Bianchi, 1993). We can train and educate people to be productive workers. This process will also generate new tax revenue and reduce welfare costs.

Consider, for example, the Earned Income Tax Credit (EITC). The EITC is a refundable tax credit for low-income families with children. It is an earned income support program that encourages work and self-sufficiency. Best of all, the EITC has been effective in alleviating poverty, and its expansion would do much to help reduce child poverty. Another way to help poor children is to enforce child support laws that require absent parents (almost always fathers) to contribute to the economic security of their children. The Family Support Act of 1988 was a step in the right direction, and recent initiatives at the federal and state levels crack down even harder on parents who owe child support. Some states do much better than others at enforcing child support laws, and the success of these states should be emulated more broadly across the country. Even with these efforts, there will still be cases wherein the absent parent cannot or will not pay support. To address that fact, the United States must act, as a number of European countries have, to institute a minimum guaranteed level of child support to single parents (Garfinkel et al., 2010; Clearinghouse on International Developments in Child, Youth and Family Policies, 2010). Although assured child support of this type has been proposed in Wisconsin and New York, such policies were never adopted in those or any states in the United States (see Garfinkel, 1992; Garfinkel et al., 2010; Meyer, Garfinkel, Oellerich, & Robins, 1994, for a discussion of the benefits of assured child support for children).

Probably the most difficult problem for working poor families and their children in the United States is the lack of affordable health care. Until recently the United States subsidized the cost of health care for only certain segments of the population (the disabled, the very poor, and the aged) through programs such as Medicaid and Medicare. Other citizens have medical insurance as part of their employment benefits, and a sizable group, whose employers do not provide this benefit, must buy insurance on the open market. Many in this last group are the working poor who cannot afford medical insurance and try to get by without it. The children in these families often see a doctor only when it is absolutely necessary. If a child becomes seriously ill, the parents can be thrown into serious debt and even bankruptcy. For the poor children of single parents, a child's illness may often mean leaving a job and turning to welfare to collect Medicaid (Dugger, 1992; Rosier, 2000).

Under the Obama administration the United States adopted a major health care policy in March 2010, which when fully in place by 2014, will provide health care for all Americans. Meanwhile there has been a major improvement for children's health care. In February 2009 President Obama, in his first major act as president, signed the expansion of the States Children's Health Insurance Program, a $33 billion bill that will provide health coverage for more than half of the 8 million children who will remain uninsured in 2012. So we are not quite there yet, but the United States will soon join all other major industrialized countries in the world and ensure health care for all children.

We also need to know more about children with health problems and how these problems affect children's lives in their families and peer groups. Although there is a substantial body of research in medical sociology, until recently children have been relatively neglected. The work of Mayall (2002) in the United Kingdom has been important, as have American studies on children with chronic illnesses (Bluebond-Langner, 1996; C. Clark, 2003).

Family Leave, Child Care, and Early Education. Although contributions to children's physical health and economic well-being can be seen as national investments in any society's future, a major theme of this book is that children's lives in the "here and now" are also worthy of appreciation, support, and enrichment. This fact holds true especially during children's first 6 years of life. As we have seen in previous chapters, the preschool years are a time of exploration and spontaneity. They are also a time of negotiation, accommodation, and communal sharing. Most of us have only vague memories of our experiences when we were young children. But positive experiences in these earlier years instill in us a spirit and a sense of security and confidence that we carry with us throughout our lives. Yet the United States does less than most every other country in the industrialized world to support families with preschool children (Garfinkel et al., 2010).

What can be done? As is the case with children's economic well-being, the United States has active programs to build on and several good models from western Europe to emulate. What is most needed in the United States is an integrated and comprehensive policy that addresses maternity and family leave, child care, and early education. The Family and Medical Leave Act of 1993, which ensures job security for up to 12 weeks of unpaid leave, was a step in the right direction. However, the fact that the leave is unpaid discriminates against poor and working-class families and children. The United States needs to go beyond limited employer-mandated programs and devise a policy that offers a substantial period of paid leave with opportunities for additional unpaid leave during the child's 1st year.

Most European countries have extensive family leave programs that are financed with contributions from employers, workers, and the government. Extended parental leave guarantees that a newborn infant can remain with her mother (or father) during most if not all of her 1st year of life. Not only is the period important for the infant's development; it is also the most demanding period for her parents and siblings. Thus, parental leave reduces stress and provides all family members with more time to accommodate to and to savor this important change in their lives.

What can be done to better address the child care and early education needs of 1- to 6-year-old children in the United States? The United States currently offers tax credits, which primarily benefit middle-income families, and limited child care programs at the state level for poor families. It also has a compensatory education program, Head Start, for poor children, and all children can attend at least half-day kindergarten programs in their 6th year. As we saw in Chapter 10, however, a major problem in the United States is the poor quality of the affordable private child care and early education services that are available. The situation is quite different in Europe, where child care and early education programs are often directly subsidized by national or local governments. Although child care for 1- to 3-year-olds is normally available only to working mothers, there has been a general expansion in the availability and quality of such care throughout Europe. High-quality early education programs for 3- to 6-year-old children are widely available at low cost in Europe. France and Italy, for example, have developed excellent early childhood education programs for 3- to 6-year-olds with near universal attendance (Clawson & Gerstel, 2002; Corsaro, 2003; Corsaro & Emiliani, 1992; Corsaro & Molinari, 2005; Edwards, Gandini, & Forman, 1998). Presently in Italy there is a movement away from a custodial to a more educational approach in the country's asilo nido programs for 1- to 3-year-olds. This model refines educational ideas and philosophies first developed for the scuola materna for the needs of younger children (Gandini & Edwards, 2001).

The Italian preschool system did not spring up overnight. It was instituted in the late 1960s and has been expanded and improved during a 30-year period. Any change in the United States would also be gradual and would build on the present system. A first step for the United States should be the identification of high-quality, not-for-profit child care and early education programs. Not-for-profit programs are generally higher in quality, and they are better able to train, compensate, and retain teachers and staff compared to for-profit centers, where the curriculum and staff salaries are primarily based on profit margin. High-quality, not-for-profit programs could be targeted for government subsidies to support curriculum expansion, lower fees, and provide scholarships for economically disadvantaged children. Recently we have seen an important expansion of the Head Start program. Head Start now covers many 3- and 4-year-olds, and a new Early Head Start program has been established for babies and infants. With federal stimulus funds through the American Recovery and Reinvestment Act of 2009, Early Head Start now provides care for more than 110,000 babies and infants. The Obama budget for 2011 requests $8.2 billion for Head Start, which is a $989 million boost compared to the 2010 budget. This increase, if passed, would sustain funds for Head Start and Early Head start, which were part of the American Recovery and Reinvestment Act (Guernsey, 2010). Head Start served slightly more than 908,000 children in 2007, which covered an estimated 50% of all eligible children. Ideally, Head Start should be expanded to cover all eligible children. Although some full-day programs now exist, Head Start should also be expanded from a half- to a full-day program and made available year round to help working parents (Bianchi, 1993). Some not-for-profit early education programs also could serve as models for an expanded Head Start that still would focus on children from poor families but would move away from some of the negative aspects of its compensatory curriculum (Corsaro, Molinari, & Rosier, 2002). Finally, subsidized early education programs could be coordinated with kindergartens to smooth children's transition into elementary school. Many kindergarten programs that are now offered for only half days need to be expanded to full-day programs to better meet the needs of families and children.

Although such programs would be costly, European examples have demonstrated creative ways of sharing such costs among employers, parents, and average taxpayers. The European programs not only support families and enrich children's lives but also free more parents to work and create satisfying and well-paying full- and part-time jobs in the area of child care and early education (Bergmann, 1996; Corsaro & Emiliani, 1992; Hewlett, 1993). Recently in the United States, one state, Georgia, has instituted the goal of universal government-supported preschool for all 4-year-olds (see Raden, 1999), and other programs have been proposed in Oklahoma, New York, and California (Lekies & Cochran, 2001). Progress in reaching the goal of universal preschool for 4-year-olds has been slow, but now four states (Oklahoma, Florida, Georgia, and Vermont) enroll 50% or more of all their 4-year-olds; in Oklahoma 71% of all 4-year-olds are enrolled in state prekindergarten programs (National Institute for Early Education, 2008). Also, there have been thoughtful discussions and analyses of why universal preschool education should, and how it can, be instituted in the United States (Corsaro & Molinari, 2005; Garfinkel et al., 2010; Helburn & Bergmann, 2002; Kamerman & Kahn, 1995; Mitchell, 2001).

Combating Child Poverty in Developing Countries

As we saw in the last chapter, child poverty in developing nations can be linked to a number of factors, including rapid urbanization, the global debt crisis, government corruption, ethnic violence, and the spread of infectious diseases such as HIV/AIDS. The best way to combat these problems and the resulting poverty is with increased aid from wealthy nations. Such aid is often referred to as official development assistance (ODA). ODA refers to aid from governments for humanitarian and development purposes. Military aid is specifically excluded. About two thirds of ODA is given directly from one government to another; the remainder is channeled to various countries via international organizations and United Nations agencies. In addition, some aid is provided by voluntary organizations in the wealthy nations (UNICEF, 1995a).

Although the United States gave more total aid ($26.01 billion) than any other country in 2008, the United States ranks very low in terms of aid as a percentage of gross national income (GNI, a measure of overall economic productivity and wealth). The Scandinavian countries stand out, with Sweden contributing aid in the amount of 0.98% of its GNI and Norway 0.88% of its GNI, whereas the United States contributed only 0.18% of its GNI in 2002 (Organization for Economic Cooperation and Development, 2008).

The amount of foreign aid is far from the only issue to consider when talking about child poverty in developing countries. Just as important is how aid is distributed. A major problem in many countries in the developing world is that the aid is not used for programs that assist children, such as health and education programs. Even worse, substantial funds often are siphoned off by corrupt government officials. At the World Summit for Social Development in 1995, Norway introduced a 20/20 formula in which an allocation of an average of 20% of the recipient governments' national budgets and 20% of the donor countries' aid budgets would go to basic social services. Norway's argument was that an increased allocation to basic social programs would substantially contribute to the objective of reaching the poorest people (UNICEF, 1995a). Others have argued that foreign donors and the international financial community should not give funds directly to national governments.

Instead, donors should distribute the money themselves or give it to trusted nongovernmental organizations (Bradshaw, Buchmann, & Mbatia, 1994). As we saw in the last chapter, nongovernmental organizations are coming to play a central role as advocates for children and youth in many developing countries.

Another important objective to support the world of children would be for the United States to ratify the United Nations Convention on the Rights of the Child.

> Prior to the Convention on the Rights of the Child, human rights standards to all members of the human family have been expressed in legal instruments such as covenant, conventions and declaration, as did standards relating to the specific concerns of children. But it was only in 1989 that the standards concerning children were brought together in a single legal instrument, approved by the international community and spelling out in an unequivocal manner the right to which every child is entitled, regardless of where born or to whom, regardless of sex, religion, or social origin. The body of rights enumerated in the Convention are the rights of all children *everywhere*. The idea of *everywhere* is important. In too many countries, children's lives are plagued by armed conflict, child labor, sexual exploitation, and other human rights violations. Elsewhere, for example, children living in rural areas may have fewer opportunities to obtain an education of good quality or may have less access to health services than children living in cities. The Convention states that such disparities—within societies—are also a violation of human rights. In calling on governments to ensure the human rights of all children, the Convention seeks to correct these kinds of inequities. (UNICEF, 2004; the full text of the convention can also be found at the following website: www.unicef.org/crc/crc.htm).

The United States signed the Convention in 2000, but it still has not ratified it. Basically, this means that the United States endorses the Convention on the Rights of the Child and will seriously consider a legally binding ratification, but the U.S. Congress has yet to vote on ratification. The United States is the only country except for Somalia to not ratify the Convention. There is much debate about why the United States has been slow to ratify it. Many members of Congress have some mistrust about following the lead of the United Nations on many issues. The Obama administration has discussed pushing Congress to take up ratification on its agenda. We can only hope that the United States will move forward and ratify the Convention; our support of this comprehensive and important document on children's rights would be highly symbolic.

Some More Modest Proposals to Enrich Children's Lives

We have discussed the need for major investments in children's economic, physical, and social well-being. It is clear that short-term investments, though costly, will more than pay off in the long run because they greatly increase the likelihood that children will become productive members of their societies. However, years of neglecting a significant proportion of our children means we cannot expect immediate results. It will take great resolve, hard work, and patience. We need to get started.

Nations, communities, and individuals are already doing a wide range of things to enrich the lives of children. There are also some new ideas that have yet to be tested. Many of these demand some degree of investment of time and energy, but they have only modest economic costs. Let's discuss these proposals under the general categories of (a) enhancing the lives of families and children and (b) supporting families and children at risk.

Enhancing the Lives of Families and Children

One of the most important things that adults can do to enhance children's lives is to give them more of their time. What is needed most is everyday time for routine activities, talk, and play. Parents also need more time to participate in their children's lives outside the family, most especially in schools and community organizations. What children want and need is to engage in a little conversation at dinner, to play a game of catch or cards, to watch a TV show or DVD together, to take a walk in the park or to get an ice cream, to be tickled or tossed about before a bath, or to be read a story before bed. Children want attention. They want adults to even act silly and laugh with them now and then—to show they care. What children get, though, time and time again, are promises: "I'll buy you that new toy tomorrow," "We'll go to a museum on Saturday," "We'll see that movie next Sunday, I promise." Sometimes parents deliver on these special promises and sometimes not; however, what children need are routine, relentless reminders that they are important and that they are loved. Demanding work schedules and the hectic pace of everyday life in modern societies work against the natural expression of how much almost all parents really do love their children.

Another problem is family isolation. Families are smaller, grandparents and relatives often do not live nearby, and neighborhoods are less cohesive and communal than in the past. Children need more opportunities and space to collectively "weave their webs" with others. They need more diverse and supportive social fields and locales that can support their intricate weavings and that can allow them to establish secure places in their local family, peer, school, and neighborhood cultures. Family isolation is intensified by the class, gender, and age segregation that exists in most modern societies. Let's look at these problems—lack of family time and family isolation—and discuss some proposals to lessen their negative effects on children's lives.

Work Time, Family Time. Recently, child advocates have called for "family-friendly" workplaces that better integrate parenting and paid work in modern societies (Hertz & Marshall, 2001; Hewlett, 1993; Leach, 1994; Louv, 1990). A key to their arguments is the general acceptance of the fact that modern postindustrial societies need not require or ensure consistent full-time employment for every adult. Such acceptance would allow for more part-time work, periods of unpaid work leave, and more diversity in types of employment (Hertz & Marshall, 2001). Many of these advocates point to family leave policies in Sweden and other countries, which we discussed earlier. Employers in these countries have found that accommodation to such policies improves worker morale and productivity. The result is sustained economic growth despite what most American employers would see as excessive government regulation. In Sweden, for example, the gross national product per capita has remained one of the highest in the world and is clearly competitive with that of the United States (Hewlett, 1993).

Sweden, of course, is not the United States. American business leaders resent what they see as government mandates and intrusion; unions worry about layoffs or benefit reductions for full-time workers. Many are concerned that women who opt for part-time work or unpaid leaves will suffer losses of seniority and promotions. The United States need not enact the full-scale social welfare programs of countries such as Sweden to make the workplace more family friendly. However, at least two of the three major challenges we noted previously (paid family leave, universal health care for children, and government-subsidized child care and early education) need to be addressed. We have now made the commitment and will soon have universal health care for children. If we can make major headway on the other goals, a whole range of additional modest proposals could result in more time for parents to be with and nurture their children.

Consider how the enactment of policies such as paid family leave and universal health care could bring about ripple effects in the workplace that benefit families more generally. If the United States adopted paid family leave whose costs were shared by employers, workers, and the government, many businesses could temporarily replace full-time employees who need to be with their infants with part-time workers who are parents of preschool or elementary school children. These part-time employees would soon be able to enter the workforce with the assurance that their children's health care needs were covered. The parents would also gain valuable work experience.

Affordable government-subsidized child care and early education programs create a whole range of options for parents. They would allow some to opt for full-time work and others part-time work, and the programs would allow some parents the opportunity to further their education and job skills. Also, as we noted earlier, government subsidy of not-for-profit child care and early education programs can result in the much-needed professionalization of child care workers and early education teachers. With better training, pay, and promotion possibilities, many talented and caring adults would have the opportunity to enter a profession they find rewarding and satisfying. In addition, a range of full- or part-time job opportunities for support staff could be created. This is a good example of how programs that help children and families can put people to work in a variety of public- and private-sector jobs.

Although the United States strives to meet these major challenges, a number of more modest experiments designed to make the workplace more family friendly are already being tried out here and in other countries. Most of these new ideas involve various types of flexible work schedules. For example, some companies in the United States and Europe offer flexible working hours, compressed work weeks, job sharing, and at-home arrangements to give their employees more blocks of time to be with their children. In Europe, for example, some companies offer weekend work that pays the same for two and a half 10-hour work days as it does for a full week. Companies can afford to do this because they reduce the number of hours of overtime pay. A number of studies have found that such programs and others that address family needs reduce job turnover and absenteeism, improve recruitment, increase worker morale and productivity, and enhance company image (Hewlett, 1993, p. 47; Leach, 1994, pp. 225–239).

Flexible work hours can give at least one parent the opportunity to routinely pick up the children from day care, early education, and elementary school programs with less haste and tension. Picking up children from day care and school is often a wearisome task for parents in a hurry. I am reminded of a story I once heard about a physician who rushed into a day care center, grabbed his child's coat and hat and called out to his 5-year-old son, "Coat, hat, we're out of here!" The boy, happily constructing a house out of building blocks with two other children and a teacher, looked up and said, "I don't want to be a doctor when I grow up!" But with more flexible work hours and more time, this mundane and often tedious activity (from the parents' perspective) can be transformed into a routine that is exciting for young children and relaxing and emotionally satisfying for parents. Instead of picking up children and rushing home to fix dinner, parents and kids can take a quick trip to the store to pick up some ice cream for dessert, stop by a nearby park to play, swing by grandparents' or friends' homes for a short visit, or just drive or walk around the neighborhood.

Breaking Down the Isolation of Families With Children. Most modern industrialized societies have seen increased segregation of families with children from other members of society by class, race, ethnicity, gender, and age. Such segregation is especially difficult for poor families in the United States, who often live in neighborhoods where drug dealers and violent crime threaten the futures and the very lives of their children. Our discussion in Chapter 11 of Nicholas and his family clearly depicted the minimal support available in many inner-city neighborhoods. Many studies have found that the resiliency of the extended Black family structure, and especially the supportive role of grandmothers, is being severely challenged by the extreme poverty and violence of many inner-city areas (Heath, 1989; Hill, 1990; Rosier, 2000; Stack, 1974). Single working mothers struggling to survive in such circumstances often "resent their status as invisible women, going unnoticed in neighborhoods most often portrayed as havens for crime, drugs, and welfare dependency, rarely for workaday striving" (Dugger, 1992; also see Edin & Kefalas, 2007; Hays, 2004). In her highly insightful ethnography of nine families living in poverty, Katherine Rosier found that single mothers often purposefully cut themselves and their children off from neighbors whom they saw as bad and threatening influences (Rosier, 2000). The mothers contrasted their own values of hard work and decency with what they saw as the irresponsibility of others, who had given in to drugs, crime, or welfare dependency (also see Anderson, 1994). This survival strategy further isolated these mothers, however, who felt they could not risk venturing into the community to seek out others like themselves.

In cases such as these, community organizations are needed to bring such families together for mutual support and to reach out to other families who have succumbed to the difficult challenges of poverty. As we saw with Nicholas's family, religious organizations offer spiritual and community support of this type. In many cases, however, churches have abandoned inner-city areas and have moved to more stable working- and middle-class neighborhoods. Those that remain often offer basic religious services to congregations that live primarily outside the inner-city area, and community social services are often curtailed. A major reason, of course, is high rates of violent crime, a problem we take up in the next section.

A major contributor to family isolation among all social classes in industrialized societies is age segregation. The fragmentation of institutions according to age and the high level of social mobility in modern societies "has meant that interaction of persons of different ages occurs less and less frequently and is of diminishing social significance" (Schildkrout, 1975/2002, p. 346). Most societies will never again experience the close personal relations among generations (in terms of responsibilities and obligations) that prevailed in preindustrial societies. Some have argued that most people would not find a return to such close relations desirable (Qvortrup, 1994b). The degree of age segregation that exists in the United States is truly unfortunate, however, because the young and the elderly have so much to offer each other.

One thing that has continually struck me during my stays in Italy is the active involvement of older people in everyday life. In the cities in northern Italy where I have lived, the elderly are everywhere: in parks, public squares, churches, and shops. It is not unusual to see 60-, 70-, and even 80-year-old men and women navigating bicycles through heavy city traffic. When they are out and about, many of Italy's elderly are on their way to visit grandchildren or to pick them up from school. During my many hours of participant observation in Italian preschools, I have found that the two most common phrases in the children's vocabularies are *mia nonna* and *mio nonno* (my grandma and my grandpa). And grandparent involvement does not stop with preschool; at least 40% of the adults who took children to and then picked them up from my daughter's elementary school in Modena, Italy, were grandparents. Grandparents caring for and spending time with their grandchildren are so much a part of everyday life in Italy that their activities are even depicted on street signs. As we see in Exhibit 12.1, signs that mark bike and walking paths in Modena clearly depict frequent users of these lanes: granddads and their granddaughters.

Even Italy, however, is experiencing increased social mobility, so some grandparents live in towns and cities other than those in which their grandchildren live. But this change does not mean that activities cannot be devised to bring children and the elderly together, even if they are not all directly related. In the introduction to this chapter, I discussed my recollection of festa di nonni (party for grandparents or Grandparents Day) at a scuola materna in Modena. As we can see from the pictures in

Exhibits 12.2 and 12.3, which show some of the activities that occurred that day, all of the children at Grandparents Day benefited from interaction with the grandparents, even if their own grandparents could not attend. In Exhibit 12.2, a grandmother smiles proudly as her grandson whips up her traditional family dessert; another child (an immigrant from Egypt) looks on. In Exhibit 12.3, a young boy sits at a table where his grandfather has been making kites; several of his classmates pose for a picture with them.

Undoubtedly there are Grandparents Days in schools in the United States. But these rare occasions need to be expanded to become annual traditions in all schools. We also need to reach out to the elderly in our communities, many of whom are isolated, to serve as surrogate grandparents

Exhibit 12.1   Sign Marking Bicycle and Walking Paths in Modena, Italy

for neighborhood children whose own grandparents may live far away. Such programs could involve safe transportation for the elderly where public transit is limited and there are concerns about security. Why should we stop with programs such as Meals on Wheels when the elderly need companionship as much as if not more than nutrition? We all need more opportunities to engage in routine collective activities with others.

We need not stop with programs for the very young and the elderly. It would be highly useful to bring the elderly together with preadolescents and adolescents, an age group many of the elderly have come to fear in the United States. Some years ago in Belleville, New Jersey, the local high school sponsored its second annual "senior prom" for all elderly members of this community of 34,000 near Newark. Teenage students were on hand to serve refreshments, chat, and dance with "the strangers of their grandparents' or, maybe, great grandparents' era" (Hanley, 1996). The elderly also have an open invitation to attend classes at the Belleville high school at no cost, and many have taken the high

Exhibit 12.2   Grandmother and Grandson Prepare Dessert in *Scuola Materna* in Modena, Italy

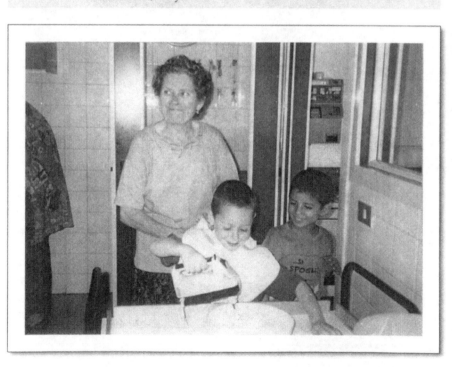

Exhibit 12.3   Grandfather Makes a Kite for Children in a *Scuola Materna* in Modena, Italy

school up on its offer. Such programs turn strangers into friends and, as Belleville's school superintendent noted, the programs have done a lot to allay older citizens' concerns about education budgets.

Supporting Families and Children at Risk

Families and children need special help and support at times of major disruption and instability, which put families and children at physical, emotional, and social risk. Unemployment, family illness, family conflict, separation and divorce, and living in threatening and violent environments all take a toll on families and children. During these times, parents and children need to help one another, and to do that they also need support from outside the family. Communities, including voluntary and government organizations, need to play more of a role than they do now. What is needed, most especially in the United States, is a reinvigoration and celebration of civic engagement, that is, people's connections with and participation in the life of their communities (Putnam, 1996).

As I argued earlier, although there has been a long debate about the breakdown of family values, only recently have some begun to discuss our collective responsibility as citizens to act to help families and children in times of need. What often clouds fruitful debate about the need for civic participation, however, is an insistence that the traditional two-parent family is best. Many children in single-parent families are, for all sorts of reasons, better off than they would have been if their parents had entered into loveless marriages or had continued in failed and unhappy ones. Furthermore, families with caring adults are what are important for children. When there is more than one caring adult, all the better. In fact, as we saw in Chapter 5, children in many societies are cared for by a wide range of adult and peer caretakers. We can appreciate family diversity and still help children in need. Let's consider some of the major risks that families and children face and evaluate some proposals for how communities can help families at risk help themselves and their children.

Supporting Families and Children of Divorce. The ease with which marriages can be dissolved and men can avoid supporting their families in the United States is shameful. There is much debate about returning to more restrictive divorce laws and especially to doing away with what is called "no-fault" divorce. Under no-fault divorce statutes, a divorce is granted even if only one spouse wants it. I believe that doing away with no-fault laws is unwise because the end result of such action may well be more expensive and acrimonious divorces.

Still, there is reason to question the quickness with which divorces are currently granted in the United States. Many European countries require a 2- to 5-year waiting period in granting divorces, whereas in the United States most states have done away with waiting periods of a year or more. Waiting periods require married couples to carefully evaluate their marital problems and to consider the effects of divorce on their children, and they prevent fathers and mothers from rushing quickly into new marriages. In many troubled marriages, compelling circumstances (such as intense conflict and spouse or child abuse) might exist that require that legal separations be easily and swiftly obtained. Even in these cases, however, quick divorce and remarriage are usually not in the best interest of children. In Italy and France, longer waiting periods are closely tied to strict rules of child support. In France, for example, divorce requires a 6-year waiting period, and the husband is bound to support his wife and children in their current lifestyle (Glendon, 1987; Hewlett, 1993).

In addition to benefiting from longer waiting periods, children of families undergoing divorce would also benefit from their parents' having to attend court-ordered classes or workshops in which they learn how to cope with their children's needs during the divorce process. Such courses are now required by law in 26 states, and bills requiring parental participation in such courses are now pending in a number of additional states. Some court jurisdictions require such courses in nearly all states (Gardiner, Fishman, Nikolov, Glosser, & Laud, 2002). The courses focus on getting parents to view their situation from their children's perspective. They often include showing parents videotaped skits of typical parental conflicts occurring in front of children as well as interviews of real children who have experienced bitter divorces. They also stress the benefits of parents' working together to raise their children, and the costs (financial and emotional) of court battles to work out custody agreements.

In programs of this type, however, there is always a danger of espousing formulaic solutions and what some observers see as the "unpleasant tinge of the therapeutic state" (Lewin, 1995a, p. A8). Also, some parents and their lawyers resent the classes and see them as intrusions in the legal process of divorce. Surveys of parents who have completed divorce education, however, show that they strongly approve of the courses. In Connecticut, for example, 90% of the parents surveyed after completing the classes approved of the requirement. As one father noted,

> when they show you these heartbreaking interviews with real kids, you see how devastating it is for the kids, and you think a little less about your next move in court, and more about how it will be for your child. (Lewin, 1995a, p. A8)

Reducing the Risk of Child Abuse. Every time I teach my course on childhood in contemporary society or the sociology of childhood, I ask my students (normally around 80 people) if they had a course on driver's education in high school. The hand of nearly every student immediately shoots up. Then I ask how many had a course on children, child development, or child care and child rearing. Now there are far fewer hands, usually about 35 or 40 at most. And this is in classes that are normally 75% to 80% female! It seems we feel it is more important to prepare our children to be drivers than parents.

One of the reasons many school districts shy away from teaching parenting is that it can be controversial. The same people who want religion and morality in the schools often balk at courses on parenting. A course on children and parenting? Why, that's an invasion of parents' rights. Child rearing is a private matter.

Surely, courses that prepare children and adolescents for parenthood can be developed and encouraged as important options if they are not required classes. What should be the nature of the curricula in such courses? We certainly need to get beyond courses that are often aimed at less-academic female students and that focus only on practical skills. We need courses that both inform students about children and also celebrate the wonder of children. Students need to do more than bathe a borrowed baby or make a one-time trip to a day care center.

What is needed is a series of projects that involve reading, discussing, doing, re-creating, and evaluating. Especially useful would be to require students to engage in a series of activities with young children and to reflect on and evaluate those experiences. Because of small families and the age segregation that exists in American society, such activities do not occur routinely in preadolescents' and adolescents' (especially males') everyday lives. But here again, a little ingenuity can go a long way. Boys can babysit as well as girls. And most adolescents have relatives, friends, or neighbors who have young children with whom they can spend time and whom they can get to know better. Think back to our earlier discussion of how nice it would be if parents could routinely pick up their young children from day care, preschool, or elementary school and then spend time with them in conversation and play. Why couldn't an adolescent relative or friend take the role of parent in this routine once or twice a week? This would be an excellent field project in a course on children and parenting. In such a project everyone benefits—the young child, the older adolescent friend or relative, and the parents. It is also just one of many possible ways to prepare preadolescents and adolescents for parenting.

Classes on childhood, children, and parenting in middle school and high school can do much to prepare youth for their coming transition to parenthood. But how can we help today's parents deal with the major responsibilities and demands of caring for infants and young children? We know from our earlier discussion in Chapter 10 that the most common form of child abuse is neglect. A frequent factor in neglect is family isolation, stress, and substance abuse. How can we reach out to families in need of help because of one or several of these factors?

Great Britain reaches out to families with newborns through its program of national health visitors. Health visitors spend time talking with and advising all new parents (usually mothers) before and after the birth of a child. Again, there is some debate about costs of the program, the intrusion of the state into private family affairs, and the feminization and middle-class therapeutic aspects of these services (Mayall, 1996). Still, such services provide attention, care, and advice to many families, especially those living in poverty and isolation.

Although such universal child health programs do not exist in the United States, voluntary programs to help families at risk for child abuse and neglect are becoming more widespread. Such programs usually involve social workers who make house calls to troubled families or family resource centers where parents can go to seek help. Many existing programs are modeled after one begun in Hawaii in the mid-1980s and after another project sponsored by the National Committee to Prevent Child Abuse in Chicago, which refined and expanded the Hawaii program. Such programs are controversial because of their expense, the fear of government intrusion, and difficulties in evaluating their effectiveness. Yet there have been reductions in reports of child abuse in the communities served.

Programs to prevent child abuse may be the most important thing we can do to help America's children. As James Garbarino has most eloquently stated,

> If you take almost any major social problem in America and treat it like those nested Russian dolls, what you will get to is that child abuse would be the last doll—because it is such a profound wound in developing children. (quoted in Lev & Brandon, 1994, p. D5)

Protecting Children From Abuse and Violence Outside the Family. As we discussed in Chapter 11, many children's lives are disrupted, permanently scarred, or brought to an end by persistent abuse and violence in their schools, neighborhoods, and communities. Children are abused and harassed by peers and teachers in schools, exploited by employers in the workplace, assaulted and murdered by criminals, and maimed and killed by the bombs and bullets of wars. What can be done to reduce the shameful record of violence against children? A first step is speaking up and challenging world leaders and all citizens to become more aware of the extent of the problem. The next step is the enactment of a range of programs that, little by little, may help to turn the tide and make the world safer for children and youth.

Some gains have been made in the area of abuse and harassment in schools through growing recognition of the problem, research on its extensiveness and underlying causes, and programs to educate students about their rights and responsibilities (Ambert, 1995; Besag, 1989; Eder, 1995). These developments may lead to some of the same positive results that occurred after the long-neglected problem of sexual abuse in the workplace was finally addressed in a serious manner.

Although the exploitation of child workers can occur anywhere in the world, as we saw in Chapter 10, it is primarily concentrated in developing countries. Ultimately, the political leaders, parents, and children in these countries will have to lead the way in combating this evil. This has already occurred in countries such as Pakistan and India. In these countries, children have actively proclaimed their rights even when this has meant sacrificing their lives for the cause (as in the case of young Iqbal Masih). Nonetheless, we can all fight against this problem by pushing for legislation that would ban the sale of goods produced by child labor in our country and by lobbying American companies to stop contracting work to countries where children are exploited.

How do we help children of war? The world seems never at peace, and children are the chief victims of its conflicts. I have touched only indirectly on this issue in this book, yet there clearly are things to be done. We can support a ban on the production of land mines in the United States and throughout the world; we can support the United Nations Convention on the Rights of the Child, which specifically addresses children's rights in wartime; and we can inform ourselves and take responsibility for our own government's military actions and policies in regard to children.

Finally, there are the war zones of America. The number of children and youth who are victims of violent crimes in the United States is appalling, shameful, and devastatingly sad. The causes of this tragedy are many, and they are intricately interrelated: poverty, abuse, drugs, guns, fear, and despair. In Chapter 11 we saw all these elements played out in the life of Robert, the 11-year-old hit man who was himself executed. Stories like Robert's, although almost incomprehensible, are becoming more and more common. Two Chicago boys, ages 12 and 13, dropped a 5-year-old from a high-rise building because he wouldn't steal candy for them. In Richmond, California, a 6-year-old boy and his twin 8-year-old brothers slipped into a neighbor's apartment to steal a tricycle. The 6-year-old dumped the neighbor's newborn baby from his bassinet and beat the infant nearly to death. Increasingly in American war zones both the victims and the perpetrators are children.

What's to be done? First and foremost, we need to get beyond our own emotions and concentrate on the children who have to deal with such violence every day of their lives. As sad as it may be, we need to focus less on the actual victims and perpetrators of these crimes once they have occurred and more on the children who continue to deal with relentless violence in their neighborhoods long after our memories of the shocking events begin to fade. We need to use the sad victimization of our children to spur us to help those still at risk rather than pointing fingers at our political enemies and shouting, "Moral breakdown!"

How can we help these children? How do we keep them safe? How do we prevent them from being tomorrow's victims or tomorrow's executioners? What these children need in their communities are more police, fewer guns, more caring adults, and more secure places to play and to be children.

Residents of high-crime areas have long lamented the lack of police attention and protection in their communities (Anderson, 1994). Recently there has been a call to hire more police and to increase their visibility in high-crime areas. Many experts point to recent drops in violent crime throughout the country as an indication that this policy is working. The police, however, must focus on helping and defending minority children and youth, not on intimidating them.

We also must address the easy availability of handguns and assault weapons. As gun violence and crime have increased among youth, so has the belief among youth who are not involved in crime that they need guns to protect themselves. Recent restrictions on gun sales, as well as legislation such as the Brady bill, which requires a waiting period and also a background check, have helped. But it is still much easier to sell, buy, and own a handgun or assault weapon in the United States than it is to buy, sell, or own a car. In 1994 handgun legislation offered up in Congress by Senator Bill Bradley (D-NJ) and Representative Charles Schumer (D-NY) would have mandated, essentially, many of the same restrictions for handgun sale and ownership that exist for selling and owning a car. Unfortunately, the legislative initiative never became law. I can think of no worse crime than selling a gun to a minor. Yet it happens all the time, often without real threat of criminal prosecution.

Throughout this book I have argued for the importance of appreciating children's active construction of their own peer worlds and cultures. We have seen how children's construction of and participation in their peer cultures also contributes to reproduction and change in adult society. Children who live in violent communities are restricted from creating and participating in such cultures. There are few safe places in their worlds for them to be children. A New York City grade school teacher, Sara Mosle (1994), wrote that her third-grade students lived under virtual house arrest. Their neighborhoods were filled with violence and crime, and they were afraid to spend much time outdoors. Thus, they lacked the everyday opportunities most of us had as children to play and to learn to get along with their peers. These children missed the rudiments of social interaction such as "how not to hog the ball, how to stop teasing a friend before it became unpleasant, how to settle a disagreement without resorting to a fight" (Mosle, 1994, p. 19). As a result, Mosle found that her students were continually upset about minor slights from their peers, and she spent a lot of time teaching "conflict resolution" in her class. Still, her students loved school. They begged her to let them stay after school so that they could "have a chance to talk to one another, to talk to me, to watch the fish in the aquarium, play (if Miss Mosle was in a good mood) for just a little" (p. 19).

Many of the preadolescents and adolescents who have been placed in the Camden County Youth Center in New Jersey, where Mary Taylor Previte is the administrator, have a lot in common with Sara Mosle's third graders (Previte, 1994). They too need a safe place to learn, to play, and to be children. Compared to the third graders, however, these youth have seen more violence, are more likely to have experienced death firsthand, and have been in trouble themselves. In the detention center, they talk about the violent experiences in their lives, trying to rid themselves of memories of domestic abuse or drive-by shootings. In these painful reflections, some children even contemplate their own funerals. However, they also make desperate attempts to catch up on lost childhood during leisure activities, and they make dramatic academic gains. Like the third graders who want to stay after school, these youth often prefer the lockup center to their homes and neighborhoods. Consider the response of one 14-year-old after two former residents of the center were gunned down on a Camden street corner: "Good thing I be here. Mighta been me dead out there" (Previte, 1994, p. E17).

The best havens from violence in the inner city are youth organizations. We know from the research of Heath and McLaughlin (1993) that youth organizations such as Boys and Girls Clubs, Police Athletic League clubs, and YMCAs have been very successful in serving inner-city youth. These organizations often tailor program content and institutional processes to the interests of the youth in the community, and they incorporate young people into participatory roles of all sorts. Activities in the organizations provide youth a sense of self-worth from being members of a group or team, a sense of belonging from being needed within the organization, and a sense of responsibility from being held accountable for contributing to the group and adhering to set rules and expectations. Such organizations are also often administered by excellent role models who are committed to giving something back to the communities in which they grew up (Marsiglio, 2008).

Big problems for youth organizations in inner cities are uncertain budgets and lack of continuous support from local communities and from national chapters of various organizations. Such organizations are, of course, not cure-alls for the problems of violence and crime in inner-city areas. With strong financial support from federal, state, and local governments and from individuals, however, they may very well be the best hope for providing the security so many of our children desperately need.

Acting Right Now

In this section we have evaluated programs for supporting families and children. Many of these programs are already in place and are working well. Most are administered by private voluntary organizations or local governments, and the overwhelming majority do not carry heavy costs for taxpayers. These programs and future initiatives that promise to help families and children do, however, need the support of all of us.

Recently the debate about family values has expanded and blossomed into a public discourse with great potential. Conservatives, mostly Republicans, deserve credit for initiating the debate. However, their views about the limits of big government and the decline of personal responsibility capture only one side of the issue. Liberals, mostly Democrats, who at first were mainly on the defensive, have now responded that the problems American families face are deeply rooted in the economic conditions of modern societies. Now the debate has become more constructive, and modest (but real) proposals such as workplace flexibility and leave time for parents may become a reality (Dionne, 1996).

Another positive outcome of the family values debate is that both sides have challenged the media, most especially the visual media of television and film, to be more responsible. Here both liberals and conservatives have assailed the media's position that their products only reflect the violent and sexual themes of our society. In many ways the media are a mirror of society and culture, but that mirror needs to be wide enough to reflect the diversity of our culture. Furthermore, the media, because of their great power, have an obligation to go beyond entertainment; they are obligated to inform and to educate their audiences. In short, the media need to join the debate about families and children rather than to reflect, sensationalize, and contribute to the problems families and children face.

As individual citizens, we all must heed this same challenge. We need to increase our civic engagement by contributing our time and money to a wide range of community organizations that help families with children. Many political leaders are calling for such civic involvement, and there is some evidence that volunteerism may be increasing in the United States, especially among young people (see Youniss & Levine, 2009; Youniss & Yates, 1997). We need to celebrate this fact and join the process.

CONCLUSION

In this final chapter I have presented many ideas and proposals for how we can invest in children and their childhoods. In line with the belief that children are active participants in society, I have argued that we need to enrich children's appropriations from the adult world, to encourage their constructions of their own peer cultures, and to better appreciate the contributions that children can and do make to our adult worlds. Many of the social problems of children can seem overwhelming. Yet the truth is that the majority of the world's children are actively creating and enjoying their childhoods. We need to do our best to create a commitment of responsibility among adults so that we can provide all children these same opportunities and experiences.

Our children are our future. How often we hear this obvious but true proverb. Cultures that invest in their children; that shelter, nourish, and challenge their young; and that hold high expectations for their future generations will survive and flourish. All children live their childhoods only once. We adults have had our childhoods; for some they were happy and enriching, and for others, unfortunately, sad and oppressive. We cannot have them back to live another way, nor can we live the lives of our children.

All too often, individuals and societies try to justify their actions in terms of their effects on children's futures as adults. This focus on the future, on what our children will become, can often blind us to how we treat and care for our children in the present. Enriching the lives of all our children will produce better adults and will enable our children to participate actively and fully in their own childhoods and contribute to the quality of our adult lives.

Cultures that appreciate and celebrate their children for who they are as well as for who they will become are the cultures that will lead us most successfully as we proceed further into this new century. Yes, our children are our future. And if there is one point, moral, or insight that I would have you take from this book it is, The future of childhood is the present.

Glossary

Access strategies: A variety of strategies that young children employ to gain access to play groups in preschool settings. These strategies are complex and are designed to overcome the resistance of other children who are attempting to protect their interactive space.

Approach-avoidance play: A primarily nonverbal pretend play routine in the peer culture of preschool children in which children identify, approach, and then avoid a threatening agent or monster.

As-if assumption: Assumption or attitude in person-to-person interaction wherein something that is potentially true or possible is treated as if it were really true or possible. For example, infants are often treated by adult caretakers as though they were socially competent (that is, fully capable of social exchanges). Because of this, children eventually progress from limited to full participation in cultural routines. In peer activities, preschool and preadolescent children pretend that certain facts are real as a way of exploring and testing their relations with each other and their developing places in the world.

Blaming the victim: The tendency to hold children personally responsible for the complex social and economic forces and problems that so dramatically affect their lives.

Bogeyman syndrome: The general fear of the victimization of children in contemporary industrialized societies, most especially in the United States.

Borderwork: Activities that mark and strengthen boundaries between groups. Thorne found that borderwork among preadolescent children heightened awareness of "the girls" and "the boys" as opposite and even antagonistic sides in play and peer relations.

Child abuse laws: Laws or regulations prohibiting the misuse of parental authority. Most laws specify that parental authority is misused when it is employed to damage the child either physically or emotionally or is administered in any manner that reduces or limits the child's opportunity for normal growth and development.

Child neglect: The most common form of child abuse, best defined as parents' failure to meet their children's needs in regard to health, development, and physical safety.

Childhood: The socially constructed period in which children live their lives.

Childhood as structural form: Description of childhood as a category or part of society. Children are active members of their childhoods; however, childhood is merely a temporary period of their lives. For society, however, childhood is a permanent structural form or category that never disappears, even though its members change continuously and its nature and conception vary historically. As a structural form, childhood is interrelated with other structural categories such as class, gender, and age groups. Thus, the structural arrangements of these categories and changes will affect the nature of childhood.

Childhood material culture: Clothing, books, artistic and literary tools (crayons, pens, paper, paints), and most especially toys. Children can and often do use some of these objects to produce other material artifacts of childhood culture (for example, pictures, paintings, block structures, improvised games, routines, and so forth).

Childhood symbolic culture: Various representations or expressive symbols of children's beliefs, concerns, and values. These primary sources of childhood symbolic culture are children's media (cartoons, films, and so on), children's literature (especially fairy tales), and mythical figures and legends (Santa Claus, the tooth fairy, and others).

Children's games as situated activities: Children's games are situated in real time and place by children who often have long interactional histories.

Children's lore: Shared aspects of children's cultures, such as games, jokes, chants, rhymes, riddles, songs, and other verbal routines that are created and transmitted by children over time and across societies. Such lore has been well documented by child folklorists.

Constructivist and interpretive theoretical perspectives: Theoretical approaches in sociology that carefully examine assumptions about the genesis of everything from friendship to scientific knowledge as social constructions rather than biological givens or obvious social facts. From this perspective, childhood and all social objects (including class, gender, race, and ethnicity) are thought to be interpreted, debated, and defined in processes of social action. In short, they are viewed as social products or constructions.

Constructivist model: Model of socialization in which the child is seen as an agent and eager learner. In this view, the child actively constructs his or her social world and his or her place in it.

Cultural routines: Repetitive everyday activities collectively produced by members of a culture. The habitual, taken-for-granted character of the routines provides children and all social actors with the security and shared understanding of belonging to a social group. On the other hand, this predictability empowers routines and provides a framework for producing, displaying, and interpreting a wide range of sociocultural knowledge.

Deterministic model: Model of socialization in which the child plays a basically passive role. In this view, the child is simultaneously a novice with potential to contribute to the maintenance of society and an untamed threat who must be controlled through careful training.

Discussione: Highly stylized and dramatic public discussions and debates that occur in the everyday lives of Italian adults and children. Having been exposed to and included in discussione by parents, teachers, and other adults in their community, preschool children generate and value the activity in their peer cultures.

Earned Income Tax Credit (EITC): Refundable tax credit for low-income families with children. It is an earned income support program that encourages work and self-sufficiency.

Equilibrium: Concept from Piaget's theory that is seen as the central force propelling the child through the stages of cognitive development. It is the compensation resulting from the activities of the child in response to external intrusions.

Externalizing disorders: Psychological effects on children resulting from parents' divorce and normally involving acting-out behaviors such as aggression, disobedience, lying, and so on.

Functionalist models: Models of socialization that focus on what the child needs to internalize and which parental child-rearing or training strategies are used to ensure such internalization.

He-said-she-said confrontations: A type of gossip dispute routine among American Black female preadolescents documented by Goodwin. A he-said-she-said confrontation can be defined as a type of gossip dispute routine that is brought about when one party to a dispute gossips about the other party in her or his absence. The he-said-she-said confrontation comes about when the absent party challenges his or her antagonist at a later point in time.

Internalization: Vygotsky's concept that holds that every function in the child's psychological and social development appears twice: first on the social level (between the child and others) and later on the individual level (inside the child). By this, Vygotsky meant that all our psychological and social skills (cognitive, communicative, and emotional) are always acquired from our interactions with others. We first develop and use such skills at the interpersonal level before internalizing them at the individual level.

Internalizing disorders: Psychological effects on children resulting from parents' divorce and normally involving depression, anxiety, or withdrawal.

Interpretive reproduction: A concept offered as an alternative to the notion of socialization. The term *interpretive* captures the innovative and creative aspects of children's participation in society and points to the fact that children create and participate in their own unique peer cultures by creatively taking or appropriating information from the adult world to address their own peer concerns. The term *reproduction* captures the idea that children are not simply internalizing society and culture but actively contributing to cultural production and change. The term also implies that children are, by their very participation in society, constrained by societal reproduction. That is, children and their childhoods are affected by the societies and cultures of which they are members.

Linear view of developmental process: Assumption that the child must pass through a preparatory period in childhood before he or she can develop into a socially competent adult. In this view, the period of childhood consists of a set of developmental stages in which cognitive skills, emotions, and knowledge are required in preparation for adult life.

Means-tested programs: Social welfare programs that distribute money and other types of resources to the poor and near poor.

Mental structures: Concept developed by Jean Piaget. Refers to the mental or cognitive representations or concepts that children construct of their physical and social worlds.

New history of childhood: Historical accounts that focus directly on the collective actions of children with adults and each other.

Nongovernmental organizations: Often referred to as NGOs, organizations that have no governmental affiliation; they promote change and address various social and economic problems at the community or grassroots level. These organizations have pressed for change and new legislation to improve the lives of children in many countries.

Oppositional talk: Playful teasing and confrontational talk that some African American children use to construct social identities, cultivate friendships, and both maintain and transform the social order of their peer cultures.

Orb web model: A graphic model that depicts interpretive reproduction as children's collective weaving of an orb web. In the model, the orb webs of peer cultures are collectively spun on the framework of the knowledge and institutions of adult society.

Out-group: Concept offered by Leach in reference to children's treatment by adults. When treated as an out-group, children are not just seen as adults in the making or as junior selves but also as inferior and not worthy of the same respect as adults.

Posttax and transfer poverty rate: Poverty measures that take taxes and income transfer resources (such as medical coverage and food stamps) into account in estimating poverty levels.

Protection of interactive space: Tendency on the part of preschool children to protect their ongoing play from the intrusions of others. This tendency is directly related to the fragility of peer interaction, the multiple possibilities of disruption in most preschool settings, and the children's desire to maintain control over shared activities.

Reproductive models: Models of socialization that focus primarily on access to cultural resources and the differential treatment of individuals in social institutions (especially the educational system), which reflects and supports the prevailing class system.

Rituals of pollution: Play routines or rituals in which specific individuals or groups are treated as contaminated (as in "having cooties"). Pollution games have been observed in many parts of the world, and Thorne found the variants of cootie games were very much a part of cross-gender conflict and teasing.

Secondary adjustments: Concept from Goffman that refers to efforts on the part of a member of an organization to employ unauthorized means, or obtain unauthorized ends, in an attempt to get around the organization's assumptions about what he or she should do and what he or she should be. Children attempt to evade adult rules through collaboratively produced secondary adjustments that enable them to gain a certain amount of control over their lives.

Sharing rituals: Children's collective activities that involve patterned, repetitive, and cooperative expressions of the shared values and concerns of childhood.

Social insurance programs: Government income redistribution programs such as social security and Medicare. Such programs are financed by payroll taxes and are paid out by those currently employed and by their employers. The benefits are provided to the retired, to dependents of deceased workers, and to the insured unemployed.

Socialization: Process by which children adapt to and internalize society. Most theories of socialization see the child as something apart from society who must be shaped and guided by external forces to become a fully functioning member.

Strange situation experiment: Experiment in which an infant is brought by her mother to a playroom setting in a laboratory, engaged in play with some toys by the mother, and then left alone with a strange female researcher. The infant's responses to the mother's brief absence and to the mother's return are seen as indicators of the child's attachment to the mother.

Zone of proximal development: Vygotsky's concept that estimates the child's level of development. The zone of proximal development is the distance between the child's actual developmental level as determined by independent problem solving and the level of potential development as determined by problem solving under adult guidance or collaboration with more capable peers.

References

Aaron, H. (2009). *Comments on "Spending on Children and the Elderly: An Issue Brief"* *by Julia Isaacs.* Washington, DC: Brookings Institution.

Abrahams, R. (1975). Negotiating respect: Patterns of presentation among Black women. In C. Farrer (Ed.), *Women and folklore* (pp. 58–80). Austin: University of Texas Press.

Adler, P. A., & Adler, P. (1998). *Peer power: Preadolescent culture and identity.* New Brunswick, NJ: Rutgers University Press.

Agnvall, E. (2006, May 16). Is teen sex bad? *The Washington Post.*

Ahrons, C. (1994). *The good divorce.* New York: HarperCollins.

Ahrons, C. (2004). *We're still family: What grown children have to say about their parents' divorce.* New York: HarperCollins.

Ainsworth, M., Blehar, M., Waters, E., & Wall, S. (1978). *Patterns of attachment: A psychological study of the strange situation.* Hillsdale, NJ: Lawrence Erlbaum.

Alan Guttmacher Institute. (1994). *Sex and America's teenagers.* New York: Author.

Alan Guttmacher Institute. (2010). *U.S. teenage pregnancies, births, and abortions: National and state trends by race and ethnicity.* Retrieved January 26, 2010, from www.guttmacher.org

Alanen, L. (1990). Rethinking socialization, the family and childhood. In P. A. Adler, P. Adler, N. Mandell, & S. Cahill (Eds.), *Sociological studies of child development* (Vol. 3, pp. 13–28). Greenwich, CT: JAI Press.

Alanen, L. (1994). Gender and generation: Feminism and the "child question." In J. Qvortrup, M. Bardy, & H. Wintersberger (Eds.), *Childhood matters: Social theory, practice and politics* (pp. 27–42). Brookfield, VT: Avebury.

Alanen, L. (2000). Visions of a social theory of childhood. *Childhood, 7,* 493–505.

Alanen, L. (2009). Generational order. In J. Qvortrup, W. Corsaro, & M. Honig (Eds.), *The Palgrave handbook of child studies* (pp. 159–174). Basingstoke, UK: Palgrave.

Alanen, L., & Mayall, B. (Eds.). (2001). *Conceptualizing child-adult relations.* London: Falmer.

Alderson, P. (2000). Children as researchers: The effects of participation rights on research methodology. In P. Christensen & A. James (Eds.), *Research with children: Perspectives and practices* (pp. 241–257). London: Falmer.

Alston, L. (1992). Children as chattel. In E. West & P. Petrick (Eds.), *Small worlds* (pp. 208–231). Lawrence: University Press of Kansas.

Ambert, A. (1986). Sociology of sociology: The place of children in North American sociology. In P. Adler & P. Adler (Eds.), *Sociological studies of child development* (Vol. 1, pp. 11–31). Greenwich, CT: JAI Press.

Ambert, A. (1995). Toward a theory of peer abuse. *Sociological Studies of Children, 7,* 177–205.

American Psychological Association. (1995, February 3). *Strategies for reducing nonmarital childbearing among adolescents: Effective policy responses.* Testimony submitted to the House of Representatives Ways and Means Subcommittee on Human Resources.

Amorim, K., Anjos, A., & Rossetti-Ferreira, M. (2008). *Do babies interact with babies?* [Didactic/Scientific DVD]. Riberão Preto, Brazil: Pseudo Video.

Anderson, D. R., Huston, A. C., Schmitt, K. L., Linebarger, D. L., & Wright, J. C. (2001). Early childhood television viewing and adolescent behavior: The recontact study. *Monographs of the Society for Research in Child Development, 68*(1), 1–143.

Anderson, E. (1994, May 5). The code of the streets. *Atlantic Monthly, 273,* 81–94.

Anderson, S., & Musi, A. (2005). Interpreting the continued decline in the average age at menarche: Results from two nationally representative surveys of U.S. girls studied 10 years apart. *Journal of Pediatrics, 147,* 753–760.

Ariès, P. (1962). *Centuries of childhood.* New York: Vintage.

Asher, S., & Coie, J. (Eds.). (1990). *Peer rejection in childhood.* New York: Cambridge University Press.

Ataöv, A., & Haider, J. (2006). From participation to empowerment: Critical reflections on a participatory action research project with street children in Turkey. *Children, Youth, and Environments, 16,* 127–152. Retrieved December 27, 2006, from www.colorado.edu/journals/cye

Aydt, H., & Corsaro, W. (2003). Differences in children's construction of gender across culture: An interpretive approach. *American Behavioral Scientist, 46,* 1306–1325.

Barlow, K. (1985, November). *Play and learning in a Sepik society.* Paper presented at the annual meetings of the American Anthropological Association, Washington, DC.

Barnes, M. M., & Vangelisti, A. (1995). Speaking in a double-voice: Role-making as influence in preschoolers' fantasy play situations. *Research on Language and Social Interaction, 28,* 351–389.

Barnes, P. (2003). Children's friendships. In M. Kehily & J. Swaan (Eds.), *Children's cultural worlds* (pp. 47–85). Chichester, UK: John Wiley.

Bass, L. (2003). Child labor and household survival strategies in west Africa. *Sociological Studies of Children and Youth, 9,* 127–148.

Bass, L. (2004). *Child labor in sub-Saharan Africa.* Boulder, CO: Lynne Rienner.

Bateson, G. (1956). This is play. In B. Schaffner (Ed.), *Group processes: Transactions of the second conference* (pp. 145–152). New York: Joseph Macey, Jr. Foundation.

Baumgartner, M. P. (1992). War and peace in early childhood. *Virginia Review of Sociology, 1,* 1–38.

Bazalgette, C., & Buckingham, M. (Eds.). (1995). *In front of the children: Screen entertainment and young audiences.* London: BFI.

Bearman, P., & Brückner, H. (2001). Promising the future: Virginity pledges and first intercourse. *American Journal of Sociology, 106,* 859–912.

Bell, E., Haas, L., & Sells, L. (Eds.). (1995). *From mouse to mermaid.* Bloomington: Indiana University Press.

Belsey, M. (1993). Child abuse measuring a global problem. *World Health Statistics Quarterly, 46,* 69–77.

Belsky, J., & Rovine, M. (1988). Nonmaternal care in the first year of life and the security of infant-parent attachment. *Child Development, 59,* 1157–1167.

Benin, M., & Edwards, D. (1990). Adolescents' chores: The difference between dual- and single-earner families. *Journal of Marriage and the Family, 52,* 361–373.

Berentzen, S. (1984). *Children constructing their social world* (Bergen Studies in Social Anthropology, No. 36.). Bergen, Norway: University of Bergen.

Bergmann, B. (1996). *Saving our children from poverty: What the United States can learn from France.* New York: Russell Sage Foundation.

Berne, L., & Huberman, B. (1999). *European approaches to adolescent sexual behavior and responsibility.* Washington, DC: Advocates for Youth. Retrieved February 12, 2010, from www.advocatesforyouth.org

Bernstein, B. (1981). Codes, modalities, and the process of cultural reproduction: A model. *Language in Society, 10,* 327–363.

Besag, V. (1989). *Bullies and victims in schools: A guide to understanding and management.* Philadelphia: Open University Press.

Best, A. (2007). *Representing youth: Methodological issues in critical youth studies.* New York: New York University Press.

Best, J. (1990). *Threatened children: Rhetoric and concern about child-victims.* Chicago: University of Chicago Press.

Best, J. (1994). Troubling children: Children and social problems. In J. Best (Ed.), *Troubling children: Studies of children and social problems* (pp. 3–19). New York: Aldine De Gruyter.

Best, R. (1983). *We've all got scars.* Bloomington: Indiana University Press.

Bettelheim, B. (1976). *The uses of enchantment: The meaning and importance of fairy tales.* New York: Knopf.

Bianchi, S. (1993). Children of poverty: Why are they poor? In J. Chafel (Ed.), *Child poverty and public policy* (pp. 91–106). Washington, DC: Urban Institute.

Blair, S. (1992). The sex-typing of children's household labor: Parental influence on daughters' and sons' housework. *Youth & Society, 24,* 178–203.

Blanchflower, D., & Freeman, R. (Eds.). (2000). *Youth employment and joblessness in advanced countries.* Chicago: University of Chicago Press.

Bluebond-Langner, M. (1996). *In the shadow of illness: Parents and siblings of the chronically ill child.* Princeton, NJ: Princeton University Press.

Blum-Kulka, S., & Snow, C. (2004). Introduction: The potential of peer talk. *Discourse Studies, 6,* 291–306.

Bohlen, C. (1995, March 24). Tell these Italians communism doesn't work. *New York Times,* p. A7.

Boocock, S., & Scott, K. (2005). *Kids in context: The sociological study of children and childhoods.* Lanham, MD: Rowman & Littlefield.

Boonstra, H. (2002). *Teen pregnancy: Trends and lessons learned* (The Guttmacher Report on Public Policy). Retrieved February 12, 2010, from www.guttmacher.org

Boonstra, H. (2009). Advocates call for a new approach after the era of "abstinence-only" sex education. *Policy Review, 12,* 6–11. Retrieved February 12, 2010, from www.guttmacher.org

Bourdieu, P. (1977). *Outline of a theory of practice.* New York: Cambridge University Press.

Bourdieu, P. (1991). *Language and symbolic power.* Cambridge, MA: Harvard University Press.

Bourdieu, P. (1993). Concluding remarks: For a sociogenetic understanding of intellectual works. In C. Calhoun, E. LiPuma, & M. Postone (Eds.), *Bourdieu: Critical perspectives* (pp. 263–275). Chicago: University of Chicago Press.

Bourdieu, P., & Passeron, J. C. (1977). *Reproduction in education, society, and culture.* Beverly Hills, CA: Sage.

boyd, d. (2010). Friendship. In M. Ito et al. (Eds.), *Hanging out, messing around, and geeking out: Kids living and learning with new media* (pp. 79–115). Cambridge, MA: MIT Press.

Boyle, D., Marshall, N., & Robeson, W. (2003). Fourth-grade girls and boys on the playground. *American Behavioral Scientist, 46,* 1326–1345.

Bradshaw, Y. (1993). New directions in international developmental research: A focus on children. *Childhood, 1,* 134–142.

Bradshaw, Y., Buchmann, C., & Mbatia, P. (1994). A threatened generation: Impediments to children's quality of life in Kenya. In J. Best (Ed.), *Troubling children: Studies of children and social problems* (pp. 23–45). New York: Aldine De Gruyter.

Bradshaw, Y., Noonan, R., Gash, L., & Sershen, C. B. (1993). Borrowing against the future: Children and third world indebtedness. *Social Forces, 71,* 629–656.

Bradshaw, Y., & Wallace, M. (1996). *Global inequalities.* Thousand Oaks, CA: Pine Forge Press.

Briggs, J. (1998). *Inuit morality play: The emotional education of a three-year-old.* New Haven, CT: Yale University Press.

Browne, K., & Hamilton-Giachritsis, C. (2005). The influence of violent media on children and adolescents: A public-health approach. *Lancet, 365,* 702.

Brückner, H., & Bearman, P. (2005). After the promise: The STD consequences of adolescent virginity pledges. *Journal of Adolescent Health, 36,* 271–278.

Bruner, J. (1986). *Actual minds, possible worlds.* Cambridge, MA: Harvard University Press.

Bruner, J., & Sherwood, V. (1976). Peekaboo and the learning of rule structure. In J. Bruner, A. Jolly, & K. Sylva (Eds.), *Play: Its role in development and evolution* (pp. 277–285). New York: Basic Books.

Buckingham, D. (1996). *Moving images: Understanding children's emotional responses to television.* Manchester, UK: Manchester University Press.

Buckingham, D. (1997). Dissin' Disney: Critical perspectives on children's media culture. *Media, Culture, and Society, 19,* 285–293.

Buckingham, D. (2000). *After the death of childhood: Growing up in the age of electronic media.* Cambridge, UK: Polity.

Buckingham, D. (2009). Children and television. In J. Qvortrup, W. Corsaro, & M. Honig (Eds.), *The Palgrave handbook of child studies* (pp. 347–359). Basingstoke, UK: Palgrave.

Budwig, N., Strage, A., & Bamberg, M. (1986). The construction of joint activities with an age-mate: The transition from caregiver-child to peer play. In J. Cook-Gumperz, W. Corsaro, & J. Streeck (Eds.), *Children's worlds and children's language* (pp. 83–108). Berlin, Germany: Mouton.

Bukowski, W., Newcomb, A., & Hartup, W. (Eds.). (1996). *The company they keep: Friendship in childhood and adolescence.* Cambridge, MA: Cambridge University Press.

Bureau of Justice Statistics. (2009). *Violent victimization rates by age, 1973–2008.* Retrieved January 10, 2010, from http://bjs.ojp.usdoj.gov

Bureau of Labor Statistics. (2009). *Employment characteristics of families in 2008.* Retrieved January10, 2010, from www.bls.gov/cps

Bureau of Labor Statistics. (2010). *Child day care services.* Retrieved April 19, 2010, from www.bls.gov/oco/cg/cgs032.htm#earnings

Burtless, G. (1994). Public spending on the poor: Historical trends and economic limits. In S. Danziger, G. Sandefur, & D. Weinberg (Eds.), *Confronting poverty: Prescriptions for change* (pp. 51–84). New York: Russell Sage Foundation.

Butler, C. (2008). *Talk and social interaction in the playground.* Burlington, VT: Ashgate.

Cahill, S. (1986). Childhood socialization as a recruitment process: Some lessons from the study of gender development. *Sociological Studies of Child Development, 1,* 163–186.

Cancian, M., & Reed, D. (2001). Changes in family structure: Implications for poverty and related policy. In S. Danziger & R. Haveman (Eds.), *Understanding poverty* (pp. 69–96). Cambridge, MA: Harvard University Press.

Carlsson-Paige, N., & Levin, D. (1987). *The war play dilemma: Children's needs and society's future.* New York: Teachers College Press.

Carlton-Ford, S. (2004). Armed conflict and children's life chances. *Peace Review, 16,* 185–191.

Carvalho, A., Império-Hamburger, A., & Pedrosa, M. (1998). Interaction, regulation and correlation in the context of human development: Conceptual discussion and empirical examples. In M. Lyra & J. Valsiner (Eds.), *Child development within culturally structured environments* (Vol. 4, pp. 155–180). Stamford, CT: Ablex.

Center on Budget and Policy Priorities. (1998). *Strengths of the safety net: How the EITC, social security and other government programs affect poverty.* Retrieved April 28, 2004, from www.cbpp.org

Center on Media for Child Health. (2005). *The effects of electronic media on children ages zero to six: A history of research.* Menlo Park, CA: Henry Kaiser Family Foundation. Retrieved February 25, 2010, from www.kff.org/entmedia/7239 .cfm

Chau, M. (2009). *Low-income children in the United States.* Retrieved January 30, 2010, from www.nccp.org/publications/pub_907.html

Cherlin, A. (2009). *The marriage-go-round: The state of marriage and the family in America today.* New York: Knopf.

Cherlin, A., & Furstenberg, F. (1986). *The new American grandparent: A place in the family, a life apart.* New York: Basic Books.

Child Trends. (2003). *Infant homicide.* Retrieved April 28, 2004, from www.childrends databank.org

Chin, E. (2001). *Purchasing power: Black kids and American consumer culture.* Minneapolis: University of Minnesota Press.

Chin, T., & Phillips, M. (2003). Just play? A framework for analysing children's time use. *Sociological Studies of Children and Youth, 9,* 149–178.

Chin, T., & Phillips, M. (2004). Social reproduction and childrearing practices: Social class, children's agency, and the summer activity gap. *Sociology of Education, 77,* 185–210.

Chira, S. (1996, April 21). Infant's trust found unhurt by child care. *New York Times,* TimesFax Internet ed., p. 1.

Christensen, P., & James, A. (2008a). Childhood diversity and commonality: Some methodological insights. In P. Christensen & A. James (Eds.), *Research with children: Perspectives and practices* (2nd ed., pp. 156–172). New York: Routledge.

Christensen, P., & James, A. (Eds.). (2008b). *Research with children: Perspectives and practices* (2nd ed.). New York: Routledge.

Christensen, P., & James, A. (2008c). Researching children and childhood: Cultures of communication. In P. Christensen & A. James (Eds.), *Research with children: Perspectives and practices* (2nd ed., pp. 1–9). New York: Routledge.

Christensen, P., & O'Brien, M. (Eds.). (2003). *Children in the city: Home, neighborhood and community.* New York: Routledge.

Christensen, P., & Prout, A. (2002). Working with ethical symmetry in social research with children. *Childhood, 9,* 477–497.

Chudacoff, H. (2007). *Children at play: An American history.* New York: New York University Press.

Cicirelli, V. (1995). *Sibling relationships across the life span.* New York: Plenum.

Clark, A., Kjørholt, A.-T., & Moss, P. (2005). *Beyond listening: Children's perspectives on early childhood services.* Bristol, UK: Policy Press.

Clark, C. (1995). *Flights of fancy, leaps of faith*. Chicago: University of Chicago Press.

Clark, C. (1999). The autodriven interview: A photographic viewfinder into children's experience. *Visual Sociology, 14*, 39–50.

Clark, C. (2003). *In sickness and in play: Children coping with chronic illness*. New Brunswick, NJ: Rutgers University Press.

Clarke-Stewart, A., & Brentano, A. (2006). *Divorce: Causes and consequences*. New Haven, CT: Yale University Press.

Clarke-Stewart, K. A. (1989). Infant day care: Maligned or malignant? *American Psychologist, 44*, 66–73.

Clawson, D., & Gerstel, N. (2002). Caring for our young children: Child care in Europe and the United States. *Contexts, 1*, 28–35. Retrieved April 28, 2004, from www.childpolicy.intl.org

Clearinghouse on International Developments in Child, Youth and Family Policies. (2010). *Comparative child, youth, and family policies and programs: Benefits and services*. Retrieved February 12, 2010, from www.childpolicyintl.org

Clerkx, L., & Van Ijzendoorn, M. (1992). Child care in a Dutch context: On the history, current status, and evaluation of nonmaternal child care in the Netherlands. In M. Lamb, K. Sternberg, C. Hwang, & A. Broberg (Eds.), *Child care in context: Cross-cultural perspectives* (pp. 55–80). Hillsdale, NJ: Lawrence Erlbaum.

Cohen, S. (2009). The Obama administration's first budget proposal prioritizes sex education and family planning but not abortion access. *Guttmacher Policy Review, 12*(2). Retrieved February 12, 2010, from www.guttmacher.org

Coie, J., & Dodge, K. (1988). Multiple sources of data on social behavior and social status in the school: A cross-age comparison. *Child Development, 54*, 1400–1416.

Connell, R. (1987). *Gender and power: Society, the person and sexual politics*. Stanford, CA: Stanford University Press.

Connolly, K., & Smith, P. (1978). Experimental studies of the preschool environment. *International Journal of Early Childhood, 10*, 86–95.

Cook, D. (2004). *The commodification of childhood*. Durham, NC: Duke University Press.

Cook, D. (2008). The missing child in consumption theory. *Journal of Consumer Culture, 8*, 219–243.

Cook, D. (2009). Children as consumers. In J. Qvortrup, W. Corsaro, & M. Honig (Eds.), *The Palgrave handbook of child studies* (pp. 332–346). Basingstoke, UK: Palgrave.

Coontz, S. (1992). *The way we never were: American families and the nostalgia trap*. New York: Basic Books.

Coontz, S. (1997). *The way we really are: Coming to terms with America's changing families*. New York: Basic Books.

Corsaro, W. (1979). "We're friends, right?" Children's use of access rituals in a nursery school. *Language in Society, 8*, 315–336.

Corsaro, W. (1985). *Friendship and peer culture in the early years*. Norwood, NJ: Ablex.

Corsaro, W. (1988). Routines in the peer culture of American and Italian nursery school children. *Sociology of Education, 61,* 1–14.

Corsaro, W. (1990). The underlife of the nursery school: Young children's social representations of adult rules. In G. Duveen & B. Lloyd (Eds.), *Social representations and the development of knowledge* (pp. 11–26). Cambridge, UK: Cambridge University Press.

Corsaro, W. (1992). Interpretive reproduction in children's peer cultures. *Social Psychology Quarterly, 55,* 160–177.

Corsaro, W. (1993). Interpretive reproduction in children's role play. *Childhood, 1,* 64–74.

Corsaro, W. (1994). Discussion, debate, and friendship: Peer discourse in nursery schools in the US and Italy. *Sociology of Education, 67,* 1–26.

Corsaro, W. (1996). Transitions in early childhood: The promise of comparative, longitudinal, ethnography. In R. Jessor, A. Colby, & R. Shweder (Eds.), *Ethnography and human development* (pp. 419–457). Chicago: University of Chicago Press.

Corsaro, W. (2003). *"We're friends, right?" Inside kids' culture.* Washington, DC: Joseph Henry Press.

Corsaro, W. (2009a). Italian children and the mysterious La Befana. In R. Shweder (Ed.), *The child: An encyclopedic companion* (p. 659). Chicago: University of Chicago Press.

Corsaro, W. (2009b). Peer culture. In J. Qvortrup, W. Corsaro, & M. Honig (Eds.), *The Palgrave handbook of child studies* (pp. 301–315). Basingstoke, UK: Palgrave.

Corsaro, W., & Eder, D. (1990). Children's peer cultures. *Annual Review of Sociology, 16,* 197–220.

Corsaro, W., & Emiliani, F. (1992). Child care, early education, and children's peer culture in Italy. In M. Lamb, K. Sternberg, C. Hwang, & A. Broberg (Eds.), *Child care in context: Cross-cultural perspectives* (pp. 81–115). Hillsdale, NJ: Lawrence Erlbaum.

Corsaro, W., & Fingerson, L. (2003). Development and socialization in childhood. In J. Delamater (Ed.), *Handbook of social psychology* (pp. 125–156). New York: Kuwer/Plenum.

Corsaro, W., & Johannesen, B. O. (2007). The creation of new cultures in peer interaction. In J. Valsiner & A. Rosa (Eds.), *The Cambridge handbook of socio-cultural psychology* (pp. 444–459). Cambridge, UK: Cambridge University Press.

Corsaro, W., & Maynard, D. (1996). Format tying in discussion and argumentation among Italian and American children. In D. Slobin, J. Gerhardt, A. Kyratzis, & J. Guo (Eds.), *Social interaction, social context and language: Essays in honor of Susan Ervin-Tripp* (pp. 157–174). Mahwah, NJ: Lawrence Erlbaum.

Corsaro, W., & Molinari, L. (1990). From *seggiolini* to *discussione:* The generation and extension of peer culture among Italian preschool children. *International Journal of Qualitative Studies in Education, 3,* 213–230.

Corsaro, W., & Molinari, L. (2000). Priming events and Italian children's transition from preschool to elementary school: Representations and action. *Social Psychology Quarterly, 63,* 16–33.

Corsaro, W., & Molinari, L. (2005). *I compagni: Understanding Italian children's transition from preschool to elementary school.* New York: Teachers College Press.

Corsaro, W., & Molinari, L. (2008). Entering and observing in children's worlds: A reflection on a longitudinal ethnography of early education in Italy. In P. Christensen & A. James (Eds.), *Research with children: Perspectives and practices* (2nd ed., pp. 237–259). New York: Routledge.

Corsaro, W., Molinari, L., Hadley, K., & Sugioka, H. (2003). Keeping and making friends in Italian children's transition from preschool to elementary school. *Social Psychology Quarterly, 66,* 272–292.

Corsaro, W., Molinari, L., & Rosier, K. (2002). Zena and Carlotta: Transition narratives and early education in the United States and Italy. *Human Development, 45,* 323–348.

Corsaro, W., & Nelson, E. (2003). Children's collective activities in early literacy in American and Italian preschools. *Sociology of Education, 76,* 209–227.

Corsaro, W., & Rizzo, T. (1988). *Discussione* and friendship: Socialization processes in the peer culture of Italian nursery school children. *American Sociological Review, 53,* 879–894.

Corsaro, W., & Rizzo, T. (1990). Disputes in the peer culture of American and Italian nursery school children. In A. Grimshaw (Ed.), *Conflict talk* (pp. 21–66). New York: Cambridge University Press.

Corsaro, W., & Rosier, K. (1994, July). *Transition narratives and reproductive processes in the lives of Black families living in poverty.* Paper presented at the XIII World Congress of Sociology, Bielefeld, Germany.

Corsaro, W., & Rosier, K. (2002). Priming events, autonomy, and agency in low income African-American children's transition from home to school. In R. Edwards (Ed.), *Children, home and school: Regulation, autonomy or connection?* (pp. 138–154). New York: Routledge.

Critcher, C. (2008). Making waves: Historical aspects of public debates about children and mass media. In K. Drotner & S. Livingstone (Eds.), *The international handbook of children, media, and culture* (pp. 91–104). Thousand Oaks, CA: Sage.

Cromdal, J. (2001). Can I be with? Negotiating play entry in a bilingual school. *Journal of Pragmatics, 33,* 515–543.

Cromdal, J. (2004). Building bi-lingual oppositions: Code-switching in children's disputes. *Language in Society, 33,* 33–58.

Cross, G. (1997). *Kids' stuff.* Cambridge, MA: Harvard University Press.

Damon, W. (1977). *The social world of the child.* San Francisco: Jossey-Bass.

Darroch, J., Singh, S., & Frost, J. (2001). Differences in teenage pregnancy rates among five developed countries: The roles of sexual activity and contraceptive use. *Family Planning Perspectives, 33,* 244–281.

Davies, B. (1982). *Life in the classroom and playground: The accounts of primary school children.* Boston: Routledge Kegan Paul.

Davies, B. (1989). *Frogs and snails and feminist tales: Preschool children and gender.* Boston: Allen and Unwin.

De Castell, S., & Jenson, J. (2003). Serious play. *Journal of Curriculum Studies, 6,* 649–665.

deMause, L. (1974). The evolution of childhood. In L. deMause (Ed.), *The history of childhood* (pp. 1–74). New York: Harper & Row.

DeVault, M. (2000). Producing family time: Practices of leisure activity beyond the home. *Qualitative Sociology, 23,* 485–503.

Dionne, E., Jr. (1996, June 29–30). A healthy "family values" debate. *The International Herald Tribune,* p. 6.

Dobson, J. (1996). *The new dare to discipline.* Wheaton, IL: Tyndale House.

Dodge, C., & Raundalen, M. (1991). *Reaching children in war: Sudan, Uganda and Mozambique.* Uppsala, Sweden: Scandinavian Institute of African Studies.

Dorais, M., & Lajeunesse, S. (2004). *Dead boys can't dance.* Montreal, Canada: McGill-Queen's University Press.

Drotner, K. (2009). Children and digital media: Online, on site, on the go. In J. Qvortrup, W. Corsaro, & M. Honig (Eds.), *The Palgrave handbook of child studies* (pp. 360–373). Basingstoke, UK: Palgrave.

Drotner, K., & Livingstone, S. (2008). *The international handbook of children, media and culture.* Thousand Oaks, CA: Sage.

Droz, Y. (2006). Street children and the work ethic: New policy for an old moral, Nairobi (Kenya). *Childhood, 13,* 349–363.

Dugger, C. (1992, March 31). Tiny incomes, little help for single mothers. *New York Times,* pp. A1, A16.

Dunn, J. (1988). *The beginnings of social understanding.* Cambridge, MA: Harvard University Press.

Dunn, J. (2004). *Children's friendships: The beginnings of intimacy.* Malden, MA: Blackwell.

Dunn, J., & Kendrick, C. (1982). *Siblings: Love, envy and understanding.* Cambridge, MA: Harvard University Press.

Dunn, J., and Plomin, R. (1990). *Separate lives: Why siblings are so different.* New York: Basic Books.

Eder, D. (1988). Building cohesion through collaborative narration. *Social Psychology Quarterly, 51,* 225–235.

Eder, D. (1995). *School talk: Gender and adolescent culture.* New Brunswick, NJ: Rutgers University Press.

Eder, D., & Fingerson, L. (2002). Interviewing children and adolescents. In J. Gubrium & J. Holstein (Eds.), *Handbook of interview research* (pp. 181–201). Thousand Oaks, CA: Sage.

Eder, D., & Nenga, S. (2003). Socialization in adolescence. In J. Delamater (Ed.), *Handbook of social psychology* (pp. 157–182). New York: Kuwer/Plenum.

Eder, D., & Parker, S. (1987). The cultural production and reproduction of gender: The effects of extra-curricular activities on peer group culture. *Sociology of Education, 60,* 200–213.

Edin, K., & Kefalas, M. (2007). *Promises I can keep: Why women put motherhood before marriage.* Berkeley: University of California Press.

Edwards, C. (2000). Children's play in cross-cultural perspective: A new look at the *sick cultures* study. *Cross-Cultural Research, 34,* 318–338.

Edwards, C., Gandini, L., & Forman, G. (Eds.). (1993). *The hundred languages of children.* Norwood, NJ: Ablex.

Edwards, C., Gandini, L., & Forman, G. (Eds.). (1998). *The hundred languages of children: The Reggio-Emilia approach—Advanced reflections.* Greenwich, CT: Ablex.

Einarsdottir, J. (2005). Playschool in pictures: Children's photographs as a research method. *Early Childhood Development and Care, 175,* 523–541.

Elder, G., & Conger, R. (2000). *Children of the land: Adversity and success in rural America.* Chicago: University of Chicago Press.

Ellis, S., Rogoff, B., & Cromer, C. (1981). Age segregation in children's social interaction. *Developmental Psychology, 17,* 399–407.

Evaldsson, A. (1993). *Play, disputes and social order: Everyday life in two Swedish after-school centers.* Linköping, Sweden: Linköping University.

Evaldsson, A. (2002). Boy's gossip telling: Staging identities and indexing (unacceptable) masculine behavior. *Text, 22,* 199–225.

Evaldsson, A. (2003). Throwing like a girl? Situating gender differences in physicality across game contexts. *Childhood, 10,* 475–497.

Evaldsson, A. (2009). Play and games. In J. Qvortrup, W. Corsaro, & M. Honig (Eds.), *The Palgrave handbook of child studies* (pp. 316–331). Basingstoke, UK: Palgrave.

Evaldsson, A., & Corsaro, W. (1998). Play and games in the peer cultures of preschool and preadolescent children: An interpretive approach. *Childhood, 5,* 377–402.

Evans, R. (2006). Negotiating social identities: The influence of gender, age, and ethnicity on young people's "street careers" in Tanzania. *Children's Geographies, 4,* 109–128.

Eyer, D. (1993). *Mother-infant bonding: A scientific fiction.* New Haven, CT: Yale University Press.

Fass, P. (Ed.). (2003). *Encyclopedia of children and society: In history and society.* New York: Macmillan.

Fein, G. (1981). Pretend play: An integrative review. *Child Development, 52,* 1095–1118.

Ferguson, A. (2000). *Bad boys: Public schools in the making of Black masculinity.* Ann Arbor: University of Michigan Press.

Fernie, D., Davies, B., Kantor, R., & McMurray, P. (1993). Becoming a person in the preschool: Creating integrated gender, school culture, and peer culture positionings. *Qualitative Studies in Education, 6,* 95–110.

Fernie, D., Kantor, R., & Whaley, K. (1995). Learning from classroom ethnographies: Same places, different times. In A. Hatch (Ed.), *Qualitative research in early education settings* (pp. 155–172). Westport, CT: Greenwood.

Fields, J. (2003). *Children's living arrangements and characteristics: March 2002* (Current Population Reports). Washington, DC: U.S. Census Bureau.

Fine, G., & Sandstrom, K. (1988). *Knowing children: Participant observation with minors*. Newbury Park, CA: Sage.

Fine, G. A. (1987). *With the boys: Little league baseball and preadolescent culture*. Chicago: University of Chicago Press.

Fingerson, L. (1999). Active viewing: Girls' interpretations of family television programs. *Journal of Contemporary Ethnography, 28,* 389–418.

Fingerson, L. (2009). Children's bodies. In J. Qvortrup, W. Corsaro, & M. Honig (Eds.), *The Palgrave handbook of child studies* (pp. 217–227). Basingstoke, UK: Palgrave.

Finkelhor, D., & Dziuba-Leatherman, J. (1994). Victimization of children. *American Psychologist, 49,* 173–183.

Finkelhor, D., & Jones, L. (2006). Why have child maltreatment and child victimization declined? *Journal of Social Issues, 62,* 685–716.

Fish, S. (1980). *Is there a text in this class? The authority of interpretive communities*. Cambridge, MA: Harvard University Press.

Formanek-Brunell, M. (1992). Sugar and spite: The politics of doll play in nineteenth-century America. In E. West & P. Petrik (Eds.), *Small worlds: Children and adolescents in America, 1850–1950* (pp. 107–124). Lawrence: University Press of Kansas.

Freeman, M. (2009). Children's rights as human rights: Reading the UNCRC. In J. Qvortrup, W. Corsaro, & M. Honig (Eds.), *The Palgrave handbook of child studies* (pp. 377–393). Basingstoke, UK: Palgrave.

Freese, J., Powell, B., & Steelman, L. (1999). Rebel without a cause or effect: Birth order and social attitudes. *American Sociological Review, 64,* 207–231.

Fromberg, D., & Bergen, D. (2006). *Play from birth to twelve: Contexts, perspectives, and meanings* (2nd ed.). New York: Routledge.

Fromby, P., & Cherlin, A. (2007). Family instability and child well-being. *American Sociological Review, 72,* 181–204.

Frønes, I. (1995). *Among peers: On the meaning of peers in the process of socialization*. Oslo, Norway: Scandinavian University Press.

Furstenberg, F., Brooks-Gunn, J., & Chase-Landale, L. (1989). Teenaged pregnancy and childbearing. *American Psychologist, 44,* 313–320.

Furstenberg, F., & Cherlin, A. (1991). *Divided families: What happens to children when parents part*. Cambridge, MA: Harvard University Press.

Gagon, J. (1972). The creation of the sexual in early adolescence. In J. Kagan & R. Coles (Eds.), *Twelve to sixteen* (pp. 231–257). New York: Norton.

Gandini, L., & Edwards, C. (Eds.). (2001). *Bambini: The Italian approach to infant/toddler care*. New York: Teachers College Press.

Garbarino, J., Dubrow, N., Kostelny, K., & Pardo, C. (1992). *Children in danger: Coping with the consequences of community violence.* San Francisco: Jossey-Bass.

Garbarino, J., Kostelny, K., & Dubrow, N. (1991). *No place to be a child: Growing up in a war zone.* Lexington, MA: Lexington Books.

Gardiner, K., Fishman, M., Nikolov, P., Glosser, A., & Laud, S. (2002). *State policies to promote marriage: Final report.* Retrieved April 28, 2004, from http://aspe.hhs .gov/hsp/marriage02f

Garfinkel, I. (1992). *Assuring child support: An extension of social security.* New York: Russell Sage Foundation.

Garfinkel, I., Rainwater, L., & Smeeding, T. (2010). *Wealth and welfare states: Is America a laggard or leader?* New York: Oxford University Press.

Garnsey, P. (1991). Child rearing in ancient Italy. In D. Kertzer & R. Saller (Eds.), *The family in Italy* (pp. 48–65). New Haven, CT: Yale University Press.

Garofalo, J., Siegel, L., & Laub, J. (1987). School-related victimizations among adolescents: An analysis of National Crime Survey narratives. *Journal of Quantitative Criminology, 3,* 321–338.

Garvey, C. (1984). *Children's talk.* Cambridge, MA: Harvard University Press.

Gaskins, S., Miller, P., & Corsaro, W. (1992). Theoretical and methodological perspectives in the interpretive study of children. In W. Corsaro & P. Miller (Eds.), *Interpretive approaches to children's socialization* (pp. 5–23). San Francisco: Jossey-Bass.

Gee, J. (2003). *What video games have to teach us about learning and literacy.* New York: Palgrave/Macmillan.

Gee, J. (2008). Learning theory, video games, and popular culture. In K. Drotner & S. Livingstone (Eds.), *The international handbook of children, media, and culture* (pp. 196–211). Thousand Oaks, CA: Sage.

Geertz, C. (1973). *The interpretation of cultures.* New York: Basic Books.

General Accounting Office. (1994, May). *Families on welfare: Sharp rise in never-married women reflects societal trend.* Report to the Chairman, Subcommittee on Human Resources, Committee on Ways and Means, House of Representatives.

Genovese, E. (1974). *Roll, Jordan, roll: The world that slaves made.* New York: Pantheon.

Gibbs, N. (2008, July 18). The pursuit of teen girl purity. *Time.* Retrieved February 12, 2010, from www.time.com/time/magazine/article/0,9171,1823930-2,00.html

Giddens, A. (1991). *Modernity and self identity.* Stanford, CA: Stanford University Press.

Gilligan, C. (1982). *In a different voice: Psychological theory and women's development.* Cambridge, MA: Harvard University Press.

Gillis, J. (1985). Review of *Forgotten Children* by Linda Pollock. *Journal of Interdisciplinary History, 16,* 142–144.

Gillis, J. (2009). Transitions to modernity. In J. Qvortrup, W. Corsaro, & M. Honig (Eds.), *The Palgrave handbook of child studies* (pp. 114–126). Basingstoke, UK: Palgrave.

Ginsburg, H., & Opper, S. (1988). *Piaget's theory of intellectual development* (3rd ed.). Englewood Cliffs, NJ: Prentice Hall.

Giroux, H. (1996). *Fugitive cultures: Race, violence, and youth.* New York: Routledge.

Gladwell, M. (1998, August). Do parents matter? *The New Yorker, 17,* 54–64.

Glassner, B. (2010). *The culture of fear: Why Americans are afraid of the wrong things* (Rev. ed.). New York: Basic Books.

Glendon, M. (1987). *Abortion and divorce in Western law: American failures, European challenges.* Cambridge, MA: Harvard University Press.

Goffman, E. (1961). *Asylums.* Garden City, NJ: Anchor.

Goffman, E. (1967). *Interaction ritual: Essays on face-to-face behavior.* New York: Anchor.

Goffman, E. (1974). *Frame analysis.* New York: Harper & Row.

Goldman, L. (2000). *Child's play: Myth, mimesis, and make-believe.* New York: Oxford University Press.

Goldstein, J. (Ed.). (1994). *Toys, play, and child development.* New York: Cambridge University Press.

Göncü, A. (1993). Development of intersubjectivity in social pretend play. *Human Development, 36,* 185–198.

Göncü, A., & Gaskins, S. (Eds.). (2006). *Play and development: Evolutionary, sociocultural, and functional perspectives.* Mahwah, NJ: Lawrence Erlbaum.

Göncü, A., Mistry, J., & Mosier, C. (2000). Cultural variations in the play of toddlers. *International Journal of Behavioral Development, 24,* 321–329.

Goodnow, J. (1988). Children's household work: Its nature and functions. *Psychological Bulletin, 103,* 5–26.

Goodwin, M. (1985). The serious side of jump rope: Conversational practices and social organization in the frame of play. *Folklore, 98,* 315–330.

Goodwin, M. (1990). *He-said-she-said: Talk as social organization among Black children.* Bloomington: Indiana University Press.

Goodwin, M. (1998). Games of stance: Conflict and footing in hopscotch. In S. Hoyle & C. Adger (Eds.), *Kids talk: Strategic language use in later childhood* (pp. 23–46). New York: Oxford University Press.

Goodwin, M. (2003). The relevance of ethnicity, class, and gender in children's peer negotiations. In J. Holmes & M. Meyerhoff (Eds.), *Handbook of language and gender* (pp. 229–251). London: Blackwell.

Goodwin, M. (2006). *The hidden life of girls: Games of stance, status, and exclusion.* Malden, MA: Blackwell.

Gottman, J. (1983). How children become friends. *Monographs of the Society for Research in Child Development, 48*(3), 1–86.

Gottman, J. (1986). The world of coordinated play: Same- and cross-sex friendships in young children. In J. Gottman & J. Parker (Eds.), *Conversations among friends: Speculations on affective development* (pp. 139–191). New York: Cambridge University Press.

Gotz, M., Lemish, D., Moon, H., & Aidman, A. (2005). *Media and the make-believe worlds of children: When Harry Potter meets Pokeman in Disneyland.* New York: Routledge.

Gough, K., & Franch, M. (2005). Spaces of the street: Socio-spatial mobility and exclusion of youth in Recife. *Children's Geographies, 3,* 149–166.

Grant, L. (1984). Gender roles and statuses in school children's peer interactions. *Western Sociological Review, 14,* 58–76.

Gray, M. (1999). *In your face: Stories from the lives of queer youth.* Binghamton, NY: Haworth.

Greenberger, E., & Steinberg, J. (1986). *When teenagers work.* New York: Basic Books.

Greene, S., & Hogan, D. (Eds.). (2005). *Researching children's experience: Approaches and methods.* London: Sage.

Greenspan, S. (2003). Child care research: A clinical perspective. *Child Development, 74,* 1064–1068.

Greenstein, R., & Shapiro, I. (2004, January). *The new, definitive CBO data on income and tax trends.* Retrieved April 28, 2004, from www.inequality.org

Greenwood, A. (1998). Accommodating friends: Niceness, meanness, and discourse norms. In S. Hoyle & C. Adger (Eds.), *Kids talk: Strategic language use in later childhood* (pp. 68–91). New York: Oxford University Press.

Griswold, W. (1994). *Cultures and societies in a changing world.* Thousand Oaks, CA: Pine Forge Press.

Gubrium, J., & Holstein, J. (1990). *What is family?* Mountain View, CA: Mayfield.

Guernsey, L. (2010). *A closer look at Obama's FY11 budget: Head Start.* Washington, DC: New America Foundation. Retrieved April 12, 2010, from http://earlyed .newamerica.net/blogposts/2010/a_closer_look_at_obama_s_fy11_budget_he ad_start-27490

Hadley, K. (2003). Children's word play: Resisting and accommodating Confucian values in a Taiwanese kindergarten classroom. *Sociology of Education, 76,* 193–208.

Hagan, J. (1994). *Crime and disrepute.* Thousand Oaks, CA: Pine Forge Press.

Hagerman, M. (2010). "I like being intervieeeeeeewed!" Kids' perspectives on participating in social research. In H. B. Johnson (Ed.), *Children and youth speak for themselves* (Sociological Studies of Children and Youth, Vol. 13, pp. 61–104). Bingley, UK: Emerald.

Hall, K. (2002). *Lives in transition: Sikh youth as British citizens.* Philadelphia: University of Pennsylvania Press.

Hanawalt, B. (1993). *Growing up in medieval London.* New York: Oxford University Press.

Handel, G., Cahill, S., & Elkin, F. (2007). *Children and society: The sociology of children and childhood socialization.* Los Angeles: Roxbury.

Hanley, R. (1996, May 10). With a prom and classes, schools court elderly for budget support. *New York Times,* TimesFax Internet ed., p. 6.

Hao, L., & Cherlin, A. (2004). Welfare reform and teenage pregnancy, childbirth, and school dropout. *Journal of Marriage and the Family, 66,* 179–194.

Harkness, S., & Super, C. (1992). Shared child care in east Africa: Sociocultural origins and developmental consequences. In M. Lamb, K. Sternberg, C. Hwang, &

A. Broberg (Eds.), *Child care in context: Cross cultural perspectives* (pp. 441–459). Hillsdale, NJ: Lawrence Erlbaum.

Harris, J. (1998). *The nurture assumption.* New York: Free Press.

Harrisson, J., Reubens, B., & Sparr, P. (1983). Trends in numbers employed, 1960–1980. In B. Reubens (Ed.), *Youth at work: An international survey* (pp. 17–18). Totowa, NJ: Rowman & Allanheld.

Haskins, R. (1992). Similar history, similar markets, similar policies yield similar results. In M. Lamb, K. Sternberg, C. Hwang, & A. Broberg (Eds.), *Child care in context: Cross-cultural perspectives* (pp. 267–280). Hillsdale, NJ: Lawrence Erlbaum.

Hatch, A. (1986). Affiliation in a kindergarten peer group. *Early Child Development and Care, 25,* 305–317.

Hays, S. (2004). *Flat broke with children: Women in the age of welfare reform.* New York: Oxford University Press.

Heath, S. (1983). *Ways with words: Language, life and work in communities and classrooms.* New York: Cambridge University Press.

Heath, S. (1989). Oral and literate traditions among Black Americans living in poverty. *American Psychologist, 44,* 367–373.

Heath, S. (1990). The children of Trackton's children: Spoken and written language in social change. In J. Stigler, R. Shweder, & G. Herdt (Eds.), *Cultural psychology: Essays on comparative human development* (pp. 496–519). New York: Cambridge University Press.

Heath, S., & McLaughlin, M. (Eds.). (1993). *Identity & inner-city youth: Beyond ethnicity and gender.* New York: Teachers College Press.

Hecht, T. (1998). *At home in the street: Street children of northeast Brazil.* New York: Cambridge University Press.

Helburn, S., & Bergmann, B. (2002). *America's child care problem: The way out.* New York: Palgrave.

Hendrick, H. (2008). The child as a social actor in historical sources: Problems of identification and interpretation. In P. Christensen & A. James (Eds.), *Research with children: Perspectives and practices* (2nd ed., pp. 40–65). New York: Routledge.

Hendrick, H. (2009). The evolution of childhood in western Europe c. 1400–c. 1750. In J. Qvortrup, W. Corsaro, & M. Honig (Eds.), *The Palgrave handbook of child studies* (pp. 99–113). Basingstoke, UK: Palgrave.

Henton, J., & Cate, R. (1983). Romance and violence in dating relationships. *Journal of Family Issues, 4,* 467–481.

Herbert, B. (1995, April 22). The terrorists failed. *New York Times,* p. 15.

Hernandez, D. (1993a). *America's children: Resources from family, government, and the economy.* New York: Russell Sage Foundation.

Hernandez, D. (1993b). *We, the American children* (U.S. Bureau of the Census, WE-10). Washington, DC: Government Printing Office.

Hernandez, D. (1994). Children's changing access to resources: A historical perspective. *Social Policy Report, Society for Research in Child Development, 8*(1), 1–23.

Hernandez, D., & Charney, E. (Eds.). (1998). *From generation to generation: The health and well-being of children in immigrant families.* Washington, DC: National Academies Press.

Hernandez, D., Denton, N., & Macartney, S. (2007a). Child poverty in the U.S.: A new family budget approach with comparison to European countries. In H. Wintersberger, L. Alanen, T. Olk, & J. Qvortrup (Eds.), *Childhood, generational order and the welfare state: Exploring children's social and economic welfare* (pp. 109–140). Odense: University Press of Southern Denmark.

Hernandez, D., Denton, N., & Macartney, S. (2007b). Young Hispanic children in the 21st century. *Journal of Latinos and Education, 6,* 209–228.

Hertz, R., & Marshall, N. (Eds.). (2001). *Working families: The transformation of the American home.* Berkeley: University of California Press.

Hetherington, E., & Kelly, J. (2002). *For better or for worse: Divorce reconsidered.* New York: Norton.

Hewlett, S. (1993). *Child neglect in rich nations.* New York: UNICEF.

Hill, R. (1990). Economic forces, structural discrimination and Black family instability. In H. Cheatham & J. Stewart (Eds.), *Black families: Interdisciplinary perspectives* (pp. 87–105). New Brunswick, NJ: Transaction Books.

Hilton, J., & Haldeman, V. (1991). Gender differences in the performance of household tasks by adults and children in single-parent and two-parent and two-parent, two-earner families. *Journal of Family Issues, 12,* 114–130.

Hochschild, A. (1989). *The second shift.* New York: Viking.

Hofferth, S. (1995). Caring for children at the poverty line. *Children and Youth Services Review, 17,* 61–90.

Hofferth, S., Brayfield, A., Deich, S., & Holcomb, P. (1991). *National Child Care Survey, 1990.* Washington, DC: Urban Institute Press.

Hofferth, S., & Hayes, C. (Eds.). (1987). *Risking the future* (Vol. 2). Washington, DC: National Academies Press.

Hofferth, S., Reid, L., & Mott, F. (2001). The effects of early childbearing on schooling over time. *Family Planning Perspectives, 33,* 259–267.

Hofferth, S., & Sandberg, J. (2001a). Changes in American children's time, 1981–1997. In T. Owens & S. Hofferth (Eds.), *Children at the millennium: Where have we come from, where are we going?* (pp. 193–229). New York: Elsevier.

Hofferth, S., & Sandberg, J. (2001b). How American children spend their time. *Journal of Marriage and the Family, 63,* 295–308.

Holmes, R. (1995). *How children perceive race.* Thousand Oaks, CA: Sage.

Holmes, R. (1998). *Fieldwork with children.* Thousand Oaks, CA: Sage.

Holson, L. (2008, March 9). Text generation gap: U R 2 OLD (JK). *New York Times.* Retrieved July 21, 2010, from www.nytimes.com/2008/03/09/business/09cell.html?sq=U R 2 Old&st=nyt&scp=1&pagewanted=print

Honig, A., & Thompson, A. (1993, December). *Toddler strategies for social engagement with peers.* Paper presented at the Biennial National Training Institute of the National Center for Clinical Infant Programs, Washington, DC.

Honig, M. (2009). How is the child constituted in childhood studies? In J. Qvortrup, W. Corsaro, & M. Honig (Eds.), *The Palgrave handbook of child studies* (pp. 62–77). Basingstoke, UK: Palgrave.

Hoover, S., & Clark, L. (2008). Children and media in the context of the home and family. In K. Drotner & S. Livingstone (Eds.), *The international handbook of children, media, and culture* (pp. 105–120). Thousand Oaks, CA: Sage.

Hoover, S., Clark, L., Alters, D., Champ, J., & Hood, L. (2004). *Media, home, and family.* New York: Routledge.

Horn, P. (1994). *Children's work and welfare, 1780–1880s.* London: Macmillan.

Horst, H. (2010). Families. In M. Ito et al. (Eds.), *Hanging out, messing around, and geeking out: Kids living and learning with new media* (pp. 149–194). Cambridge, MA: MIT Press.

Horst, H., Herr-Stephenson, B., & Robinson, L. (2010). Media ecologies. In M. Ito et al. (Eds.), *Hanging out, messing around, and geeking out: Kids living and learning with new media* (pp. 29–78). Cambridge, MA: MIT Press.

Howard, A. (1974). *Ain't no big thing: Coping strategies in a Hawaiian-American community.* Honolulu: University of Hawaii Press.

Hoyle, S. (1998). Register and footing in role play. In S. Hoyle & C. Adger (Eds.), *Kids talk: Strategic language use in later childhood* (pp. 47–67). New York: Oxford University Press.

Hunt, P., & Frankenberg, R. (1990). It's a small world: Disneyland, the family, and the multiple re-representations of American childhood. In A. James & A. Prout (Eds.), *Constructing and reconstructing childhood: Contemporary issues in the sociological study of childhood* (pp. 107–125). London: Falmer.

Hutchby, I. (2005). Children's talk and social competence. *Children & Society, 19,* 66–73.

Inkeles, A. (1968). Society, social structure and child socialization. In J. A. Clausen (Ed.), *Socialization and society* (pp. 73–129). Boston: Little, Brown.

Isaacs, J. (2009). *How much do we spend on children and the elderly?* Washington, DC: Brookings Institution.

Ito, M. (2009). *Engineering play: A cultural history of children's software.* Cambridge, MA: MIT Press.

Ito, M., & Bittanti, M. (2010). Gaming. In M. Ito et al. (Eds.), *Hanging out, messing around, and geeking out: Kids living and learning with new media* (pp. 195–242). Cambridge, MA: MIT Press.

Ito, M., et al. (Eds.). (2010). *Hanging out, messing around, and geeking out: Kids living and learning with new media.* Cambridge, MA: MIT Press.

James, A., Jenks, C., & Prout, A. (1998). *Theorizing childhood.* New York: Teachers College Press.

Jemmott, J., & Jemmott, L. (2010). Efficacy of a theory-based abstinence-only intervention over 24 months. *Archives of Pediatric Adolescent Medicine, 164,* 152–159.

Johannesen, B. O. (2004, August). *On shared experiences and intentional actions emerging within a community of Lego-playing children.* Paper presented at the Third International Conference on the Dialogical Self, Warsaw, Poland.

Jones, E., Forrest, J., Goldman, N., Henshaw, S., Lincoln, R., Rosoff, J., et al. (1985). Teenage pregnancy in developed countries: Determinants and policy implications. *Family Planning Perspectives, 17,* 53–63.

Jones, R., & Brayfield, A. (1997). Life's greatest joy? European attitudes toward the centrality of children. *Social Forces, 73,* 1239–1270.

Kamerman, S. (2000). *Parental leave policies: An essential ingredient in early childhood education and care policies* (Social Policy Report). Ann Arbor, MI: Society for Research in Child Development.

Kamerman, S., & Kahn, A. (1995). *Starting right: How America neglects its youngest children and what we can do about it.* New York: Oxford University Press.

Kaplan, E. (1997). *Not our kind of girl: Unraveling the myths of Black teenage motherhood.* Berkeley: University of California Press.

Katriel, T. (1985). *Brogez:* Ritual and strategy in Israeli children's conflicts. *Language in Society, 16,* 467–490.

Katriel, T. (1987). *"Bexibùdim!"* Ritualized sharing among Israeli children. *Language in Society, 16,* 305–320.

Katz, C. (2004). *Growing up global: Economic restructuring and children's everyday lives.* Minneapolis: University of Minnesota Press.

Kelle, H. (2000). Gender and territoriality in games played by nine- to twelve-year-old schoolchildren. *Journal of Contemporary Ethnography, 29,* 164–196.

Kelly, P., Buckingham, D., & Davies, H. (1999). Talking dirty: Children, sexual knowledge and television. *Childhood, 6,* 221–242.

Kinder, M. (1991). *Playing with power in movies, television, and video games: From Muppet babies to Teenage Mutant Ninja Turtles.* Berkeley: University of California Press.

Kinney, D. (1993). From nerds to normals: The recovery of identity among adolescents from middle school to high school. *Sociology of Education, 66,* 21–40.

Kisker, E. (1985). Teenagers talk about sex, pregnancy, and contraception. *Family Planning Perspectives, 17,* 83.

Klein, W., Graesch, A., & Izquierdo, C. (2009). Children and chores: A mixed-method study of children's household work in Los Angeles families. *Anthropology of Work Review, 30,* 98–109.

Kline, S. (1993). *Out of the garden: Toys, TV, and children's culture in the age of marketing.* New York: Verso.

Knapp, M., & Knapp, H. (1976). *One potato, two potato: The secret education of American children.* New York: Norton.

Kulkin, H., Chauvin, E., & Percie, G. (2000). Suicide among gay and lesbian adolescents and young adults: A review of the literature. *Journal of Homosexuality, 40,* 1–29.

Kutner, L., & Olson, C. (2008). *Grand theft childhood: The surprising truth about violent video games.* New York: Simon & Schuster.

Kyratzis, A. (2004). Talk and interaction among children and the co-construction of peer groups and peer culture. *Annual Review of Anthropology, 33,* 625–649.

Kyratzis, A., & Guo, J. (2001). Preschool girls' and boys' verbal conflict strategies in the United States and China. *Research on Language and Social Interaction, 34*, 45–74.

Labov, W. (1972). *Language in the inner city: Studies in Black English vernacular.* Philadelphia: Pennsylvania University Press.

Ladd, G. (1992). Themes and theories: Perspectives on processes in family-peer relationships. In R. Parke & D. Ladd (Eds.), *Family-peer relationships: Modes of linkage* (pp. 1–34). Hillsdale, NJ: Lawrence Erlbaum.

Ladd, G., Profilet, S., & Hart, C. (1992). Parents' management of children's peer relations: Facilitating and supervising children's activities in the peer culture. In R. Parke & D. Ladd (Eds.), *Family-peer relationships: Modes of linkage* (pp. 215–254). Hillsdale, NJ: Lawrence Erlbaum.

LaFrenier, P., & Charlesworth, W. (1983). Dominance, attention, and affiliation in a preschool group: A nine-month longitudinal study. *Ethology and Sociobiology, 4*, 55–67.

Lamb, M., Sternberg, K., Hwang, C., & Broberg, A. (Eds.). (1992). *Child care in context: Cross-cultural perspectives.* Hillsdale, NJ: Lawrence Erlbaum.

Lamb, M., Sternberg, K., & Ketterlinus, R. (1992). Child care in the United States: The modern era. In M. Lamb, K. Sternberg, C. Hwang, & A. Broberg (Eds.), *Child care in context: Cross-cultural perspectives* (pp. 207–222). Hillsdale, NJ: Lawrence Erlbaum.

Landau, E. (1994). Many factors contribute to child abuse. In K. de Koster (Ed.), *Child abuse: Opposing viewpoints* (pp. 114–122). San Diego, CA: Greenhaven Press.

Lange, A., & Mierendorff, J. (2009). Method and methodology in childhood research. In J. Qvortrup, W. Corsaro, & M. Honig (Eds.), *The Palgrave handbook of childhood studies* (pp. 78–95). Basingstoke, UK: Palgrave.

Lareau, A. (2003). *Unequal childhoods: Class, race, and family life.* Berkeley: University of California Press.

Larson, R., Richards, M., Sims, B., & Dworkin, J. (2001). How urban African American young adolescents spend their time: Time budget for locations, activities, and companionship. *American Journal of Community Psychology, 29*, 565–597.

Lave, J., & Wenger, E. (1991). *Situated learning: Legitimate peripheral participation.* New York: Cambridge University Press.

Leach, P. (1994). *Putting children first: What our society must do—and is not doing—for our children today.* New York: Knopf.

Lee, L. (2009). Young American immigrant children's interpretations of popular culture: A case study of Korean girls' perspectives on royalty in Disney films. *Journal of Early Childhood Research, 7*, 200–213.

Lee, N. (2001). *Childhood and society.* Buckingham, UK: Open University Press.

Lee, Y., Schneider, B., & Waite, L. (2003). Children and housework: Some unanswered questions. *Sociological Studies of Children and Youth, 9*, 105–125.

Lekies, K., & Cochran, M. (2001). *Collaborating for kids: New York state universal prekindergarten, 1999–2000.* Ithaca, NY: Cornell Early Childhood Program, Department of Human Development, Cornell University.

Lemish, D. (2008). The mediated playground: Media in early childhood. In K. Drotner & S. Livingstone (Eds.), *The international handbook of children, media, and culture* (pp. 152–167). Thousand Oaks, CA: Sage.

Lenhart, A. (2009). *Teens and sexting* (Pew Internet & American Life Project). Washington, DC: Pew/Internet. Retrieved March 22, 2010, from www.pew internet.org/~/media//Files/Reports/2008/PIP_Writing_Report_FINAL3.pdf .pdf

Lenhart, A., Arafeh, S., Smith, A., & McGill, A. (2008). *Writing, technology, and teens* (Pew Internet & American Life Project). Washington, DC: Pew/Internet. Retrieved March 22, 2010, from www.pewinternet.org/~/media//Files/Reports/ 2008/PIP_Writing_Report_FINAL3.pdf.pdf

Lev, M., & Brandon, K. (1994, September 18). Teaching parents not to abuse. *The Indianapolis Star*, pp. D1, D5.

Lever, J. (1978). Sex differences in the complexity of children's play and games. *American Sociological Review, 43,* 471–483.

Levi, G., & Schmitt, J. (Eds.). (1997). *A history of young people: Ancient and medieval rites of passage.* Cambridge, MA: Harvard University Press.

Lewin, T. (1990, March 15). Panel asks $5 billion to improve child care. *New York Times*, pp. B1, B7.

Lewin, T. (1995a, April 24). Now divorcing parents must learn how to cope with children's needs. *New York Times*, p. A8.

Lewin, T. (1995b, December 7). Parents poll finds child abuse to be more common. *New York Times*, p. A17.

Lewin-Epstein, N. (1981). *Youth employment during high school: An analysis of high school and beyond* (Report No. NCES-81-249). Washington, DC: National Center for Educational Statistics.

Lewis, A. (2003). *Race in the schoolyard.* New Brunswick, NJ: Rutgers University Press.

Lewis, V., Kellett, M., Fraser, S., Ding, S., & Robinson, C. (2003). *Doing research with children and young people.* Thousand Oaks, CA: Sage.

Li, J. A. (2007). *The kids are ok: Divorce and children's behavior problems.* Santa Monica, CA: RAND. Retrieved February 21, 2010, from www.rand.org/pubs/working_ papers/WR489

Lichter, D., & Eggebeen, D. (1992). Child poverty and the changing rural family. *Rural Sociology, 57,* 151–172.

Lindop, L. (2007). *Gay, lesbian, bisexual, transgender youth suicide.* Retrieved February 14, 2010, from www.healthyplace.com/gender/gay-is-ok/gay-lesbian- bisexual-transgender-youth-suicide/

Ling, R. (2007). Children, youth, and mobile communication. *Journal of Children and Media, 1,* 60–67.

Ling, R., & Haddon, L. (2008). Children, youth, and the mobile phone. In K. Drotner & S. Livingstone (Eds.), *The international handbook of children, media, and culture* (pp. 137–151). Thousand Oaks, CA: Sage.

Livingstone, S. (2007). Do the media harm children? Reflections on new approaches to an old problem. *Journal of Children and Media, 1,* 5–14.

Livingstone, S., & Drotner, K. (2008). Editor's introduction. In K. Drotner & S. Livingstone (Eds.), *The international handbook of children, media, and culture* (pp. 1–16). Thousand Oaks, CA: Sage.

Löfdahl, A. (2005). The funeral: A study of children's shared meaning-making and its developmental significance. *Early Years, 25,* 5–16.

Löfdahl, A., & Hägglund, S. (2006). Power and participation: Social representations among children in pre-school. *Social Psychology of Education, 9,* 179–194.

Løkken, G. (2000a). The playful quality of the toddling "style." *International Journal of Qualitative Studies in Education, 13,* 531–542.

Løkken, G. (2000b). Tracing the social "style" of toddler peers. *Scandinavian Journal of Educational Research, 2,* 163–176.

Lollis, S., Ross, H., & Tate, E. (1992). Parents' regulation of children's peer interactions: Direct influences. In R. Parke & D. Ladd (Eds.), *Family-peer relationships: Modes of linkage* (pp. 255–281). Hillsdale, NJ: Lawrence Erlbaum.

Louv, R. (1990). *Childhood's future.* New York: Anchor.

Louv, R. (2008). *Lost child in the woods: Saving our children from nature-deficit disorder.* Chapel Hill, NC: Algonquin Books.

Luker, K. (1991, Spring). Dubious conceptions: The controversy over teen pregnancy. *American Prospect, 2,* 73–83.

Luker, K. (2006). *When sex goes to school: Warring views on sex—and sex education—since the sixties.* New York: Norton.

Lurie, A. (1990). *Don't tell the grown-ups: Subversive children's literature.* Boston: Little, Brown.

Maccoby, E. (1999). *The two sexes: Growing up apart, coming together.* Cambridge, MA: Harvard University Press.

Maccoby, E., & Lewis, C. (2003). Less day care or different day care? *Child Development, 74,* 1069–1075.

Males, M. (1999). *Framing youth: Ten myths about the next generation.* Monroe, ME: Common Courage Press.

Mandell, N. (1988). The least-adult role in studying children. *Journal of Contemporary Ethnography, 16,* 433–467.

Manning, W. (1990). Parenting employed teenagers. *Youth & Society, 22,* 184–200.

Marquardt, E. (2005). *Between two worlds: The inner lives of children of divorce.* New York: Crown.

Marriott, M. (2004, October 28). Weaned on video games. *New York Times.* Retrieved July 21, 2010, from www.nytimes.com/2004/10/28/technology/circuits/28kids.html?scp=1&sq=M.+Marriott+Weaned+on+Video+Games&st=nyt

Marshall, L. (1976). *The !Kung of Nyae Nyae.* Cambridge, MA: Harvard University Press.

Marsiglio, W. (2008). *Men on a mission: Valuing youth work in our communities.* Baltimore: Johns Hopkins University Press.

Martin, J., Hamilton, B., Sutton, P., Ventura, S., Menacker, F., Kirmeyer, S., et al. (2009). *Births: Final data for 2006* (National Vital Statistics Reports, Vol. 57, No. 7). Hyattsville, MD: National Center for Health Statistics.

Martin, J., Park, M., & Sutton, P. (2002). *Births: Preliminary data for 2001* (National Vital Statistics Reports, Vol. 50, No. 10). Hyattsville, MD: National Center for Health Statistics.

Martin, K. (1998). Becoming a gendered body: Practices of preschools. *American Sociological Review, 63,* 494–511.

Martin, S. (2004). *Growing evidence for a divorce divide?* (Working Paper). New York: Russell Sage Foundation. Retrieved July 14, 2010, from www.russell sage.org/programs/main/inequality/workingpapers/martinexecsumm1/document_view

Martínez, K. (2010). The Garcia family: A portrait of urban Los Angeles. In M. Ito et al. (Eds.), *Hanging out, messing around, and geeking out: Kids living and learning with new media* (pp. 158–162). Cambridge, MA: MIT Press.

Martini, M. (1994). Peer interactions in Polynesia: A view from the Marquesas. In J. Roopnarine, J. Johnson, & F. Hooper (Eds.), *Children's play in diverse cultures* (pp. 73–103). Albany: State University of New York Press.

Mason, K., & Kuhlthau, K. (1989). Determinants of child care ideals among mothers of preschool-aged children. *Journal of Marriage and the Family, 51,* 593–603.

Matthews, H., Limb, M., and Taylor, M. (2000). The street as thirdspace. In S. Holloway & G. Valentine (Eds.), *Children's geographies: Playing, living, learning* (pp. 63–79). New York: Routledge.

Mayall, B. (1996). *Children, health, and the social order.* Philadelphia: Open University Press.

Mayall, B. (2002). *Towards a sociology for childhood: Thinking from children's lives.* Philadelphia: Open University Press.

Mayall, B. (2008). Conversations with children: Working with generational issues. In P. Christensen & A. James (Eds.), *Research with children: Perspectives and practices* (2nd ed., pp. 109–124). New York: Routledge.

Mayall, B. (2009). Generational relations at family level. In J. Qvortrup, W. Corsaro, & M. Honig (Eds.), *The Palgrave handbook of child studies* (pp. 175–187). Basingstoke, UK: Palgrave.

Maynard, D. (1985). On the functions of social conflict among children. *American Sociological Review, 50,* 207–223.

Maynard, D. (1986). Offering and soliciting collaboration in multi-party disputes among children (and other humans). *Human Studies, 9,* 261–285.

Maynard, R. (Ed.). (1997). *Kids having kids: Economic costs and social consequences of teen pregnancy.* Washington, DC: Urban Institute Press.

McDowell, J. (1979). *Children's riddling.* Bloomington: Indiana University Press.

McKendrick, J. (2009). Localities: A holistic frame of reference for appraising social justice in children's lives. In J. Qvortrup, W. Corsaro, & M. Honig (Eds.), *The Palgrave handbook of child studies* (pp. 238–255). Basingstoke, UK: Palgrave.

McLanahan, S., & Sandefur, G. (1994). *Growing up with a single parent: What hurts, what helps.* Cambridge: Harvard University Press.

Meintjes, H., & Giese, S. (2006). Spinning the epidemic: The making of mythologies of orphanhood in the context of AIDS. *Childhood, 13,* 407–430.

Mergen, B. (1992). Made, bought, and stolen: Toys and the culture of childhood. In E. West & P. Petrick (Eds.), *Small worlds: Children and adolescents in America, 1850–1950* (pp. 86–106). Lawrence: University Press of Kansas.

Merleau-Ponty, M. (1967). *Les relatons avec autrui chez l'enfant.* Paris: Centre de Documentation Universitaire.

Messner, M. (2000). Barbie girls versus sea monsters: Children constructing gender. *Gender & Society, 14,* 765–784.

Meyer, D., Garfinkel, I., Oellerich, D., & Robins, P. (1994). Who should be eligible for an assured child support benefit? In I. Garfinkel, S. McLanahan, & P. Robins (Eds.), *Child support and child well-being* (pp. 175–205). Washington, DC: Urban Institute Press.

Miller, P. (1982). *Amy, Wendy, and Beth: Learning language in South Baltimore.* Austin: University of Texas Press.

Miller, P. (1986). Teasing as language socialization and verbal play in a White, working-class community. In B. Schieffelin & E. Ochs (Eds.), *Language socialization across cultures* (pp. 199–212). New York: Cambridge University Press.

Miller, P., & Moore, B. (1989). Narrative conjunctions of caregiver and child: A comparative perspective on socialization through stories. *Ethos, 17,* 428–449.

Miller, P., Potts, R., Fung, H., Hoogstra, L., & Mintz, J. (1990). Narrative practices and the social construction of self in childhood. *American Ethnologist, 17,* 292–311.

Miller, P., & Sperry, L. (1987). The socialization of anger and aggression. *Merrill-Palmer Quarterly, 33,* 1–33.

Miller, P., Wiley, A., Fung, H., & Liang, C. (1997). Personal storytelling as a medium of socialization in Chinese and American families. *Child Development, 68,* 557–568.

Milner, M. (2004). *Freaks, geeks, and cool kids.* New York: Routledge.

Mintz, S. (2004). *Huck's raft: A history of American children.* Cambridge, MA: Harvard University Press.

Mishler, E. (1979). "Won't you trade cookies with the popcorn?" The talk of trades among six year olds. In O. Garnica & M. King (Eds.), *Language, children, and society: The effects of social factors on children's learning to communicate* (pp. 21–36). Elmsford, NY: Pergamon.

Mitchell, A. (2001). *Education for all young children: The role of states and the federal government in promoting pre-kindergarten and kindergarten.* New York: Foundation for Child Development.

Mizen, P., Pole, C., & Bolton, A. (2001). *Hidden hands: International perspectives on children's work and labour.* London: Routledge Falmer.

Moore, V. (2001). "Doing" racialized and gendered age to organize peer relations: Observing kids in summer camp. *Gender & Society, 15,* 835–858.

Moore, V. (2002). The collaborative emergence of race in children's play: A case study of two summer camps. *Social Problems, 49,* 58–78.

Morgan, J., & Zedner, L. (1992). *Child victims: Crime, impact, and criminal justice.* Oxford, UK: Clarendon.

Morgenthaler, S. (2006). The meanings of play with objects. In D. Fromberg & D. Bergen (Eds.), *Play from birth to twelve: Contexts, perspectives, and meanings* (2nd ed., pp. 65–74). New York: Routledge.

Morrow, V. (2008). Ethical dilemmas in research with children and young people about their social environments. *Children's Geographies, 6,* 49–61.

Mosle, S. (1994, June 4). Who's playing games? *New York Times,* p. 19.

Mueller, E. (1972). The maintenance of verbal exchanges between young children. *Child Development, 43,* 930–938.

Murray, C. (1984). *Losing ground: American social policy, 1950–1980.* New York: Basic Books.

Mussati, T., & Panni, S. (1981). Social behavior and interaction among day care center toddlers. *Early Child Development and Care, 7,* 5–27.

Nansel, T., Overpeck, M., Pilla, R., Raun, W., Simons-Morton, B., & Scheidt, P. (2001). Bullying behavior among US youth: Prevalence and association with psychosocial adjustment. *Journal of the American Medical Association, 285,* 2094–2100.

Nasaw, D. (1985). *Children of the city.* New York: Anchor.

National Campaign to Prevent Teen and Unplanned Pregnancy. (2010). [Teen pregnancy, birth, and sexual activity data]. Retrieved February 8, 2010, from www.thenationalcampaign.org

National Center for Education Statistics. (1996). *Marriage and divorce ratios in selected countries: 1960 to 1992.* Retrieved April 28, 2004, from www.nces.ed .gov/pubs98/yi/y9605a.asp

National Center for Health Statistics. (2010). *Health, United States, 2009: With special feature on medical technology.* Retrieved March 2, 2010, from www.cdc .gov/nchs/data/hus/hus09.pdf#listtables

National Committee to Prevent Child Abuse. (1996). *Annual fifty-state survey of child welfare officials.* Chicago: Author.

National Institute for Early Education. (2008). *The state of preschool 2008.* New Brunswick, NJ: Rutgers Graduate School of Education. Retrieved April 11, 2010, from http://nieer.org/yearbook/pdf/yearbook.pdf

National Institute of Child Health and Human Development Early Child Care Research Network. (2003). Does amount of time spent in child care predict socioemotional adjustment during the transition to kindergarten? *Child Development, 74,* 976–1005.

National Research Council. (1995, April 10). *Report on workshop on child care for low-income families*. Washington, DC: Institute of Medicine, Board on Children and Families.

Ness, D., & Farenga, S. (2007). *Knowledge under construction: The importance of play in developing children's spatial and geometric thinking*. Lanham, MD: Rowan & Littlefield.

New, R. (1994). Child's play—*una cosa naturale:* An Italian perspective. In J. Roopnarine, J. Johnson, & F. Hooper (Eds.), *Children's play in diverse cultures* (pp. 123–147). Albany: State University of New York Press.

Newman, K., Fox, C., Roth, W., Mehta, J., & Harding, D. (2004). *Rampage: The social roots of school shootings*. New York: Basic Books.

Nieuwenhuys, O. (1993). To read and not to eat: South Indian children between secondary school and work. *Childhood, 1,* 100–109.

Nieuwenhuys, O. (2005). The wealth of children: Reconsidering the child labour debate. In J. Qvortrup (Ed.), *Studies in modern childhood* (pp. 167–183). London: Palgrave.

Nieuwenhuys, O. (2009). From child labour to working children's movements. In J. Qvortrup, W. Corsaro, & M. Honig (Eds.), *The Palgrave handbook of child studies* (pp. 289–300). Basingstoke, UK: Palgrave.

Nightingale, V., Dickenson, D., & Griff, C. (2000). *Children's views about media harm*. Sydney: University of Western Sydney, Australian Broadcasting Company.

Nilsen, R. (2005). Searching for analytic concepts in the research process: Learning from children. *International Journal of Social Research Methodology, 8,* 117–135.

Nsamenang, B. (1992a). Early childhood care and education in Cameroon. In M. Lamb, K. Sternberg, C. Hwang, & A. Broberg (Eds.), *Child care in context: Cross cultural perspectives* (pp. 419–440). Hillsdale, NJ: Lawrence Erlbaum.

Nsamenang, B. (1992b). *Human development in cultural context: A third world perspective*. Newbury Park, CA: Sage.

Nsamenang, B. (2006). Human ontogenesis: An indigenous African view on development and intelligence. *International Journal of Psychology, 41,* 293–297.

Nsamenang, B. (2010). The importance of mixed-age groups in Cameroon. In M. Kernan & E. Singer (Eds.), *Peer relationships in early childhood education* (pp. 61–73). London: Routledge.

Nukaga, M. (2008). The underlife of kids' school lunchtime: Negotiating ethnic boundaries and identity in food exchange. *Journal of Contemporary Ethnography, 37,* 342–380.

Ochs, E. (1988). *Culture and language development: Language acquisition and language socialization in a Samoan village*. New York: Cambridge University Press.

Olesen, J. (1999). *Children and media risks* (Child and Youth Culture Working Paper No. 7). Odense, Denmark: Odense University.

Olweus, D. (1993). *Bullying at school: What we know and what we can do*. Malden, MA: Blackwell.

Opie, I., & Opie, P. (1959). *The lore and language of schoolchildren.* New York: Oxford University Press.

Opie, I., & Opie, P. (1969). *Children's games in street and playground.* Oxford, UK: Clarendon.

Organization for Economic Cooperation and Development. (2008). *Developmental aid at its highest level ever in 2008.* Retrieved April 11, 2010, from www.oecd .org/document/35/0,3343,en_2649_34487_42458595_1_1_1_1,00.html

Oswald, H., Krappman, L., Chowdhuri, I., & von Salisch, M. (1987). Gaps and bridges: Interactions between girls and boys in elementary school. In P. A. Adler & P. Adler (Eds.), *Sociological studies of child development* (Vol. 2, pp. 205–223). Greenwich, CT: JAI Press.

Pakistanis silence youthful voice against child labor. (1995, April 1). *Chicago Tribune,* p. 6.

Paley, V. (1984). *Boys and girls: Superheroes in the doll corner.* Chicago: University of Chicago Press.

Paley, V. (1992). *You can't say, you can't play.* Cambridge, MA: Harvard University Press.

Parke, R., & Ladd, G. (Eds.). (1992). *Family-peer relationships: Modes of linkage.* Hillsdale, NJ: Lawrence Erlbaum.

Parker, S. (1991). *Early adolescent male cultures: The importance of organized and informal sport.* Unpublished doctoral dissertation, Indiana University, Bloomington.

Parsons, T., & Bales, R. F. (1955). *Family, socialization and interaction process.* New York: Free Press.

Pascoe, C. J. (2007). *"Dude, you're a fag": Masculinity and sexuality in high school.* Berkeley: University of California Press.

Pascoe, C. J. (2010). Intimacy. In M. Ito et al. (Eds.), *Hanging out, messing around, and geeking out: Kids living and learning with new media* (pp. 117–148). Cambridge, MA: MIT Press.

Paternoster, R., Bushway, S., Brame, R., & Apel, R. (2003). The effect of teenage employment on delinquency and problem behaviors. *Social Forces, 82,* 297–335.

Pear, R. (1994, February 2). Audit of day care centers finds widespread problems. *New York Times,* p. 24.

Pellegrini, A., & Long, J. (2002). A longitudinal study of bullying, dominance, and victimization during the transition from primary school through secondary school. *British Journal of Developmental Psychology, 20,* 259–280.

Peterson, P. (1999). *Gray dawn.* New York: Random House.

Piaget, J. (1932). *The moral judgment of the child.* London: Routledge Kegan Paul.

Piaget, J. (1968). *Six psychological studies.* New York: Vintage.

Plomin, R., & Daniels, D. (1987). Why are children in the same family so different from one another? *Behavioral and Brain Sciences, 10,* 1–60.

Polakow, V. (2007). *Who cares for our children? The child care crisis in the other America.* New York: Teachers College Press.

Pollock, L. (1983). *Forgotten children.* New York: Cambridge University Press.

Pontecorvo, C., Fasulo, A., & Sterponi, L. (2001). Mutual apprentices: The making of parenthood and childhood in family dinner conversations. *Human Development, 44,* 340–361.

Pontecorvo, C., & Sterponi, L. (2002). Learning to argue and reason through discourse in educational settings. In G. Wells & G. Claxton (Eds.), *Learning for life in the 21st century* (pp. 127–140). Hoboken, NJ: John Wiley.

Popenoe, D. (1992, December 26). The controversial truth: Two-parent families are better. *New York Times,* p. 13.

Postman, N. (1994). *The disappearance of childhood.* New York: Vintage.

Poveda, D. (2001). *La ronda* in a Spanish kindergarten classroom with a cross-cultural comparison to sharing time in the U.S.A. *Anthropology & Education Quarterly, 32,* 301–325.

Poveda, D., & Marcos, M. (2005). The social organization of a "stone fight": *Gitano* children's interpretive reproduction of ethnic conflict. *Childhood, 12,* 327–349.

Preston, S. (1984). Children and the elderly in the U.S. *Scientific American, 251,* 44–49.

Previte, M. (1994, August 7). What will they say at my funeral? *New York Times,* p. E17.

Proctor, B., & Dalaker, J. (2003). *Poverty in the United States: 2002.* Retrieved April 28, 2004, from www.census.gov/prod/2003pubs/p60–222.pdf

Prosecutors gone wild. (2010, March 25). *New York Times.* Retrieved July 2, 2010, from www.nytimes.com/2010/03/25/opinion/25thur2.html?scp=1&sq=Prosecutors %20Gone%20Wild&st=cse

Prout, A. (Ed.). (2000). *The body, childhood, and society.* London: Macmillan.

Prout, A. (2005). *The future of childhood.* London: Routledge.

Pugh, A. (2009). *Longing and belonging: Parents, children, and consumer culture.* Berkeley: University of California Press.

Punch, S. (2000). Children's strategies for creating playspaces: Negotiating independence in rural Bolivia. In S. Holloway & G. Valentine (Eds.), *Children's geographies: Playing, living, learning* (pp. 48–62). New York: Routledge.

Putnam, R. (1996). The strange disappearance of civic America. *American Prospect, 24,* 34–50.

Qvortrup, J. (1991). *Childhood as a social phenomenon—An introduction to a series of national reports* (Eurosocial Report No. 36). Vienna, Austria: European Centre for Social Welfare Policy and Research.

Qvortrup, J. (1993a). Nine theses about "childhood as a social phenomenon." In J. Qvortrup (Ed.), *Childhood as a social phenomenon: Lessons from an international project* (Eurosocial Report No. 47, pp. 11–18). Vienna, Austria: European Centre for Social Welfare Policy and Research.

Qvortrup, J. (1993b). Societal position of childhood: The international project childhood as a social phenomenon. *Childhood, 1,* 119–124.

Qvortrup, J. (1994a). Childhood matters: An introduction. In J. Qvortrup, M. Bardy, G. Sgritta, & H. Wintersberger (Eds.), *Childhood matters: Social theory, practice, and politics* (pp. 1–23). Brookfield, VT: Avebury.

Qvortrup, J. (1994b). A new solidarity contract? The significance of a demographic balance for the welfare of both children and the elderly. In J. Qvortrup, M. Bardy, G. Sgritta, & H. Wintersberger (Eds.), *Childhood matters: Social theory, practice, and politics* (pp. 319–334). Brookfield, VT: Avebury.

Qvortrup, J. (2000). Macroanalysis of children. In P. Christensen & A. James (Eds.), *Research with children: Perspectives and practices* (pp. 77–97). London: Falmer.

Qvortrup, J. (2009). Childhood as a structural form. In J. Qvortrup, W. Corsaro, & M. Honig (Eds.), *The Palgrave handbook of child studies* (pp. 21–33). Basingstoke, UK: Palgrave.

Qvortrup, J., Corsaro, W., & Honig, M. (Eds.). (2009). *The Palgrave handbook of child studies*. Basingstoke, UK: Palgrave.

Raden, A. (1999). *Universal pre-kindergarten in Georgia: A case study of Georgia's lottery-funded pre-k program*. New York: Foundation for Child Development.

Rainwater, L., & Smeeding, T. (1995). *Doing poorly: The real income of American children in a comparative perspective* (Luxembourg Income Study Working Paper No. 127). Walferdange, Luxembourg: Luxembourg Income Study.

Rainwater, L., & Smeeding, T. (2003). *Poor kids in a rich country: America's children in comparative perspective*. New York: Russell Sage Foundation.

Rampton, B. (1995). *Crossing: Language and ethnicity among adolescents*. London: Longman.

Ramsey, P. (1991). *Making friends in school: Promoting peer relationships in early childhood*. New York: Teachers College Press.

Rasmussen, K. (2004). Places for children—Children's places. *Childhood, 11,* 155–173.

Ratcliff, D. (1994). *An elementary school hallway: Social formations and meanings outside the classroom*. Unpublished doctoral dissertation, University of Georgia, Athens.

Ratner, N., & Bruner, J. (1977). Games, social exchanges and the acquisition of language. *Journal of Child Language, 5,* 391–401.

Remafedi, G. (Ed.). (1994). *Death by denial: Studies of suicide in gay and lesbian teenagers*. Boston: Alyson.

Resnick, M., Bearman, P., Blum, R., Bauman, K., Harris, M., Jones, J., et al. (1997). Protecting adolescents from harm: Findings from the national longitudinal study on adolescent health. *Journal of the American Medical Association, 278,* 823–832.

Richert, S. (1990). *Boys and girls apart: Children's play in Canada and Poland*. Ottowa, Canada: Carleton University Press.

Rideout, V., Foehr, U., & Roberts, D. (2010). *Generation M²: Media in the lives of 8- to 18-year-olds*. Menlo Park, CA: Kaiser Family Foundation. Retrieved February 27, 2010, from www.kff.org/entmedia/mh012010pkg.cfm

Rideout, V., Vandewater, E., & Wartella, E. (2003). *Zero to six: Electronic media in the lives of infants, toddlers, and preschoolers*. Menlo Park, CA: Henry Kaiser Family Foundation. Retrieved February 25, 2010, from www.kff.org/entmedia/entmedia 102803pkg.cfm

Rigby, K. (2002). *New perspectives on bullying*. London: Jessica Kingsley.

Rivara, F., & Joffe, A. (2010). Research, policy, and adolescent sexual behavior. *Archives of Pediatric Adolescent Medicine, 164*, 2000.

Rizzini, I., & Butler, U. (2003). *Life trajectories of children and adolescents living on the streets of Rio de Janeiro*. Retrieved December 27, 2006, from www.colorado.edu/journals/cye

Rizzini, I., Rizzini, I., Munoz-Vargas, M., & Galeano, L. (1994). Brazil: A new concept of childhood. In C. Blanc (Ed.), *Urban children in distress: Global predicaments and innovative strategies* (pp. 55–100). Langhorne, PA: Gordon and Breach.

Rizzo, T. (1989). *Friendship development among children in school*. Norwood, NJ: Ablex.

Rogoff, B. (1995). Observing sociocultural activity on three planes: Participatory appropriation, guided participation, and apprenticeship. In J. Wertsch, P. del Rio, & A. Alvarez (Eds.), *Sociocultural studies of mind* (pp. 139–164). Cambridge, UK: Cambridge University Press.

Rogoff, B. (1996). Developmental transitions in children's participation in sociocultural activities. In A. Sameroff & M. Haith (Eds.), *The five to seven year shift: The age of reason and responsibility* (pp. 273–294). Chicago: University of Chicago Press.

Rogoff, B. (2003). *The cultural nature of human development*. New York: Oxford.

Rogoff, B., Mosier, J., & Göncü, A. (1989). Toddlers' guided participation in cultural activity. *Cultural Dynamics, 2*, 209–237.

Rosier, K. (2000). *Mothering inner-city children: The early school years*. New Brunswick, NJ: Rutgers University Press.

Rosier, K. (2009). Children as problems, problems of children. In J. Qvortrup, W. Corsaro, & M. Honig (Eds.), *The Palgrave handbook of child studies* (pp. 256–272). Basingstoke, UK: Palgrave.

Rosier, K., & Corsaro, W. (1993). Competent parents, complex lives: Managing parenthood in poverty. *Journal of Contemporary Ethnography, 22*, 171–204.

Rossetti-Ferreira, C., Oliveira, Z., Campos-de-Carvalho, M., & Amorim, K. (2010). Peer relations in Brazilian daycare centres. In M. Kernan & E. Singer (Eds.), *Peer relationships in early childhood education* (pp. 74–87). London: Routledge.

Sacks, C. (2001). Interracial relationships and racial identity processes in an urban mother-and-child rehabilitation program. *Sociological Studies of Children and Youth, 8*, 43–68.

Saez, E. (2009). *Striking it richer: The evolution of top incomes in the United States*. Retrieved April 11, 2010, from http://elsa.berkeley.edu/~saez/saez-UStopincomes-2007.pdf

Sanders, B. (1995). *A is for ox: The collapse of literacy and the rise of violence in an electronic age*. New York: Vintage.

Santelli, J., Lindberg, L., Finer, L., & Singh, S. (2007). Explaining recent declines in adolescent pregnancy in the United States: The contribution of abstinence and improved contraceptive use. *American Journal of Public Health, 97*, 150–156.

Santelli, J., Ott, M., Lyon, M., Rogers, J., Summers, D., & Schleifer, R. (2006). Abstinence and abstinence-only education: A review of US policies and programs. *Journal of Adolescent Health, 38*, 72–81.

Sawyer, C. K. (1997). *Pretend play as improvisation: Conversation in the preschool classroom*. Mahwah, NJ: Lawrence Erlbaum.

Sawyer, C. K. (2002). Improvisation and narrative. *Narrative Inquiry, 12*, 319–349.

Schäfer, N., & Yarwood, R. (2008). Involving young people as researchers: Uncovering multiple power relations among youths. *Children's Geographies, 6*, 121–135.

Schalet, A. (2004). Must we fear adolescent sexuality? *Medscape General Medicine, 6*, 44.

Schieffelin, B. (1990). *The give and take of everyday life: Language socialization of Kalui children*. New York: Cambridge University Press.

Schieffelin, B., & Ochs, E. (Eds.). (1986). *Language socialization across cultures*. New York: Cambridge University Press.

Schildkrout, E. (2002). Age and gender in Hausa society: Socio-economic roles of children in urban Kano. *Childhood, 9*, 344–368. (Original work published 1975)

Schofield, J. (1982). *Black and white in school*. New York: Praeger.

Schor, J. (2004). *Born to buy*. New York: Scribner.

Schwartzman, H. (1978). *Transformations: The anthropology of children's play*. New York: Plenum.

Scott, J. (2008). Children as respondents: The challenge for quantitative methods. In P. Christensen & A. James (Eds.), *Research with children: Perspectives and practices* (pp. 87–108). New York: Routledge.

Scott, K. (2002). "You want to be a girl and not my friend": African-American/Black girls' play activities with and without boys. *Childhood, 9*, 397–414.

Scott, K. (2003). In girls, out girls, and always Black: African-American girls' friendships. *Sociological Studies of Childhood and Youth, 9*, 179–207.

Seiter, E. (1993). *Sold separately: Parents & children in consumer culture*. New Brunswick, NJ: Rutgers University Press.

Seiter, E. (1999). *Television and new media audiences*. New York: Oxford University Press.

Selman, R. (1980). *The growth of interpersonal understanding*. New York: Academic Press.

Serpell, R. (1992). African dimensions of child care and nurturance. In M. Lamb, K. Sternberg, C. Hwang, & A. Broberg (Eds.), *Child care in context: Cross-cultural perspectives* (pp. 463–474). Hillsdale, NJ: Lawrence Erlbaum.

Sgritta, G. (1994). The generational division of welfare: Equity and conflict. In J. Qvortrup, M. Brady, G. Sgritta, & H. Wintersberger (Eds.), *Childhood matters: Social theory, practice and politics* (pp. 335–362). Brookfield, VT: Avebury.

Sgritta, G. (1997). The generation question. In J. Commaille & F. de Singly (Eds.), *The European family: The family question in the European community* (pp. 151–166). Boston: Kluwer.

Shaffer, D. (2006). *How computer games help children learn.* New York: Palgrave/ Macmillan.

Shahar, S. (1990). *Childhood in the middle ages.* London: Routledge.

Shanahan, S. (2007). Lost and found: The sociological ambivalence toward childhood. *Annual Review of Sociology, 33,* 407–428.

Shantz, C. (1987). Conflicts among children. *Child Development, 58,* 283–305.

Sheldon, A. (1997). Talking power: Girls, gender, enculturation and discourse. In R. Wodak (Ed.), *Gender and discourse* (pp. 225–244). London: Sage.

Shelton, B. (1992). *Women, men, and time: Gender differences in paid work, housework, and leisure.* Westport, CT: Greenwood.

Shorter, E. (1977). *The making of the modern family.* New York: Basic Books.

Shusterman, G., & Fluke, J. (2005). *Male perpetrators of child maltreatment: Findings from NCANDS, Walter R. McDonald and Associates.* Retrieved April 19, 2010, from http://aspe.hhs.gov/hsp/05/child-maltreat/

Sidel, R. (1992). *Women and children last.* New York: Penguin.

Simmons, R. (2002). *Odd girl out: The hidden culture of aggression in girls.* New York: Harcourt.

Simpson, B. (2000). Regulation and resistance: Children's embodiment during the primary-secondary school transition. In A. Prout (Ed.), *The body, childhood, and society* (60–78). New York: St. Martin's.

Skocpol, T., & Wilson, W. (1994, February 9). Welfare as we need it. *New York Times,* p. 16.

Skolnick, A. (1991). *Embattled paradise: The American family in an age of uncertainty.* New York: Basic Books.

Smeeding, T. (2002). *Real standards of living and public support for children: A cross-national comparison* (Luxembourg Income Study Working Paper Series No. 345). Syracuse, NY: Syracuse University.

Smeeding, T., Rainwater, L., & Burtless, G. (2001). U.S. poverty in a cross-national context. In S. Danziger & R. Haveman (Eds.), *Understanding poverty* (pp. 162–189). New York: Russell Sage Foundation.

Solberg, A. (1990). Negotiating childhood: Changing constructions of age for Norwegian children. In A. James and A. Prout (Eds.), *Constructing and reconstructing childhood* (pp. 118–137). New York: Falmer.

Spigel, L. (1992). *Make room for TV.* Chicago: University of Chicago Press.

Stacey, J. (1991). *Brave new families: Stories of domestic upheaval in late twentieth century America.* New York: Basic Books.

Stack, C. (1974). *All our kin: Strategies for survival in a Black community.* New York: Harper & Row.

Stamback, M., & Verba, M. (1986). Organization of social play among toddlers: An ecological approach. In E. Mueller & C. Cooper (Eds.), *Process and outcome in peer relationships* (pp. 229–247). New York: Academic Press.

Stanley, B., & Sieber, J. (1992). *Social research on children and adolescents: Ethical issues.* Newbury Park, CA: Sage.

Stein, N. (1993). No laughing matter: Sexual harassment in K-12 schools. In E. Buchwald (Ed.), *Transforming a rape culture* (pp. 313–314). Minneapolis, MN: Milkweed Editions.

Stein, N., & Albro, E. (2001). The origins and nature of arguments: Studies in conflict understanding, emotion, and negotiation. *Discourse Processes, 33*, 113–133.

Stephens, S. (1993). Children at risk: Constructing social problems and policies. *Childhood, 1*, 246–251.

Stern, D. (1985). *The interpersonal world of the infant: A view from psychoanalysis and developmental psychology.* New York: Basic Books.

Stern, D. (2004). *The present moment in psychotherapy and everyday life.* New York: Norton.

Sternheimer, K. (2003). *It's not the media: The truth about pop culture's influence on children.* Boulder, CO: Westview.

Sternheimer, K. (2010). *Connecting social problems and popular culture: Why media is not the answer.* Boulder, CO: Westview.

Stone, L. (1977). *Family, sex and marriage in England, 1500–1800.* New York: Harper & Row.

Strandell, H. (1994, July). *What are children doing? Activity profiles in day care centres.* Paper presented at the XIII World Congress of Sociology, Bielefeld, Germany.

Strandell, H. (1997). Doing reality with play: Play as a children's resource in organizing everyday life in daycare centres. *Childhood, 4*, 445–464.

Straus, M., & Donnelly, D. (2001). *Beating the devil out of them: Corporal punishment in American families and its effects on children.* New Brunswick, NJ: Transaction Books.

Strayer, F., & Strayer, S. (1976). An ethological analysis of social agonism and dominance relations among preschool children. *Child Development, 47*, 980–989.

Sutton-Smith, B. (1976). *The dialectics of play.* Schorndoff, Germany: Verlag Hoffman.

Sutton-Smith, B. (1986). *Toys as culture.* New York: Gardner Press.

Tannen, D. (1990). *You just don't understand: Women and men in conversation.* New York: Morrow.

Tatar, M. (1992). *Off with their heads! Fairy tales and the culture of childhood.* Princeton, NJ: Princeton University Press.

Tejada-Vera, B., & Sutton, P. (2008). *Births, marriages, divorces, and deaths: Provisional data for 2007* (National Vital Statistics Reports, Vol. 56, No. 21). Hyattsville, MD: National Center for Health Statistics.

Terry, D. (1994a, February 3). 19 children found in squalid Chicago apartment. *New York Times,* pp. A1, A11.

Terry, D. (1994b, September 1). When children kill children: Boy, 11, is wanted in Chicago. *New York Times,* p. A1.

Tesson, G., & Youniss, J. (1995). Micro-sociology and psychological development: A sociological interpretation of Piaget's theory. *Sociological Studies of Children and Youth, 7*, 101–126.

Thompson, M., O'Neill, C., & Cohen, L. (2001). *Best friends, worst enemies: Understanding the social lives of children.* New York: Ballantine.

Thorne, B. (1986). Girls and boys together . . . but mostly apart: Gender arrangements in elementary schools. In W. Hartup & Z. Rubin (Eds.), *Relationships and development* (pp. 167–184). Hillsdale, NJ: Lawrence Erlbaum.

Thorne, B. (1987). Re-visioning women and social change: Where are the children? *Gender & Society, 1,* 85–109.

Thorne, B. (1993). *Gender play: Girls and boys in school.* New Brunswick, NJ: Rutgers University Press.

Thorne, B. (2001). Pick-up time at Oakdale elementary school: Work and family from the vantage points of children. In R. Hertz & N. Marshall (Eds.), *Working families: The transformation of the American home* (pp. 354–376). Berkeley: University of California Press.

Tobin, J. (2000). *"Good guys don't wear hats": Children's talk about the media.* New York: Teachers College Press.

Trenholm, C., Devaney, B., Fortson, K., Clark, M., Quay, L., & Wheeler, J. (2008). Impacts of abstinence education on teen sexual activity, risk of pregnancy, and risk of sexually transmitted diseases. *Journal of Policy Analysis and Management, 27,* 255–276.

Tronick, E., Morelli, G., & Winn, S. (1987). Multiple caretaking of Efe (Pygmy) infants. *American Anthropologist, 89,* 96–106.

Tucker, C., Marx, J., & Long, L. (1998). "Moving on": Residential mobility and children's school lives. *Sociology of Education, 71,* 111–129.

Tynes, S. (2001). The colors of the rainbow: Children's racial self-classification. *Sociological Studies of Children and Youth, 8,* 69–85.

UNICEF. (1995a). *The progress of nations 1995.* Retrieved April 28, 2004, from www.unicef.org/pon95/progtoc.html

UNICEF. (1995b). *The state of the world's children.* Oxford, UK: Oxford University Press.

UNICEF. (2003). *The state of the world's children, 2003.* Retrieved April 28, 2004, from www.unicef.org

UNICEF. (2004). *Convention of the rights of the child.* Retrieved April 28, 2004, from www.unicef.org/crc/crc.htm

UNICEF. (2009). *The state of the world's children, special edition: Celebrating 20 years of the Convention on the Rights of the Child.* Retrieved February 8, 2010, from www.unicef.org

United Nations Statistics Division. (2006). *Demographic yearbook 2006.* New York: United Nations.

United Nations Statistics Division. (2007). *Demographic yearbook 2007.* New York: United Nations.

U.S. Census Bureau. (1992). *Statistical abstract of the United States, 1992.* Washington, DC: Government Printing Office.

U.S. Census Bureau. (2002). *Statistical abstract of the United States, 2001.* Washington, DC: Government Printing Office.

U.S. Census Bureau. (2003). *Statistical abstract of the United States, 2002.* Washington, DC: Government Printing Office.

U.S. Census Bureau. (2009). *Current Population Survey, 2009 Annual Social and Economic Supplement.* Washington, DC: Government Printing Office.

U.S. Department of Health and Human Services. (2009). *Child maltreatment: 2007.* Washington, DC: Government Printing Office.

U.S. Department of Labor. (2000). *Report on the youth labor force.* Retrieved April 18, 2010, from www.bls.gov/opub/rylf/pdf/rylf2000.pdf

U.S. Office of Management and Budget. (2010). *The president's budget for fiscal year 2011.* Retrieved February 6, 2010, from www.whitehouse.gov/omb/budget/?print=1

Valenti, J. (2009). *The purity myth: How America's obsession with virginity is hurting young women.* Berkeley, CA: Seal Press.

Van Ausdale, D., & Feagin, J. (2001). *The first R: How children learn race and racism.* Lanham, MD: Rowman & Littlefield.

Van Blerk, L. (2005). Negotiating spatial identities: Mobile perspectives on street life in Uganda. *Children's Geographies, 3,* 5–21.

Vandell, D. (2004). Early child care: The known and the unknown. *Merrill-Palmer Quarterly, 50,* 387–414.

Vecchiotti, S. (2003). Kindergarten: An overlooked educational policy priority. *Social Policy Report, 17,* 3–19.

Voss, L. (1997). Teasing, disputing, and playing: Cross-gender interactions and space utilization among first and third graders. *Gender & Society, 11,* 238–256.

Vygotsky, L. S. (1978). *Mind in society.* Cambridge, MA: Harvard University Press.

Waldfogel, J. (2006). *What children need.* Cambridge, MA: Harvard University Press.

Walkerdine, V. (1986). Post-structuralist theory and everyday practices: The family and the school. In S. Wilkinson (Ed.), *Feminist social psychology* (pp. 57–76). Philadelphia: Open University Press.

Walkerdine, V. (1990). *Schoolgirl fictions.* New York: Verso.

Walkerdine, V. (1997). *Daddy's girl: Young girls and popular culture.* Cambridge, MA: Harvard University Press.

Walkerdine, V. (1998). Children in cyberspace: A new frontier. In K. Lesnik-Oberstein (Ed.), *Children in culture: Approaches to childhood* (pp. 231–247). London: Macmillan.

Walkerdine, V. (2004). Remember not to die: Young girls and video games. *Papers: Explorations into Children's Literature, 14,* 28–37.

Walkerdine, V. (2009). *Children, gender, video games: Towards a relational approach to multimedia.* New York: Palgrave/Macmillan.

Wallerstein, J., Lewis, J., & Blakeslee, S. (2001). *The unexpected legacy of divorce: A 25-year landmark study.* New York: Hyperion.

Waskler, F. (Ed.). (1991). *Studying the social worlds of children: Sociological readings.* London: Falmer.

Wasko, J. (2008). The commodification of youth culture. In K. Drotner & S. Livingstone (Eds.), *The international handbook of children, media, and culture* (pp. 460–474). Thousand Oaks, CA: Sage.

Wasko, J., Phillips, M., & Meehan, E. (Eds.). (2001). *Dazzled by Disney? The global Disney audiences project.* London: Leicester University Press.

Watson-Gegeo, K., & Gegeo, D. (1986). The social world of Kwara'ae children: Acquisition of language and values. In J. Cook-Gumperz, W. Corsaro, & J. Streeck (Eds.), *Children's worlds and children's language* (pp. 109–128). Berlin, Germany: Mouton.

Weaver, H., Smith, G., & Kippax, S. (2005). School-based sex education policies and indicators of sexual health among young people: A comparison of the Netherlands, France, Australia and the United States. *Sex Education, 5,* 171–188.

Weisner, T., & Gallimore, R. (1977). My brother's keeper: Child and sibling caretaking. *Current Anthropology, 18,* 169–190.

Wentworth, W. M. (1980). *Context and understanding: An inquiry into socialization theory.* New York: Elsevier.

West, E. (1992). Children on the plains frontier. In E. West & P. Petrik (Eds.), *Small worlds* (pp. 26–41). Lawrence: University Press of Kansas.

West, E., & Petrick, P. (1992). Introduction. In E. West & P. Petrik (Eds.), *Small worlds* (pp. 1–8). Lawrence: University Press of Kansas.

White, L., & Brinkerhoff, D. (1981). Children's work in the family: Its significance and meaning. *Journal of Marriage and the Family, 43,* 789–798.

Whiting, B., & Edwards, C. P. (1988). *Children of different worlds: The formation of social behavior.* Cambridge, MA: Harvard University Press.

Wiehe, V. (2002). *What parents need to know about sibling abuse: Breaking the cycle of violence.* Springville, UT: Cedar Fort.

Wiggins, D. (1985). The play of slave children in the plantation communities of the old South, 1820–1860. In N. Hiner & J. Hawes (Eds.), *Growing up in America: Children in historical perspective* (pp. 173–192). Urbana: University of Illinois Press.

Wight, V., Chau, M., & Aratani, Y. (2010). *Who are America's poor children?* Retrieved February 7, 2010, from www.nccp.org/publications/pdf/text_912.pdf

Wilcox, W. B. (2009, Fall). The evolution of divorce. *National Affairs, 1,* 81–94. Retrieved February 7, 2010, from www.NationalAffairs.com

Wilkerson, I. (1993, April 4). First born, fast grown: The manful life of Nicholas, 10. *New York Times,* pp. 1, 16.

Wilkerson, I. (2005, June 12). Angela Whitiker's climb. *New York Times.* Retrieved July 21, 2010, from www.nytimes.com/2005/06/12/national/class/ANGELA-FINAL.html?ref=isabel_wilkerson

Williams, S., & Bendelow, G. (1998). Malignant bodies: Children's beliefs about health, cancer and risk. In S. Nettleton & J. Watson (Eds.), *The body in everyday life* (pp. 103–123). London: Routledge.

Winn, M. (1984). *Children without childhood*. New York: Penguin.

Winnicott, D. W. (1951). *Collected papers*. New York: Basic Books.

Wiseman, R. (2002). *Queen bees & wanabes: Helping your daughter survive cliques, gossip, boyfriends, and other realities of adolescence*. New York: Crown.

Wober, M. (1975). *Psychology in Africa*. London: International African Institute.

Wolf, S., & Heath, S. (1992). *The braid of literature: Children's worlds of reading*. Cambridge, MA: Harvard University Press.

Wootton, A. (1986). Rules in action: Orderly features of actions that formulate rules. In J. Cook-Gumperz, W. Corsaro, & J. Streeck (Eds.), *Children's language and children's worlds* (pp. 147–168). Berlin, Germany: Mouton.

World Health Organization. (2002). *World report on violence and health*. Retrieved February 10, 2010, from www.who.int/violence_injury_prevention

Wu, L., & Li, J. (2005). Children of the NLSY79: A unique data resource. *Monthly Labor Review, 128*, 59–62.

Wulff, H. (1988). *Twenty girls: Growing up, ethnicity and excitement in a south London microculture*. Stockholm, Sweden: University of Stockholm.

The young and the damned. (1996, April 15). *Time, 148*, 36–39.

Youniss, J., & Damon, W. (1994). Social construction and Piaget's theory. In B. Puka (Ed.), *Moral development: Vol. 5. New research in moral development* (pp. 407–426). New York: Garland.

Youniss, J., & Levine, P. (2009). *Engaging young people in civic life*. Nashville, TN: Vanderbilt University Press.

Youniss, J., & Yates, M. (1997). *Community service and social responsibility in youth*. Chicago: University of Chicago Press.

Zelizer, V. (1985). *Pricing the priceless child: The changing social value of children*. New York: Basic Books.

Zukow, P. (Ed.). (1989). *Sibling interaction across cultures: Theoretical and methodological issues*. New York: Springer-Verlag.

Index

About the Author

William A. Corsaro is the Robert H. Shaffer Class of 1967 Endowed Chair in the Department of Sociology at Indiana University, Bloomington, where he won the President's Award for Distinguished Teaching in 1988. He teaches courses on the sociology of childhood, childhood in contemporary society, and ethnographic research methods. His primary research interests are the sociology of childhood, children's peer cultures, the sociology of education, and ethnographic research methods. Corsaro is the author of *Friendship and Peer Culture in the Early Years* (1985), author of *"We're Friends, Right?" Inside Kids' Culture* (2003), and coauthor with Luisa Molinari of *I Compagni: Understanding Children's Transition From Preschool to Elementary School* (2005). He is the coeditor with Jens Qvortrup and Michael-Sebastian Honig of *The Palgrave Handbook of Childhood Studies* (2009). Corsaro was a Fulbright Senior Research Fellow in Bologna, Italy, in 1983–1984 and a Fulbright Senior Specialist Fellow in Trondheim, Norway, in 2003.